Transformations of Security Studies

This volume brings together a group of distinguished scholars to engage in a dialogue on key developments in the study of security.

The book provides a comprehensive overview of theoretical, empirical and methodological developments within security studies, the political and societal importance of which has grown significantly in recent years. By bringing together scholars who hold differing perspectives on security, this volume provides insights into a variety of approaches and their newest developments, including 'mainstream' as well as heterodox perspectives on security. Thus, it aims to build bridges of communication between different 'camps' by initiating a dialogue on the identity and diversity of security studies. It does so in three parts. The first part of the book includes paradigmatic approaches to security that are closely connected to major debates in international relations such as realism, institutionalism and constructivism as well as approaches to the culture and ethics of security and critical security studies. The second part places emphasis on the broadening and deepening of the concept of security in recent decades. It discusses key empirical frontiers including the continued centrality of the state, the link between democracy and security, and environmental security as well as financial security. The third part of the book presents various methodological approaches to the question of security and peace. It provides an overview of new approaches such as the visual turn, quantifying security and method combinations.

This book will be of much interest to students of critical security studies, international relations and research methods.

Gabi Schlag is Teaching Associate and Research Fellow at the Otto von Guericke University Magdeburg, Germany, and holds a PhD from the Goethe University Frankfurt, Germany.

Julian Junk is a Researcher at both the Peace Research Institute Frankfurt and the Goethe University Frankfurt, Germany.

Christopher Daase is Professor of International Organization at the Goethe University Frankfurt, Germany, and co-editor of *Rethinking Security Governance: The problem of unintended consequences*, (Routledge, 2010, co-edited with Cornelius Friesendorf).

PRIO New Security Studies
Series Editor: J. Peter Burgess, PRIO, Oslo

The aim of this book series is to gather state-of-the-art theoretical reflection and empirical research into a core set of volumes that respond vigorously and dynamically to the new challenges to security scholarship.

The Geopolitics of American Insecurity
Terror, power and foreign policy
Edited by François Debrix and Mark J. Lacy

Security, Risk and the Biometric State
Governing borders and bodies
Benjamin J. Muller

Security and Global Governmentality
Globalization, governance and the state
Edited by Miguel de Larrinaga and Marc G. Doucet

Critical Perspectives on Human Security
Rethinking emancipation and power in international relations
Edited by David Chandler and Nik Hynek

Securitization Theory
How security problems emerge and dissolve
Edited by Thierry Balzacq

Feminist Security Studies
A narrative approach
Annick T. R. Wibben

The Ethical Subject of Security
Geopolitical reason and the threat against Europe
J. Peter Burgess

Politics of Catastrophe
Genealogies of the unknown
Claudia Aradau and Rens van Munster

Security, the Environment and Emancipation
Contestation over environmental change
Matt McDonald

Securitization, Accountability and Risk Management
Transforming the public security domain
Edited by Karin Svedberg Helgesson and Ulrika Mörth

Commercialising Security
Political consequences for European military operations
Edited by Anna Leander

Transnational Companies and Security Governance
Hybrid practices in a postcolonial world
Jana Hönke

Citizenship and Security
The constitution of political being
Edited by Xavier Guillaume and Jef Huysmans

Security, Emancipation and the Politics of Health
A new theoretical perspective
João Nunes

Security, Technology and Global Politics
Thinking with Virilio
Mark Lacy

Critical Security and Chinese Politics
The Anti-Falungong Campaign
Juha A. Vuori

Governing Borders and Security
The politics of connectivity and dispersal
Edited by Catarina Kinnvall and Ted Svensson

Contesting Security
Strategies and logics
Edited by Thierry Balzacq

Conflict Resolution and Ontological Security
Peace anxieties
Edited by Bahar Rumelili

Biopolitics of Security
A political analytic of finitude
Michael Dillon

Security Expertise
Practice, power, responsibility
Edited by Trine Villumsen Berling and Christian Bueger

Transformations of Security Studies
Dialogues, diversity and discipline
Edited by Gabi Schlag, Julian Junk and Christopher Daase

Transformations of Security Studies

Dialogues, diversity and discipline

Edited by Gabi Schlag, Julian Junk and Christopher Daase

LONDON AND NEW YORK

First published 2016
by Routledge
2 Park Square, Milton Park, Abingdon, Oxon OX14 4RN

and by Routledge
711 Third Avenue, New York, NY 10017

Routledge is an imprint of the Taylor & Francis Group, an informa business

© 2016 selection and editorial material, Gabi Schlag, Julian Junk and Christopher Daase; individual chapters, the contributors

The right of the editors to be identified as the authors of the editorial material, and of the authors for their individual chapters, has been asserted in accordance with sections 77 and 78 of the Copyright, Designs and Patents Act 1988.

All rights reserved. No part of this book may be reprinted or reproduced or utilised in any form or by any electronic, mechanical, or other means, now known or hereafter invented, including photocopying and recording, or in any information storage or retrieval system, without permission in writing from the publishers.

Trademark notice: Product or corporate names may be trademarks or registered trademarks, and are used only for identification and explanation without intent to infringe.

British Library Cataloguing in Publication Data
A catalogue record for this book is available from the British Library

Library of Congress Cataloguing in Publication Data
Transformations of security studies : dialogues, diversity and discipline / edited by
   Gabi Schlag, Julian Junk, and Christopher Daase.
     pages   cm. – (PRIO new security studies)
   Includes bibliographical references and index.
   1. Security, International.   2. Security, International–Social aspects.
   3. Security, International–Research.   4. International relations.
   I. Schlag, Gabi.   II. Junk, Julian.   III. Daase, Christopher.
   JZ5588.T73124 2016
   355'.033–dc23   2015019529

ISBN: 978-1-138-89949-0 (hbk)
ISBN: 978-1-315-70783-9 (ebk)

Typeset in Times LT Std
by Out of House Publishing

Contents

List of figures	ix
List of contributors	x
Acknowledgements	xiv

Transformations of security and security studies: an introduction to the volume 1
GABI SCHLAG, JULIAN JUNK AND CHRISTOPHER DAASE

PART I
Paradigmatic Approaches to Security   33

1 Realism: not expanding, but still evolving   35
   CHARLES L. GLASER

2 Is the crisis of security institutions a crisis of institutional theory?   51
   CAROLINE FEHL

3 Is there life beyond language? Discourses of security   70
   KARIN M. FIERKE

4 On paradox and pathologies: a cultural approach to security   82
   CHRISTOPHER DAASE

5 An ethics of security   94
   J. PETER BURGESS

PART II
Subjects of Security   109

6   Power politics revisited: are realist theories really at odds with the new security threats?   111
CARLO MASALA

7   Democratic distinctiveness and the new security agenda   126
ANNA GEIS AND WOLFGANG WAGNER

8   Securing the environment: from defense to resilience   142
CHRIS METHMANN AND ANGELA OELS

9   Financial security   156
NINA BOY

PART III
Methodologies of Studying Security   171

10   Imaging security: a visual methodology for security studies   173
GABI SCHLAG

11   Global, state, and individual security in quantitative conflict research   190
HÅVARD HEGRE AND IDUNN KRISTIANSEN

12   Combining methods: connections and zooms in analysing hybrids   216
JULIAN JUNK AND VALENTIN RAUER

     A dialogue on the identity and diversity of security studies: a conclusion to the volume   233
JULIAN JUNK, GABI SCHLAG AND CHRISTOPHER DAASE

     Index   246

List of figures

0.1	The four dimensions of extended security	8
0.2	The four dimensions of extended security studies	13
9.1	The Capital Market Line and the Market Portfolio	162
11.1	Number of state-based armed conflicts by type, 1946–2013	192
11.2	Number of direct battle-related deaths in state-based armed conflicts, 1946–2013	192
11.3	Battle-related deaths in non-state and one-sided conflicts, 1946–2013	193
11.4	Number of coups, 1950–2013	194
11.5	Regime types, 1800–2013	194
12.1	Connective actions	221
12.2	Zooms	222

List of contributors

Nina Boy is a Senior Researcher at the Peace Research Institute Oslo (PRIO), Norway. She holds a PhD in Politics from Lancaster University, UK. Her work explores the security dimensions of sovereign creditworthiness, financial security/securitisation, social imaginaries and the modern co-evolution of finance, society and the public. As management team member of the COST Action *System risk, financial credit and crisis* from 2010–2014 she led the working group 'Credit, crisis & culture – historical, sociological and literary perspectives'. She co-edited a special issue of *Security Dialogue* on the global governance of security and finance in 2011.

J. Peter Burgess is Research Professor at the Peace Research Institute Oslo (PRIO), Norway, and Senior Researcher at the Institute for European Studies of the Vrije Universiteit Brussels, Belgium. He is Editor of *Security Dialogue*. His research and writing concern the meeting place between culture and politics in particular in Europe, focusing most recently on the theory and ethics of security and insecurity. He has published in the fields of philosophy, political science, gender studies, cultural history, security studies and cultural theory. He has developed and directed a range of collaborative research projects with Norwegian and European partners.

Christopher Daase is Professor of International Organization at the Goethe University Frankfurt, Germany, as well as member of the executive board and head of research department "International Institutions" at the Peace Research Institute Frankfurt (PRIF). His research interests include security studies with an emphasis on security culture and security policy as well as theories of International Relations with a focus on international norms and international organizations. He is co-editor of the journal *Zeitschrift für Internationale Beziehungen*. He is the co-editor of *Rethinking Security Governance: The Problem of Unintended Consequences*, London/New York: Routledge, 2010 (co-edited with Cornelius Friesendorf). Together with James Davis, he has translated Clausewitz' work on small wars into English (published by Oxford University Press).

Caroline Fehl is Senior Researcher at the Peace Research Institute Frankfurt (PRIF), Germany. Her research interests focus on norms and institutions in

List of contributors xi

the field of international security policy and on (power) inequalities in global institutional orders. Before joining PRIF, she held postdoctoral research fellowships at the University of Oxford, UK and Goethe University Frankfurt. She holds a DPhil in International Relations from the University of Oxford. Her work has been published by Oxford University Press and in journals such as the *European Journal of International Relations* and the *Review of International Studies*.

Karin M. Fierke is a Professor of International Relations in the School of International Relations at the University of St. Andrews, UK. She is author of five books, including *Political-Self Sacrifice: Agency, Body and Emotion in International Relations* (Cambridge University Press 2013), which was awarded the Sussex International Theory Prize 2014; *Critical Approaches to International Security* (Polity 2007, 2nd edition 2015); and *Changing Games, Changing Strategies: Critical Investigations in Security* (Manchester University Press 1998), as well as numerous articles in internationally recognized journals relating to constructivism and security and emotion, trauma and memory as they relate to political violence.

Anna Geis is Professor of International Relations at the University of Magdeburg, Germany. She received her PhD from the University of Hamburg, Germany. Her fields of interests are theories of peace and war, critical theory, democratic theory, constructivism, and international political theory. Her publications include *Democratic Wars: Looking at the Dark Side of Democratic Peace* (co-edited with Lothar Brock and Harald Müller, Palgrave Macmillan, 2006); *The Militant Face of Democracy: Liberal Forces for Good* (co-edited with Harald Müller and Niklas Schörnig, Cambridge University Press, 2013); and articles in *International Politics*, *International Relations*, *Review of International Studies*, and *Zeitschrift für Internationale Beziehungen*.

Charles L. Glaser is Professor of Political Science and International Affairs in the Elliott School of International Affairs and the Department of Political Science at George Washington University, USA, where he directs the Institute for Security and Conflict Studies. Glaser's recent book *Rational Theory of International Politics: The Logic of Competition and Cooperation* (Princeton University Press, 2010) explores how both states' motives and the material structure of the international system influence states' choices between competition and cooperation. His security policy research addresses the implications of China's rise for US foreign and defense policy, energy security, and US strategic nuclear policy.

Håvard Hegre is Dag Hammarskjöld Professor of Peace and Conflict Research at the Uppsala University and Research Professor at the Peace Research Institute Oslo (PRIO), Norway. He received his PhD from the University of Oslo in 2004. Hegre has published in international journals including *American Journal of Political Science*, *American Political Science Review*, *Journal of Conflict Resolution*, *Journal of Peace Research*, *Political Geography*, and

World Development in addition to several book chapters. His research interests include democracy and conflict, development and conflict, democratization, conflict forecasting, conflict dynamics, trade and conflict, and conflict research methodology.

Julian Junk is a Researcher at both the Peace Research Institute Frankfurt (PRIF) and Goethe University Frankfurt, Germany. His research interests include security studies with a focus on foreign policy analysis, international organizations, the responsibility to protect, and method combinations. He recently co-edited two special issues on 'Micropolitics meets Geopolitics: Internal dynamics and dysfunctions of international organizations' (*Journal of International Organization Studies*) and 'Organizing Peace: Organization Theory and International Peace Operations' (*Journal of Intervention and Statebuilding*).

Idunn Kristiansen is a Researcher at the Peace Research Institute Oslo (PRIO), Norway, and Managing Editor for the *Journal of Peace Research*. She holds an MA degree in Comparative Politics from the University of Bergen (2013), and her thesis research focused on the Israeli–Palestinian conflict. She has previously also worked at the Norwegian Embassy in Tel Aviv. Her more general research interests include the relationship between political institutions and armed conflict.

Carlo Masala is Professor of International Relations at the University of the German Bundeswehr, Munich, Germany. His main research areas are realist theories and security studies with a special focus on alliances and the use of force. Over the past 20 years he has been a consultant to various international and regional organizations (NATO, EU, AU), and national Ministries of Defense as well as the Armed Forces.

Chris Methmann works as an environment campaigner at the German online movement Campact. He holds a PhD in political science from the University of Hamburg. His research interests centre on discourses of climate change, climate security and climate-induced migration. His work has been published, among others, in *International Political Sociology*, the *European Journal of International Relations* and *Security Dialogue*.

Angela Oels is Visiting Professor at the Department of Political Science and at the Lund University Centre on Sustainability Studies (LUCSUS), Sweden, the professorship is financed by Riksbankens Jubileumsfond. Angela holds a PhD in Environmental Sciences from the University of East Anglia in Norwich, UK. She has taught at the universities of Berlin (FU), Hamburg (UH), Halle (MLU) and Hagen. Her current research focuses on the construction of climate change as a security issue in international political and scientific discourses, with a particular focus on climate change-induced migration. She has published in *Security Dialogue*, *GEOFORUM* and the *Journal of Environmental Policy and Planning* amongst others.

List of contributors xiii

Valentin Rauer is a Researcher at the interdisciplinary Cluster of Excellence 'The Formation of Normative Orders' at Goethe University Frankfurt, Germany. His current research project is focused on the diffused responsibility in security related action-chain-networks. Selected publications include *The Visualization of Uncertainty* (in: J. C. Alexander et al., eds., 2012, Iconic Power: Materiality and Meaning in Social Life, New York: Palgrave); *Interobjektivität: Sicherheitskultur aus Sicht der Akteur-Netzwerk-Theorie* (in: C. Daase et al., eds., 2012, Sicherheitskultur: Soziale und politische Praktiken der Gefahrenabwehr, Frankfurt, Campus).

Gabi Schlag is Teaching Associate and Research Fellow at the Otto von Guericke University Magdeburg, Germany. She holds a PhD from the Goethe University Frankfurt. Her research and teaching interests include International Political Theory, securitization theory and visual culture in IR. Her most recent works focus on a Western security community, the re-constitution of NATO, disaster images and visual securitization and have been published in journals such as the *European Journal of International Relations* and *Journal of International Relations and Development*. She currently co-edits a special issue on visuality in IR.

Wolfgang Wagner is Professor of International Security at VU University Amsterdam, the Netherlands. He holds an MA in Political Science and German Literature from the University of Tübingen, Germany and a PhD from the Goethe University in Frankfurt am Main. Before assuming a position at VU University Amsterdam, he worked at the universities of Tübingen, Frankfurt am Main and Konstanz and at the Peace Research Institute Frankfurt (PRIF). His research interests include comparative foreign policy analysis and the interplay between democratic politics and international conflict in particular.

Acknowledgements

The idea for this edited volume grew out of a lively discussion about the state of the art of security studies within the research project "The Transformation of Security Culture", at the Goethe University Frankfurt. Puzzled by the diagnosed fragmentation of the field, we organized a workshop at the Goethe University Frankfurt with scholars from different camps and strands of security studies. This workshop has been a very inspiring and thought provoking event – one of the rare but desirable gatherings where a real and honest dialogue about the identity and diversity of security as a research field started. We are very thankful to all contributors to and participants of this workshop.

This edited volume would not have been possible without the help and support of many people and institutions. The Federal Ministry of Education and Research in Germany funded the workshop and the Goethe University Frankfurt hosted the meeting. At the Annual Convention of the ISA in San Francisco, 2013, Peter J. Burgess – who has also been a sponsor of and contributor to this volume – discussed some drafts of chapters. Most importantly, without the contributions by the authors and their engagement with different perspectives, this book would be a bland monologue by the editors.

Many research assistants have assisted us in organizing the workshop and in adapting the chapters to the requirements of the publisher – in particular (in alphabetical order) Johannes Haaf, Fabian Hanschen, Wencke Müller, Ariel Pate, Thea Riebe, and Martin Schmetz.

It goes without saying that many colleagues and friends have inspired this project, consciously and unconsciously as well, when we discussed our ideas with them. We are particularly thankful to the anonymous reviewers for their suggestions on how to improve the overall framing of the book as well as for their constructive critique of individual chapters.

Last but not least, Andrew Humphrys and Hannah Ferguson at Routledge have been most helpful in the last months. They patiently and immediately responded to our many questions.

Nevertheless, all remaining shortcomings belong to the responsibility of the editors who are very much looking forward to continuing a dialogue on security studies beyond narrowly defined academic camps and intellectual traditions.

Gabi Schlag, Julian Junk, Christopher Daase
Magdeburg and Frankfurt

Transformations of security and security studies
An introduction to the volume

Gabi Schlag, Julian Junk and Christopher Daase

In the beginning, there was ... security

In his book '*People, States and Fear*' (first published in 1983),[1] Barry Buzan stated that security is an essentially contested concept (Buzan 2007: 29). This 'contestedness' has, however, not deterred political decision makers, policy experts or academics from undertaking, analyzing and theorizing security. From the very beginning, a general interest in the meaning of security has been accompanied by an ever-expanding political security agenda and by a growth of security studies as a field of research. This broadening of the meaning of security has had consequences for both actual security policy and politics as well as for security studies. As the concept of security has become more all-encompassing, an increased number of sub-disciplines within political science, in general, and International Relations (IR), in particular, have become involved in re-shaping the theoretical and methodological research agenda(s) of security studies. This development has indeed made security one of the key contested concepts within academia and politics in the last century. This has likewise made the matter of security and its study a continually changing subject.

The other side of this development, however, has been a pluralization of theories and methodologies that have often led to ambivalent consequences for the identity and integrity of a, more or less, coherent research field. The contestedness of the primary subject matter of security studies, along with its theories and methodologies, has not vanished in recent years – and is unlikely to be resolved anytime soon. As Ole Waever warned, '[t]he risk is real that the present security boom will lead to a multiplication of uncoordinated theories, a-theoretical policy analysis and theory disconnected from practice (and from other theorists) [...]. Current stakes are high, and the possibilities of both fragmentation and a "second golden age" are real' (Waever 2010: 656).

The present introduction retraces and systematizes a 'double extension' within security and security studies, which is meant to set the stage for discussing the diversity, identity and discipline of security studies. The driving force behind our idea of inviting a group of scholars from various areas within the academic landscape to a *dialogue on security* was twofold: to consider the ambivalent relation between the omnipresence of security and security politics, on the one hand, and the diversity of questions, approaches and methodologies relating to security studies on the other hand.

While there is a growing volume of literature related to the field, its history, structure and sociology, this edited volume emphasizes three specific aspects of the current state of international security studies, moving beyond the assessment and fear of an ever more fragmented research field. This does not imply, however, that the authors fail to recognize the diversity of approaches; rather, they acknowledge contributions from diverse sub-fields (theoretical, methodological and empirical) to the area of security studies. Accordingly, this volume is meant to provide a basis for critical debate surrounding varied approaches to security. Indeed many different – even conceptually, methodologically, empirically and normatively competing – 'camps' are in existence. All too often, we think, security studies is characterized by silence rather than a lively discussion between 'critical/Critical' and 'mainstream' scholars. Despite this, ongoing dialogue about the possibilities and the limits of the intellectual and political value of security studies should, at the very least, remain a common goal. In order to do so, this edited volume has brought together scholars who hold differing perspectives on security. It intends to foster both an intra- and an inter-disciplinary dialogue between various communities within security studies, helping to further mutual understanding between self-proclaimed 'mainstream' and heterodox perspectives on security. While taking stock of the field's immense variety, this volume also incorporates new conceptual, methodological and empirical perspectives on how security is conceptualized and analyzed.

This introduction has two goals. First, it takes the current state of security studies as the starting point and highlights its contested disciplinary status. Disciplines are not fixed – rather, they are always in flux. Secondly, through this introduction, we are interested in more closely connecting the conceptual history of security to the development of (international) security studies. This is guided by the assumption that changes in social and political realities have implied shifts in research, i.e. how security has been and is currently theorized and studied – and *vice versa*. The introduction concludes with an overview and summary of the contributions that comprise this edited volume.

The current state of international security studies

Numerous high-quality handbooks, edited volumes, monographs and articles have been written about the history, evolution and state of security studies in the last decades (Burgess 2010; Collins 2013a; Dunn Cavelty and Mauer 2009; Fierke 2015; Peoples and Vaughan-Williams 2015; Williams 2013; Shepherd 2013). This continued – perhaps even growing – interest implies that security represents a central value within modern societies, having fostered scholarly attention for nearly a century. Most scholars date the beginning of international security studies to the period after the Second World War, pointing to two definitive moments: the invention of the atomic bomb and mounting ideological tensions (Prins 1998: 784). While nuclear issues led to theorizing security in terms of deterrence and mutual destruction (Brodie 1959), the ideological clash between the 'East' and the 'West' induced theories of alliance-formation in the 1950s and early 1960s (Osgood 1962).

The tradition of security-related research extends back much further and is more versatile than analyses focusing on the consequences of the nuclear revolution and bipolarity – one must merely consider war studies and military history. Some scholars have remarked that security studies and strategic studies were synonymous in the early period of their (joint) development with deterrence theory characterized as an inter- and trans-disciplinary project (Nye and Lynn-Jones 1988: 6–7). Today, these two topics seem to be distinct fields of research; strategic studies have been limited to a narrow focus on national security strategies and cultures whereas the 'cottage industry' (Baldwin 1997: 5) related to the notion of security is constantly expanding.[2]

The most recent and comprehensive reconstruction of the development of security studies is a joint contribution by Barry Buzan and Lene Hansen. They distinguish five drivers that have been instrumental in the development of international security studies (Buzan and Hansen 2009: 50), namely: changes in great power politics, innovations in technology, crucial events, conflicting academic debates about the core of security studies, and the institutionalization of an academic and scientific discipline.[3] These drivers are quite obviously intertwined. Historical events and academic debates had an impact on the institutionalization of security studies as a distinct research field. The development of organizational structures (universities and policy-oriented think tanks), funding opportunities, publications, public outreach and research networks assume an essential role in the establishment of any discipline; this holds true for security studies as well (Buzan and Hansen 2009: 60). Waever and Buzan (2013) show that public and private funding of research projects and institutes has been a crucial factor in the development of theories – as well as the rise and perceived decline of security studies. Scholars often overlook that teaching practices, the definition of a core curriculum for study programs, and the attractiveness of PhD programs are important factors for recruiting young scholars to the field of security studies as well (Waever 2010: 656).

Commonly, the history of security studies is compartmentalized into distinct periods (e.g. Baldwin 1995; Waever and Buzan 2013; Walt 1991): the inter-war period, the post-war decade, the so-called golden age in the 1950s and 1960s, the rise of non-military issues and arms control in the 1970s and 1980s, the end of the Cold War, and the post-9/11 era.[4] Recent introductions to the evolution of security studies emphasize deterrence theory as a founding myth, followed by intellectual stagnation between 1965 and the 1980s. Then, starting in the 1980s, the debate between advocates of a narrow and a wide concept of security is said to have reanimated the field, serving as the starting point for ambitious theorizing in the 1990s (Waever and Buzan 2013). At her ISA presidential address in 1990, Helga Haftendorn said that '[s]ecurity studies as an academic field is in need of clarification: what is to be studied, how is it to be studied, and how is security studies to be distinguished from various subfields' (Haftendorn 1991: 15). This need for clarification gave rise to a lasting debate on the subject matter, theories and methodologies of security studies as well as the field's disciplinary status.

In comparing various approaches to the evolution and state of security studies, most studies make use of a combination of historicizing and theorizing the field. Some authors are explicit about their assumptions while others have a more implicit understanding of the history and sociology of security studies as a scientific endeavour. While Haftendorn (1991), Walt (1991) and Baldwin (1997) speak of a history of progress (and degeneration), Buzan, Hansen and Waever have focused on the sociological dimension of the development of security studies. Most introductions to this research field touch on its history, key approaches and various subject matters (e.g. Collins 2013a; Williams 2013). Accordingly, the prefix 'critical' has been used by many scholars in an attempt to indicate a distinction between conventional security studies and *critical* security studies based on a different collection of theories, methods and subject matters (e.g. Aradau et al. 2015; Peoples and Vaughan-Williams 2015; Shepherd 2013).

The evolution of security studies has neither been random nor a purely progressive process. In many ways, its development mirrors the widening and deepening of the concept of security itself. This co-constitution between theory and practice is not surprising given the fact that theorizing is, at the same time, always a social and political endeavour (Cox 1981: 128–9; Horkheimer ([1937] 1977). Thus, as a research field with close connections to changing 'political realities', security studies is characterized by the continuous broadening of theories, methods and research objects while its disciplinary status remains essentially contested.

The disciplinary question

Disciplines often prove to be elusive phenomenona: attempts to capture them are repelled by their diffuse and murky character. While it has become a matter of course to describe IR as a distinct discipline, this is a far more contested claim in the case of security studies. On the one hand, security (studies) is often implicitly perceived as a topic that defines IR. The *Oxford Handbook of International Relations* (Reus-Smit and Snidal 2010), for example, does not classify security studies as a subfield but refers to the more narrowly defined field of 'strategic studies'. *The Handbook of International Relations* (Carlsnaes et al. 2002) includes two issue-related chapters on 'War and Peace' (by Jack Levy) and 'Security Cooperation' (by Harald Müller), and its second edition (2012) has kept this the same.

On the other hand, developments in Europe, the USA, Latin America, Asia and Africa point to the fact that IR and security studies are institutionalized differently and that academic debates have taken a differing course (for IR see Waever 1998). Some critics have even argued that IR (and certainly security studies) have been a 'Westphalian project'; scholars in the USA and Europe have paid less attention to the body of thought originating from regions outside of Europe (Darby 2010: 95; for non-Western perspectives, see Tickner and Waever 2009). Whether 'African or Asian approaches to the study of security' (Collins 2013b: 4) will emerge remains an open question. However, if academic disciplines are not, in fact, trans-historic and trans-regional containers of objective knowledge but rather always entrenched in contingent political and social structures, the overall focus on 'states', 'war', 'security' and 'cooperation' must be understood as an expression of the specific historical circumstances in North America and Europe over the last three centuries. Despite this criticism, the concept of security has had a lasting attraction for policy makers and academics alike – a unique 'metaphysical punch' and 'disciplinary power' as Der Derian (1995: 24–5) writes. Taking these arguments seriously raises the question of whether security studies constitutes a (sub-) discipline at all, or as Nye and Lynn-Jones (1988: 6) nicely put it with reference to a conference participant: 'international security is not a discipline but a problem'. We have thus far used the terms research field, discipline and sub-discipline interchangeably. But what exactly *is* security studies?

While research field is certainly an uncontroversial notion, often used in a quotidian sense,[5] academic disciplines and sub-disciplines are powerful notions for different reasons. Collins, for example, pointedly writes that security studies is '*the* sub-discipline of International Relations' (Collins 2013b: 1). Some scholars would even suggest that security studies represent an inter- and trans-disciplinary project itself in which international security studies (associated with IR) is simply the most visible expression of a much broader research field. According to Stephen Toulmin (1972: 175), a discipline is characterized by three related indicators: an explanatory goal; a repertoire of concepts, theories and methods; and the accumulated experience of scholars that they constitute an academic community.

(1) *A common explanatory goal*: Traditional security studies has focused on explaining 'the threat, use and control of military force' (Walt 1991: 212), or, more broadly conceived, any phenomena of 'international violence' (Nye and Lynn-Jones 1988: 6), including the causes, effects of and responses to military threats on an inter-state level. In his introduction, Collins argues that 'a consensus has emerged on what security studies entails – it is to do with threats' (2013b: 1). This joint subject matter has not disappeared but rather expanded along many dimensions. This expansion is not *per se* a rejection of a common goal; though it may well be a rejection of *explaining* it. In formal terms, security studies is about 'security': ranging from the threat, use and control of force up to the discourses and practices of violence and insecurities in a broader sense. As a common starting point, all scholars either implicitly or explicitly theorize the core meaning of security – though in a variety of ways (Huysmans 1998). In various handbooks, security studies is defined on the basis of its key notion while alternative concepts such as peace and risk have been part of related debates; in a way, they question the centrality of security as a political concept today.

(2) *A shared repertoire of concepts, theories and methods*: The formal identity of security studies raises the next question: what *is* security, what does it mean (Waever 1995)? Boundaries of the concept itself are permeable and changing. While Baldwin (1997) intended to define security according to common

elements existent within varied conceptualizations, conceptual history tends to approach the meaning of security in a different way. It is interested in uncovering how concepts are used, reflecting changing political, societal and historical circumstances (Daase 2010; Huysmans 1998). Thus, security studies is increasingly being characterized by a plurality of theories and methods, expanding the formerly rather narrow focus on military threats, national security and the state. However, it is crucial to note that the *repertoire* of approaches appears quite stable. Many recent handbooks encompass a similar choice that range from classical realism to post-structuralism, quantitative to qualitative methods and include a plurality of concepts with different security foci – e.g. national security, human security and cyber security (Burgess 2010; Collins 2013a; Dunn Cavelty and Mauer 2009; Peoples and Vaughan-Williams 2015; Williams 2013).[6]

(3) *A community of scholars*: Shared identity among scholars is visible across numerous forms of institutionalization. This is particularly evident in journals that place special focus on security – such as *International Security* (founded in 1976) or *Security Dialogue* (founded in 1970 as *Bulletin of Peace Proposals*)[7] – in research programs, conferences, centers and institutes, study and PhD programs. Being both a research *and* teaching community, security studies encompass many well-known Master- and PhD-programs worldwide and also comprise major departments, research institutes and think tanks. Accordingly, security studies developed as an inter-disciplinary enterprise from the very beginning, incorporating military experts – even scholars from the natural sciences – and maintained a close connection to think tanks and practitioners (Buzan and Hansen 2009: 60; Nye and Lynn-Jones 1988: 6; Waever 2010).

Although Toulmin's first and second criteria for defining a discipline might generally apply to security studies, it would be inaccurate to speak of a clearly bounded community of scholars. There are many scholars who have specialized in international security politics (and policies) across various disciplines (mainly political science, but also sociology and the humanities) but the broadening of approaches has made the field more diverse (see the statements in the *conclusion*). Thus, anything akin to a 'community' of scholars has to be characterized by varying degrees of identity *and* diversity. Such a plurality requires more exchange and, as we recommend, *dialogue* beyond old-fashioned dualistic 'oppositions' between realists and institutionalists, positivists and post-positivists, or between the often-invoked 'mainstream' and 'its critics'. If not, academic fragmentation and political irrelevance could well be the result.

While Toulmin's approach to disciplines tends to be analytical, it was Michel Foucault who introduced a genealogical approach to knowledge and its relation to society. In many ways, academic disciplines are permeated by what Foucault understood to be the power/knowledge-nexus. While disciplines are not mere objective institutionalizations of knowledge, they do entail disciplinary machineries in the ways they impose a specific repertoire of concepts, theories and methods understood as the (identifiable) core of a discipline: the greater the coherence of the identity of a research and teaching community, the higher the disciplinary effects and dangers of stagnation or even degeneration. As Foucault aptly wrote: 'We should admit rather that power produces knowledge (and not simply by encouraging it because it serves power or by applying it because it is useful); that power and knowledge directly imply one another' ([1975] 1995: 27). Disciplines regulate what can be meaningfully said – for example about the definition of security, security politics and policies – constituting subjects that can be acted upon.[8] What these arguments tell us is that critique is primarily directed at *how* power/knowledge constitutes a field of research, its inclusive and exclusive discourses and practices; it poses 'the "meta-question" about security studies: why it has the boundaries that it has' (Prins 1998: 782).

Extending the meaning of security – a contested semantic field

It is often assumed that security comprises the core value of our modern – or rather post-modern – society, having a strong legacy in continental philosophy (Der Derian 1995; Dillon 1996). This has not always been the case. For centuries, it was not security but spiritual and secular peace that dominated theological, philosophical and even political thinking. The Latin noun *securus* means 'freedom from pain'. Historically the meaning of security was closely associated with the political peace order that the Roman Emperor Augustus created some 2000 years ago (Conze 1984). While security and peace were closely related to each other over the centuries, each concept has been used differently in strategic debates and political programs since the early twentieth century. Security was often branded the conservative term while peace became the political slogan of a young generation in the 1960s – proclaiming justice, participation and the reform of political systems in Western societies. Today, global security is often regarded as an undisputed value while peace is often perceived as only suited (and suitable) for political sermons.[9]

Our analysis of the changing meaning of security starts from a very narrow understanding of the concept as it was established after the Second World War in strategic debates and public discourse. In the late 1940s and early 1950s, the meaning of security narrowed to the greatest degree possible, focusing on the national survival of states and communities in the face of existential threats such as world wars and nuclear annihilation. It is no wonder, then, that external security became the key concept within international politics throughout the second half of the twentieth century and remained separated from social notions of security for quite some time (Conze 2009; Frei 1977; Haftendorn 1983). This separation has gradually disappeared; meanings of internal and external, national and human, military and economic, territorial and global security have emerged to form an extended concept of security over the last fifty years.

Systematically analyzed, the notion of security broadened with regard to four dimensions (see also Daase 2010). First, the scope of security expanded along the

8 *Gabi Schlag, Julian Junk and Christopher Daase*

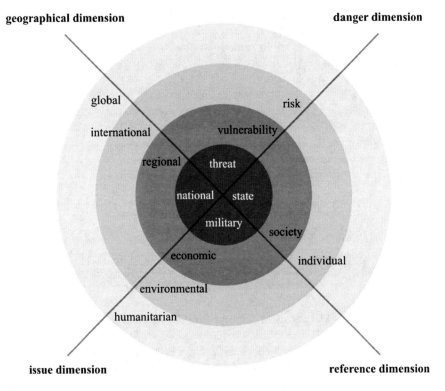

Figure 0.1 The four dimensions of extended security (Adapted from Daase 2010)

dimension of the *referent object*, relating to the question of whose security is to be guaranteed. Here, the state was joined by society and society, in turn, by the individual as the main referent object of security. Secondly, the *issue area* widened as well: perceptions of insecurity gradually extended from military dangers to economic, environmental and humanitarian concerns. Thirdly, the *spatial scope* of security changed its focus from the national level to regional, international and global security. Fourthly, the very *conceptualization of danger* changed: the purpose of security shifted from mere defence against threats to matters such as the reduction of vulnerabilities and the management of risks. Figure 0.1 summarizes these four dimensions.

Beyond the state – the reference dimension

The first dimension in which such conceptual extension is evident is the reference dimension that determines *whose* security should be safeguarded. Historically, the concept of security has closely been linked to the consolidation of the nation state as the only legitimate actor in international politics. In early modern times, the state established itself as a guarantor of the safety of its citizens, as Thomas

Hobbes famously described. The security of the state, however, remained precarious in the context of an interstate system without strong central authority. Thus, security in international relations, first and foremost, meant state security, i.e. the safeguarding of the nation's territory and the defence of national borders vis-à-vis other states. This is the understanding of *national security* advocated by so-called political realists such as Hans Morgenthau (1954), John Herz (1950) and others following the Second World War and throughout the Cold War (see Glaser's contribution to this volume). In the absence of an international monopoly of power and authority, they claim, all states live in a self-help system, and their primary duty is to assure national survival. As Kenneth Waltz famously wrote: 'In anarchy, security is the highest end' (Waltz 1979: 126).

This idea of national security as the absence of threats to the sovereignty and territorial integrity of a state did not go unchallenged. Historically, liberal theorists such as John Locke and Immanuel Kant stressed that the state is only an instrument for providing safety to the public. Liberal theorists in the 1970s took up this idea and challenged state-centric realist thinking by arguing that society should be the main reference point for security policy, while the focus of international politics in general should be society (Doyle 1983; Keohane and Nye 1977). *Societal security* was thus understood as a situation in which a collective of citizens lives in safety and freedom so that it can develop its productivity and wealth (Waever 1993).

This line of argument was taken a step further when the concept of *human security* became prominent after the end of the Cold War. In this view, the referent object of security policy is not the state and not even social collectives but rather the individual human being. The human security approach challenges both a traditional state-centric view and also the focus on social groups. Championed by the United Nations and a number of expert commissions (among them the *Commission on Global Governance* and the *Commission on Human Security*), the concept is closely tied to a cosmopolitan understanding of international politics, i.e. the conviction that human beings, not states, possess intrinsic values and should be protected (Beitz 1979; Pogge 2001). In this view, wherever state rights and human rights come into conflict, human rights should take priority. Thus, human security does not only refer to the protection of individuals and communities from war and other forms of violence but likewise to the protection of 'the vital core of all human lives in ways that advance human freedoms and human fulfillment' (Thakur and Newman 2004: 37).

Beyond the military – the issue dimension

The conceptual extension in terms of the referent objects has implications for the issue of areas comprising security. Traditional security threats were mainly perceived in *military* terms. This stems from the fact that by far the greatest security concerns for states are military attacks and the danger of being conquered. Thus, traditional national security interests are military in nature. Military security, in turn, is deemed to be most under threat from hostile states. In particular, the focus on nuclear weapons underlined the realist perspective on state-to-state threats and deterrents throughout the Cold War, focusing on Soviet nuclear strategy and decision making (Brodie 1959; Kissinger 1957). Non-state military threats only came into view when 'national liberation movements' in the Third World in the 1960s were perceived to be 'communist' threats to US and Western interests, bringing with them the imperative for developing new strategies of 'limited war' and 'counter-insurgency' (Blaufarb 1977; Deitchman 1962). As the terrorist attacks of 9/11 have shown, even small groups have gained the capacity to inflict disproportional damage and thereby seriously challenge a state's security. This is the reason that the concept of security nowadays not only refers to hostile states but also non-state actors as a source of military threats.

The traditional focus on military threats changed in the early 1970s when *economic security* gained in importance (see Boy's contribution to this volume). The oil crises of 1973 and 1979 made people aware that their well-being was jeopardized by economic vulnerabilities as well as by military threats (Wolf 1977). The concept of security was therefore broadened to include access to so-called 'vital resources'. The objective of resource security was to mitigate or dominate vulnerabilities to supply disruptions (Maull 1989). States and societies can be vulnerable in this sense, through embargoes or by unintentionally getting cut off from resources as a result of natural catastrophes, civil wars or simply shortages. Thus, many scholars draw the conclusion that in order to safeguard energy security, economic, political and military instruments had to be integrated into a single framework of comprehensive security (Nye 1982).

A further step towards extending the meaning of security occurred with the introduction of the notion of *environmental security* (see Methmann and Oels' contribution to this volume). The Brundtland Report in 1987 stated that 'environmental threats to security are now beginning to emerge on a global scale' (Brundtland Report 1987). Since then, environmental degradation and climate change have been discussed as national and international security issues (Myers 1989; Renner 1989). The key argument here is that the increasing destruction of human beings' natural habitat may directly lead to conflict (Tuchmann Mathews 1989: 166). However, the empirical link between environmental degradation and the risk of violent conflict has remained controversial (Deudney and Matthew 1999; Homer-Dixon 1999). Nevertheless, advocates of environmental security defend the securitization of the environment by pointing to the magnitude of potential consequences and the urgent need to rally public support for more resolute environmental policies. Richard Ullman nicely redefined security in 1983 by specifying the newly perceived threats: 'A threat to national security is an action or sequence of events that (1) threatens drastically and over a relatively brief span of time to degrade the quality of life for the inhabitants of a state, or (2) threatens significantly to narrow the range of policy choices available to the government of a state or to private, nongovernmental entities (persons, groups, corporations) within the state' (Ullman 1983: 133). In his view, and in the view of many of his colleagues at the time, environmental degradation and climate change can have exactly these effects, therefore making them legitimate security issues.

A more recent development is the extension of security into the humanitarian field. With this move, the last great issue area of international politics – namely human rights – comes under the influence of a security discourse. *Humanitarian security* refers to the human rights situation of groups and individuals (as the term human security does) as well as to the security of development aid volunteers and disaster relief workers in crisis areas. However, another intended purpose of humanitarian security is the protection of so-called safe-havens and humanitarian zones (Simon 2003). The conceptual affinity of humanitarian security and humanitarian intervention demonstrates how easy it would be to imagine 'military humanism' (Chomsky 1999) and even 'humanitarian wars' (Woodward 2001) when linking human rights and security (see Geis and Wagner's contribution to this volume).

Beyond the national – the geographical dimension

A third dimension of extended security is its geographical scope. The question is: what is the extent of security concerns geographically? Traditional security policy only applied to the national level. Realists deemed it misguided to design security policies beyond the nation state; even if global security problems existed, the international system would only allow for national solutions: 'World-shaking problems cry for global solutions, but there is no global agency to provide them' (Waltz 1979: 109). National security therefore strictly refers to the security of the territorial state and derives its ends and means from so-called national interests.

This limitation proves problematic as soon as states develop joint strategies to defend their common interests at a regional level. With the founding of NATO in 1949, a process was set into motion that gradually led to the development of a transatlantic 'security community' (Deutsch 1954). Security communities develop when states integrate with each other politically by renouncing violence as a means of settling conflicts among themselves and by developing common ideas of how to establish and maintain regional stability. Security communities have emerged in many regions of the world, overcoming the narrow notion of national security (Adler and Barnett 1998).

The term *international security* more broadly refers to inter-state cooperation on security issues (see Fehl's contribution to this volume). It departs from realist assumptions by arguing that cooperation among security-seeking states is possible even in the absence of an overarching framework for coercing states to keep their promises (Axelrod and Keohane 1986). International security thus redirects the focus from purely national and regional concerns to the stability of the international system as a common good. The question then is no longer how to maximize national security but how to create international conditions in which all states enjoy a high degree of security. Institutions – such as conventions, regimes and organizations – are seen as the principal tools for the multilateral preservation of international security (Haftendorn et al. 1999; Martin 1992).

Finally, the concept of *global security* even goes beyond the idea of international security. While international security still primarily refers to states, global security refers to human beings. The Palme Commission argued as early as 1982 for a notion of 'common security' that would transform a reigning inter-state society into a world society. The concept of global security gave rise to strategies for enhancing living conditions for world society, i.e. for all human beings. Global security often goes hand in hand with human security and integrates measures that protect the environment and climate, secure access to food and clean water, and end civil strife and violent conflict.

Beyond threats – the danger dimension

The fourth, and arguably most important dimension of conceptual change, concerns the meaning of danger. Traditionally, political challenges to the state had been defined as *threats*, measured on the basis of what was known about the enemy actor, their hostile intentions and their military capabilities (Cohen 1979; Knorr 1976). This case was paradigmatic during the Cold War when 'East' and 'West' stood heavily armed in opposition to one another. Defusing threats either by counter-threats and deterrence or by threat-reduction and détente became a crucial undertaking during the Cold War (Gaddis 1987).

However, once more diffuse dangers to the well-being of societies were perceived, this concept of insecurity as a symmetrical threat became untenable. In times of great social and economic interdependence, dangers do not necessarily emanate from hostile actors or through military capabilities – as the oil crises demonstrated. Thus, insecurity had to be measured in alternative ways, including as the degree of *vulnerability* to externalities, whatever their sources might be (Keohane and Nye 1977). With this, the security debate shifted from enemy strength to one's own alleged weakness. The famous 'window of vulnerability' was a by-product of détente, as disarmament raised fears that the good-will of cooperation could be exploited by an enemy.

With the concept of vulnerability, it is only a small step to the paradigmatic shift in security policy after the Cold War (Daase 2002; Kessler and Daase 2007). Today, *risks*, not threats, dominate discourses about international politics. The 'clear and present danger' of the Cold War has been replaced by unclear and future 'risks and challenges'. The proliferation of weapons of mass destruction, transnational terrorism, organized crime, environmental degradation and many other issues are discussed in terms of uncertainty and risk. Their similarity lies in their relative indeterminableness (see Burgess' contribution to this volume).

In sum, the notion of security expanded greatly as a consequence of transformations in policy – the resultant semantic shifts probably influenced this transformation as well. As we elaborate in the following section, this expansion occurred in tandem with changes to the boundaries of security studies itself.

Mapping extending security studies – a brief intellectual history

Simply stated, the broadening of the meaning of security (figure 0.1) was paralleled by a widening of security *studies* as a research field (see figure 0.2 below). In this section, we focus on the relation between academic debates and the meaning of security as the two main drivers for the evolution of security studies as a (sub-) discipline. Comparable to the four dimensions of an extended meaning of security, we distinguish an *ontological, epistemological, methodological* and *theoretical* dimension.[10] The typological selection of these dimensions, however, is contested and raises many questions. Philosophy of (social) science students would certainly criticize its oversimplification. However, any attempt at mapping is, to an extent, a simplification in essence. A map is a two-dimensional representation of a given terrain that intends to provide spatial orientation, not to inscribe conclusive truth claims or normative judgments about intellectual progression (or degeneration). In using a map, we stress that boundaries between differing

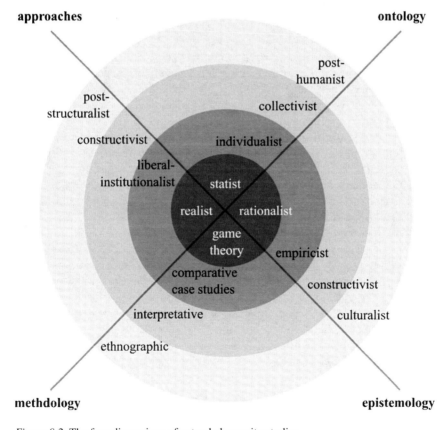

Figure 0.2 The four dimensions of extended security studies

positions are permeable; even intellectual boundaries are not given facts but must be delineated. Thus, sites of ontology, epistemology and methodology do not add up to any static meta-theoretical picture but symbolize (the possibility of) movements in different directions.

By *ontology*, we refer to the basic assumptions of what and who are regarded as the central subjects and referent objects of security. As a theory of being, ontology is concerned with the questions of: 'what is the world made of? what objects do we study?' (Kurki and Wight 2010: 15). Ontological claims are not empirically grounded, hence they are assumptions about what is granted. Common ontological positions include the dichotomy of materialism and idealism as well as the differentiation between statism, individualism and collectivism.[11]

Epistemology and methodology are often used interchangeably (Wight 2002: 26) but direct our attention to different aspects of knowledge (production). As a theory of knowledge, epistemology is concerned with the question 'how do we come to have knowledge of the world?' (Kurki and Wight 2010: 15). This often includes the distinction between objectivism and subjectivism but also between (scientific) realist and (meta-) constructivist positions in answering the question of how we are able to know things about the world.[12]

Methodology, then, is used as a hinge between ontological and epistemological claims. It explicates how being and knowing are related in a way that allows for scientific results and knowledge production. Methodological positions are often focused on the question of methods, i.e. 'what methods do we use to unearth data and evidence?' (Kurki and Wight 2010: 15). In the social sciences, the classic divide is drawn between qualitative and quantitative methods as well as between causal analysis and hermeneutic approaches. Methodology, however, entails more than mere technical questions regarding the application of the right and appropriate methods; it is a focal point for the basic question of scientific inquiry, the practices of knowledge and science itself (Jackson 2011).

Such debates on the philosophy of science in IR had an ambivalent impact on the field of security studies during the Cold War. In terms of central *approaches* and debates, security studies moved from a rather coherent realist core to a pluralist and inter-disciplinary research field. Major IR approaches were largely dominated by questions of security and had a visible impact on the evolution of security studies as well. While the first debate between realists and idealists was only implicitly present in the opposition between strategic studies and peace research, neo-realism, liberal institutionalism, constructivism and post-structuralism comprise variably prominent theoretical positions within international security studies today. With the end of the Cold War, security studies became a much more diversified research field. Feminist and post-colonial approaches as well as Critical Theory, even *Critical Security Studies* as a unique research field, are often perceived as outliers within security studies depending on one's viewpoint (Krause and Williams 2005). Before we return to the question of discipline, let us describe each dimension and its expansion in greater detail.

From statism to post-humanism – the ontological dimension

It might not be surprising that the *state* and its security has been the central subject and referent object of international security studies, closely associated with the realist paradigm in IR (Morgenthau 1954; Waltz 1979).[13] Statism is most obviously symbolized by the concept of 'national security' and the field of 'strategic studies' maintaining a focus on the 'national security strategy' of major powers (Wolfers 1962).[14] Conceptualizing the state as the central and most important factor in international security politics continues, and research on changing security strategies, often in a comparative perspective, has not vanished (see Glaser's contribution to this volume).

With the development of liberal approaches in IR as well as foreign policy analysis as a distinct research field, this state-centred perspective has often included an interest in *individual* motivations and *collective* decision-making as well (see Masala's contribution to this volume). While the question of whether individuals make a difference has mostly been relegated to historically informed analyses and policy studies, people remain a powerful source of collective action. Allison (1969), for example, discussed different models for explaining the Cuban missile crisis with reference to individual frames of reference and collective decision making. Jervis (1976), on the other hand, emphasized modes and processes of perception and misperception and their impact on political outcomes.[15]

A more pronounced focus on collective actors is often associated with the rise of constructivist approaches and their interest in understanding the formation of collectivities through social and discursive processes (Weldes et al. 1999). Here, *collectivism* directs our attention to the structural forces constituting collective actors as well as to the discursive practices of reproducing meaningful representations. Hence, collectivism is not limited by an understanding of the state as a central actor but often shifts perspectives to the ways in which subjects and subjectivities – either states or groups – are constituted by discourses of security (Campbell 1998; Doty 1996).

While all of these perspectives on ontology presume a human being to some extent, recent debates on surveillance technologies have furthered the interest in *post-human* agents and material-object based conditions of security (Aradau 2010; see Junk and Rauer's contribution to this volume). Advocates of the Actor-Network-Theory, for example, emphasize that machines and objects fundamentally challenge our common conceptions of actorness and agency while cognitive research on the mind questions the freedom of choice in the first place.

From rationalism to culturalism – the epistemological dimension

While epistemological perspectives have been central to IR, security studies is only implicitly shaped by these debates. A primary focus on the material resources of the state for the sake of maintaining security was often narrowed to the question of military capabilities. Defining and detecting objective threats and dangers to national security as a *rationalist* approach describes the major epistemological position of security studies for the first three decades. Neo-realists as well as liberal institutionalists did not doubt that a scientific approach could detect 'real' threats and dangers. Thus, rationalism becomes closely associated with *empiricism*, i.e. conducting empirical research grounded in (comparative) case studies that place the dominance of formal modelling and game theory in perspective.

This rationalist-objectivism was followed by a more sociological approach which emphasized that subjective factors drive politics as well. Wendt's *constructivism* implied a revival of 'structural idealism' (Wendt 1999: 1) claiming that ideas, norms and rules are constitutive structures shaping the behaviour of agents. Nevertheless, he described himself as a 'positivist' and 'scientific realist', building a so-called *via media* towards IR's rationalist' mainstream (Wendt 1999: 39, 51). Security studies' take on the constructivist turn was moderate and tended to be empirically directed at the importance of the social constructions of threats and dangers as well as the distinct causal mechanisms of security communities (Adler and Barnett 1998; Katzenstein 1996). While a rationalist epistemology is commonly associated with (neo-) positivism, constructivist perspectives vary according to their methodological positions between a positivist pole (prominently advocated by Wendt) and a hermeneutic pole (see below).

The opening of epistemological positions towards a constructivist approach gave rise to a lasting debate on discourses and practices, and on how structures of meaning enable and constrain political action. Such a *cultural approach* often delimits itself from the objective/subjective dichotomy and accentuates the inter-subjectivity of agency and the importance of contingency (see Fierke's as well as Schlag's contributions to this volume). A cultural approach is primarily interested in taking constitutive processes seriously, thereby departing from the positivist straitjacket that Wendt put on his version of thin constructivism. The notion of culture, however, should not be understood as a shorthand for value-based communities (e.g. civilizations) but as an analytical perspective on the meanings that produce the discourses and practices (Bueger and Gadinger 2014; Reckwitz 2002; Weldes et al. 1999). The post-structural strand of collectivism is thus inherently based on a cultural epistemology, often implying a rejection of ontological confessions of any kind.

From game theory to anthropology – the methodological dimension

As already stated, methodological questions should not be reduced solely to the selection of correct methods and techniques. Methodology and epistemology share many arguments but direct attention to different aspects of knowledge-production. While IR's founding years were mostly characterized by historically informed methods that led to the second debate about the 'scientific rigor' of the discipline, security studies took a slightly different lead. According to its materialist-rational and state-centred focus on nuclear threats, *game theory* provided the key methodology for calculating probabilities of a nuclear showdown and the strategic choices available to players under the conditions of anarchy (Brodie 1959; Jervis

1978; Snyder 1971). Formal modelling and quantitative methods helped incorporate scholars from different disciplines to the study of security (see Hegre and Kristiansen's contribution to this volume). Nevertheless, this also had strong disciplining effects, as Powell's (1999: 97) statement shows: 'Models serve […] as a tool for disciplining our thinking about the world, and formal models install a particular type of discipline' – and such a rigorous discipline often included empirical pitfalls and instances of a normative-political naiveté.[16]

With the rise of (neo-) *positivism* and the scientific revolution in IR, methodological issues became even more concentrated on explaining and predicting security politics (King et al. 1994). *Comparative case study* designs evolved as the preferred method for understanding the driving forces – in particular the cause and effect-relations – of security-related issues (Achen and Snidal 1989; George and Bennett 2004; Blatter and Haverland 2012). Most prominently, the formulation of an alliance of threat-theory by Stephen Walt (1985, 1987, 1988), with clear statements on testable hypotheses, has had a lasting impact on the style of research in security studies.

Quite similar to the third debate in IR, critique from various sources also rose along with the hegemony of positivism. Hermeneutic and discursive approaches, often summarized under the *ex negativo* label of *post-positivism*, entered international security studies (Smith et al. 1996). In particular, receptions of Wittgenstein, Foucault and Derrida gave rise to deconstruction as a form of theorizing in which the boundaries between analytical and normative, epistemological and methodological dimensions were often dissolved.

One recent trend has been a growing interest in *anthropology* and its methods, redefining the role of the researcher as part of his/her research rather than as an objective and neutral observer (Salter and Mutlu 2013). Accordingly, methodological choices and methods are not value-neutral techniques waiting to be used for a rigor analysis. Aradau and Huysmans (2014: 598) argue 'that method and methodological reflections can be a key site of revisiting critique and politics in IR research'. Methods, then, are 'performative practices experimentally connecting and assembling fragments of ontology, epistemology, theories, techniques and data through which substantive effects are obtained' (Aradau and Huysmans 2014: 3). Hence, questions of methodology and the choice of methods must be understood as an inherently reflexive endeavour.

From monism to pluralism – the theoretical dimension

Ontological, epistemological and methodological positions relate to the development of different theories and approaches to security. Indeed, they established security studies as a distinct field in relation to war studies and military history with a quite differing repertoire of approaches.[17] Strategic studies was (and is) about the 'choices between alternative strategies for states' (Nye and Lynn-Jones 1988: 7) and was largely synonymous with *realist approaches* to national security and state strategies (Glaser 2013; Prins 1998: 786). At the core of security studies lay a realist approach with a clear focus on a state's strategic choices in the nuclear age. Deterrence theory was the most prominent explication of this joint endeavour; it focused on US grand strategy, NATO's security strategy of massive retaliation and alliance formation in a broader sense (Kaufmann 1973; Kissinger 1957; Osgood 1962; Schelling 1962). The influence of bureaucratic decision-making approaches was great (Allison 1969) and at times also included psychological insights (Jervis 1976). Behaviourism dominated most of the methodological debates during the first two decades of security studies.

While deterrence theory was closely associated with rational choice and game theory – including extrapolations of decision making in the Kremlin and Soviet military doctrine – alliance theory had a clear positivist leaning (Snyder 1971, Walt 1985, Waltz 1979). With détente, the Harmel report and the invocation of flexible response, *liberal institutionalism* developed as a main challenger to realist approaches, emphasizing the impact of institutions and regimes (Haftendorn et al. 1999). Security studies was strongly associated with IR's focus on states and decision makers based on a rationalist epistemology and positivist methodology. As Waever (2013) has argued, the neo-neo debate between neo-realism and neo-liberal institutionalism dominated the 1970s and 1980s until academic and political critique formed around a rather vast and heterogeneous constructivist paradigm. This critique coincided with the rapid development of the peace movement, particularly in Western Europe in response to NATO's double track decision and its implementation in 1982.

Following the distinction between conventional and critical constructivism by Ted Hopf (1998), *conventional constructivism* was primarily interested in the impact of ideas, identities and norms (Desch 1998; Farrell 2002; Katzenstein 1996). It still was state-oriented (although collectivities played a more significant role through the key notion of 'collective identity') and based on a mixture of constructivist epistemology and positivist methodology. This breed of constructivism formed a new middle ground (Checkel 1998) and created linkages in different directions.

In the mid- to late-1990s, the rational and positivist core of security studies was more explicitly attacked by critical approaches; this included feminist, post-colonial and deconstructivist perspectives that often had a focus on the political and normative dimensions of security politics and studies. Critical constructivists emphasized the power of discourse and the social constructions of threats and enmity. Parallel to the various movements within critical constructivism, most scholars shared a commitment to the contested meaning and contestedness of key political notions such as security and the state (Buzan et al.1998; Jones 1999; Krause and Williams 2005; Weldes et al. 1999). In essence, the new movement was interested in the formation of collectivities, with close links to constructivist and culturalist epistemologies explicating the methodological diversity of 'post-positivism'. *Post-structuralism* quickly became a focal point for critical constructivism, with securitization theory as its most prominent expression (Buzan et al. 1998; Campbell 1998; Der Derian 1995; Dillon 1996; Hansen 2006).[18] Recent theoretical trends suggest that security studies is moving into ontological debates on *post-humanism*. It exhibits a growing interest in a post-rational rather than a post-positivist methodology and a clear connection to other (sub-) disciplines such as science and technology studies, surveillance studies and more broadly conceived cultural studies and sociology.

Before turning to an overview of the single contributions to the volume, one word of caution is needed: One might expect to find a systematic selection and positioning of the contributors to this volume within our map, along with an assessment of the 'rise and fall' or 'progression and degeneration' of security studies' research programs. However, this has not been our intention. The everyday practices of carrying out research do not lead to a neat, static image on which positions can clearly be distinguished. Certain combinations of ontological, epistemological and methodological positions are more coherent and practicable, while others are more ambivalent and abstract. In the end, approaches to theorizing security have mostly utilized ontology, epistemology and methodology as forms of academic reflection and criticism, not as an essential(ized) positioning. Hence, security studies was and still is mainly *problem-driven* – depending on what and how we define and describe the central 'problem' that security studies is meant to deal with.

Dialogues on the identity and diversity of security studies – an overview of the volume

This edited volume provides an overview of some theoretical strands of, conceptual challenges to and methodological trends in security studies.[19] Taking the field's pluralism seriously, this volume is the starting point of a *dialogue* about the theoretical, empirical and methodological identity and diversity of security studies, the political and societal importance of which has grown significantly in recent years. While security scholars generally share the notion of a wide empirical concept of security,[20] theoretical and methodological gaps and rifts are obvious. In many ways, debates within international security studies and IR have moved from a rather simple bipolar constellation – realism/strategic studies vs. 'all the others' – to an immense variety of paradigms, theories and methodologies. It may often appear that there are as many 'approaches' as there are researchers trying to find a 'new' (not yet used) theory or method on how to study security.

This initial depiction of security studies as an expanding and probably inter- and trans-disciplinary field leads to the impression that most of these communities and 'sub-cultures' do not speak to one another (any more). Some have never shared common ground for debates; others have furthered a specialized language often unintelligible to outsiders. We posit that such silence between different schools of thought, theories and methodologies is unproductive. It heightens an artificial division of debates on the meaning and practices of 'security', often by making use of each of their idiosyncratic vocabularies.[21]

In order to overcome this situation, a multifaceted dialogue is necessary. Dialogue on security does not only bring politics back in, it also enables the self-reflection of a scientific community on its 'proper' research objects, approaches and methods. As mentioned above, although scholars relate to a wide concept of security, the very meaning of 'security' remains contested. Such contestedness is not problematic *per se*; rather it brings to mind the idea that any political concept is essentially contested – as it should be since it opens up the possibility of a critical conversation and of a critical stance towards politics. This book aims at building bridges of communication between different 'camps' by initiating a dialogue on the identity *and* diversity of security studies. It does so in three parts, introducing paradigmatic approaches to security, discussing advances on different subjects of security, and, lastly, outlining methodological challenges in studying security.

Paradigmatic approaches to security

The first part of the book includes paradigmatic approaches to security that are closely connected to major IR debates. The first chapter by *Charles Glaser* responds to many critics of realist thought and its alleged incapability to explain current security politics. In essence, he argues that although the core concepts of realism have not expanded, the theory has indeed evolved significantly over the past few decades. The chapter begins by reviewing realism's core assumptions and explaining how they are related to the expansion of security studies. Glaser explores realism's understanding of security and explains the distinguishing features of various strands of realism. He takes a closer look at the security dilemma, specifically the role of information about the motives of other states in driving the security dilemma; he relates realism's continuing analytic value for understanding and responding to on-going changes in international politics, particularly to the rise of China.

Caroline Fehl's contribution outlines an institutionalist approach to security. It stands beyond doubt that the evolution of security institutions and organizations – in particular NATO and the UN – have fundamentally changed the ways that security is actually provided. Nevertheless, many scholars have criticized how these institutions and organizations fail to live up to their promises; they find themselves in an acute crisis, wedged between states' willingness to cooperate and the impact of international norms. Fehl argues that rationalist institutionalism can make sense of this 'crisis' by emphasizing that states are rational actors that act strategically in pursuit of their preferences in the context of decision-making about institutions (even if these decisions are constrained and the outcomes often uncontrollable); she also argues that institutions 'matter' in the sense of exercising an autonomous causal effect irreducible to the material capabilities of individual states. Owing precisely to the fact that power is often exercised through institutions, policy outcomes would radically differ if these institutions were absent, as Fehl illustrates by the non-proliferation regime.

While realist and (rational) institutionalist approaches have been central to the field of security studies for decades, constructivist approaches challenge the rationalist assumptions inherent in both approaches. Maintaining that constructivism is a pluralistic family of different approaches, *Karin Fierke* takes side with a language-based approach to security. The notion of discourses and speech acts has tremendously influenced debates on the very meaning of security since the late 1980s and provoked many critical comments by realists. In her contribution in Chapter 3, Fierke differentiates among three progressive layers of debate: In the first layer, which started in the 1980s, critical scholars attempted to dismantle the taken-for-granted, hegemonic status of the language of security and IR. In a second layer, emphasis shifted to an examination of how the language of security operates in the world, including a more explicit theorization of the relationship between language and embodiment. A third layer of the debate represents a return to materiality, but departing from the material capabilities that earlier generations of realist scholarship were interested in. The debate, which began over a question of whether language is important, has evolved into an emphasis on the 'embodiment' of security, Fierke argues. The abstract, disembodied individual – whether state or person – has given way to the human subject who not only speaks, but also sees, feels and acts within a social, cultural, historical and material context.

The next chapter, by *Christopher Daase*, introduces a culturalist approach to security as an interdisciplinary research programme. It first delineates a conceptual change of security in order to show that the return of culture into security studies corresponds to social and political transformations in domestic and international politics. Second, it outlines the development of security studies as a discipline and discusses various ways in which culture has been used to explain divergence and convergence in security policy. Third, the chapter defines security culture as 'those values, discourses and practices of individuals and institutions that determine what issue is a danger and how and by which means it is best tackled'. Situating security culture between the more comprehensive term 'political culture' and the more narrow term 'strategic culture', the chapter uncovers the added value of a culturalist approach by showing how legal, historical and ethical issues can productively be integrated into security analyses.

Peter Burgess accentuates ethical issues and directs our attention to the relation between ethics, security and knowledge. His chapter revisits the basic premises for understanding security in our time in order to answer questions of epistemology, knowledge and ignorance in relation to issues of security. Burgess argues that the foundation of the politics of security today is an epistemology of the unknown; this epistemology imposes changes in the way that we are to understand ethics, in general, and the ethics of security in particular. Thus, his reflections make clear that the preoccupation with certainty will naturally have consequences on the way that we study security, the kinds of security research questions asked, by whom and for whom, and the status that answers to such questions can actually have.

Subjects of security

The second part of the volume places more emphasis on the subject of security and the broadening and deepening of the concept of security in recent decades. While Glaser's contribution outlines realism's core assumptions *Carlo Masala* focuses more deeply on the empirical value of realist approaches. Many scholars doubted that there would be any new contribution by realist theories to security politics in the twenty-first century. Masala argues that in times when most security studies scholars are preoccupied with non-military, societal and individual, regional and global security issues, realists remind us of the continued centrality of the use of force and the state in world politics. Failed states, ethnic conflicts, the return of religion, the rise of new great powers, global and regional power shifts – all of these phenomena have characterized the international systems for centuries. Realist scholars, especially those who work with historical case studies, make the point that most of the issues labelled as new are actually 'not-that-new', having already been a security concern of policy makers in the past. For these reasons, security studies can still profit from realist scholarship in the future but, at the same time, requires openness to dialogue on the part of realist scholars, as Masala concludes.

Chapter 7 by *Anna Geis* and *Wolfgang Wagner* addresses a core phenomenon in security politics, namely the distinctive approach to security taken by democracies. Much has been written on the Democratic Peace and, more recently, on democratic wars, as Geis and Wagner summarize. Liberal researchers maintain that this 'peculiarity' is no coincidence but instead the result of democratic domestic institutions and norms. The authors are interested in assessing the success of the 'democratic distinctiveness programme' in dealing with the new security agenda that has arisen since the end of the Cold War. Geis and Wagner argue that, although rooted in the state-centric world of international relations of pre-globalization, the 'democratic distinctiveness programme' has done remarkably well in applying its key causal mechanisms to a changing security agenda. It would therefore seem more fruitful to replace the Democratic Peace research programme with a much more comprehensive liberal approach to security challenges in a globalizing world.

The most challenging development in security politics has been the evolution of 'new' risks and dangers often associated with climate change and humanitarian catastrophes. *Chris Methmann* and *Angela Oels* take a look at environmental security, a success story within a broadening security agenda. Based on a genealogy of environmental security discourses, the authors challenge the emancipatory notion of human security on two accounts: First, Methmann and Oels show that security has not simply appropriated environmental concerns but that both notions of environment and security have undergone significant changes and influenced each other along the way. Second, they argue that the succession of these discourses does not necessarily imply a more emancipatory take on securing the environment. Instead, each contains a different version of the domination of Southern populations. The most recent discourse on climate security, for example, invokes a neo-liberal framework of resilience and opens the back door for military interventions.

The breakdown of financial markets is certainly indicative of the most recent security-related problem societies and governments face. *Nina Boy* focuses on the notion of financial security and shows that economics have been related to state security issues for centuries. As such, she returns to the state as a subject of security; with an emphasis on sovereign creditworthiness, she goes well beyond the traditional issue areas of security studies. Even though the on-going sovereign debt crisis brought renewed attention to the topic, Boy shows that this issue extension within security can be traced back several centuries. She describes four historical and present manifestations of this financial concept of security: the historical term of public credit, the liquid government bond, the risk-free asset of financial-economic textbooks, and the 'safe haven' role assumed by the bond market in times of uncertainty. By analysing the interlinkages between these concepts, Boy shows how financial and political security are interwoven.

Methodologies of studying security

While conceptual and empirical issues constitute the core of security studies as a research field, questions of methodology and methods are equally important. The third part of the volume presents some new avenues of and challenges to methods and methodology in the study of security (and peace).

In her chapter, *Gabi Schlag* argues that a turn towards visuality is highly relevant for IR and critical security studies. It opens the rather narrow perspective on speech acts and grants more attention to the symbolic and cultural practices that constitute the very meaning of security in the first place. In recent years, there has been growing academic interest in the visual politics of security – especially since the iconic images of '9/11'. It is often assumed that images construct social reality and influence political decision makers. Moreover, images are used to enforce and criticize contested policies, and their usage has been accused of entailing propaganda and digital manipulation. Apart from conceptualizing images as iconic acts, the most profound challenge to the growing interest in visuality by security studies is that of methodology, Schlag states. Based on discourse analysis and iconology, she outlines how security studies could systematically include visual cultures into the research design, demonstrating the importance of images for constructing visual representations of insecurities, identity and otherness, as well as violence and pain.

Although security has long been the core term within security studies, alternative concepts have had an important impact on how security-related issues have actually been studied. Peace and conflict studies certainly represent the most sophisticated field in terms of methodological clarification. *Håvard Hegre* and *Idunn Kristiansen* discuss opportunities and challenges of quantifying security as a methodological choice. They provide an overview of quantitative conflict research to illustrate how indicators have been created to measure global, state and individual security. A trend supported by many empirical findings on all levels of analysis exists in global security: though the number of conflicts remains high, security has improved over the past decades. Hegre and Kristiansen analyze in greater depth the variety of contributing factors behind this trend. While quantitative methods have been helpful for analyzing these factors (even though adjusting some indicators can lead to differing results), the temporal dimension of conflict escalation has so far escaped the analysis of this methodological choice and has tended to be tackled by qualitative methods. In their chapter, Hegre and Kristiansen go well beyond the traditional state security scope, and discuss matters such as individual level indicators as well.

The chapter by *Julian Junk* and *Valentin Rauer* outlines the consequences of perpetuating the alleged incompatibility of hermeneutic interpretive and positivist causal explanatory methods. One of the most prominent – though, from a social science perspective, not completely understood – developments are drones or 'unmanned area vehicles' (UAVs). These robotic systems are increasingly capable of autonomous actions. As such, they are not actors in the sense of human beings but constitute 'hybrids' or 'actants', which are, in part, capable of intentional and autonomous decision making, as the Actor-Network Theory (ANT) has shown. This phenomenon of hybridity, Junk and Rauer argue, demands the combination of methods in a controlled and systematic way, particularly through connections and zooms as methodological lenses and through method triangulation and parallelization as research strategies. They show that the extension of security studies goes hand in hand with a need for more inclusive research designs that harvest the plurality of methodological tools and integrate them into one coherent research project.

The dialogical approach

Along these lines, this book commences as a dialogue – one between (international) security studies and what we identify as some of the most prominent and promising approaches to security and security politics in IR. A dialogue presupposes different perspectives; it also presupposes that there is something important and valuable to discuss. A dialogue, however, likewise implies that, following all these debates, authors maintain their approaches, defending them against critique but also rethink theoretical claims and empirical results. Thus, a dialogue is not meant to outline a new grand theory but rather strengthen the ability to communicate with one another. We think that a comprehensive and critical understanding of security policy and security studies requires no less. Our *conclusion* is thus designed to engage all authors and participants of the initial workshop of the volume in a 'live' dialogue, presenting new avenues for further debate beyond paradigmatic straitjackets.

A final note on where this book and the map it presents fall short is also necessary. First, though we intended to fill some gaps with this introduction, a broader historical perspective on the concept of security and security-related issues has been rather absent in international security studies and IR. A comprehensive *'begriffsgeschichte'* of security – including its related notions – is yet to be written (Conze 1984). A broader sociological approach should look back and forth to sub-disciplines of history, in particular to war studies and military history and how approaches and scholars generally traverse different disciplines with ease. Second, non-Western and non-European approaches to security are of growing interest in various disciplines (Barkawi and Laffey 2006). This also directs more attention to locally and regionally specific issues of security. It demonstrates that the notion of security has often been limited to American and European, hence historically contingent, experiences regarding dangers and threats. Last but not least, a reader might be surprised that gender-related approaches and the debate on human security have not been included in this volume (Paris 2001; Sjoberg 2009). These absences are not meant to be discrimination but are the unavoidable, albeit regretful, result of a limited choice of contributions. A critical and fertile dialogue regarding security studies will hopefully continue far beyond the limits of this volume.

Notes

1 The book was first published in 1983 with the subtitle 'The National Security Problem in International Relations' which changed to 'An Agenda for International Security Studies in the Post Cold War Era' in its second edition in 1991.
2 While publications and edited volumes on security studies have thrived, this has not been true for strategic studies to the same extent.
3 Buzan and Hansen present the evolution of security studies in terms of a post-Kuhnian sociology of science based on these different internal and external, material and ideational drivers.
4 Interestingly, Baldwin (1995: 124) understands the 1970s as a 'decline' while Walt (1991: 216) dates a 'renaissance' of security studies already with the end of the Vietnam War. Haftendorn (1991: 5) distinguishes security studies' history according to its subject matter, changing from national security (seventeenth century to 1960s), to international (since 1970s) and global security today (Haftendorn 1991: 12).
5 Bourdieu has developed a more sophisticated notion of a social field.
6 An innovative exception is the edited volume by Aradau et al. (2015) and its focus on new methodologies instead of paradigms, concepts and research fields as well as the edited volume by Salter and Mutlu (2013) whose contributors describe how they are actually doing research.
7 The first issue of IS included articles on arms control and US grand strategy but also a contribution by Singer on peace research. Security Dialogue, by contrast, started with sections on science and development, the Vietnam war, human environment and non-military defense.
8 Jackson (2011: 9) has emphasized that the notion 'scientific' has been the central rhetorical commonplace used to distinguish science from non-science, disciplining what can be researched, how, and why.
9 One could claim that the conceptual victory of security over peace is cause and effect of political change (Daase 2010). The crucial point of this change is that the liberal state – and along with it the international liberal society – are becoming the victims of their own success, for the social process of emancipation depends on a relatively peaceful and secure environment. Societal security demands are only articulated if the fundamental security needs of the state – i.e. peace in the traditional sense – are fulfilled. As soon as this is the case, however, further security demands are articulated, which tend to overburden the capacities of states and international organizations. While in the 1950s and 1960s a narrow concept of security referred mainly to military threats to national territory, today an extended concept of security also captures the individual risk of global human rights violations.
10 Colin Wight has argued that in IR 'these terms are often thrown around like philosophical hand grenades, with little consideration given to how they are deployed, or to what end' (Wight 2002: 26). Wight says: 'Ontology, in philosophical terms, was originally

understood as a branch of metaphysics; it is the science of being in general, embracing such issues as the nature of existence and the categorical structure of reality. In the philosophy of science and the philosophy of social science, it is used to refer to the set of things whose existence is claimed, or acknowledged, by a particular theory or system of thought: it is in this sense that one speaks of "the" ontology of a theory, or of a theory having such-and-such an ontology (for example, an ontology of anarchical structures, or of material substances). The term epistemology comes from the Greek word epistêmê, meaning knowledge. In simple terms, epistemology is the philosophy of knowledge or of how we come to know. Methodology is also concerned with how we come to know, but is much more practical in nature. Methodology is focused on the specific ways – the methods – that we can use to try to understand our world better. Epistemology and methodology are intimately related: the former involves the philosophy of how we come to know the world and the latter involves the practice. It is common in IR for these aspects to be conflated and confused' (Wight 2002: 42, Fn12).

11 Ontological debates are often focused on the agency–structure debate and the constitutive relation between agents and social structures (Wendt 1987).
12 As our map indicates, constructivism is a highly contested term indicating quite different levels of theorizing. For an overview, see Joergensen (2001).
13 For an interesting assessment and critical theorizing of ontological security, see Steele (2007).
14 In his reflections about Buzan's "Peoples, States, and Fear", Martin Shaw has made a strong case against statism as well as individualism in international security studies: 'What is needed is a deepening as well as a broadening of the agenda. The concept of "social relations" (or "society") needs to be interposed between and around the terms "state" and "individual" within which the debate has been conducted' (Shaw 1993: 160).
15 The recent interest of security study scholars in the power and role of emotions probably revives the individual level of analysis with a pronounced sociological (rather than a strict psychological) approach (Hutchison 2010).
16 For a comprehensive discussion of the pitfalls of formal modeling, see Walt (1999). He argues: 'The central aim of social science is to develop knowledge that is relevant to understanding important social problems. Among other things, this task requires theories that are precise, logically consistent, original, and empirically valid. Formal techniques facilitate the construction of precise and deductively sound arguments, but recent efforts in security studies have generated comparatively few new hypotheses and have for the most part not been tested in a careful and systematic way. The growing technical complexity of recent formal work has not been matched by a corresponding increase in insight, and as a result, recent formal work has relatively little to say about contemporary security issues' (Walt 1999: 8). To overcome this division between quantitative and qualitative approaches, Gaddis has argued to extend the 'data base' and build an archive 'that would be equally relevant to the respective concerns of historians, political scientists, and policymakers, from which hypotheses could be constructed and tested, and on the basis of which we could begin a sustained dialogue among all three groups about how what we do could be made relevant to the very real problems all of us, as the ultimate "consumers" of what we hope will be peace and security, are likely to confront' (Gaddis 1987: 15).
17 Unfortunately, we do not have the space to go into this deeper but on first sight it seems that war studies and military history as part of History were mostly defined in methodological terms.
18 Securitization theory has obviously more roots than post-structuralism.
19 This book is closer to the edited volume by Ronnie D. Lipschutz (1995) than to the many excellent textbooks published in the last five years. Lipschutz states that 'we [...] tried to bring together a diverse group of individuals whose approaches to security

policy and practice ranged from realist to "interdependista" to postmodern' (Lipschutz 1995: xi).
20 It was not until 1983 that a wider notion of security entered the debates in International Security (Ullmann 1983).
21 This is truly paradoxical: while security becomes all-encompassing and its various extensions more and more interdependent in the social and political world, the academic world locks itself into many boxes falling once more into the trap of irrelevance for real world problems. How security is actually *done* is thus much different from how it is *studied*.

References

Achen, C.H and Snidal, D. (1989) 'Rational Deterrence Theory and Comparative Case Studies', *International Organization*, 41 (2): 143–69.
Adler, E. and Barnett, M. (1998) 'Security Communities in Theoretical Perspective', in E. Adler and M. Barnett (eds) *Security Communities*, Cambridge: Cambridge University Press: 2–28.
Allison, G.T (1969) 'Conceptual Models and the Cuban Missile Crisis', *The American Political Science Review*, 63 (3): 689–718.
Aradau, C. (2010) 'Security That Matters: Critical Infrastructure and Objects of Protection', *Security Dialogue*, 41 (5): 491–514.
Aradau, C. and Huysmans, J. (2014) 'Critical Methods in International Relations: The Politics of Techniques, Devices and Acts', *European Journal of International Relations*, 20 (3): 596–619.
Aradau, C., Huysmans, J., Neal, A. and Voelkner, N. (2015) (eds) *Critical Security Methods: New Frameworks for Analysis*, London and New York: Routledge.
Axelrod, R. and Keohane, R.O. (1986) 'Achieving Cooperation under Anarchy: Strategies and Institutions", in K. Oye (ed.) *Cooperation under Anarchy*, Princeton: Princeton University Press: 226–54.
Baldwin, D.A. (1995) 'Security Studies and the End of the Cold War', *World Politics*, 48 (1): 117–41.
—— (1997) 'The Concept of Security', *Review of International Studies*, 23: 5–26.
Barkawi, T. and Laffey, M. (2006) 'The Postcolonial Moment in Security Studies, *Review of International Relations*, 32 (2): 329–52.
Beitz, C. (1979) *Political Theory and International Relations*, Princeton: Princeton University Press.
Blatter, J. and Haverland, M. (2012) *Designing Case Studies – Explanatory Approaches in Small-N Research*, Basingstoke: Palgrave Macmillan.
Blaufarb, D. (1977) *The Counterinsurgency Era: U.S. Doctrine and Performance*, New York: Free Press.
Brodie, B. (1959) *Strategy in the Missile Age*, Princeton: Princeton University Press.
Brundlandt Report (1987) 'Our Common Future', available at: http://www.un-documents.net/ocf-11.htm (accessed 15 December 2014).
Bueger, C. and Gadinger, F. (2014) *International Practice Theory: New Perspectives*, Basingstoke and New York: Palgrave Macmillan.
Burgess, P.J. (ed.) (2010) *The Routledge Handbook of New Security Studies*, London and New York: Routledge.
Buzan, B., O. Waever and J. de Wilde (1998) *Security: A New Framework for Analysis*, Boulder: Lynne Rienner.

Buzan, B. (2007) *People, States and Fears*, 2nd edn, Colchester: ECPR Press.
Buzan, B. and Hansen, L. (2009) *The Evolution of International Security Studies*, Cambridge: Cambridge University Press.
Campbell, D. (1998) *Writing Security: United States Foreign Policy and the Politics of Identity*, Minneapolis: University of Minnesota Press.
Carlsnaes, W. Risse, T. and Simmons, B. (eds) (2002/2012) *Handbook of International Relations*, London: SAGE.
Checkel, J.T. (1998) 'The Constructivist Turn in International Relations Theory', *World Politics*, 50 (2): 324–48.
Chomsky, N. (1999) *The New Military Humanism: Lessons from Kosovo*, Monroe: Common Courage Press.
Collins, A. (ed.) (2013a) *Contemporary Security Studies*, 3rd edn, Oxford: Oxford University Press.
—— (2013b) 'Introduction: What is Security Studies?', in A. Collins (ed.) *Contemporary Security Studies*, 3rd edn, Oxford: Oxford University Press: 1–11.
Cohen, R. (1979) *Threat Perception in International Crisis*, Milwaukee: University of Wisconsin Press.
Conze, E. (2009) *Die Suche nach Sicherheit. Eine Geschichte der Bundesrepublik Deutschland von 1949 bis in die Gegenwart*, Berlin: Siedler.
Conze, W. (1984) 'Sicherheit/Schutz', in O. Brunner, W. Conze and R. Koselleck (eds) *Geschichtliche Grundbegriffe. Historisches Lexikon zur politisch-sozialen Sprache in Deutschland*, Vol. 5, Stuttgart: Klett- Cotta: 831–862.
Cox, R.W. (1981) 'Social Forces, States and World Orders: Beyond International Relations Theory', *Millennium – Journal of International Studies*, 10 (2): 126–55.
Daase, C. (2002) 'Internationale Risikopolitik. Ein Forschungsprogramm für den sicherheitspolitischen Paradigmenwechsel', in C. Daase, S. Feske and I. Peters (eds) *Internationale Risikopolitik*, Baden-Baden: Nomos: 9–35.
—— (2010) 'National, Societal, and Human Security: On the Transformation of Political Language', *Historical Social Research*, 35 (4): 22–37.
Darby, P. (2010) 'A Disabling Discipline', in C. Reus-Smit and D. Snidal (eds) *The Oxford Handbook of International Relations*, Oxford: Oxford University Press: 94–105.
Deitchman, S.J. (1962) *Limited War and American Defense Policy: Building and Using Military Power in a World at War*, Cambridge (MA): MIT Press.
Der Derian, J. (1995) 'The Value of Security: Hobbes, Marx, Nietzsche, and Baudrillard', in R.D. Lipschutz (ed.) *On Security*, New York: Columbia University Press: 24–45.
Desch, M.C. (1998) 'Culture Clash: Assessing the Importance of Ideas in Security Studies', *International Security*, 23 (1): 141–70.
Deudney, D.H. and Matthew, R.A. (eds) (1999) *Contested Grounds: Security and Conflict in the New Environmental Politics*, Albany: State University of New York Press.
Deutsch, K.W. (1954) *Political Community at the International Level: Problems of Definition and Measurement*, Garden City: Doubleday.
Dillon, M. (1996) *Politics of Security: Towards a Political Philosophy of Continental Thought*, London and New York: Routledge.
Doty, R.L. (1996) *Imperial Encounters: The Politics of Representation in North-South Relations*, Minneapolis: University of Minnesota Press.
Doyle, M. (1983) 'Kant, Liberal Legacies, and Foreign Affairs', *Philosophy and Public Affairs*, 12 (3/4): 205–35 and 323–53.
Dunn Cavelty, M. and Mauer, V. (eds) (2009) *The Routledge Handbook of Security Studies*, London and New York: Routledge.

Farrell, T. (2002) 'Constructivist Security Studies: Portrait of a Research Program', *International Studies Review*, 4 (1): 49–72.

Frei, D. (1977) *Sicherheit. Grundfragen der Weltpolitik*, Stuttgart: Kohlhammer.

Fierke, K.M. (2015) *Critical Approaches to International Security*, 2nd edn, Cambridge: Polity Press.

Foucault, M. ([1975] 1995) *Discipline and Punish: The Birth of the Prison*, New York: Vintage Books.

Gaddis, J.L. (1987) 'Expanding the Data Base: Historians, Political Scientists, and the Enrichment of Security Studies', *International Security*, 12 (1): 3–21.

George, A. and Bennett, A. (2004) *Case Studies and Theory Development in the Social Sciences*, Cambridge (MA): MIT Press.

Glaser, C. (2013) Realism, in A. Collins (ed.) *Contemporary Security Studies*, 3rd edn, Oxford: Oxford University Press: 13–27.

Haftendorn, H. (1983) *Sicherheit und Entspannung. Zur Außenpolitik der Bundesrepublik Deutschland 1955–1982*, Baden-Baden: Nomos.

(1991) 'The Security Puzzle: Theory-Building and Discipline-Building in International Security', *International Studies Quarterly*, 35 (1): 3–17.

Haftendorn, H., Keohane, R.O. and Wallander, C. (eds) (1999) *Imperfect Unions: Security Institutions Over Time and Space*, Oxford: Oxford University Press.

Hansen, L. (2006) *Security as Practice: Discourse Analysis and the Bosnian War*, London and New York: Routledge.

Herz, J. (1950) 'Idealist Internationalism and the Security Dilemma', *World Politics*, 2 (2): 157–80.

Homer-Dixon, T. (1999) *Environment, Scarcity, and Violence*, Princeton: Princeton University Press.

Hopf, T. (1998) 'The Promise of Constructivism in International Relations Theory', *International Security*, 23 (1): 171–200.

Horkheimer, M. ([1937] 1977) 'Traditionelle und kritische Theorie', in M. Horkheimer, A. Schmidt (eds) *Kritische Theorie*, Vol. 2, Frankfurt/M.: Fischer: 521–75.

Hutchison, E. (2010) 'Trauma and the Politics of Emotions: Constituting Identity, Security and Community after the Bali Bombing', *International Relations*, 24 (1): 65–86.

Huysmans, J. (1998) 'Security! What Do You Mean? From Concept to Thick Signifier', *European Journal of International Relations*, 4 (2): 226–255.

Jackson, P. (2011) *The Conduct of Inquiry in International Relations*, London and New York: Routledge.

Jervis, R. (1976) *Perception and Misperception in International Politics*, Princeton: Princeton University Press.

(1978) 'Cooperation under the Security Dilemma', *World Politics*, 30 (2): 167–214.

Joergensen, K.E. (2001) 'Four Levels and a Discipline', in K.M. Fierke and K.E. Joergensen (eds) *Constructing International Relations: The Next Generation*, Armonk and New York: ME Sharpe: 36–53.

Jones, R.W. (1999) *Security, Strategy and Critical Theory*, London: Lynne Rienner.

Katzenstein, P.J. (ed.) (1996) *The Culture of National Security: Norms and Identity in World Politics*, New York: Columbia University Press.

Kaufmann, F.-X. (1973) *Sicherheit als soziologisches und sozialpolitisches Problem: Untersuchungen zu einer Wertidee hochdifferenzierter Gesellschaften*, 2nd edn, Stuttgart: Enke.

Keohane, R.O. and Nye, J.S. (1977) *Power and Interdependence: World Politics in Transition*, Boston: Little, Brown & Co.

Kessler, O. and Daase, C. (2007) 'From Insecurity to Uncertainty: Risk and the Paradox of Security Politics', *Alternatives*, 33(2): 211–232.

King, G., Keohane, R.O. and Verba, S. (1994) *Designing Social Inquiry*, Princeton: Princeton University Press.

Kissinger, H.A. (1957) *Nuclear Weapons and Foreign Policy*, New York: Harper and Row.

Knorr, K. (1976) 'Threat Perception', in K. Knorr (ed.) *Historical Dimensions of National Security Problems*, Lawrence: University Press of Kansas: 78–119.

Krause, K. and Williams, M. (eds) (2005) *Critical Security Studies: Concepts and Cases*, Minneapolis: University of Minnesota Press.

Kurki, M. and Wight, C. (2010) 'International Relations and Social Sciences', in T. Dunne, M. Kurki and S. Smith (eds) *International Relations Theories: Discipline and Diversity*, Oxford: Oxford University Press: 14–35.

Lipschutz, R.D. (1995) (ed.) *On Security*, New York: Columbia University Press.

Martin, L.L. (1992) 'Interests, Power, and Multilateralism', *International Organization*, 46 (4): 765–92.

Maull, H.W. (1989) 'Energy and resources: The strategic dimensions', *Survival*, 31(6): 500–518.

Mearsheimer, J.J. (1991) Back to the Future: Instability in Europe after the Cold War, in *International Security*, 15(1): 5–56.

Morgenthau, H.J. (1954) *Politics among Nations*, 2nd edn, New York: Knopf.

Myers, N. (1989) 'Environment and Security', *Foreign Policy*, 74: 23–41.

Nye, J.S. (1982) 'Energy and Security Strategy', in S.P. Huntington (ed.) *The Strategic Imperative: New Policies for American Security*, Cambridge (MA): 301–29.

Nye, J.S. and Lynn-Jones, S.M. (1988) 'International Security Studies: A Report of a Conference on the State of the Field', *International Security*, 12 (4): 5–27.

Osgood, R.E. (1962) *NATO: The Entangling Alliance*, Chicago: Chicago University Press.

Paris, R. (2001) 'Human Security: Paradigm Shift or Hot Air?', *International Security*, 26 (2): 87–102.

Peoples, C. and Vaughan-Williams, N. (2015) *Critical Security Studies*, rev. 2nd edn, London and New York: Routledge.

Pogge, T. (2001) *Global Justice*, Malden: Blackwell.

Powell, R. (1999) 'The Modeling Enterprise and Security Studies', *International Security*, 24 (2): 97–106.

Prins, G. (1998) 'The Four-Stroke Cycle in Security Studies', *International Affairs*, 74 (4), 781–808.

Reckwitz, A. (2002) 'Toward a Theory of Social Practices: A Development in Culturalist Theorizing', *European Journal of Social Theory*, 5 (2): 243–63.

Renner, M. (1989) *National Security: The Economic and Environmental Dimensions*, Washington: Worldwatch Institute.

Reus-Smit, C. and Snidal, D. (eds) (2010) *The Oxford Handbook of International Relations*, Oxford: Oxford University Press.

Salter, M. and Mutlu, C.E. (eds) (2013) *Research Methods in Critical Security Studies: An Introduction*, London and New York: Routledge.

Schelling, T.C. (1962) Nuclear Strategy in Europe, in *World Politics*, 14 (3): 421–432.

Shaw, M. (1993) 'There Is No Such Thing as Society: Beyond Individualism and Statism in International Security Studies', *Review of International Studies*, 19 (2): 159–75.

Shepherd, L.J. (2013) *Critical Approaches to Security: An Introduction to Theories and Methods*, London and New York: Routledge.

Simon, A. (2003) *UN-Schutzzonen – Ein Schutzinstrument für verfolgte Personen?*, Heidelberg: Springer.
Sjoberg, L. (ed) (2009) *Gender and International Security: Feminist Perspectives*, London and New York: Routledge.
Smith, S., Booth, K. and Zalewski, M. (eds) (1996) *International Theory: Positivism and Beyond*, Cambridge: Cambridge University Press.
Snyder, G. (1971) '"Prisoner's Dilemma" and "Chicken" Models in International Politics', *International Studies Quarterly*, 15 (1): 66–103.
Steele, B. (2007) *Ontological Security in International Relations: Self Identity and the IR State*, London and New York: Routledge.
Tickner, A. and Waever, O. (eds) (2009) *International Relations Scholarship around the World*, London and New York: Routledge.
Thakur, R., and Newman, E. (2004) 'Introduction: Non-Traditional Security in Asia', in R. Thakur and E. Newman (eds) *Broadening Asia's Security Discourse and Agenda: Political, Social, and Environmental Perspectives*, Tokyo: United Nations University Press: 1–15.
Toulmin, S. (1972) *Human Understanding: The Collective Use and Evolution of Concepts*, Princeton: Princeton University Press.
Tuchman Mathews, J. (1989) 'Redefining Security', *Foreign Affairs*, 68 (2): 162–77.
Ullman, R.H. (1983) 'Redefining Security', *International Security*, 8 (1): 129–53.
Waever, O. (1993) 'Societal Security: The Concept', in O. Waever, B. Buzan, M. Kelstrup and P. Lemaitre (eds) *Identity, Migration and the New Security Agenda in Europe*, London: Pinter: 17–40.
(1995) 'Securitisation and Desuritisation', in R.D. Lipschutz (ed.) *On Security*, New York: Columbia University Press: 46–86.
(1998) 'The Sociology of a Not So International Discipline: American and European Developments in International Relations', *International Organization*, 52 (4): 687–727.
(2010) 'Towards a Political Sociology of Security Studies', *Security Dialogue*, 41 (6): 649–58.
(2013) Still A Discipline after all these Debates? in T. Dunne, M. Kurki and S. Smith (eds) *International Relations Theory: Discipline and Diversity*, 3rd edn, Oxford: Oxford University Press, 306–328.
Waever, O. and Buzan, B. (2013) 'After the Return to Theory: The Past, Present and Future od Security Studies', in A. Collins (ed.) *Contemporary Security Studies*, 3rd edn, Oxford: Oxford University Press: 393–409.
Walt, S.M. (1985) 'Alliance Formation and the Balance of World Power', *International Security*, 9 (4): 3–43.
(1987) *The Origins of Alliances*, Ithaca: Cornell University Press.
(1988) 'Testing Theories of Alliance Formation: The Case of Southwest Asia', *International Organization*, 42 (2): 275–316.
(1991) 'The Renaissance of Security Studies', *International Studies Quarterly*, 35 (2): 211–39.
(1999) 'Rigor or Rigor Mortis?: Rational Choice and Security Studies', *International Security*, 23 (4): 5–48.
Waltz, K.N. (1979) *Theory of International Politics*, New York: Random House.
Weldes, J. et al. (1999) *Cultures of Insecurity: States, Communities, and the Production of Danger*, Minneapolis: University of Minnesota Press.
Wendt, A. (1987) 'The Agent-Structure Problem in International Relations Theory', *International Organization*, 41 (3): 335–70.

(1999) *Social Theory of International Politics*, Cambridge: Cambridge University Press.
Wight, C. (2002) 'Philosophy of Social Sciences and International Relations', in W. Carlsnaes, T. Risse and B. Simmons (eds) *Handbook of International Relations*, London: SAGE: 23–52.
Williams, P.D. (2013) *Security Studies: An Introduction*, 2nd edn, London and New York: Routledge.
Wolf, J.J. (1977) *The Growing Dimensions of Security*, Washington: The Atlantic Council's Working Group on Security.
Wolfers, A. (1962) 'National Security as an Ambiguous Symbol', in A. Wolfers (ed.) *Discord and Collaboration: Essays on International Politics*, Baltimore: The Johns Hopkins University Press: 147–65.
Woodward, S.L. (2001) 'Humanitarian War: A New Consensus?', *Disasters*, 25 (4): 331–44.

Part I
Paradigmatic Approaches to Security

1 Realism
Not expanding, but still evolving

Charles L. Glaser

The purpose of this chapter is to lay out how realists understand 'security' – specifically, the meaning of the term itself, the factors that influence a state's ability to be secure, and the strategies that states can pursue to achieve security. Realism is the longest standing and arguably the best developed of the various approaches for understanding international security. As the editors of this volume argue in the Introduction, realist approaches were at the core of security studies as it developed during the nuclear age. Realism is frequently described as the dominant paradigm in the fields of international relations and security studies. Consequently, realism has often been the target against which new approaches to security have been launched (for example, see Chapter 3 by K.M. Fierke in this volume, which explores how critical scholarship has approached realism).

The Introduction to this volume lays out four dimensions along which the concept of security has been expanded over the past twenty-plus years. With very limited exceptions, realism has not joined this exercise in expansion: it has continued to focus on the security of states, not on society and individuals; it has continued to emphasize military dangers, not economic and environmental dangers (on these topics, see Chapter 8 in this volume by Methmann and Oels, and Chapter 9 by Boy); it has continued to view regional and global security primarily as byproducts of national security and/or means for producing national security, and therefore retained its focus on states' security; and it has continued to envision defending against threats, as opposed to managing vulnerability and risk, as the key to achieving security. In terms of the figure that the editors have designed to summarize these dimensions, realism lies solidly within the inner circle of the diagram. This central position reflects realism's foundational role within the field of security studies.

Although its core concepts have not expanded, realism has evolved significantly over the past few decades. This chapter begins by reviewing realism's core assumptions and explaining how they are related to the expansion of security studies which is the focus of this volume. The next section explores realism's understanding of security, and the following section explains the distinguishing features of different strands of realism. The chapter then takes a closer look at the security dilemma, specifically the role of information about other states' motives in driving the security dilemma. The final section considers realism's continuing

36   Charles L. Glaser

analytic value for understanding and responding to ongoing changes in international politics.

Core assumptions and features of realism

Reviewing realism's basic assumptions sets the stage for understanding its lack of conceptual expansion.[1] The expansion that has taken place in other strands of security studies runs contrary to some of realism's defining assumptions and against some of the most immediate implications of these assumptions. Thus, we should not be surprised that theorists who have embraced a broader understanding of certain key concepts of realism decided to move beyond realism instead of expanding it from within.

First, realism views states as the most important actors in the international system.[2] Among grand theories the primary alternative is international institutions. Realists argue that international institutions play a less important role than states; many argue that they play a relatively unimportant role, largely reflecting the international conditions facing states while doing little to independently shape them. Some realists take the central role of states as an assumption; others argue that the limited role for institutions follows deductively from the theory's basic assumptions. Either way, the dominant importance of states is an analytic claim that runs across the realist family.[3]

Obviously, theoretical efforts that have chosen to look beyond states, focusing primary attention on the security of societies and of individuals, diverge from this core realist assumption. Perhaps less obviously, realism's focus on states leads it to emphasize national security, in contrast to regional or global security. Of course, realism addresses security across these larger spaces, but it understands security arising through the choices of individual states, not grander processes.

Second, realism imagines states as essentially unitary actors. This assumption is clearly not accurate – states are made up of leaders, governing institutions, interest groups, various types of cultures, and populations. Realist theories include this assumption due to its analytic value – helpful for understanding the key features of the choices states face and, closely related, for understanding their strategic interactions. This assumption, however, means that realism does not address societies or individuals – they are abstracted away by this simplification.

Third, realism characterizes the international system as anarchic – there is no international authority that can enforce agreements and prevent the use of force. In this usage, anarchy does not refer to state behavior; describing the system as anarchic is not meant to imply that international relations are chaotic. Instead, anarchy simply describes the lack of an international authority capable of governing the international system.[4]

Fourth, largely reflecting the importance it places on the anarchic nature of the international system, realism identifies power as a defining feature of the international environment that states face. In fact, for the majority of realists power is *the* defining feature. (For divergent understandings of power, see Chapter 3 by Fierke and Chapter 11 by Schlag, which present a couple of constructivist approaches to power.) Although power is a complicated concept, it is adequately understood as the resources available to a state for building military forces.[5] The key elements that contribute to a state's power include its wealth, population, and technological sophistication. More powerful states can build larger and more technologically advanced military forces. The importance of power follows closely from the anarchic nature of the international system – states need to rely on their own military capabilities to achieve their international goals and power plays a central role in enabling states to acquire these capabilities.

The importance that realism places on power supports the common characterization of realism as a material theory. Many theoretical critiques of realism highlight the negative implications that result from limiting a theory to material factors. However, as I lay out in following sections, so-called defensive realism and a closely related rational variant have identified a central role for states' information about other states' motives. The result of this evolution of realism is a significant narrowing of the divide between material and ideational theories of international relations.

The materialist characterization is also closely related to a fifth key assumption – realist analysis 'black-boxes' opposing states, that is, states assess each other in terms of their power and military capabilities, but not in terms of the variation that exists within states, including regime type, the nature of the state's leadership, its political ideology, and so on. (On theories that take a divergent approach, emphasizing the potential differences between democratic and non-democratic states, see Chapter 7 by Geis and Wagner.) However, here again the materialist characterization is overdrawn, because black-boxing does not mean that information about opposing states is entirely unavailable. To start, the rational realist theory assumes that states have information about opposing states that they acquired prior to their strategic interaction and some of this information could be based on states' internal characteristics. The rational theory does not explain how the state acquires this initial (that is, pre-strategic interaction) information. Consequently, it is a partial theory; it can be combined with other layers of analysis to produce a more complete theory.[6] But the key point here is that the rational theory does not preclude this information. In addition, and more central to the defensive realist and rational theories, black-boxing does not prevent the state from revising its estimate of the opposing state's motives. Quite the contrary, these theories emphasize the possibility that an opposing state's actions can communicate valuable information about its motives. In other words, strategic interaction can result in a state updating its information about the opposing state's type.

Finally, realism sees states as essentially rational actors: states make decisions that are well matched to achieving their goals, given the constraints imposed by their power and the uncertainties they face about other states' capabilities and motives. States make strategic decisions – that is, they take into consideration how other states will react to their policies. Although there are realists who reject this rational actor assumption and question its importance, and others who are not clear about their position on it, the rationality assumption is widely enough employed to include it among realism's core assumptions.[7]

The rationality assumption essentially takes for granted answers to questions that other theories – including some of the expanded theories of security studies that this volume engages – take as their focus. For example, rationality means that states hold beliefs and understandings that are well matched to the evidence that is available about their international situation. These understandings would concern both the state's material situation, and the motives and goals of other states in the international system. In addition, the state should also have at least a basic understanding of how opposing states might interpret its strategy and react to it. Here again, realist theories take these understandings as given, that is, not explained by the theory itself. Research on the sources of causal beliefs, of shared understandings of the material world, and of the development of norms can therefore be viewed as complementing the rationality assumption. Similarly, research on how states organize themselves to collect and process data on their international environment, invest in technology and human capital to make possible the efficient conversion of their raw power into military capabilities, and structure themselves to make complicated decisions during crises can all be understood as contributing to our understanding of the origins of rational states (as well as flawed states that do not meet the rationality standard).

Realism and security

Realism relies on a straightforward understanding of security. Security is first and foremost about the protection of a state's territory from attacks by other states. A state is more secure when it is less likely to be attacked and will suffer less damage if attacked.[8] Under certain conditions, a state may have to protect other interests – for example, allies or lines of communication – to protect its territory. In such cases, a state is more secure when it faces smaller threats to these other vital interests. In addition to protecting its territory, a state wants to maintain the independence of its political, economic and social systems from the demands of other states. Consequently, a state is more secure when it is less vulnerable to coercion by other states. Freedom from coercion is closely related to the features noted above – for example, a state that is less vulnerable to attack is less susceptible to coercion.

Although realism envisions security in terms of threats posed by other states, this is not because scholars who employ realist theories necessarily believe that these are the only dangers states face. Terrorism, global pandemics, and weak domestic political systems, to name just a few possibilities, can pose large threats to a state's well-being. Many security studies scholars who employ realism to analyze interactions between states have used other theories to analyze these other types of dangers. Instead, realism's emphasis on states reflects at least two quite different rationales. First, states have historically posed the greatest potential danger to other states. The only external threat to a state's survival was from other states. Given the challenges in understanding interactions between states, and closely related, the strategies that a state chooses to deal with potential opponents, developing a theory that focused only on these issues was (and still is) an ambitious and challenging undertaking. Second, other dangers have sufficiently different sources and dynamics that there is likely little value in developing a single theory that attempts to explain the full range of potential threats to states. This said, there are specific issues in which realist arguments can provide leverage in understanding non-state dangers (see for example, Posen 1993).

A related set of arguments helps to explain why some scholars have preferred to maintain a narrow definition of the range of topics and dangers that should be included within the field of security studies.[9] So-called traditionalists do not deny the importance of other dangers and types of security – including environmental, economic and human security. Rather, they tend to believe that the narrow definition, which focuses on the danger posed to states by organized violence – possibly focusing on states, but also including civil war and terrorism – already includes a huge swath of important phenomena. As a result, widening the definition and scope of security studies promises to add little analytic leverage, while risking a loss of focus that could weaken the analysis of the issues that are already covered by the traditional definition. In the end, this is largely an issue of labeling – that is, describing the boundaries of various type of analysis – though there can be implications for the health and vitality of various fields and subfields of study.

Another related point addresses the common claim that states' willingness to invest in purposes other than their own security – for example, saving lives via humanitarian intervention and advancing their political ideological beliefs by spreading democracy – provides empirical evidence that undermines realism. According to this line of argument, realism claims that states only care about security, and possibly increasing their own wealth, and therefore will not engage in activities that primarily benefit other states and their citizens. However, realism provides greater leeway for states to pursue these other purposes than the critique suggests. Structural realism does assume that states give top priority to achieving security. Realists, of course, realize however that states do have other goals. The assumption that states can be envisioned as pure security seekers is chosen to enable the theory to isolate the impact of the international system. Therefore a sophisticated reading of structural realism says that states may pursue a variety of non-security objectives, but only when they have achieved a high level of security or when pursuing these other objectives would not detract from their ability to achieve and maintain their security. According to a realist analysis, we would expect that as a state's security increases, it would have greater leeway to pursue non-security objectives. Evidence from the past couple of decades provides support for this prediction. After the Cold War, NATO – reflecting the interests of its member states – could afford to place greater weight on spreading democracy, partly because the security threats it faced had been greatly reduced and partly because the risks of spreading democracy were greatly reduced. Human rights and humanitarian intervention can be understood to have gained prominence for similar reasons. With the end of the Cold War, the lack of pressing security threats allowed the Western powers to devote greater political attention and material resources to helping to resolve ethnic conflicts.[10] In a similar vein, some realist analysts have argued that US unipolarity after the Cold War, which erased security threats to US vital interests, allowed the United States to overreach – for example, by launching a costly invasion of Iraq in 2003 when its vital interests were not at stake (see for example, Posen 2007).

A state can attempt to achieve security in two basic ways. First, and most obvious, the state can acquire the military capabilities required to protect itself from other states. The capabilities can include the ability to deter attacks and to defend its territory if deterrence fails.[11] Second, and less obvious but central to much of realism, the state can try to achieve security by changing its adversary's objectives. Most important, the state may be able to achieve this by increasing the adversary's security. An adversary motivated by security can have expansionist territorial objectives and competitive military objectives that result from its insecurity. In this type of situation, the adversary's insecurity decreases the state's own security. Policies that enable the state to increase its adversary's security will, therefore, increase the state's own security.

Unfortunately, a state will often be in a situation in which pursuing one of these approaches to security will undermine its ability to simultaneously pursue the other. For example, deploying the military capabilities required for deterrence and defense can reduce the adversary's ability to deter and defend, which in turn reduces the adversary's security. The net result can be that the state ends up less secure, even though its enhanced military capabilities initially increased its ability to defend and deter. Similarly, efforts to make one's adversary more secure – for example, by reducing the size of one's military forces or accepting arms limitations that prevent a military buildup – can compromise the state's own ability to defend and deter. These tensions lie at the core of the security dilemma, which turns out to be an essential element of structural realism. I will explore the security dilemma in some detail in a later section. However, before presenting that discussion, we need to explore the significant differences within the realist family, which arise, among other reasons, due to the quite different weight they place on the security dilemma.

The key divergences within the realist family

Although realism is frequently associated with a specific bottom line – states exist in an international system that is characterized by competition and war – in fact, the evolution of realism over the past few decades has produced significant disagreement on this most basic conclusion. This section briefly sketches the divergent strands of the realist family and assesses why they disagree.

In very broad terms, realism started with what is now termed classical realism; Kenneth Waltz's *Theory of International Politics* transformed realist thinking by giving priority to the impact of international structure, as compared to individual leaders, or to the domestic political system and regime type of specific states (Waltz 1979).[12] In following decades, different formulations of structural realism – including what are termed offensive defensive and defensive realism – have challenged Waltz's theory and reached different conclusions about the extent of the competitive nature of international politics. During this same period, new strands of realist thinking have returned to the classical focus on the role of states. My recent book provides a synthesis, showing how the two approaches are complementary and interrelated (Glaser 2010).

The fundamental divide – structure versus motives

The fundamental division within realism is between the strand that focuses on the impact of the international system and the strand that focuses on the impact of states' own motives and fundamental goals. The latter, which I term 'motivational realism' (and which includes some of classical realism and neo-classical realism), gives priority to states that have an inherent desire to expand for explaining international competition and conflict. These states – 'greedy states' – are interested in territorial expansion even when they are secure in the status quo.[13] From this perspective, the international environment remains important – it will constrain these states and create opportunities for them to expand. But for motivational realism the international environment is not the key source of these states' desire to take territory and, in turn, of conflict between states.[14]

Some motivational realist theories simply posit the existence of greed states, while others offer explanations for the sources of greed itself. Classical realism envisioned greed as rooted in human nature (Morgenthau 1973). State greed, however, need not reflect the preferences of individuals. Other prominent possibilities include a state's desire for wealth and prosperity, or for international status; and a state's desire to spread its political ideology and governance system, or to spread its dominant religion. Theories that explain the sources of greedy motives are largely separate from motivational realism, but are clearly complementary to it. Such theories can be combined to produce a more complete theory.

Greedy motives can significantly influence a state's choice of strategy: under certain conditions greedy states will choose competitive strategies when a security seeker will choose more cooperative ones. Most obviously, because a greedy state will usually place greater value on gaining territory than a security seeker, it will usually be more disposed to invest in the military forces required to fight on the offense, to risk an arms race that is required to obtain military advantages, and to fight a costly war to acquire territory.[15] In addition, greedy states and security seekers are inclined to choose different alliance strategies. Unlike security seekers, which are inclined to balance against more powerful and threatening states – that is, weaker states join together to offset the advantages of a more powerful state – greedy states are inclined to 'bandwagon' – that is, join the stronger state. Greedy states bandwagon because this increases their chances of achieving territorial gains in a war, even though this strategy also places them at greater risk of being attacked by the stronger state.[16]

In contrast, the strand of realism that emphasizes the implications of international structure is termed structural realism or neorealism. Instead of emphasizing the importance of what states desire, structural realism argues that the constraints and opportunities created by a state's international environment are the key to understanding its behavior. Even states that are interested only in maintaining sovereign control of their territory can end up in arms races and war because of the pressures created by the anarchic international system. These states – the 'security seekers' – want only to be secure in the status quo. Nevertheless, competition and conflict can occur between rational security seekers because the international system generates insecurity and drives them into competition.

Divides within structural realism

Structural realism contains a number of competing theories. While less fundamental than the state versus structure divide, the divisions within structural realism are important. Structural realism has been extremely influential since the 1970s, which makes the intra-structural-realist debate important. Moreover, the divergent approaches focus on different logics of interaction and generate quite different conclusions about the likelihood of international competition and the possibilities for cooperation. Consequently, structural realism's key conclusions depend on which version of the theory is most compelling. Although this is not the place to try to fully adjudicate these arguments, my own research supports defensive realism, and its more general rational variant, over the other structural realist theories.

Waltz argues that international structure generates a general tendency towards competition between security-seeking states. The pressures and incentives created by the international system greatly limit the potential benefits of cooperation. Waltz begins with the simple, minimal assumption that all states give priority to ensuring their own survival; although states may have other goals, we can understand their interactions by focusing on the survival motive alone. Survival is a benign motive – the goal is not to take what other states have, but simply to protect what one already has. Maybe the most striking finding of Waltz's structural realism, therefore, is the seemingly counter-intuitive conclusion that international politics will have a strong tendency towards competition – arms races, alliances and war – even though the states involved lack fundamental conflicts of interest.

According to Waltz, the international system fuels competition in a variety of ways. The possibility that an adversary will cheat on an agreement is a major barrier. Even an agreement that would initially increase a state's ability to defend itself could be too risky if the adversary might not honor the agreement, leaving the state more vulnerable to attack. This inclination towards competition is reinforced by uncertainty about states' future motives and intentions. Even if confident today that other states have benign intentions, a state cannot be confident about the others' future intentions. When uncertain about the opposing state's intentions, a state must worry not only about whether cooperation will make it better off – increasing its security or prosperity – but also about which state will gain more. Even if cooperation would make the state better off – that is, provide absolute gains – the state might reject cooperation because its adversary would gain more. Allowing its adversary to achieve these *relative* gains could leave the state worse off, because in the future its adversary might use its increased capability to attack or coerce the state.

Waltz does, however, argue that states recognize the importance of not pursuing unlimited power. Power is a means for achieving security, not an end in itself. A state's acquisition of excessive power risks convincing other states to balance against it, thereby reducing the state's own security. According to Waltz, recognition of this strategic dynamic makes the international system less competitive.

By comparison, offensive realism sees a still more competitive world. John Mearsheimer, whose formulation defines offensive realism, agrees that states pursue power as a means, not an end, but concludes that states nevertheless try to maximize their power and pursue hegemony when possible (Mearsheimer 2001). Consequently, offensive realism sees international politics as still more competitive than does Waltz's neorealism. Mearsheimer reaches this conclusion by arguing not only that states face uncertainty about others' intentions, but also that states should assume the worst about these intentions. As a result, states focus solely on other states' capabilities.

According to offensive realists, therefore, states attempt to maximize their power. The reason is straightforward – the more powerful a state is, the better its prospects for defending itself if attacked. A state would be most secure if it were the dominant, hegemonic power; states will pursue competitive policies to achieve this position, if they have a reasonable probability of success. Waltz disagrees not so much because he believes additional power is undesirable, but because he believes states will be unable to acquire it, since other states will react by balancing against the power maximizer. In contrast, offensive realism holds that balancing is often insufficiently effective to make clear that territorial expansion is infeasible. Potential allies are sometimes geographically separated, which reduces their ability to come to each other's aid, thereby reducing the value of balancing. In addition, states may be slow to balance, because they disagree about how to coordinate their efforts and how to share the costs of fighting. Moreover, states may choose not to balance against an expansionist state, hoping that the state that is immediately threatened will be able to defend itself and/or that other allies will come to its aid. In other words, a state may 'pass the buck' instead of balance. Consequently, states can often succeed in maximizing their power and will choose to do so when the prospects of success are reasonably high.

Unlike both Waltz and offensive realism, defensive realism argues that international structure does not create a general tendency towards international competition. Although it starts with essentially the same assumptions, under a range of conditions, defensive realism finds that states can best achieve security by cooperating. The security dilemma lies at the heart of the defensive realist argument – competitive policies that a state pursues to increase its own security can reduce its adversary's security, which pressures the adversary to pursue compensatory measures, which in turn can reduce the state's own security. In sharp contrast to the other structural realisms, defensive realism concludes that, under a range of conditions, a state's best option can be cooperation or restraint, not competition. And, under some conditions, although the international system is anarchic, states can be quite secure.

The adversary's insecurity is a potential problem, not because the state places inherent value on its adversary's security, but because the adversary's insecurity may in turn reduce the state's own security. In other words, cooperation does not depend on altruism or shared identities; in the defensive realist story, self-interest drives cooperation.

A state's unilateral competitive policies can be counterproductive via three key mechanisms. First, in response to the state's acquisition of new military capabilities, its adversary could respond by building up its own forces. The adversary's security-driven buildup could leave the state less secure than it was before its own buildup because the adversary might turn out to be able to out build the state. Their buildups could also leave both states less secure because their new forces add more to their ability to attack than to defend, leaving both states more vulnerable to attack.

Second, the adversary's increased insecurity can lead it to pursue policies that increase the probability of crises and war. Under some conditions, expansion would increase the adversary's security – for example, by increasing its power, or by reducing the state's power, or by providing strategically valuable territory that improves its prospects for defense. Because it is now more insecure, the adversary is more willing to pursue these risky policies to regain its security.

Third, the adversary's buildup can convince the state that its adversary is more likely to be a greedy state – one that values taking territory for reasons other than increasing its security. Because a greedy state is willing to pay greater costs to expand and is therefore harder to deter, the state concludes that it is more insecure, which, as described above, can call for more competitive policies. Moreover, as a state increases its assessment that its adversary is greedy, cooperation becomes riskier, making competitive policies still more attractive. These interactions can lead to a continuing deterioration of political relations, fueling a negative political spiral.[17]

Cooperation, although bringing its own dangers, can enable a state to avoid the dangers of competition and, therefore, can under certain conditions be a state's best option. Cooperation can reduce the military dangers. More specifically, an arms control agreement that limits the size of deployed forces can provide protection against losing an arms race. An arms control agreement that limits forces that are especially effective for attacking can enhance both states' abilities to defend and deter, leaving both more secure. Cooperation can also improve states' political relations, helping to moderate negative spirals and possibly setting in motion positive spirals. Cooperation may enable a state to communicate that its motives are benign, leading the adversary to conclude that the state is more likely to be a security-seeker and therefore that it is less dangerous.

Defensive realism does not find that states should in general cooperate or compete. Instead, the benefits and risks of both types of policies need to be compared. There is not a general answer, because the benefits and risks will vary, depending on the international situation a state faces. Much of the relevant variation is in the magnitude and nature of the security dilemma.

Information and the security dilemma

As we consider how realism relates to other theories of security, it is especially important to appreciate the central role the security dilemma plays in structural realism. Among the insights that flow from the following points is that structural realism is not, and cannot be, a purely material theory. Contrary to common characterizations, structural realism depends heavily on information variables, as well as material variables.

First, the security dilemma is the key to understanding competition between security-seeking states. If states could build forces that made them secure by providing the capability to defend or deter, or both, while not providing the ability to attack, then security-seekers could increase their security without decreasing others' security. In this case, the international system could not produce insecurity or competition between rational states. Although barely mentioned by Waltz, international structure can produce competition only when there is a security dilemma.

Second, the security dilemma depends on both material and information variables. The intensity of the security dilemma depends on two material variables – the offense-defense balance and offense-defense distinguishability. When defense is much easier (that is, much less expensive to deploy) than offense, the security dilemma will be mild – a security seeker can deploy defense without posing a large threat to its adversary, because the adversary will be able to offset any increases in offensive capability with its own defense. Similarly, when the forces required for defense are different from the forces require for offense, a state will be able to increase its defensive capability without simultaneously increasing its offensive capability, thereby increasing its security without reducing that of its adversary.[18]

The intensity of the security dilemma also depends on a state's information about its adversary's motives. If a potential adversary knew with certainty that the state was a security seeker, military policies that the state pursued to increase its security would not reduce the adversary's security.[19] The adversary would know that the state had no reason to attack it and, therefore, would not be more insecure, even if the state increased its offensive military capabilities. This helps to explain why political relations between close, long-term allies are not strained by their individual military buildups. The impact of information on the state's security continues through various degrees of uncertainty. A high probability estimate that the adversary is a security seeker results in a less severe security dilemma, while a high probability estimate that the adversary is a greed state results in a more severe security dilemma.

The importance of information in determining the severity of the security dilemma creates an incentive for states to demonstrate that they are in fact security seekers. Remember that a state's own security increases as its adversary comes to believe that it is more likely to be a security seeker. Communicating this information requires the state to adopt policies that send 'costly signals' – actions that are less costly for a security-seeker than for a greedy state. Communicating information requires a costly signal because a greedy state has incentives to mislead its adversaries into believing that it is a security-seeker, because its adversaries would then be more likely to adopt policies that would leave them vulnerable, improving the greedy state's prospects for achieving its expansionist objectives. An arms control agreement can serve as a costly signal because forgoing the possibility of winning an arms race is more costly for a greedy state than a security-seeker. Similarly, an agreement that limits both sides' offensive capabilities is more costly for a greedy state, because offense is more valuable for it than for a security-seeker. Cooperative policies have the potential to generate a positive spiral – as an adversary concludes that the state is more likely to be a security-seeker, the adversary finds that cooperation would be less risky, which makes the adversary more willing to reciprocate the state's cooperation.

A state will not, however, always find that sending costly signals is its best option. When facing uncertainty about the adversary's type, cooperation is often risky because it may require that the state make itself vulnerable to cheating on arms control agreements, accept some reduction in its ability to defend against attack, and/or pursue policies that may incorrectly convince the adversary that the state lacks resolve. When the risks of signaling are too high, the state will decide to compete instead of cooperate. What we are seeing here is another face of the security dilemma – from this perspective, the security dilemma is preventing states from learning that opposing states are security seekers and, thereby, fueling competition.

Appreciating that information variables are an essential element of structural realism, and its more general rational variant, enables us to see significant similarities between these theories and structural constructivism.[20] Constructivists commonly characterize structural realism as a material theory, in contrast to their own, which focuses on ideas (Adler and Barnett 1998; Wendt 1999: 16, 30, 263) – a broad category that includes information, causal beliefs and norms. However, making the role of information about motives more explicit in the security dilemma and, in turn, in structural realism, makes clear that the material versus nonmaterial distinction does a poor job of characterizing the difference between these theories.

Moreover, many of the deductive arguments produced by these theories make similar predictions about the possibilities for cooperation and rely on similar mechanisms in reaching these predictions. Alexander Wendt argues that in contrast to neorealism – which finds that anarchy has a single logic, specifically that anarchy creates a tendency toward international competition – his constructivist theory demonstrates that anarchy does not have a unique logic – anarchy allows for cooperation and stable peace, as well as competition (Wendt 1999: 247–9). But we have seen, contrary to the standard characterization of realism, that defensive realism and the related rational theory of international politics finds that the same range of international outcomes is possible. On the similarity of mechanisms, consider Wendt's criticism of Waltz, which highlights his neglect of the possibility that information about state's motives could influence their choices between competitive and cooperative policies. Wendt argues that interaction between states can moderate or eliminate fears, thereby reducing the threat posed by other states' military capabilities, making cooperation and peace possible (Wendt 1992). As reviewed above, the rational theory sees the same possibilities in a state's costly signals.

Realism's contribution to understanding current international politics

Many observers believed that the end of the Cold War also marked the end of traditional security studies. This prediction was starkest for realism – at a minimum, the end of the Cold War marked the end of intense competition between the globe's major powers. If true, realism had little to offer because it focused specifically on security interactions between major powers.

Both sets of predictions have turned out to be wrong. Traditional security studies shifted attention to civil war and insurgencies and, following the September 11th attacks, shifted attention again to global terrorism. Of course, research and analysis of 'old' issues continued, but the weight of scholarly effort did redistribute. The fact that traditional security studies responded to dramatic changes in the real world must be considered one of its strengths. It has continued to combine a commitment to policy-relevant international relations theory with a commitment to analyzing current international dangers. While many academic fields and subfields are so far removed from real world events and concerns that they are fairly characterized as belonging to a 'cult of irrelevance,' traditional security studies has continued to address critical issues of national and international security.

We can now see with confidence that proclamations about realism's demise were equally off the mark. The first couple of decades after the Cold War might have provided support for this claim: while the end of the Cold War was not followed by agreement among scholars about the future of major power relations, there was a period of relative calm that stretched into the beginning the new century. However, following this relatively short period, China's tremendous economic and military growth have brought standard fears about major power conflict back to the forefront of international relations.

The developing debate over China's rise reflects the divergent views of many theoretical traditions, including realism, but also liberalism and constructivism.[21] Maybe of greatest interest to the themes of this chapter, the debate within realism accounts for a wide range of divergent views on China. Both Waltz's realism and offensive realism foresee China's rise generating on-going competition. Waltz predicts China building up its military capabilities to offset existing US military advantages in northeast Asia. The United States, fearing that China's efforts will undermine its ability to defend and deter in the region, will therefore build up its forces in response. This action-reaction cycle will continue, as both countries work to retain confidence in their abilities to defend. According to Waltz, the overall result will be international competition that resembles the Cold War: nuclear weapons will keep the peace, but competition and insecurity will be the defining features of the international system (Waltz 2000).

48 *Charles L. Glaser*

Offensive realism envisions a still more competitive outcome. China, acting in accordance with the theory's call for states to maximize their power, will attempt to become the hegemonic power in Northeast Asia (Mearsheimer 2001). Striving to achieve regional hegemony will require China to build military forces capable of defeating its neighbors and would thereby provide tremendous political influence. Acquiring these benefits will require China to push the United States out of Northeast Asia – China cannot be the regional hegemon if the United States continues to deploy forces in Japan and South Korea, and to maintain substantial security commitments in the region in general. The United States, however, would be threatened by Chinese hegemony and therefore will compete to maintain its position in Northeast Asia. Both sides will be insecure because they lack confidence in the adequacy of their forces, which at best will fuel intensified military competition and at worst could lead to war as China and the United States place greater instrumental value on controlling the region's sea lanes and disputed territories (Mearsheimer 2010).

In contrast, defense realism (and its more general rationalist variant) sees greater potential for a relatively calm and secure region. China need not pursue regional hegemony because high levels of security are possible without it. China's power – its geographical size, large population, and wealth – would provide it with the resources necessary for defense. In addition, China's separation from the United States by the vast Pacific Ocean makes defense against conventional attack relatively easy. Maybe most importantly, nuclear weapons will provide China with massive retaliatory capabilities, which will greatly enhance its ability to deter both conventional and nuclear attacks. In other words, geography and military technology will enable China to defend itself relatively easily. This 'defense advantage' greatly moderates the security dilemma, which reduces the competitive pressures generated by the international system (Glaser 2011).

Each of these realist theories not only makes different predictions, but also prescribes different policies for the United States. This should leave little doubt about the continuing importance of realism, and of a continuing evolution that advances these debates and resolves their disagreements.

Notes

1 Much of the review in this article draws upon Glaser (2013).
2 For a different characterization of realism's core assumptions, see Masala in this volume.
3 For two different realist perspectives that point in this direction see Mearsheimer (1994–95); and Glaser (2010: 123–6, 161–6).
4 This understanding is narrower than in Wendt (1992). Wendt focuses on the behaviors that anarchy generates, not anarchy itself. As I explain below, his finding that a spectrum of cooperative and competitive behaviors is possible under international anarchy is entirely consistent with defense realism.
5 For a broader understanding of power, see Barnett and Duvall (2005).
6 On the complementary nature of types of theories, and the partial nature of the rational theory more generally, see Glaser (2010: 21–28).

7 Importantly, although Waltz has argued that his theory does not require rational states, many theorists view his arguments as drawing heavily on a rational logic. For his view, see Waltz (1986: 330–1).
8 This seemingly simple formulation does leave open some important ambiguities; see Powell (2002: 773–8).
9 For a sampling of views on this issue see Ullmann (1983); Walt (1991); and Paris (2001).
10 I have developed this argument somewhat more fully in Glaser (2003: 412–4).
11 On the relationship between deterrence and defense, see Snyder (1961).
12 For Waltz's initial exploration of these 'levels of analysis' see Waltz (1959).
13 On the security seeker and greedy state terminology, see Glaser (2010: 35–40).
14 For an early use of this term, see Kydd (1997a). Motivational realism is distinguished from neoclassical realism partly by the latter's relaxation of the unitary actor assumption, and, closely related, its relaxation of the rationality assumption. On neoclassical realism see Taliaferro (2009).
15 On arming, see Kydd (2000); on fighting, see Schweller (1998).
16 On this type of bandwagoning, see Schweller (1994); on balancing against threat, see Walt (1987); on the dangers of bandwagoning, see Waltz (1979).
17 On the spiral model, see Chapter 3 of Jervis (1976); Glaser (1992; 2010: 68–72, 94–102) and Kydd (1997b).
18 The foundational piece is Jervis (1978); see also Van Evera (1999) and Glaser and Kaufmann (1998).
19 This would also require that the adversary knew that the state knew that it was a security seeker. Otherwise the adversary would have to worry that the state's insecurity could lead it to pursue dangerous, competitive policies.
20 For a more extensive discussion of these issues, see Glaser (2010: 166–71).
21 For reviews of the implications of different theoretical approaches, see Friedberg (2005); and Goldstein (2008).

References

Adler, E. and Barnett, M. (1998) 'Security Communities in Theoretical Perspective', in E. Adler and M. Barnett (eds) *Security Communities*, Cambridge: Cambridge University Press: 3–28.
Barnett, M. and Duvall, R. (2005) 'Power in International Politics', *International Organization*, 59 (1): 39–75.
Friedberg, A. (2005) 'The Future of U.S.-China Relations: Is Conflict Inevitable?', *International Security*, 30 (2): 7–45.
Glaser, C.L. (1992) 'Political Consequences of Military Policy: Expanding and Refining the Spiral and Deterrence Models', *World Politics*, 44 (4): 497–538.
—— (2003) 'Structural Realism in a More Complex World', *Review of International Studies*, 29 (3): 403–14.
—— (2010) *Rational Theory of International Politics*, Princeton: Princeton University Press.
—— (2011) 'Will China's Rise Lead to War? Why Realism Does Not Mean Pessimism', *Foreign Affairs*, 90 (2): 80–91.
—— (2013) 'Realism' in A. Collins (ed.) *Contemporary Security Studies*, 3rd edn, Oxford: Oxford University Press: 13–27.
Glaser, C.L. and Kaufmann, C. (1998) 'What is the Offense-Defense Balance and Can We Measure It?', *International Security*, 22 (4): 44–82.
Goldstein, A. (2008) 'Parsing China's Rise: International Circumstances and National Attributes', in R.S. Ross and Z. Feng (eds) *China's Assent: Power, Security, and the Future of International Politics*, Ithaca: Cornell University Press: 55–86.

Jervis, R. (1976) *Perception and Misperception in International Politics*, Princeton: Princeton University Press.
   (1978) 'Cooperation Under the Security Dilemma', *World Politics*, 30 (2): 167–214.
Kydd, A. (1997a) 'Sheep in Sheep's Clothing: Why Security Seekers Do Not Fight Each Other', *Security Studies*, 7 (1): 114–54.
   (1997b) 'Game Theory and the Spiral Model', *World Politics*, 49 (3): 371–400.
   (2000) 'Arms Races and Arms Control: Modeling the Hawk Perspective', *American Journal of Political Science*, 44 (2): 222–38.
Mearsheimer, J.J. (1994–95) 'The False Promise of International Institutions', *International Security*, 5 (1): 5–49.
   (2001) *The Tragedy of Great Power Politics*, New York: Norton.
   (2010) 'The Gathering Storm: China's Challenge to US Power in Asia', *The Chinese Journal of International Politics*, 3 (4): 381–96.
Morgenthau, H. (1973) *Politics Among Nations: The Struggle for Power and Peace*, 5th edn, New York: Knopf.
Paris, R. (2001) 'Human Security: Paradigm Shift or Hot Air?', *International Security*, 26 (2): 87–102.
Posen, B.R. (1993) 'The Security Dilemma and Ethnic Conflict', *Survival*, 35 (1): 27–47.
   (2007) 'The Case for Restraint', *The American Interest*, 3 (2).
Powell, R. (2002) 'Game Theory, International Relations Theory, and the Hobbesian Stylization', in I. Katznelson and H.V. Milner (eds) *Political Science: The State of the Discipline*, New York: Norton: 773–8.
Schweller, R.L. (1994) 'Bandwagoning for Profit: Bringing the Revisionist State Back In', *International Security*, 19 (1): 72–107.
   (1998) *Deadly Imbalances: Tripolarity and Hitler's Strategy of World Conquest*, New York: Columbia University Press.
Snyder, G.H. (1961) *Deterrence and Defense: Toward a Theory of National Security*, Princeton: Princeton University Press.
Taliaferro, J., Lobell, S.E. and Ripsman, N.M. (2009) 'Introduction: Neoclassical Realism, the State, and Foreign Policy', in S.E. Lobell, N.M. Ripsman, and J. Taliaferro (eds) *Neoclassical Realism, the State, and Foreign Policy*, Cambridge: Cambridge University Press: 1–41.
Ullmann, R.H. (1983) 'Redefining Security', *International Security*, 8 (1): 129–53.
Van Evera, S. (1999) *Causes of War: Power and the Roots of Conflict*, Ithaca: Cornell University Press.
Walt, S.M. (1987) *The Origins of Alliances*, Ithaca: Cornell University Press.
   (1991) 'The Renaissance of Security Studies', *International Studies Quarterly*, 35 (1): 211–39.
Waltz, K.N. (1959) *Man, the State, and War*, New York: Columbia University Press.
   (1979) *Theory of International Politics*, Boston: Addison-Wesley.
   (1986) 'Reflections on *Theory of International Politics*: A Response to my Critics', in R.O. Keohane (ed.) *Neorealism and Its Critics*, New York: Columbia University Press: 322–46.
   (2000) 'Structural Realism After the Cold War', *International Security*, 25 (1): 5–41.
Wendt, A. (1992) 'Anarchy is What States Make of It: The Social Construction of Power Politics', *International Organization*, 46 (2): 391–425.
   (1999) *Social Theory of International Politics*, Cambridge: Cambridge University Press.

2 Is the crisis of security institutions a crisis of institutional theory?

Caroline Fehl

Introduction

International security – understood here as the policy area relating to the potential or actual use of force among states or by transnational non-state actors – is the core concern of a great variety of international institutions.[1] It thus appears natural that institutionalist approaches to International Relations theory, which emphasize the central role institutions play in enabling international cooperation, have been 'remarkably influential in security studies' (Hyde-Price 2001: 31). Yet, institutionalist work on global security issues has recently become rare, in part due to the perception that many of the familiar institutions of the Western-centric global security order are 'in crisis'. This chapter argues that such crises have indeed challenged institutional theory in its conventional form, specifically its rationalist branch, by exposing it to criticism from highly diverse alternative perspectives. However, a review of recent developments within rational institutional theory suggests that proponents of this approach have taken up the challenge by advancing institutionalist thinking through a *dialogue* with these alternative approaches, yet without losing sight of core institutionalist assumptions. As a result of this productive engagement, the 'new institutionalism' has become much better able to shed light on unequal power dynamics as well as inefficiencies within global security institutions – and more open toward a research agenda shared by many of its critics.

As the introductory chapter to this volume argues, theoretical change in the academic field of security studies has often been driven by real-world developments in security policy, and the dual crisis of security institutions and the institutional theory of security (studies) is no exception to this pattern. The tableau of security institutions that marks the present global political order has emerged slowly over the course of the past century, mirroring the secular trend toward an expansion of the concept of security in terms of its objects, issue scope, spatial extension, and conceptualization of danger. Some institutional arrangements, such as the Hague Regulations Concerning the Laws and Customs of War, date back as far as 1899, while others, such as the Proliferation Security Initiative (PSI), were founded as recently as 2003 to address new types of security 'risks' that concern states as much as their interaction with (terrorist) non-state actors. At the regional level, long-established security organizations such as the North Atlantic Treaty Organization (NATO) coexist with relative newcomers such as the 2001 Shanghai Cooperation Organization, as well as recent efforts to expand the scope of existing regional organizations to security issues, for instance in the European Union or in the African Union.

The institutionalization of international security has thus been a long – and in many ways ongoing – process. Nevertheless, there is a widespread perception today that many of the older institutions that were long regarded as the backbone of international security policy are currently 'in crisis'. The crisis terminology is used widely by observers to highlight a range of different problems of effectiveness and legitimacy that established security institutions are currently struggling with and that are also closely connected to the expansion of the global security agenda.

NATO, for instance, has long fended off criticism that it is becoming less relevant to its members' security concerns and military cooperation. After the demise of the Cold War threat that it was originally directed against, the organization initially seemed to find a new role for itself by developing a robust doctrine for 'out-of-area missions' addressing new types of conflicts and risks. Yet, it was a latecomer to the Western-led interventions in Afghanistan and Libya, and was sidelined altogether in the 2003 Iraq war (Cottey 2004; Gordon and Shapiro 2004; Friedrichs 2011).

Similarly, at the United Nations (UN), the UN Security Council's authorization of multinational interventions in Iraq in 1990 as well as in the Bosnian war in 1995 engendered hope that the organ long envisioned to govern world security affairs would finally live up to its task in the post-Cold War world. Yet, the Council's inaction during the Rwandan genocide and the way its authority was circumvented in the run-up to the Western-led interventions in Kosovo (1999) and Iraq (2003) all but dissipated such hopes (Franck 2003; Glennon 2003; Malone 2004). In the recent crisis in Libya, the Council again authorized the use of military action to enforce a no-fly zone, but Council members (and non-members) quickly fell out over how the mandate was subsequently interpreted by the Western coalition executing the intervention. The result was an even more acrimonious deadlock over the ongoing crisis in Syria, not only regarding the question of military intervention. Evidently, the old global security architecture has not kept up with the rapid expansion of the global security agenda to include non-traditional risks and conflicts. Concepts such as 'human security' and the contested 'responsibility to protect' are still widely viewed as expressions of a liberal-democratic security agenda (see Chapter 7 by Geis and Wagner) and have failed to gain sufficient support in global, consensus-oriented institutional fora.

Lastly, the perceived crisis of international security institutions has also stretched to those global institutions governing ownership and use of the means of military force, that is, arms control. In this area, the challenges to established multilateral treaties and negotiating forums are manifold. The 1968 nuclear Non-Proliferation Treaty (NPT) has been troubled by problems of non-compliance at various levels: by controversies surrounding the nuclear programmes of Iran and North

Korea, by the bilateral agreement between the US and India on civilian nuclear cooperation – signed despite India's non-recognition as a Nuclear Weapons State under the NPT – and by the continued refusal of Nuclear Weapons States (NWS) to live up to their long-term disarmament commitments under the treaty (Huntley 2006; Meier 2006; Müller 2010). Meanwhile, important initiatives for new arms control agreements that would further expand the international security agenda have shipwrecked or stalled, due to domestic opposition in key participant states – as exemplified by the US Senate's rejection of the Comprehensive Test Ban Treaty in 1999 – or due to political deadlock in the relevant multilateral negotiating forums. The Conference on Disarmament in particular has been blocked on many key issues by clashes of interests between the United States and China and between larger Western and non-Western coalitions (Becker *et al.* 2008; Borrie 2006).

Another oft-cited problem is the tendency of key states, most notably the United States and its allies, to circumvent established multilateral negotiating frameworks and treaties by new types of security risks and challenges in exclusive, informal clubs of like-minded countries. This strategy can be traced back to the diverse export control arrangements set up in the 1970s, 1980s and 1990s, but has recently been reinforced with the creation of the PSI. This US-led informal agreement, designed to facilitate the interdiction of shipments suspected of carrying illegal weapons technologies, has met with strong criticism on the part of non-participating nations, who fear that the initiative might open a door to tactics not covered by contemporary international law.

Similar problems of legitimacy have plagued several recent initiatives by the UN Security Council on new security issues, including Resolution 1540 which aims to prevent the spread of non-proliferation of weapons of mass destruction to non-state actors. In this and other resolutions, the Council created general binding rules for all UN members, rather than acting on specific threats to international peace. According to the critics, the body thus overstepped its legal mandate and circumvented traditional ways of consensual law-making among equal sovereigns (Meier 2008; Talmon 2005).

In summary, the popular 'crisis' diagnosis points to a number of distinct, but related, problems of effectiveness and legitimacy that, in the eyes of critics, have plagued many established international security institutions: non-compliance with institutional rules and decisions; inaction due to internal vetoes and blockades; irrelevance due to the tendency of member states to circumvent established fora with unilateral policies, informal groupings and hierarchical rule-making; and contested legitimacy of these latter, new types of institutional initiatives. Strikingly, what 'crisis' does *not* imply is instability or even disintegration of international security institutions. In line with the 'expansion thesis' set out in the introductory chapter to this volume, the vast garden of international security institutions is flourishing and growing – but critics worry that many of the older trees are rotting from the inside out.

What does this widely perceived crisis of international security institutions imply for our theoretical perspective on security, particularly for those theoretical approaches that have been most interested in – and most optimistic about – the critical role that institutions play in facilitating cooperation on international security issues? Is the crisis of security institutions also a crisis of institutional theory? In principle, this question concerns both rationalist and non-rationalist strands of institutional theory: neoliberal institutionalism as well as constructivist arguments about 'security communities' or security-related norms (e.g. Adler and Barnett, 1998; Risse-Kappen, 1995; Tannenwald, 1999). The following discussion focuses specifically on *rational institutionalism*, the older of the two strands. This choice should not be mistaken as suggesting that other variants of institutionalism are irrelevant to contemporary security studies. Rather, the analysis zooms in on that form of institutionalist thought which has been *most* challenged by recent developments. In particular, the widely perceived dysfunctionalities of international security institutions pose a grave problem to the theory's core argument that international institutions exist because they perform useful functions for their member states. Other problems of rational institutionalism, particularly its traditional neglect of power politics through and within institutional frameworks, are shared by constructivist versions of institutionalist theory. Thus, by making a case for the continued utility of a rational institutionalist perspective on international security politics – in a sense the 'least likely case' – the analysis *also* indicates the need for a fresh look at constructivist approaches to security institutions.

Can rational institutionalism make sense of the above-cited 'crises' of security institutions? My answer is a qualified 'yes', that will be elaborated in the following steps. First, I briefly summarize the assumptions and causal conjectures that define rational institutional theory and delineate it from principal alternative approaches. Second, I elaborate on the ways in which perceived crises of security institutions challenge rational institutionalist claims, according to critics. Next, I review past attempts, made in different strands of institutional theory, to take up these challenges and address the weak points highlighted by recent developments in international security policy. I argue that such a rethinking is possible by taking on board insights from alternative theoretical perspectives on security politics and security institutions, but *without* completely renouncing core tenets of rational institutionalist thinking. Such a dialogue, I argue, can in fact improve our understanding of the current 'crisis of international security institutions'. I illustrate this argument with a revised institutionalist reading of the crisis of multilateral arms control institutions.

Rational institutionalism challenged

What is rational institutionalism? The main features of what was long one of the dominant approaches in the discipline of International Relations (IR) are well-known and need only brief mention here.[2] As the first part of the label indicates, the theory assumes that states are rational, unitary actors whose actions seek to maximize certain (material or immaterial) benefits. Two corollaries derive from this basic rationalist assumption: that states create and design international institutions purposefully and strategically so as to maximize utilities, and that institutions reflect the preferences of their creators. These propositions delineate rational institutionalism from constructivist approaches to institutions, which assume that states may follow non-instrumental logics of action in setting up or joining institutions, or that their preferences are *constituted*, rather than merely reflected, by institutional structures.

The second part of the theory's name, institutionalism, points to its core claim that 'institutions matter'. This short formula summarizes a conjecture that rational institutionalism (in IR and as well as in Comparative Politics) shares with other, non-rationalist approaches to institutions. It holds that institutions exercise independent causal effects on the behaviour of individual actors and are a structural feature of the (international) political system that cannot be reduced to the sum total of individual members' preferences, capabilities, and choices (Peters 2005:14, 19). Since rational institutionalism in IR was forged out of a controversy with realist theory, institutionalist theorists' efforts in this field have focused on demonstrating that institutions are 'partially decoupled from *power* and exercise autonomous causal effects' (Jupille and Snidal 2006). This claim, too, has several corollaries: Institutions are able to function without the leadership of dominant states, and hence to survive major power shifts (Keohane 1984; Snidal 1985). While they are often shaped by the preferences of dominant states and may well have distributional effects that benefit some members over others, they constrain *both* strong and weak states in their behaviour and provide at least some net benefits to all members (via the principle of Pareto efficiency) (Moe 2005: 225). Finally, they can effectively resolve cooperation problems that realist theory thinks insurmountable, including the *security dilemma* so central to realist thinking about international security (see Chapter 1 by Glaser).[3]

The above-cited 'crises' of international security institutions challenge both these core rational institutionalist claims in a number of ways. Most importantly, many recent developments highlight the influence of global *power inequalities* on the creation, design, and effects of international security institutions. In its conventional form, rational institutionalism appears ill-suited to capture such power-related dynamics – in contrast to alternative theoretical approaches to security. Not only realism, the traditional antagonist of institutionalism, but also newer, critical and postmodernist approaches to security studies put unequal power relations and structures of domination at the centre of analysis (see Chapter 1 by Glaser and Chapter 3 by Fierke), and have accordingly advanced explanations of recent institutional crises that challenge institutionalist thinking.

With regard to NATO, the persistence of the organization after 1992 initially seemed to indicate a triumph of institutional theory (of rationalist *and* constructivist shade) over the *realist* prediction that the organization would dissolve as soon as the need to 'balance' jointly against the erstwhile principal opponent faded (Duffield 1994–95; Keohane and Wallander 1999; Risse-Kappen 1995; McCalla 1996). Reversing this argument, it appears only logical that recent tensions within the alliance over interventions in Iraq and Libya, and the fact that it was sidelined in other crises, should then be interpreted as indicating that realism was right after all, that dominant states see no need to act through security institutions in an era of unipolarity, and that tensions such as those over Iraq or over the European

Union's Security and Defence Policy signal the return of balancing or at least 'soft balancing' dynamics among the former allies (e.g. Brooks and Wohlforth 2008; Kagan 2002; Kelley 2005; Pape 2005; Posen 2006).[4] Some of the same conclusions could be drawn from disputes within the UN Security Council. Both its frequent deadlock and the tendency of state coalitions to bypass its authority in deciding on military interventions indicate to *realists* that powerful states use, veto, and circumvent international security institutions as they see fit, and that the constraining effect of international institutions on the policies of (powerful) member states is ultimately very weak.

Unilateralism and disregard for institutional rules on the part of great powers have also plagued the multilateral arms control regime – as illustrated by the non-compliance of NWS with their disarmament commitments and by various US-led initiatives that circumvent established multilateral fora and treaties. Yet, some recent challenges to the established institutional order in this particular policy area have also come from weaker actors, including rising powers such as India or nuclear dissidents such as Iran and North Korea. The policies of these states apparently aim to reverse a nuclear regime which both realists (e.g. Paul, 1998) and postmodernist scholars (e.g. Keeley, 1990) interpret as a discriminatory, hegemonic order favouring a small number of nuclear 'top dogs'. Either reading of the non-proliferation regime – a paper tiger too weak to constrain great powers, or a strong tool of great power domination – appears hard to square with rational institutionalist reasoning.

But it is not only the evident influence of power inequalities on international security institutions that poses a problem to rational institutionalism in its conventional form. Particularly, but not only in the United States, critics have argued that quite independently from power struggles between strong and weak states, many traditional multilateral institutions have proven ineffective in managing global problems – too slow, too inflexible, too big to reach agreement beyond a lowest common denominator (e.g. Daase 2009; Finnemore 2005; Van Oudenaren 2012). These 'dinosaurs' have in some cases been complemented by like-minded initiatives that participants hope will be more effective, and yet they have not been replaced. Certainly this longevity cannot be explained in a rational institutionalist manner by the useful functions they perform.

In summary, prominent accounts of recent crises of international security institutions represent a clear challenge to rational institutionalist conjectures: to the assumption that institutions reflect the preferences of their state creators and provide efficient solutions to cooperation problems, to the claim that they benefit strong and weak states alike, and to the assertions that institutions can effectively constrain powerful states.

Institutionalist responses

How can institutionalists reply to this challenge? The easiest counterargument would emphasize that despite indicators of crisis, many traditional security institutions continue to exist and function well enough and that security cooperation has even been expanding and deepening at a rapid speed outside the Euro-Atlantic region (see introductory chapter). In other words: the crisis is only partial. Such a counterargument however, amounts to a discussion of whether the glass is half full or half empty. The more interesting challenge for institutionalists to take up is in addressing precisely those theoretical weaknesses highlighted by recent crises of security institutions – the theory's apparent overstatement of institutional effectiveness and its understatement of the role of power – by taking on board insights from realist as well as critical/postmodern challengers, but without throwing overboard core institutionalist assumptions.

In fact, both challenges have been key areas of theory development and debate within institutionalist IR scholarship over the past decade. Starting with the more prominent line of discussion, that about the relationship between power and institutions, we should first recall that even mainstream rational institutionalists never denied the importance of power or its potential influence on institutions, but argued for the 'partial decoupling' of institutions from power (see above). For instance, early rational institutionalist works, such as Robert Keohane's *After hegemony* (Keohane 1984), still conceded an important role in creating – albeit less in maintaining – cooperative institutions to dominant hegemonic states. Other contributions have sought to take on board the realist objection that institutionalized cooperation among states can be impeded by distribution problems, that is, by the problem that some states may derive more benefits from it than others. In the *Rational Institutional Design* framework, for instance, the severity of distribution problems is treated as a key variable that influences states' collective choice of institutional design features such as membership size or issue scope (Koremenos et al. 2001). These conventional institutionalist approaches to incorporating power remain unsatisfying, however, in that they either cede part of their explanatory power to realism – as Keohane does – or conceive of distribution problems as something that will be *resolved*, one way or other, in the process of institutional design, thus effectively 'institutionalizing away' power struggles over policy outcomes.

Such problems, together with the long-standing tradition of testing rational institutionalist against realist propositions, gave rise to renewed criticisms, in the mid-2000s, that (rational and constructivist) institutionalism neglects the role of power in the creation and operation of international institutions (Hurrell 2005: 48; Moe 2005: 225). Unlike institutionalism's traditional realist antagonists, however, these recent critiques did not demand that institutionalism be discarded in favour of a perspective which viewed institutions as epiphenomenal to or mere servants of state power (understood as capabilities). Instead, the new critics proposed to redirect attention to 'institutional power', that is, to the complex ways in which power works *in* and *through* institutional frameworks, as well as to 'structural' and 'productive' forms of power that do not work through direct coercion but indirectly through constitutive social structures and discourses (Barnett and Duvall 2005).

Reviewing rational institutionalist work conducted over the course of the past decade, a number of contributions stand out that have taken on this challenge: taking seriously the critique regarding the neglect of power, but without altogether dropping core institutionalist insights. John Ikenberry, for instance, argues that the powers emerging victorious from major conflict – such as the US after the Second World War – can use institutions to alleviate fears of domination on the part of weaker states, and thus 'lock in' an international (economic and security) order in line with their preferences. By showing how 'institutions are [...] critical in [...] securing cooperation between unequal states' (Ikenberry 2001: 17), he puts power at the heart of his explanation of institutionalized cooperation, but *without* reducing institutions to mere instruments of domination.

A similar line of argument is advanced by contributions that draw attention to the phenomenon of *hierarchical* institutional arrangements according different rights and privileges to different member states (e.g. Lake 2009; Viola 2008; Weber 2000). From a rationalist point of view, hierarchical institutions are based on a rational bargain in which subordinate states agree to obey the commands of a superordinate state in exchange for the latter's provision of order (Lake 2009). Here, the focus is on understanding when and how, in the absence of coercion, unequal material capabilities are translated into unequal institutional arrangements.

While both accounts still uphold the institutionalist claim of Pareto efficiency – that both strong and weak states benefit from institutionalized cooperation – another institutionalist contribution relaxes this key assumption. Lloyd Gruber (2000) shows how cooperation among a limited number of states can produce negative externalities that ultimately force other states to join, even though they would have been better off without cooperation – something he terms 'go-it-alone power'. In Gruber's account, institutions clearly *are* instruments of domination. And yet, unlike realism, his theory conceives of power as a *function* of institutions – it cannot unfold its effects, or does not even exist, outside the institutional context within which it is exercised.

The rationality assumption underlying rational institutionalist frameworks, and the related functionalist argument that institutions mirror the interests of their state creators, has been another focus of debate within the institutionalist camp. First, institutionalist scholars have begun to embrace the assumption of 'bounded rationality', a concept originally proposed by Herbert Simon in 1957, that highlights decision-makers' inability to follow a strict utility–maximization strategy in a highly complex environment and under conditions of limited time and information. Instead of choosing the optimal among all available outcomes, decision-makers are thought to employ complexity-reducing search strategies, particularly 'satisficing', the search for the most easily available outcome more satisfying than the status quo. One exemplary application to institutionalist theorizing can be found in Joseph Jupille and Duncan Snidal's work on *forum shopping*. Because states are 'boundedly rational', they contend, they will only create a new institution upon confronting a new political problem after having explored and rejected as unsatisfactory *relative* to the status quo strategies for addressing the issue within existing institutions. This satisficing strategy can explain why states do not always choose to create the theoretically optimal institution for addressing a given problem (Jupille and Snidal 2006).

Bounded rationality is also one of the key ingredients of *historical institutionalism*, a school of thought that highlights how institutional choices are shaped by institutional legacies of the past, which has only recently begun to be received and applied systematically by IR scholars.[5] Bounded rationality, 'veto points' embedded in existing institutional structures and 'sunk costs' invested in the creation of existing institutions are all factors that make institutions resilient to reform, even if they no longer reflect members' interests in a changed environment (Fioretos 2011: 373–5; Ikenberry 2001: 69–72; Pierson 2004: 142–6). Change, if it happens at all, tends to be incremental and 'path dependent', that is, conditioned by contingent choices that were made at 'critical junctures' in the past. At the same time, institutional resilience sometimes makes it easier for actors to add new institutions rather than reform old ones, leading to institutional 'layering' (Fioretos 2011: 377–8, 389; Pierson 2004: 137). Among other things, these arguments imply that the assumption of 'rational institutional design' is as misplaced as the functionalist claim that institutions reflect state interests, because both overestimate states' abilities to foresee and control institutional effects. With regard to the relationship between power and institutions, historical institutionalism is agnostic, allowing for different mutual effects. On the one hand, powerful actors may sometimes be able to impose institutional rules that further deepen power asymmetries over time via 'positive feedback' effects (Pierson 2004: 36–7); on the other, unanticipated consequences and uncontrollable institutional dynamics should lead us to 'expect that substantial gaps will often emerge between the functioning of institutions and the preferences of powerful political actors' (Pierson 2004: 105). Institutional dynamics may thus help or obstruct the exercise of power, depending on circumstances.

Drawing together these diverse attempts to remedy the weaknesses of conventional institutional theory, an obvious question is: in what sense can these revised versions of the theory still be classified as 'rational institutionalist'? I argue that they can be. Although the modifications relax earlier rational institutionalist assumptions about institutional effectiveness, Pareto efficiency, and independence from power, they still uphold a theoretical core that cannot be subsumed under alternative approaches: the notion that states are rational actors which act strategically in pursuit of their preferences in their decision-making about institutions (even if these decisions are constrained and the outcomes often uncontrollable), and the claim that institutions 'matter' in the sense of exercising an autonomous causal effect irreducible to the material capabilities of individual states. Precisely because power is often exercised *through* institutions, policy outcomes would radically differ if these institutions were absent.

Thus, the 'new institutionalism' takes on board insights generated by theoretical challengers while remaining clearly distinguishable from the latter – both from realism and from critical and postmodernist approaches to security which emphasize the *constitutive* effect of unequal power structures on states' definitions of their identities and interests. At the same time, the recent developments in institutionalist thinking also open up space for a more far-reaching dialogue with alternative perspectives on security – for instance, for a joint exploration of how

60 *Caroline Fehl*

constitutive discourses, institutional structures and strategic choices conditioned by both interact in reproducing or transforming global power inequalities.

The 'crisis' of multilateral arms control: an institutionalist reading

As we have seen, the deficits of conventional institutionalist hypotheses that are highlighted by recent crises of international security institutions can and have been addressed from *within* the rational institutionalist paradigm. Institutionalists' dialogue with theoretical challengers has thus enabled them to rethink the relationship between institutions and power and assumptions about institutional effectiveness without abandoning rational institutionalism altogether.

To illustrate how a reformulation of institutionalist theory can help us to understand key aspects of much-discussed institutional crises, and how they can serve as a starting point for building further bridges toward other theories, the following section focuses on developments surrounding the multilateral arms control regime, specifically the establishment, evolution and contemporary problems of the nuclear regime resting on the 1968 NPT.

As discussed at the outset of the paper, realist readings of the challenges currently facing the nuclear non-proliferation regime emphasize the apparent inability of the treaty to effectively constrain the policies of the powerful NWS or, alternatively, the NWS' ability to use the NPT as means of domination, which has prompted repeated 'rebellions' against the treaty by members and non-members. The latter interpretation is also shared by postmodernist analyses of the global nuclear order.

From an institutionalist perspective, by contrast, the NPT is neither without effect on the behaviour of its powerful members nor a mere instrument of their power. Its stark in-built inequality, that is, the differentiation between legitimate NWS and the remainder of nuclear 'have-nots', is a form of institutionalized hierarchy that is at least in part explained by a rational exchange between the original parties, rather than by coercion. Arms control experts often describe the NPT as the product of a 'bargain' in which the Non-Nuclear Weapon States (NNWS) agreed to forego an independent nuclear capability in return for access to peaceful uses of nuclear technology, for the NWS' long-term disarmament promise, and for the latters' implicit promise to protect non-nuclear states with extended deterrence guarantees (Müller 2008; Paul 2003; Smith 1987). These arguments closely resemble Lake's 'submission for order' argument. The NPT represented a clear departure from the earlier US policy of limiting the spread of nuclear weapons through technological denial and bilateral cooperation agreements under the 'Atoms for Peace' programme. When it became clear that these unilateral and bilateral control strategies were insufficient to prevent the dissemination of nuclear weapons, 'that the "non-proliferation line" could not be held just through exercise of American power and persuasion' (Walker 2008: 38), the US sought the *consent* of the NNWS to their non-nuclear status through the NPT – a classic institutionalist move of substituting coercion with authority (Lake 2009: 182).

The institutionalist story does not end here, however. As I have argued elsewhere (Fehl 2015), the 'bargain' between nuclear and non-nuclear states that enabled the NPT did not only involve the swapping of direct, issue-specific economic and security benefits, but it also had a *procedural* dimension which fulfilled non-nuclear states' demands for a recognition of their *equal status* in multilateral arms control negotiations, and in global affairs more broadly. The institutionalization of nuclear inequality was crucially conditioned on and embedded in procedural innovations. To obtain consent of the NNWS to the unequal treaty, the superpowers had to give them a voice in the negotiations by making the global negotiating machinery on arms control matters *more* equal. The NPT was negotiated in the Eighteen Nation Disarmament Committee (ENDC), a new body that included, for the first time in post-war global arms control negotiations, not only the superpowers and their allies, but also non-aligned states representing a large part of the global South. It was therefore seen as the first genuinely multilateral negotiating forum for arms control issues (Verona 1978: 201). Once involved in the negotiations, the newcomers to the ENDC insisted on a system of Review Conferences, based on equal participation of all member states, to oversee the treaty's implementation (Carnahan 1987).[6]

What does this rational institutionalist reading of the NPT's creation in 1968 imply for our understanding of the regime's widely perceived present-day 'crisis'? As I argue in the following, the fact that both nuclear powers and weaker states have recently expressed frustration with the evolution of the regime should not lead us to the conclusion that the institutionalist explanation was wrong in the first place. On the contrary, an understanding of the NPT as resting on a rational bargain between strong and weak states and particularly a recognition of the procedural dimension of this 'deal' can help us to better understand the sources of contemporary problems and controversies.

First, the primary importance that non-nuclear states placed on the recognition of their procedural equality within the NPT itself, as well as in the negotiating process leading up to its adoption, explains their angry response to recent rhetoric and behaviour on the part of nuclear states, most notably on the subject of NWS disarmament commitments. The inclusion of the disarmament article in the NPT had been important to non-NWS not only as a potential remedy to the 'security dilemma' they faced in unilaterally renouncing nuclear weapons (Müller 2008: 71). It also reflected their insistence on a principle of procedural equality whereby all parties to a multilateral negotiation must make at least *some* concessions, even if different in size and character (Fehl 2015). This principle was openly challenged when nuclear powers, under the leadership of the George W. Bush administration, refused to recognize the previously agreed "Thirteen Steps" toward disarmament at the 2005 NPT Review Conference, and sought to promote a revisionist reading of the NPT that viewed non-proliferation as the historical core of the treaty and as primary to the other two 'pillars', disarmament and peaceful use of nuclear energy (Franceschini 2012: 6–7). The NWS' open challenge to the deal agreed in 1968 explains why the 2005 Review Conference eventually collapsed amidst heated controversies (Müller *et al.* 2012: 105–8).

A second, related but distinct consequence of the procedural dimension of the foundational NPT bargain was that it made it difficult for the great powers to maintain control over the evolution of the treaty, and over global arms control negotiations more broadly, further down the road. The creation of the ENDC had started an enlargement process that was difficult to stop, with more and more states demanding access to the official forum for UN arms negotiations – both newly independent states from the global South and states that were angry to have been skipped in the first round of admissions, such as Japan (Quester 1973: 110). As a consequence, the ENDC was replaced by the Conference of the Committee on Disarmament in 1969 and eventually by today's Conference on Disarmament in 1979, increasing its membership to 40 states in the process. Furthermore, while negotiations within these forums were initially still marked by an informal domination of the superpowers (Ungerer 2007), China and other Southern states began to play increasingly active and assertive roles in the 1980s, as Cold War tensions began to soften. While this development still benefited the negotiations on the Chemical Weapons Convention and the Comprehensive Test Ban Treaty in the early 1990s, by the turn of the millennium, clashes of interests between the US and the rising powers had all but jammed the Conference's machinery (Borrie 2006).

Within the NPT itself, the accession of more and more non-NWS from the global South enabled the Non-Aligned Movement to exert a growing influence on the agenda of NPT Review Conferences. This influence was reflected, most notably, in the gradual specification of the initially very vague formulation of a long-term disarmament commitment for the NWS in the treaty's Article VI, most importantly in the 'Thirteen Steps' discussed above. The nuclear powers were naturally opposed to such a (modest) concretization of the NPT's disarmament dimension. And yet, their efforts to underline the primacy of the treaty's non-proliferation dimension were routinely blocked by clear majorities at NPT Review Conferences (see above). This experience testifies to the limited ability of major powers to maintain control of hierarchical institutions over time. Despite the NWS' continued material dominance, they could not help but accept the 'imposition' of accountability for their compliance with NPT Article VI by the majority of non-NWS (Müller et al. 2012: 114) – which explains some of their recent outspoken discontent with the state of the treaty.

An important caveat is in order here. While much about the disarmament debate within the NPT can be illuminated from (revised) rationalist institutionalists, the case also *also* points to certain limitations of the revised rationalist approach – and to possibilities for continued dialogue and discussion with alternative perspectives on security. Arguably, the NNWS' ability to strengthen the disarmament agenda in the face of NWS opposition was facilitated not only by the NPT's decision-making procedures, but also by its early institutionalization of disarmament as a focal *discourse* in its Article IV – a discourse that the NNWS could subsequently draw on to legitimize and develop their own agenda. Such discursive dynamics remain outside the theoretical reach of the revised rational institutionalist approach – but they point to a rich agenda for discussion and cooperation with critical, discourse-oriented approaches to security. In the case at hand, it would seem promising to explore at greater depth how institutional decision-making procedures and discursive shifts have interacted (or counteracted each other) in driving the evolution of the nuclear non-proliferation regime.

In summary, the 'new' rational institutionalist rationalist reading of multilateral arms control regime can shed light on the sources of the regime's various recent 'crises'. Understanding the NPT as the product of a rational bargain between strong and weak states makes it easier to explain the non-NWS' recent discontent with the NWS' reneging on their substantive as well as procedural commitments. At the same time, a revised rational institutionalist view which draws inspiration from historical institutionalism, can best capture the evolutionary dynamics of the global arms control regime. The self-reinforcing institutionalization of equal decision-making procedures in the multilateral arms control regime created multiple veto points – both within and outside the NPT – that made it increasingly difficult for dominant states to either control the arms control agenda or reform existing institutions to align with their interests. This evolution can explain why key contemporary arms control institutions are no longer perceived as reflecting the interests of their powerful creators, and why they have nevertheless proven rather resilient. At the same time, it also accounts for a variety of strategies used by these dominant states to circumvent the procedural restrictions of the existing multilateral arms control framework: shifting key nuclear issues from multilateral to direct bilateral talks during the Cold War era (Verona 1978), governing through informal, exclusive clubs such as the diverse export control arrangements or the PSI, and the use of the UN Security Council as a quasi-legislator. All these strategies have been cited as evidence of the crisis of multilateral arms control, and as indications that great powers either ignore institutional constraints as they see fit or create institutions that are perfectly fitted to their interests. From an institutionalist perspective, such a reading is too short-sighted, however, as it ignores the decisive impact that pre-existing institutional constraints had on the choice of these institutional strategies. True, dominant states attempt to shape and use institutions strategically to pursue their interests. But both the ways in which they do so and the extent to which they succeed are deeply conditioned by past institutional legacies.

As a final illustration of the constraining impact of international arms control institutions in the current 'crisis', consider the case of the 2003 Proliferation Security Initiative. This US-led informal arrangement was highly controversial, not because it sought to coordinate the activities of like-minded states in interdicting weapons shipments in their own territorial waters, but because initial remarks by senior American government figures suggested that the US intended to use this initiative to push the boundaries of customary international law by allowing for ship interdictions on the high seas without flag state consent. This attempt at back door law-making was clearly rebutted by international legal opinion, however, and was not reaffirmed in later US statements (Byers 2004). Not least due to the widespread criticism of the PSI's questionable legality, the US government subsequently sought to strengthen states' non-proliferation obligations through UN Security Council Resolution 1540, designed to ground the

PSI's counter-proliferation measures in a firmer and more consensual basis (Daase 2009: 301; Joyner 2005: 540). Thus, rather than ignoring and abusing international institutions at will, US institutional strategies for pursuing its non-proliferation agenda were critically shaped by the constraining impact of pre-existing international law and by the opportunities provided by pre-existing institutional structures.

Summarizing the account of the crisis of multilateral arms control provided here, an institutionalist perspective recognizes that states' decisions with regard to international institutions are made strategically in pursuit of egoistic preferences, and that dominant states seek to use institutions as instruments of control. At the same time, it also underlines the non-coercive strategies through which unequal institutional structures are put in place, and highlights how such structures can escape the control of their creators over time and unfold autonomous effects that shape and channel the further institutional evolution of the field.

To what extent can this more complex institutionalist argument be transferred to other areas of international security policy? The field of arms control, with its long history of institutional innovations and reforms, obviously provides a particularly fruitful ground for demonstrating its analytical utility. Yet, a closer look is likely to reveal similar dynamics in other issue-areas.

NATO, for instance, has been discussed both as the product of a rational constitutional 'bargain' (Ikenberry 2001) and, in historical institutionalist terms, as a case of path-dependent institutional resilience after the Cold War (Ikenberry 2001; McCalla 1996; Wallander 2000). Alternatively, it could also be viewed as a case of path-dependent institutional *change*. By broadening its scope to out-of-area missions, the organization apparently successfully adapted its role to post-Cold War realities. Against the background of ethnic strife in the former Yugoslavia, this seemed an obvious choice with clear contours – yet it proved to be a choice with potentially dangerous self-reinforcing effects. In Afghanistan, NATO was confronted with a whole new array of 'out of area' challenges that prompted it to further expand its portfolio of tasks to jobs as diverse as counterinsurgency, civilian aid and reconstruction. The apparent difficulty of living up to expectations raised on all of these fronts has already triggered new calls for institutional reforms and reinforcements – a feedback loop that some argue can only lead to NATO losing the credibility it hoped to re-establish in the out-of-area 'business' (Menon and Welsh, 2011).

Conclusion

The argument I have made suggests that (rationalist) institutional theory remains an important and useful analytical tool within the field of security studies. In view of widely perceived recent crises of established global security institutions, security scholars could be tempted to abandon institutionalism in favour of either a realist approach that denies the importance of institutions or critical/postmodern approaches that dispose of both the rationality assumption and the epistemology underlying past work in the institutionalist tradition. This, however, would mean throwing out the baby with the bathwater. True, recent crises of major international security institutions have presented difficult challenges for conventional institutionalist arguments. Yet, they have also driven rational institutionalists to engage with both realist and critical theoretical challengers and to take on board important insights generated within these other research traditions – albeit with a distinctive institutionalist twist. These developments, I have sought to demonstrate, can actually lead us to a deeper understanding of recent and ongoing developments within and around international security institutions. More specifically, the revised institutionalist approach advocated here highlights the importance of power, as exercised through and within institutional frameworks, and relaxes the assumption of institutional efficiency in favour of a view of institutional choice as being constrained by bounded rationality and path dependency. Both theoretical adaptations can help us to understand contemporary crises of security institutions as resulting from rational and strategic actors' imperfect attempts to design, use and control these institutions for their own benefit.

While recent institutionalist work has been strongly influenced by engagement with other strands of security studies, the 'new institutionalism' still remains distinguishable from these other approaches. In particular, it holds that formal institutional structures remain central features of global security politics, and that they unfold effects, both positive and negative, on possibilities for cooperation and on the (re)production of unequal power that are reducible neither to material capabilities nor discourse. Insisting on institutionalism's distinctiveness should *not* be read as denying the analytical utility of theoretical approaches that put these other factors at the centre of analysis. On the contrary, sharpening the institutionalist take on institutional power and institutional dynamics is a prerequisite for continuing, more far-reaching dialogue with alternative perspectives on security studies. For instance, it could be illuminating for rational institutionalist and discourse theorists to tackle a joint research agenda by asking how formal institutional veto points and discursive dynamics interact to produce stability (or change) in security institutions. This point was illustrated above with the example of the disarmament debate in the NPT. As long as such an engagement is analytically productive, the longevity of the rational institutionalist approach to security studies can only be welcomed by all in the field, its proponents as well as its critics.

Notes

1 International institutions are understood here as sets of explicit, formal or informal rules regulating inter-state relations.
2 Prominent examples of rational institutionalist work in IR include, for instance, Keohane (1984), Martin (1992), or the recent cooperative projects on legalization (Abbott and Snidal 2000) and on the 'rational design' of international institutions (Koremenos *et al.* 2001).
3 One might object that moderate realists such as Robert Jervis have long accepted the proposition that 'institutions matter' under certain circumstances. However, the effort to demonstrate the *independence* of institutions from power-as-capabilities is the core concern of the institutionalist, not the realist, project.

4 NATO's alleged irrelevance poses less of a problem to the constructivist prediction that the transatlantic allies would preserve the alliance out of a commitment to the shared liberal-democratic identity it embodied, rather than for practical purposes (e.g. Risse-Kappen 1995).
5 For overviews of key historical institutionalist concepts and for reviews of historical institutionalist work in Comparative Politics and International Relations, see Pierson (2004), Thelen (1999), and Fioretos (2011).
6 The argument that concerns for equal recognition formed part of the "rational bargain" underlying the NPT is based on an interpretation of rational institutionalism which is ontologically open regarding the nature of states' utility functions: strategic institutional choices may be made to maximize material *or* immaterial gains.

References

Abbott, K.W. and Snidal, D. (2000) 'Hard and Soft Law in International Governance', *International Organization*, 54(3): 421–56.
Adler, E. and Barnett, M. (1998) A Framework for the Study of Security Communities, in: E. Adler and Barnett, M. (eds.) *Security Communities*, Cambridge: Cambridge University Press: 30–66.
Barnett, M. and Duvall, R. (2005) 'Power in Global Governance', in M. Barnett and R. Duvall (eds) *Power in global governance*, Princeton: Princeton University Press: 1–32.
Becker, U., Müller, H. and Rosert, E. (2008) 'Einleitung: Rüstungskontrolle im 21. Jahrhundert', in U. Becker and H. Müller (eds) *Rüstungskontrolle im 21. Jahrhundert, Die Friedenswarte special issue*, 83(2–3): 13–33.
Byers, M. (2004) 'Policing the High Seas: The Proliferation Security Initiative', *American Journal of International Law*, 98(3): 526–45.
Borrie, J. (2006) 'Cooperation and Defection in the Conference on Disarmament', in J. Borrie and V.M. Randin (eds) *Thinking Outside the Box in Multilateral Disarmament and Arms Control Negotiations*, Geneva: United Nations Institute for Disarmament Research (UNIDIR).
Brooks, S.G. and Wohlforth, W.C. (2008) *World out of Balance: International Relations and the Challenge of American Primacy*, Princeton: Princeton University Press.
Carnahan, B.M. (1987) 'Treaty Review Conferences', *The American Journal of International Law*, 81(1): 226–30.
Cottey, A. (2004) 'Nato: Globalization or Redundancy?', *Contemporary Security Policy*, 25(3): 391–408.
Daase, C. (2009) 'Die Informalisierung internationaler Politik – Beobachtungen zum Stand der internationalen Organisation', in K. Dingwerth, D. Kerwer and A. Nölke (eds) *Die Organisierte Welt: Internationale Beziehungen und Organisationsforschung*, Baden-Baden: Nomos: 289–307.
Duffield, J.S. (1994–95) 'NATO's Functions after the Cold War', *Political Science Quarterly*, 109(5): 763–87.
Fehl, C. (2015) 'Understanding the Puzzle of Unequal Recognition: The Case of the Nuclear Non-Proliferation Treaty', in C. Daase, C. Fehl, A. Geis and Georgios Kolliarakis (eds) *Recognition in International Relations. Rethinking a Political Concept in a Global Context*, Basingstoke: Palgrave Macmillan: 104–22.
Friedrichs, H. (2011) 'Libyen-Einsatz: Die NATO, der gefesselte Riese', *Die Zeit*, 22 March.

Finnemore, M. (2005) 'Fights about Rules: The Role of Efficacy and Power in Changing Multilateralism', *Review of International Studies*, 31(S1): 187–206.
Fioretos, O. (2011) 'Historical Institutionalism in International Relations', *International Organization*, 65(2): 367–99.
Franceschini, G. (2012) 'The NPT Review Process and Strengthening the Treaty: Peaceful Uses', Non-Proliferation Papers No. 11, Paris: EU Non-Proliferation Consortium, February.
Franck, T.M. (2003) 'What happens now? The United Nations after Iraq', *American Journal of International Law*, 97(3): 607–20.
Glennon, M.J. (2003) 'Why the Security Council failed', *Foreign Affairs*, 82: 16–35.
Gordon, P. and Shapiro, J. (2004) *Allies at War: America, Europe, and the Crisis over Iraq*, New York: McGraw-Hill.
Gruber, L. (2000) *Ruling the World: Power Politics and the Rise of Supranational Institutions*, Princeton: Princeton University Press.
Huntley, W. (2006) 'Rebels without a Cause: North Korea, Iran and the NPT', *International Affairs*, 82(4): 723–42.
Hurrell, A. (2005) 'Power, Institutions, and the Production of Inequality', in M. Barnett and R. Duvall (eds) *Power in Global Governance*, Princeton: Princeton University Press: 33–58.
Hyde-Price, A. (2001) '"Beware the Jabberwock!" Security Studies in the Twenty-First Century', in H. Gärtner, A. Hyde-Price and E. Reiter (eds) *Europe's New Security Challenges*, Boulder: Lynne Rienner: 27–54.
Ikenberry, G.J. (2001) *After Victory*, Princeton: Princeton University Press.
Joyner, D.H. (2005) 'The Proliferation Security Initiative: Nonproliferation, Counterproliferation, and International Law', *Yale Journal of International Law*, 39: 507–48.
Jupille, J. and Snidal, D. (2006) *The Choice of International Institutions: Cooperation, Alternatives and Strategies*, unpublished manuscript, University of Colorado at Boulder: University of Chicago, 7 July.
Kagan, R. (2002) 'Power and Weakness', *Policy Review*, 113: 3–28.
Keeley, J.F. (1990) 'Toward a Foucauldian Analysis of International Regimes', *International Organization*, 44(1): 83–105.
Kelley, J. (2005) 'Strategic Non-cooperation as Soft Balancing: Why Iraq was not just about Iraq', *International Politics*, 42(2): 153–73.
Keohane, R.O. (1984) *After Hegemony: Cooperation and Discord in the World Political Economy*, Princeton: Princeton University Press.
Keohane, R.O. and Wallander, C.A. (1999) 'Risk, Threat, and Security Institutions', in H. Haftendorn, R.O. Keohane and C.A. Wallander (eds) *Imperfect Unions. Security Institutions over Time and Space*, Oxford: Oxford University Press: 21–47.
Koremenos, B., Lipson, C. and Snidal, D. (2001) 'The Rational Design of International Institutions', *International Organization*, 55(4): 761–99.
Lake, D.A. (2009) *Hierarchy in International Relations*, Ithaca and London: Cornell University Press.
Malone, D.M. (ed.) (2004) *The UN Security Council. From the Cold War to the 21st Century*, Boulder: Lynne Rienner.
Martin, L.L. (1992) *Coercive Cooperation: Explaining Multilateral Economic Sanctions*, Princeton: Princeton University Press.
McCalla, R.B. (1996) 'NATO's Persistence after the Cold War', *International Organization*, 50(3): 445–75.

Meier, O. (2006) 'The US-India Nuclear Deal: The End of Universal Non-proliferation Efforts?', *Internationale Politik und Gesellschaft*, 4: 28–43.
— (2008) 'Non-integrative Arms Control: Assessing the Effectiveness of New Approaches to Preventing the Spread of Weapons of Mass Destruction', *S+F Sicherheit und Frieden/ Security and Peace*, 26: 53–118.
Menon, A. and Welsh, J. (2011) 'Understanding NATO's Sustainability: The Limits of Institutionalist Theory', *Global Governance*, 17: 81–94.
Moe, T.M. (2005) 'Power and Political Institutions', *Perspectives on Politics*, 3(2): 215–33.
Müller, H. (2008) 'The Future of Nuclear Weapons in an Interdependent World', *The Washington Quarterly*, 31(2): 63–75.
— (2010) 'Between power and justice: Current problems and Perspectives of the NPT Regime', *Strategic Analysis*, 34(2): 189–201.
Müller, H., Becker-Jakob, U. and Seidler-Diekmann, T. (2012) 'Regime Conflicts and Norm Dynamics: Nuclear, Biological and Chemical Weapons', in H. Müller and C. Wunderlich (eds) *Norm dynamics in Multilateral Arms Control: Interests, Conflicts, Justice*, Athens (GA): University of Georgia Press: 100–56.
Pape, R.A. (2005) 'Soft Balancing against the United States', *International Security*, 30(1): 7–45.
Paul, T.V. (1998) 'The Systemic Bases of India's Challenge to the Global Nuclear Order', *Nonproliferation Review*, 6(1): 1–11.
— (2003) 'Systemic Conditions and Security Cooperation: Explaining the Persistence of the Nuclear Non-proliferation Regime', *Cambridge Review of International Affairs*, 16(1): 135–54.
Peters, G.B. (2005) *Institutional Theory in Political Science. The 'New Institutionalism'*, London: Continuum.
Pierson, P. (2004) *Politics in Time. History, Institutions, and Social Analysis*, Princeton and Oxford: Princeton University Press.
Posen, B.R. (2006) 'European Security and Defense Policy: Response to Unipolarity?', *Security Studies*, 15(2): 149–86.
Quester, G. (1973) *The Politics of Nuclear Proliferation*, Baltimore: Johns Hopkins University Press.
Risse-Kappen, T. (1995) *Cooperation Among Democracies: The European Influence on U.S. Foreign Policy*, Princeton: Princeton University Press.
Smith, R.K. (1987) 'Explaining the Non-proliferation Regime: Anomalies for Contemporary International Relations Theory', *International Organization*, 41(2): 253–81.
Snidal, D. (1985) 'The Limits of Hegemonic Stability', *International Organization*, 39(4): 579–614.
Talmon, S. (2005) 'The Security Council as World Legislature', *American Journal of International Law*, 99(1): 175–93.
Tannenwald, N. (1999) 'The Nuclear Taboo: The United States and the Normative Basis of Nuclear Non-Use', *International Organization*, 53(3): 433–68.
Thelen, K. (1999) Historical Institutionalism in Comparative Politics, *Annual Review of Political Science*, 2(1): 369–404.
Ungerer, C. (2007) 'Influence without Power: Middle Powers and Arms Control Diplomacy during the Cold War', *Diplomacy and Statecraft*, 18(2): 393–414.
Van Oudenaren, J. (2012) 'Effectiveness and Ineffectiveness of the UN Security Council in the last 20 Years: A US perspective', in J. Krause and N. Ronzitti (eds) *The EU, the UN and Collective Security: Making Multilateralism Effective*, London: Routledge: 53–70.

Verona, S. (1978) 'Structural Negotiating Blockades to Disarmament', *Security Dialogue*, 9(3): 200–9.

Viola, L.A. (2008) *Governing the Club of Sovereigns: Inequality and the Politics of Membership in the International System*, Ph.D. dissertation, The University of Chicago: United States Dissertations & Theses Publication, No. AAT 3309115.

Wallander, C.A. (2000) 'Institutional Assets and Adaptability: NATO After the Cold War', *International Organization*, 54(4): 705–35.

Walker, W. (2008) 'The Quest for International Nuclear Order', in U. Becker and H. Müller (eds) *Rüstungskontrolleim 21. Jahrhundert, Die Friedenswarte special issue*, 83(2–3): 35–55.

Weber, K. (2000) *Hierarchy Amidst Anarchy: Transaction Costs and Institutional Choice*, Albany: State University of New York Press.

3 Is there life beyond language?
Discourses of security
Karin M. Fierke

The title of this chapter is somewhat deceptive. The possibility of life 'beyond language' would seem to reinforce a distinction between language and materiality, which critical scholars have challenged from the beginning. The extension of security studies, as discussed in the introduction, included an emphasis on ideas and language, but, as Glaser argues, realism, and the type of materialism it assumes, still occupies the core of security studies. From this perspective, one might argue that highlighting the importance of discourse is merely an attempt to reverse the dichotomy between materiality and 'ideas.' But the dominant thrust of critical scholarship has been less about reversing the hierarchy than problematizing the role of language in an academic field where it had either been taken for granted as a mere reflection of reality, or vilified due to the relative absence of 'truth' in diplomatic language. I argue that critical security studies is not moving beyond language; rather, as debates about the role of language have unfolded, language has become less a focus of analysis in itself than one of many constitutive features of the embodied subject of security. This suggests, the importance of taking methodology seriously.

The chapter is organized around a somewhat artificial distinction between three layers of debate, while recognizing that these represent less a distinct temporal progression than the unfolding and deepening of different types of concern. These layers relate to the epistemological and methodological debates discussed in the introduction, but approach them from a somewhat different angle. During the first layer of debate, which started in the 1980s, critical scholars attempted to dismantle the taken-for-granted, hegemonic status of the language of security and International Relations theory. In a second layer, the emphasis shifted to an examination of how the language of security works in the world, including a more explicit theorization of the relationship between language and embodiment. A third layer of the debate represents a return to materiality, but in a very different form than earlier generations of realist scholarship. The debate, which began over a question of whether language is important, has evolved toward an emphasis on the 'embodiment' of security. The abstract, disembodied individual, whether state or person, has given way to the human subject who not only speaks, but sees, feels and acts within a social, cultural, historical and material context. This return to materiality is wrapped up in language and meaning and thereby takes critical security studies beyond the mind–body dichotomy. Schlag's argument about visualisation (seeing) is a good example of the latter in so far as it highlights the co-constitution of the performative act with meaning and its materialisation in images.

Approaches to language in international relations have built on a variety of traditions of thought, from the speech act theory of Austin and Searle, to the language games of Wittgenstein and the discourse of Foucault, to name a few (Austin 1962; Foucault 1979; Wittgenstein 1958). My concern in this chapter is less to explore these different approaches to language – something others have done in great detail – than to analyse arguments that have been advanced by critical scholars regarding the role of language in security studies. The chapter analyses the broader academic and political context of the debates, as well as particular pieces of work, drawn from the feminist literature on security, which highlight the language/materiality relationship.

Feminist scholars have played an important role in the reintroduction of materiality to discussions of security. Feminist understandings of materialization differ from that of traditional realists, as discussed, for instance, by Glaser, who focuses on military, economic and environmental dangers 'out there' in the world, but without reference to the co-constitution of materiality and meaning. In elaborating on the different layers of debate, I have sought to explore some of these critiques in more depth. In the first section, I examine an early process of dismantling the hegemonic metaphors of security scholarship and the Cold War, focusing in particular on the classic work of Carol Cohn, who analysed the language of defence intellectuals (Cohn 1987). In the second section I turn to the efforts of security scholars to understand how the language of security works in the world. In this context, I highlight another classic piece, 'The Little Mermaid,' by Lene Hansen, which raises questions about the Copenhagen School's focus on language to the exclusion of the body (Hansen 2000). In the third section, I explore a more ontological shift within critical security studies, and the larger world, from a focus on discourses of the state to individual and human security; the expansion of referent objects, as discussed in the introduction, was followed by a series of 'turns' that reconstitute the human subject of International Relations (IR) as well as a recent turn to the materiality of objects, as expressed in the work of Claudia Aradau.

Security language as metaphor

The first layer goes back to the 1980s and the work of Robert Cox, Richard Ashley and R.B.J. Walker, among others. Ashley (1984; 1988) explored the technologies of power that surround the abstract categories of IR theory, which were reinforced by 'scientific' assumptions. Walker (1993) dismantled the boundaries separating politics 'inside' the state from the war-like state of nature 'outside'. Cox highlighted the distinction between 'problem-solving' theory, which takes the world as it is, and thereby reifies existing power structures, and 'critical theory', which stands by those who are marginalized by dominant structures of power (Cox 1981). He argued that theory is always 'for someone, and for some purpose.'

In the 'positivist' world of International Relations at the height of the second Cold War, language was treated as a label for 'reality.'[1] The central challenge was to hold the meaning of concepts in place in order to make testing possible, and thereby to assess the truth or falsity of claims about the world. The language of political or policy actors was largely ignored in the search for 'facts' and in the attempt to avoid normativity. 'Positivists' viewed both security and power as properties that states do or don't possess, and highlighted the need to secure the state within an international structure of anarchy. Much of the critical discussion was a response to the emergence of structuralist theories of IR, particularly the publication of Waltz's *Theory of International Politics* (1979; see also: Keohane 1986). The contestation regarding the role of language within international relations overlapped with processes of contestation in the political world, where disarmament and human rights groups or movements in both the East and West sought to dismantle the reified categories of the Cold War.

Carol Cohn's classic study, 'Sex and Death in the Rational World of Defence Intellectuals', is a particularly interesting analysis from this time period for several reasons. First, Cohn is an academic who was concerned with questions of language and security. The piece does not draw explicitly on any particular approach to language, such as Foucault, although she does nod to an important and growing body of feminist theory about gender and language. Second, she analyses the gendered language of defence intellectuals. In the summer of 1984, she was one of 48 college teachers to attend a summer workshop about nuclear weapons that was taught by 'defence intellectuals,' who she refers to as 'men who use the concept of deterrence to explain why it is safe to have weapons of a kind and number it is not safe to use.' (Cohn 1987: 687) Third, she analyses the role of gendered metaphors in constructing the nuclear world of the Cold War. Just as the work of Ashley and others played a central role in revealing the power contained in the abstract categories of International Relations theory, Cohn's article played a similar role in dismantling the assumptions surrounding security discourse, not least that this was the language of a privileged elite, who, in their rationality and sophistication, stood above normal human beings. She demonstrated that many of these assumptions were in fact deeply irrational. She further challenged the myth – at the time common among disarmament activists – that one needed to use this language of euphemism and metaphor in order to engage in political debate. To a certain extent this was necessary in order to be understood in that context; however, as Cohn illustrated – not least through her own experience – once one acquired and began to use this language, it shaped and limited the world that was viewed. Most importantly, the abstract metaphoric language surrounding nuclear weapons made it impossible to see, think or feel the potential damage and human suffering that would result from a nuclear war, or to consider alternatives to nuclear defence.

The language of euphemism and metaphor was deeply gendered in its reliance on sexual categories. Her analysis was not about the psychodynamic origins of the imagery; rather her main concern was to examine how the language functioned. She points to several features of this language. The euphemisms – of clean bombs, Peacekeepers (which at that time referred to the MX missile), and surgical strikes, to name just a few – made it impossible to acknowledge the horror of nuclear war or to feel moral outrage. The sexual metaphors of, for instance, thrust-to-weight ratios, deep penetration, soft lay downs and vertical erector launchers revealed a masculine desire for domination. The domestic or soft metaphors – patting missiles, silos, Christmas tree farms, even the word 'security' itself – humanized the weapons and made it easier to ignore human bodies and lives. The religious imagery of the first atomic bomb tests, Trinity and Holy Spirit, and references to a 'nuclear priesthood,' suggested an identification with divine power.

The main thrust of her argument, like those of the IR theorists, was to dismantle the world of nuclear deterrence, so that we could begin to imagine alternatives. The point was less that language was more important than materiality, than the extent to which the language surrounding nuclear practice made it difficult to comprehend the horror of a potential nuclear war. My own analysis of the language of government bodies, peace movements and human rights initiatives in both East and West during the same time period, which was published much later, revealed that non-state-state actors also engaged in a process of dismantling the dominant security metaphors of the Cold War. These challenges played a fundamental role in opening up a space for alternative practices and policies – and eventually an end to the Cold War itself – to emerge (Fierke 1998).

The construction of security and insecurity

A second layer of debate shifted emphasis to how language works in the process of world-making. Emancipation, more than language, has been the focus of Critical Security Studies with a capital C, that is, the Frankfurt school (Booth 1991; Wynn-Jones 1999). 'Conventional' constructivists have tended to distance themselves from questions of language, claiming a social ontology but holding on to elements of positivist epistemology. However, since the 1990s, a range of more critical constructivist or post-structuralist analyses have examined how language relates to the construction of identity; how 'crises' are constructed; how practices such as intervention are enabled by assumed hierarchies of meaning; the analysis of change; and the role of speech acts in the construction of threats.[2] The Copenhagen School, whose focus is the latter, distanced themselves from 'critical' schools of thought, claiming they were not simply interested in dismantling existing concepts of security. They wanted to examine how security works in practice, that is, the dynamics of naming a security threat, a securitizing move that potentially elevates the threat to existential, thereby justifying the suspension of normal politics.[3]

Lene Hansen, one notable critic who came from within the Copenhagen School, was one of the first to argue that the focus on language had obscured important aspects of materiality. She argued that in their exclusive emphasis on the speech act, the Copenhagen School was remarkably silent about gender and forms of securitization relating to the body. She illustrates this problem through the story of the Little Mermaid, a statue that sits at the entrance to Copenhagen's harbour. For Hansen, the loss of her voice prevented the Little Mermaid from ever fully materializing as an embodied subject (Hansen 2000: 285), and furthermore made it impossible for her to communicate to the prince that his construction of her subjectivity endangered her being. Hansen argues that the Copenhagen School's reliance on the speech act, and thus the assumption that speech is possible, precludes those who do not speak from being considered worthy subjects of consideration or protection. Her purpose is less to critique the absence of gender than to point to two blindspots in the speech act framework which prevent the inclusion of gender. The silent security dilemma of the Little Mermaid is indicative of these blind spots. The first is 'security as silence,' which occurs when insecurity cannot be voiced – when articulating something as a security problem may be impossible or may even aggravate the threat being faced. The second is 'subsuming security' – which arises because gendered security problems often involve an intimate inter-linkage between gendered identity and other aspects of the subject's identity, for example, national or religious. Hansen explores these blindspots through a discussion of honour killings in Pakistan. She argues, in relation to this case, that gender insecurity is not only a concern about social redistribution but poses fundamental questions of survival. Furthermore, the security of particular individuals is deeply embedded in collective constructions of subjectivity and security (Hansen 2000: 287).

The focus of the Copenhagen School on speech is problematic in situations where the possibilities of speaking security are constrained and the conditions for becoming a referent object are such that gender often excludes one from qualifying (Hansen 2000: 300). Drawing on the work of Judith Butler, Hansen highlights the importance of the body within the speech act, which opens a space for investigating gendered security dynamics. This involves making the body an additional epistemological focus and examining the individualizing strategies employed in keeping security problems from appearing at the collective level. Butler's approach makes it possible to deal with non-verbal communication, both visual and bodily, which, Hansen argues, the Copenhagen School has not addressed.

The speech act of the Copenhagen School presumes a pre-given subject who speaks, thus not accounting for how the speaking subject is constituted. Butler, by contrast, argues that the speech 'interpellates' the subject, showing how the subject who is constituted in relation to an Other becomes a subject capable of addressing an Other (Butler 1993). In this respect, the subject is neither a pre-existing sovereign agent who uses language instrumentally nor merely an affect whose agency grows out of complicity with existing operations of power. Highlighting the constitution of the subject opens the door to addressing the politics of security. As Hansen states, 'if "security" is no longer considered a speech act taking place between given subjects – usually the state and "its" citizens – but a practice which *constructs* subjects at both "ends" of the speech act (the speaker and those spoken to), we open our theory to a consideration of the discursive and bodily practices involved in the formation of subjects.' (Hansen 2000: 303)

Hansen argues that language plays an important role in constructing the contours of the body, whether individual or collective. This builds on claims by Foucault and Butler about the role of discourse in disciplining and shaping bodies.

Foucault informed some of the dismantling efforts already discussed. Hansen's critique chimes with arguments in this genre regarding the role of language in constructing exclusions, which make dehumanization and the reification of power possible. Her critique also marks a distinction between approaches that grow out of ordinary language philosophy, informed by Wittgenstein, Austin or Searle, which examine language use as a form of action, and Foucauldian approaches that highlight the power moulded in language. The Copenhagen School highlights the performative nature of the speech act. Butler and Hansen go much further in demonstrating how the performative act not only speaks to other bodies, but constructs them in the process.

Body and ontology

Debates about language and discourse raised first and foremost an epistemological question: are we using words as labels for objects in the world, are we dismantling reified categories permeated with power, or examining the constitutive dimensions of language? The question of what we assume about the nature and role of language remains important, but arguably the more significant shift has taken place at the level of ontology, with the movement away from abstract notions of the disembodied state or individual, expressed through the abstract language of metaphor, to the embodiment of the human and political subject of security.

In the 1990s, the turn from emphasis on the state to the individual was one of the defining features of Critical Security Studies in the Frankfurt School tradition, represented in particular by the work of Ken Booth. It was also at the heart of an international political shift toward human security and the merging of security and development discourses in the 1994 UN Development Report. The increasing focus on the individual, and the coining of the term 'human security', took place against the backdrop of the intra-state wars of the post-Cold War period, in which, it came to be assumed, the percentage of civilian casualties was far greater than in earlier periods of war.[4] The emergence of terrorism as an international security threat, following the attacks on the US World Trade Center and Pentagon in 2001, only reinforced this focus on the individual, given that individual terrorists, not states, presented the most direct threat. Critical security studies and human security emerged side by side, and something of a conversation has taken place between them ever since. This conversation has revolved around a question of whether human security is a liberal concept or a critical one. The critics claim that the individual of human security, like the sovereign state of neo-realist security studies, is the abstract disembodied individual of liberalism.

While this debate has many nuances, for purposes of this argument I want to highlight a number of relevant contrasts as they relate to questions of language and the body. While the liberal approach highlights the 'observation' of scientists, the critical is more attentive to the politics of visualizing catastrophe or suffering (Hansen 2011; Schlag and Heck 2013). From the absence of politics in the liberal model, and the silencing this implies, the critical turn highlights the potential for the human political subject to speak and be heard. The absence of attention to suffering in war in security studies more generally is replaced by an emphasis on the suffering body and the communication of emotion. The containment of culture within the sovereign boundaries of the state is opened up to the multiplicity and plurality of cultural spaces of practice. In short, the debate regarding human security is about whether the concept rests on liberal theory or a fundamentally critical approach, the latter highlighting the embodiment of the 'human'. Language, while losing its central place, becomes both an expression of this humanity and a problematized site of contestation, legitimacy, speech or silence, between a form of life that, in the name of security, has increasingly reduced bodies to management, or one that holds open a potential for political speech and resistance. This deepens security beyond abstract liberal notions of the individual, as citizen or human, to the underlying vulnerability of life in relation to others. Policy problems related to human security have revolved around life and death issues of flesh and blood individuals, often in a context of war; in this respect a notion that security is embodied comes closer to the reality of human suffering.

While the concept of human security in both schools of thought does highlight suffering individuals, the liberal approaches, and policies that build on them, focus on the protection of these bodies, while the critical approaches highlight the potential to enable agency. The denial of agency and the disciplining of bodies through practices of liberal governance has been a focus of studies that examine practices of refugee management or biometric technologies for identifying terrorists (Dillon and Reid 2001; Muller 2004: 22). The disembodied abstract individual or state, which during the Cold War was a representation of security, is in these analyses transformed into the empty object of bare life (Agamben 1998), shaped by technologies of control and power, and subject to pervasive insecurity. The speaking, feeling, seeing, acting and culturally-situated body of the human subject is, by contrast, the hope of life with dignity, endowed with meaning. In Chapter 5 of this volume, Peter Burgess states that security is 'the moral, cognitive and aesthetic encapsulation of the horizon of danger that derails and re-rerails the circuits of the self,' which is consistent with this view.

While critical security studies, and human security discourses at the international level, brought the individual back in, the further 'turns' since that time have the cumulative effect of embodying the human subject of security. If the disembodied individual is subject to technologies of power and management of the body, the embodiment of security in itself becomes an act of resistance which reveals the distinction between a life of humiliation and a life of dignity. If the concentration camp is the image of bare life, then the Arab Spring, or the act of reclaiming dignity in resistance, is the image of the latter.

One does not have to look far to find resistance in practice, such as the Arab Spring, or to see the importance of a concept of dignity. My own recent work on political self-sacrifice explores the relationship between humiliation and dignity and the contestation surrounding the naming of the agent of self-sacrifice as a 'terrorist' or 'martyr' (Fierke 2013). Starting from the perspective that the logic of security is different for those who historically have been located outside sovereignty, I explore several different forms of political self-sacrifice, among them the human bomb, hunger strikes, self-immolation and forms of nonviolent resistance. Turning the speech act of securitization on its head, I analyse the perlocutionary effects of the sacrifice as an 'act of speech' that speaks louder than words but without words, communicating the experience of suffering of a marginalized community. Building on the work of Sarah Ahmed (2004), as well as Butler, I theorize about how emotions circulate out from the dying or suffering body to various audiences, possibly reshaping the boundaries and restoring the dignity and autonomy of marginalized communities. The sacrifice disrupts everyday assumptions about power and normality, thereby potentially opening a space for a larger conversation regarding the rules by which a community lives.

Language is thus not merely about hegemonic discourses imposed on empty bodies, but the possibility of conversation between vulnerable others. In a special issue of *Millennium*, Arachya and Hutchings, among others, argue that many approaches to International Relations and critical theory are informed by a Eurocentric view and this view also influences conceptions of dialogue (Arachya 2011; Hutchings 2011). From this Eurocentric perspective, it is difficult to conceive of a global conversation where people can speak from a position other than this Eurocentric platform, which relies on a binary opposition between West and non-West. This platform hides the plurality and diversity of the world and limits the potential for conversation that takes seriously other traditions of thought, such as Buddhism or Taoism. If the terms of 'security,' as derived from the hegemonic tradition, limit what is seen and who is heard, how do we meaningfully converse about security in a world of changing power relations where 'the West' no longer monopolizes this hegemonic position? The metaphors of security, found in Cold War literature and practice, projected human qualities on to abstract states. Realism has relied on a 'black-box' notion of the state which, as Glaser notes, does not dismiss internal differences between states; this treatment is nonetheless thin. The move in critical security studies away from euphemism toward human bodies means more attention to those experiences that make us human, and not least dignity. The human security discourse, in its liberal form, highlights the importance of protecting individual bodies. From a critical perspective, practices of protection potentially become an expression of hegemonic power, if in a softer form (Duffield 2001; Pupavac 2001: 25), which limits the agency of the protected and thus reproduces colonial structures of power. The critical discourse reconceptualizes the human subject of security in terms of the agency of vulnerability arising from the resistance of embodied agents.

Beyond the body

International relations and security studies appear to be forever turning, in which the turning itself is a part of a dance with mystical powers. Each turn within this dance is part of a series of larger turns, which have transformed the body of security. In the first turn, that which had been given the label security, i.e. the state, was named a potential source of insecurity. Peace movements, as well as academics, told us this in the early eighties. In a second turn, it was argued that many areas of human life are insecure and thus the meaning of security should be broadened beyond the military to a focus on the individual or the planet. In a third turn, questions were raised about the potential for emancipation from forces which render human individuals insecure and keep them from realizing their potential. In a fourth turn, the emphasis shifted away from the politicization of non-military issues as 'security,' or the expectation of progress in the emancipatory potential of humanity, to asking fundamental questions about how our humanity has been eroded by the all-encompassing search for security.

At this point the whirling dancer picks up speed. The linguistic turn in International Relations rested on a claim that the subjects of study were not simply objects in the world who could be labelled but humans who speak and bring meaning to their interactions. The practice turn revealed that these subjects not only speak but engage in meaningful practices (Adler and Pouliot 2011). The aesthetic turn highlighted that human subjects see and feel and that these experiences have some impact on their actions (Bleiker 2001; Moore and Shepherd 2010). All of these turns relate to cultural beings whose saying, doing and feeling is shaped by socialization and a location within global space. A further material turn returns to a very different point than from where we began, reinforcing the assumption that security is about location and power within the material world, but in the process recasting the subject of inquiry as a speaking, feeling, acting subject who occupies a body subject to pain, suffering or pleasure. What all of these turns represent is a turn away from the abstract body of the state and use of security as metaphor, to security as the lived experience of human and political beings.

Foucault and Butler's work has had a tremendous influence on the conceptualization of the relationship between language and body. Claudia Aradau (2010), who draws on the materialist feminism of Karen Barad to critique Butler, adds a further twist to this materialist turn. But even in this case, she does not move beyond discourse; she instead shows how 'things' or materiality emerge out of material–discursive practices. Her focus is on the importance of materiality for understanding the protection of critical infrastructure and managerial responses that call for intervention to safeguard pre-existing things and their functionality. She argues that the securitization literature has largely focused on unpacking the discursive and institutional practices that constitute what is to be secured and which threats need to be eliminated or neutralized. While emphasizing performative and intersubjective practice, the securitization literature has ignored the role of 'things' in the articulation of insecurities, as discussed by Junk and Rauer in their presentation of actor-network theory. The focus has instead been on the human as the subject of security, such that non-human objects outside the realm of securitization are understood as 'facilitating' conditions of securitization (Buzan *et al.*, 1998) or as remnants of mainstream positivism (Aradau 2010: 2). Aradau argues that 'things' are neither empty receptacles of discourse nor do they have 'essential' characteristics that set them apart from humans, but that they are themselves agential and emerge in relation to material-discursive practices. This argument requires a reformulation of Butler's analysis of performativity and Foucault's analysis of the *dispositif* or apparatus. Drawing on the work of Karen

Barad, Aradau's reconceptualization helps to show how distinctions between nature and the social, objects and subjects are not pre-given, but are materially and discursively produced. Securitization thus becomes a process of materialization which 'enacts a reconfiguration of the world in ways in which differences come to matter' (Aradau 2010: 3).

Barad argues that both Butler and Foucault, while taking into account the materiality of the body, as well as its materialization through regulative practice, fail to account for *how* both materiality and language matter (Barad 1998; 2007). Butler, for instance, shows how the body emerges through iterative performative processes, which are produced through regulatory norms, without any need for an external referent. Barad, by contrast, argues that 'materialization is not only a matter of how discourse comes to matter but how matter comes to matter.'(Barad 1998: 108) Foucault, likewise, takes the material character of objects for granted, even while considering how human bodies materialize through complex forms of power/knowledge. Aradau claims that both Foucault and Butler prioritize language as shaping the material body. She argues that materiality and language are instead co-constitutive. Matter is not a passive surface that is acted upon through discourse or an end product of discourse but an active factor in material-discursive processes, which requires that we problematize the distinction between human and non-human. Neither matter nor meaning can be reduced to the other or explained in terms of the other as they are mutually articulated (Barad 2007: 152). If matter is an open-ended practice and the historical effect of iterative materializations, the central question becomes one of which specific material practices matter and how they come to matter. Matter is generative and agentive in bringing new worlds into being, not only in bringing new things into the world. In reflecting on the different materializations of, for instance, concrete, asphalt, metal, oil, water, Aradau argues that 'agency' is not only human and institutional but the agency of grids, nodes, tubes, soil, foundations and construction materials (Aradau 2010: 12). All of these interact with forms of knowledge, with humans and with institutional practices to create particular materializations of '(critical) infrastructure' to be protected.

Conclusion

The question is whether, amidst all this turning, we have simply returned to the place where security studies began, to a focus on the material rather than language. Is security studies once again a study of life beyond language? To reach this conclusion would be to remain stuck in the either/or choice between language and materiality. The dance that has been constituted by the various turns is not linear but *circular*, not static but transformative through its movement. Our point of return is very different from where we began. The subject of security is no longer the disembodied state, whose materiality takes the form of weapons wielded in violent exchange. The language of security is no longer the abstract metaphoric representation that claims to mirror a reality from which it is detached. The human subject of security who materializes upon our arrival is the embodied subject for whom security is important precisely because of a shared vulnerability. The embodied subject sees, feels, acts, builds and destroys, all the while conversing with other human subjects and interacting with a material world. This embodied security is not isolated from a material context but fundamentally bound up in the interaction between humans and their material environment, both of which are constituted in and through language.

Notes

1 I place the word positivist in quotation marks to highlight the frequent misuse of the term and the negative connotations that came to be attached to the word within disciplinary debates.
2 On how language relates to the construction of identity, see Campbell (1998); on the construction of 'crises', see Weldes (1999); on the enabling effect of assumed hierarchies of meaning, see Doty (1993); for analysis of change, see Fierke (1998); for the role of speech acts, see Buzan et al. (1998).
3 Scholarship surrounding the Copenhagen School has become something of a cottage industry, not unlike the critiques of Waltz earlier.
4 Adam Roberts argues that the 90per cent statistic, which since the early 1990s has become an 'urban myth,' is flawed, as is the view that civilians are much worse off than in earlier periods. See Roberts (2010: 115–35; 2011).

References

Adler, E. and Pouliot, V. (2011) *International Practices*, Cambridge: Cambridge University Press.
Ahmed, S. (2004) *The Cultural Politics of Emotion*, London: Routledge.
Agamben, G. (1998) *Homo Sacer: Sovereign Power and Bare Life*, Stanford: Stanford University Press.
Arachya, A. (2011) 'Dialogue and Discovery: In Search of International Relations Theory Beyond the West', *Millennium*, 39(3): 619–37.
Aradau, C. (2010) 'Security That Matters: Critical Infrastructure and Objects of Protection', *Security Dialogue*, 41(5): 491–514.
Ashley, R. (1984) 'The Poverty of Neorealism', *International Organization*, 38(2): 225–86.
—— (1988) 'Untying the Sovereign State: A Double Reading of the Anarchy Problematique', *Millennium – Journal of International Studies*, 17(2): 227–62.
Austin, J. (1962) *How to Do Things with Words*, Oxford: Oxford University Press.
Barad, K. (1998) 'Agential Realism: Feminist Interventions in Understanding Scientific Practice', in M. Biagioli (ed.) *The Science Studies Reader*, London: Routledge.
—— (2007) *Meeting the Universe Halfway: Quantum Physics and the Entanglement of Matter and Meaning*, Durham, NC: Duke University Press.
Bleiker, R. (2001) 'The Aesthetic Turn in International Political Theory', *Millennium – Journal of International Studies*, 30(3): 509–33.
Booth, K. (1991) 'Security and Emancipation', *Review of International Studies*, 17(4): 313–26.
Butler, Judith (1993) *Bodies that Matter: On the Discursive Limits of Sex*, London: Routledge.
Buzan, B., Waever, O. and DeWilde, J. (1998) *Security: A New Framework of Analysis*, Boulder: Lynne Rienner.
Campbell, D. (1998) *Writing Security*, Manchester: Manchester University Press.

Cohn, C. (1987) 'Sex and Death in the Rational World of Defense Intellectuals', *Signs*, 12(4): 687–718.

Cox, R. (1981) 'Social Forces, States and World Orders: Beyond International Relations Theory', *Millennium – Journal of International Studies*, 10(2); 126–55.

Dillon, M. and Reid, J. (2001) 'Global Liberal Governance: Biopolitics, Security and War', *Millennium – Journal of International Studies*, 30(1): 41–66.

Doty, R. (1993) 'Foreign Policy as Social Construction: A Post-Positivist Analysis of U.S. Counterinsurgency Policy in the Philippines', *International Studies Quarterly*, 37(3): 297–320.

Duffield, M. (2001) *Global Governance and the New Wars: The Merging of Development and Security*, London: Zed Books.

Fierke, K.M. (1998) *Changing Games, Changing Strategies: Critical Investigations in Security*, Manchester: Manchester University Press.

(2013) *Political Self-Sacrifice: Agency, Body and Emotion in International Relations*, Cambridge: Cambridge University Press.

Foucault, M. (1979) *Discipline and Punish: The Birth of the Prison*, transl. Alan Sheridan, New York: Random House.

Hansen, L. (2000) 'The Little Mermaid's Silent Security Dilemma and the Absence of Gender in the Copenhagen School', *Millennium – Journal of International Studies*, 29(2): 285–306.

(2011) 'Theorizing the Image for Security Studies', *European Journal of International Relations*, 17(1): 51–74.

Hutchings, K. (2011) 'The Dialogue between Whom? The Role of the West/Non-West Distinction in Promoting Global Dialogue in IR', *Millennium – Journal of International Studies*, 39(3): 639–47.

Keohane, R. (1986) *Neorealism and its Critics*, New York: Columbia University Press.

Moore, C. and Shepherd, L. (2010) 'Aesthetics and international Relations: Towards a Global Politics', *Global Politics*, 24(3): 299–309.

Muller, B. (2004) Globalization, Security, Paradox: Towards a Refugee Biopolitics, *Refuge*, 22(1): 49–57.

Pupavac, V. (2001) Therapeutic Governance: Psycho-Social Intervention and Trauma Management, *Disasters*, 25(4): 358–72.

Roberts, A. (2010) 'Lives and Statistics: Are 90% of War Victims Civilian?', *Survival*, 52(3): 115–35.

(2011) 'The Civilian in Modern War,' in H. Strachan and S. Scheipers (eds) *The Changing Character of War*, Oxford: Oxford University Press: 357–80.

Schlag, G. and Heck, A. (2013) 'Securitizing Images of the Female Body and the War in Afghanistan', *European Journal of International Relations*, 19(4): 891–913.

Walker, R.B.J. (1993) *Inside/Outside: International Relations as Political Theory*. Cambridge: Cambridge University Press.

Waltz, K. (1979) *Theory of International Politics*. Boston: Addison-Wesley.

Weldes, J. (1999) *Constructing the National Interest*, Minneapolis: University of Minnesota Press.

Wittgenstein, L. (1958) *Philosophical Investigations*, Oxford: Blackwell.

Wynn-Jones, R. (1999) *Security, Strategy and Critical Theory*, New York: Lynne-Rienner.

4 On paradox and pathologies
A cultural approach to security

Christopher Daase

Introduction

In recent years, security has become of primary value for national and international society (see the introduction to this volume by Schlag, Junk and Daase). Through this process, both political discourses and social structures have been transformed. Despite these profound changes, research on security remains largely within the straightjacket of disciplinary perspectives. Political scientists investigate novel security policies – in most cases neatly distinguishing domestic and international challenges – while criminologists examine the modification of individual threat perceptions and sociologists analyze their impact on society. Lawyers explore recent developments in security law, while historians consider protective practices over time. What is still lacking is an integrated perspective that considers these developments as various aspects of a cultural process that produces, reproduces and transforms national and international society.

Focusing on security culture, I argue, can help overcome such limitations and open up new interdisciplinary perspectives for security research. A focus on political culture, however, is neither new nor devoid of problems. The use of culture in an unreflected way in the past has discredited the concept as arbitrarily applicable and ultimately tautological. David Elkins and Richard Simeon (1979) have long since identified four problems that haunt cultural approaches in the social sciences. Firstly, it is difficult to differentiate cultural from structural and psychological variables; secondly, culture is not directly observable and must be inferred from other observations; thirdly, for most people, culture is unconscious and implicit, meaning that they cannot be directly interviewed about it; and finally, although culture is based on individual action, it is more than the sum of aggregated individual behaviour. Yet despite these analytical complications, culture continues to enjoy popularity in the social sciences because it is useful for appreciating aspects of politics – e.g. variance despite relatively similar conditions – that other conceptualizations cannot; it therefore comes as no surprise that the concept has also found its way into security studies.

In this chapter, I will do three things. First, I will describe how the concept of culture has traditionally figured in security studies, identifying its strengths and weaknesses. Second, I will present a 'culturalist' concept of security culture, focussing on the meaning and practice of security. Third, I will outline a research program for analyzing the transformation of security culture, including the paradox and pathologies that accompany this process. The core of my argument is that recent conceptual shifts are indicative of social and political transformations; these transformations reveal specific contradictions existent within the liberal national and international order. Thus, not only the traditional *security dilemma* – i.e. the decreasing supply of security despite its increasing demand (Dalby 1997; Herz 1950) – but likewise the *security paradox* – i.e. the increasing demand despite an increasing supply of security – should serve as the focus of security studies. To be sure, the security paradox is not an alternative, but a supplement to the security dilemma insofar as it concentrates on the 'internal' dynamics and pathologies of states and societies rather than on 'external' inter-state relations. How and in what way the security dilemma and the security paradox interrelate, is a matter of further research of and dialogue between different approaches to security (see our conclusion to this volume).

Security studies and the concept of culture

Until the mid-1990s, the concept of culture did not assume any significant role in security studies. This is due to the fact that security was regarded as a natural requirement of every state, independent of its political structure or ideological outlook; this thereby excluded security from the mutability and variability of culture. Realist thinkers declared the demand for security, and the resultant dilemmas among states, to be the driver of international politics, serving as the ultimate cause of such diverse phenomena as war (Posen 1993; Waltz 1989), alliances (Mearsheimer 1983; Walt 1987) and cooperation (Glaser 1997; Jervis 1978). Unit-level characteristics – or as Kenneth Waltz famously put it: reductionist theories (Waltz 1979) –, as it was argued, could not explain the surprising conformity implicit in the international political behaviour of states (see contributions by Glaser and by Masala in this volume). At best, strong and weak states could be distinguished in order to explain both the band-wagoning and the balancing behaviour of small states as well as the expansive policies of great powers to secure their respective claims for domination (Mandelbaum 1988).

Once liberal approaches began focusing on the domestic factors influencing security behaviour, a more nuanced understanding of national security developed (Risse-Kappen 1991). It was only with the introduction of the 'constructivist turn' (Checkel 1998) that culture started being employed in International Relations and Security Studies in a more systematic fashion (see Katzenstein 1996; Lapid and Kratochwil 1997). The oft-cited definition, however, remained vague, stating that 'culture refers both to a set of evaluative standards, such as norms or values, and to cognitive standards, such as rules or models defining what entities and actors exist in a system and how they operate and interrelate' (Jepperson et al. 1996: 56). The concept thus remained closely contingent on states and, in turn, national cultures in the plural. Drawing on the scholarship of organizational as well as political culture allowed for the explanation of phenomena such as the characteristics of French military policy (Kier 1996) and Chinese great power behaviour (Johnston 1998). In a similar vein, James Sperling provides the following definition: 'National security cultures provide the lens through which national authorities refract the structural positions of the state in the international system; it explains the subjective understanding of objective threats to national security, the instruments relied upon to meet those threats, and the preferences for unilateral or multilateral action' (Sperling 2010: 11). The purpose here is to explain cooperation and conflict within global security governance with respect to conflicting security cultures: 'National security cultures produce preferences for specific forms of security governance systems that, in turn, facilitate or inhibit international cooperation' (Sperling 2010: 13).

Concurrently, however, the constructivist research program has relied on a concept of culture that does not focus on national cultures but rather on world culture as developed by John Meyer and his co-researchers at the so-called Stanford School. Meyer defines culture 'less [as] a set of values and norms, and more a set of models defining the nature, purpose, resources, technologies, controls, and sovereignty of the proper nation state' (Meyer 1999: 123). In this context, culture is not used to attain an understanding of the national specifics of individual states but to uncover the global validity of universal rules of rational behavior. According to this perspective, national interests, security concerns and the strategic behavior of states can, to a large extent, be attributed to the normative structures of international society, defined as world culture (Finnemore 1996: 19).

Thus, constructivists explain divergence in national security policies by pointing to the variety of national cultures; on the other hand, convergence is explained by referring to the uniformity of world culture. This leads to three observations. Firstly, the nation state still stands at the center of the concept of culture in constructivist security studies. Secondly, change does not significantly factor into the equation since, in both cases, culture refers to a relatively static independent variable for explaining security behaviour. Thirdly, culture is supposed to explain both differences and similarities within security policy, running the danger of ultimately explaining nothing. It is therefore no wonder that the concept of security culture has been met with skepticism. David Haglund recently even went so far as to call 'the whole thing off', arguing that the concept of security culture is not only redundant but misleading since 'there is not much of a distinction worth making between security culture and strategic culture, for the latter category contains enough suggestive elements to satisfy the intellectual curiosity of those who would seek to link culture with [...] security policies and outcomes' (Haglund 2011: 511).

To be sure, the concept of security culture is much younger than that of strategic culture. It was first introduced by an expert group investigating the nuclear accident in Chernobyl under the auspices of the International Atomic Energy Agency (IAEA 1986). The concept quickly spread in relation to denoting the institutional foundations of security management and the awareness of employees in high-tech power and production plants (Ruighaver et al. 2007). From here, the concept was appropriated by social scientists to describe 'the sum of the beliefs, values and practices of institutions and individuals that (1) determine what is considered to be a danger or insecurity in the widest sense and (2) how and by which means this danger should be handled' (Daase 2010: 23). Strategic culture, by contrast, as it has been used since the 1970s, refers to the political beliefs, opinions and patterns of behaviour demonstrated by political elites, specifically regarding military matters (Johnston 1995; Snyder 1973). The terms 'strategy' and 'strategic' may assume such broad definitions so as to entail all forms of rational behaviour. From an analytical standpoint, however, in order to grasp recent changes in the security realm, it would be wiser to restrict it to a narrow meaning relating to the military and complement the term with the more recent concept of security culture. This would allow for a description of the broader spheres of activity related to states, societies and individuals (Rauer et al. 2014). This not only prevents conceptual redundancy but also allows for a more differentiated analysis of the social meaning of security as it has changed in recent years. The conceptual history of security, as outlined in our introduction to this volume as well, together with the differentiation of strategic and security culture, demonstrate that security has been emancipated from hitherto military reductionism. To insist on the traditional, all-encompassing concept of strategic culture would obscure this shift and artificially limit the meaning of security.

The transformation of security culture

Security, as noted above, has become one of the principal normative concepts in politics, both domestically and internationally; though this has not always been the case. For centuries, it was not security but peace that dominated theological, philosophical and political thinking. At the beginning of the twentieth century, however, peace and security began to compete against one another for primacy in strategic debates and political programs. Today, security is an undisputed political value whereas peace has become subordinated to it. This conceptual shift is indicative of a more fundamental change.[1] I would argue that the reinterpretation of peace and security follows a liberal script insofar as individual rights and freedoms increasingly dominate collective claims and quests for sovereignty and self-determination. This creates grave consequences for the normative structure and legal order of international relations.

Although both peace and security are mutually laid out in the UN Charter and have traditionally been applied to legitimate military measures by the Security Council, they possess distinct historical meanings. The concept of peace has dimensions that draw on varying political, cultural, philosophical and religious traditions. The Greek concept of *eirene* captures peace as a moment between wars in a world in which hostilities were a constant feature. In contrast, the Latin word *pax* depicts peace as an order of rule and authority, in which a powerful center guarantees the rule of law. The Jewish concept *schalom* expresses peace as a way of life that includes the individual, the community and their relationship to nature and God. Medieval theories of peace distinguish between the eternal spiritual peace of the Kingdom of God and the temporary peace of the political world on earth. Drawing on Augustine (*De Civitate Dei* XIX, 11–20), Thomas Aquinas speaks of a true divine peace as opposed to a worldly peace which is spurious, at best (*Summa Theologica* II-II, qu. 29). During the Renaissance, rational schemes for 'eternal peace' on earth were created, either in analogy to an existing form of rule (like Dante's *De Monarchia* of 1318) or based on social contract theory (like Hobbes' *Leviathan* 1651) that would contribute to the development of international law (as in Hugo Grotius *De Jure Belli ac Pacis libri tres* 1625). The more ambitious peace plans from the Enlightenment (like Kant's *Eternal Peace* 1795) suggested an interconnectedness between internal peace (maintained through a democratic order) and external peace (understood as a federation of free republics). Here, the idea that a state's ability for peaceful relations depends on its domestic political system and the guarantee of personal freedoms lives on today in liberal theories of democratic peace and so-called cosmopolitan approaches to human rights. An alternative tradition can be identified (drawing on Hegel's *Philosophy of Right* 1821) that privileges states' sovereignty rights over individual human rights and that understands peace as a precarious inter-state balance of power. Today, this position is occupied by so-called Realists and communitarian theorists like Alasdair MacIntyre, Michael Sandel, Charles Taylor and Michael Walzer. In both traditions, however, *peace* refers to a social interdependence of individual or collective actors, devoid of violence and other forms of coercion, in order to achieve communal benefits.

Relatively speaking, the concept of security does not enjoy any sort of rich tradition in the history of thought. However, it has evolved in the semantic field of the Latin adjectives *tututs*, *securus* and *certus* in the meaning of security as protection, as absence from needs and as certainty. Since the seventeenth century, internal and external security have been distinguished and described as the ultimate purpose of the state, often making use of *jus naturalis* justifications as by Hobbes or Pufendorf. In a similar vein, John Locke (*Two treatises of Government* 1690, §131) argued that the state is justified by nothing else 'but the peace, safety, and public good of the people'. Here one can already detect a certain ambivalence towards security policy. Though security is needed for all people alike, on the other hand, it enables the existence of the state itself, as Wilhelm von Humboldt declared (*Ideen zum einem Versuch die Grenzen der Wirksamkeit des Staates zu bestimmen* 1792). Again, two traditions emanated from this: a Realist position emphasized the principle of self-help in international relations and, consequently, the security needs of states. Its liberal counterpart favored a broader concept of security that includes the security needs of societal groups and individuals in the international context.

At the beginning of the twentieth century until the 1970s, peace was a central political concept and described, following a narrow understanding, the absence of war and personal violence; in a broader understanding, it meant the absence of repression and distress and all that could inhibit the potential realization of human abilities (Galtung 1969). The spiritual tradition of peace lives on in this broader understanding. In treatises from the Middle Ages and the Renaissance as well as in the plans for eternal peace during the Enlightenment, peace is presented as a concrete utopia (*Realutopie*), i.e. a condition that cannot be completely described and only partially realized. As a 'regulative idea', however, the concept of peace has served as the basis for the founding documents of many twentieth century international organizations and finds itself at the core of international law. Compared to this, security refers to the existing needs of individual states and the stability of the international system. The state-centric understanding of security gained wide acceptance during the nineteenth century; it found its way into international law and the statutes of international organizations as the right to national self-determination and territorial integrity.

Hence, the ideas of peace and security mentioned in the Covenant of the League of Nations or the UN Charter refer to two different, but related, political values. Security relates, first and foremost, to the inviolability of state sovereignty and the right of national self-determination and territorial integrity. Peace, at the same time, refers to the non-violent diplomatic intercourse between states and peoples in view of a better life for all human beings. Thus, security policy was primarily related to the preservation of the political status quo and the stability of the international system while the politics of peace, on the other hand, referred to a more comprehensive strategy aimed at the transformation of the existing system.

This order has changed: the relationship between peace and security has virtually been reversed in recent years. The concept of peace has lost its utopian quality and, consequently, its visionary power. It has been replaced by an extended concept of security that increasingly represents a demand for emancipation and the promise of a better life. However, the differentiating factor is that the concept of peace entailed a social utopia in which the freedom of the individual is guaranteed through social self-determination and the sovereignty of the state while the utopia found within the new concept of security refers to individual freedom beyond all political collectives. As a consequence, state sovereignty becomes secondary.

This has been an effect of the gradual extension of the security concept over recent years, as elaborated in our introduction in greater detail. For decades, security meant the absence of military threats to the nation state. This meaning was broadened in the second part of the twentieth century along four dimensions (see the figure in the introduction to this volume): with regard to the referent object, the issue area, its geographical scope, and the nature of danger. (1) Historically, the concept of security was linked to the consolidation of the state as the sole legitimate actor in international politics. Thus, security in international relations meant, first and foremost, state security – an idea that did not go unchallenged. Liberal theorists in the tradition of Locke and Kant stressed that states are only instruments meant to provide safety for society. *Sociatal security* was therefore advocated as a situation in which a collective of citizens would live in safety and freedom in order to foster productivity and wealth. The concept of *human security* goes one step further, questioning not only the state-centric approach but also the focus on collectives; it stresses that, above all, individual human beings have intrinsic value and should be protected. (2) This comes with consequences in relation to the issue areas in which security is seen as relevant. Traditional security threats were mainly perceived in military terms; this changed in the 1970s on account of the oil crises, leading to the incorporation of *economic security*. Another step was taken when *environmental security* came into vogue in the 1980s and the Brundtland-Report stated that: 'environmental threats to security are now beginning to emerge on a global scale'. Ever since, environmental degradation has been discussed as both a national and international security issue. (3) This affected the geographical scope of security. While traditional policy applied to the national level, the term *international security*, by contrast, widely used since the 1970s, referred to inter-state relations. This therefore redirected the focus from purely national concerns towards the stability of the international system. The concept of *global security* even goes one step beyond state politics insofar as it crosses national boundaries to apply the term to human beings around the globe. (4) The final, and arguably most important, dimension of the conceptual change concerns the operationalization of danger. Traditionally, political challenges to the state had been operationalized as threats, which could be measured on the basis of what was known about the enemy actor, his hostile intentions and the military capabilities available. This concept, however, became problematic with the perception of more diffuse dangers to the wellbeing of societies. Under the condition of social and economic interdependence, dangers do not necessarily emanate strictly from hostile actors or through military capabilities. Insecurity had to be measured in alternative ways, e.g. as the degree of vulnerability to externalities, whatever their sources may be. From there, it was only a small step towards the paradigmatic shift in security policy after the Cold War. Today it is risks rather than threats that dominate the discourse about international politics. The 'clear and present danger' of the Cold War has been replaced by unclear and future 'risks and challenges'. The proliferation of weapons of mass destruction, transnational terrorism, organized crime, environmental degradation and many other issues are discussed in terms of uncertainty and risk. One common factor among them lies in their relative indeterminableness.

What this brief conceptual history has aimed to demonstrate is the fact that the perception of international and transnational risks is a culmination of a historical trend towards broadening the meaning of security, driven by the long-term emancipation of society from the state. The liberal understanding of security is conceptually denationalized, ideationally globalized, and spatially deterritorialized. Liberal security culture thus focuses on the global management of individual risks.

The paradox of security

The concept of security is the most visible aspect of security culture: depending on how insecurity and security are conceptualized, dangers come to either be emphasized or de-emphasized and specific political and social issues come to the fore or are set aside. As such, in order to analyze security culture, it is necessary to concentrate on conceptual change. However, it would be wise to go beyond the constructivist belief that security has become today's core value merely through wilful speech acts of securitization, i.e. the deliberate denomination of problems as security issues for the sake of heightening their significance within the political process (Buzan et al. 1998; Weaver 1995). While securitization might indeed be part of the process, the change of security culture runs deeper. It is the result of political and social de-nationalization and trans-nationalization which is, in turn, the unintended effect stemming from the emancipation of society from the state. The concept of security is thus cause *and* effect of political change.

The crucial consequence of this change is that the liberal state – and along with it international liberal society – are becoming victims of their own success. Since social processes of emancipation depend on relatively secure environments, new security demands are only made when more general security needs are satisfied. As soon as this becomes the case, however, more far-reaching security demands develop; these tend to overburden state and international organizations, undermining their legitimacy and security in the long run. I refer to this process as a 'security paradox', i.e. a circle of a self-increasing and concurrently self-undermining strife for security (see also Angehrn 1993: 240).

This paradox is a well-documented feature of many social situations and it is often discussed as the divergence of objective hazards and subjective security. It has been described with regard to people's perceptions of criminality, their dealings with medicine (e.g. vaccine) and the fear for social security. Those who enjoy relative security, it seems, seek absolute security and are increasingly worried because of its elusiveness. This mechanism not only applies to individuals but likewise to collective actors such as states and international organizations. The relative increase of national security after the end of the Cold War did not result in a new sense of security but, on the contrary, insecurity, especially in the US. As early as 1991, NATO declared that although the disintegration of the Soviet Union had lessened an acute threat, new 'international risks and challenges' had emerged in unexpected ways. However, the reverse phenomenon has also been identified when an enhanced sense of security increases real danger. In the insurance industry, it is well known that new safety technologies may encourage risky behaviour and increase the prospect of accidents. Again, this is not alien to collective actors. If states misjudge their relative power, they are prone to take risks and intervene in situations in which victory is unlikely (Vertzberger 1998).

There are a number of theories that attempt to explain the divergence of subjective (i.e. perceived) and objective (i.e. calculated) security. Traditionally, they proceed from the assumption that a certain type of 'bias' prevents actors from accurately judging perilous situations. The reasons for such biases are identified in psychological mechanisms (Slovic 1992), group dynamics (Janis 1982), or cultural dispositions (Douglas and Wildavsky 1982). But it could well be that the distinction between objective and subjective security is overly simplistic, especially if objective security is awarded the quality of scientific accuracy and political rationality, being juxtaposed alongside the fearful irrationality of the public at large. After all, the subjective security of laypersons may not be as irrational as one might think and the objective security of experts not as rational as it would like to portray itself. A more accurate picture of security culture emerges when scientific experts, political decision-makers and ordinary people are understood to make judgements according to their own criteria of rationality and the customs and incentives predominant in their respective sub-system, or rather sub-culture.

One way of framing the security paradox is to distinguish between two kinds of insecurity, ontological and epistemological: the danger for life and limb, freedom and welfare on the one hand and the uncertainty with which we can realize and assess these dangers on the other (Daase and Kessler 2007). This distinction allows for an explanation of how one measure that increases security by decreasing actual danger may, at the same time, increase the sense of insecurity by enhancing uncertainty about other potential dangers. The fear among parents expecting a child is thus not irrational given ever better prenatal diagnostics; it is the result of increased uncertainty in light of better knowledge. As knowledge also produces ignorance, security produces uncertainty. This is the reason why relatively secure societies are also anxious societies.

This process plays out differently in various social sub-systems; it is the interaction of those systems that 'produces' security policy and practices. Given the extended meaning of and the enhanced demand for security, policy is no longer solely the domain of states and international organizations. Rather, security policy takes place in what Richard Münch refers to as the 'interpenetration zones' of relatively autonomous functional systems (Münch 1996: 180).[2] In international relations, 'security governance' has described such interaction and the networking of different actor types into complex structures to address urgent issues (Bryden and Caparini 2006; Krahmann 2003). However, the policies emanating from the interplay of actors rooted in different functional systems also increase the unpredictability of effects and the probability of unintended consequences (Daase and Friesendorf 2010). One such consequence is the security paradox, which is not simply an unavoidable systemic feature driven by anonymous structural forces but, first and foremost, a phenomenon driven by identifiable social agents interacting in specific, or even 'pathological', ways. By applying this somewhat normatively colored term, I try to capture a process in which outputs from various social sub-systems reinforce rather than balance each other, contributing to a dynamic that undermines the system's long-term stability. The politics of anti-terrorism is a perfect example. Only because the political apparatus, the media, the academic sector and the general public interacted in such a reinforcing manner after September 11, was it possible to introduce profound social and political changes that significantly enhanced the power of control and surveillance (and objective security for that matter) while undermining global norms and civil liberties, ultimately undermining the sense of subjective security (Mueller and Steward 2015). The policing of terrorism is only one example of how sub-systems interrelate in adverse ways to reinforce threat perceptions and contribute to the transformation of security culture.

Conclusion

In this chapter, I have advocated a cultural approach to security, suggesting that an analysis of conceptual change sheds light on the causes and consequences of recent social and political transformations. In the course of the analysis, it has become evident that security is not a conventional commodity that responds to marked forces.[3] It is not the logic of demand and supply, according to which increased supply reduces the demand, that determines the degree of individual and collective security. Rather, a cultural logic seems to be at work according to which an increase in the supply of security can further bolster the demand for it. Since security is not a good readily produced but rather a general idea about the expectation of future conditions, such a thing as a saturated market can never exist. This to some extent explains the paradox of why increased efforts to supply security result in an even higher demand for it. However, the mechanisms driving this process must be analyzed in further detail, integrating not only domestic and international perspectives of politics, but also other disciplinary assessments such as historical, legal, psychological and sociological analyses of security culture. Uncovering how various actors, institutions and practices interrelate to produce security but, at the same time, undermine it is the central task for a cultural approach to security and is worth an interdisciplinary effort. A more comprehensive understanding of the security paradox remains the precondition that will allow us to escape the vicious cycle of ever-increasing yet ever-undermining security efforts and also to balance security and other social values.

Notes

1 I am drawing here on methods of conceptual history as developed by Reinhard Koselleck (1979) and Quentin Skinner (1989). For a more detailed discussion, see Daase 2010.
2 Similar to Niklas Luhmann, Münch regards society as composed of sub-systems but, similar to Fritz Scharpf, he allows for governance of the system through the interaction of political, economic and social actors.
3 I am indebted to Valentin Rauer for clarifying this point.

References

Angehrn, E. (1993) 'Das Streben nach Sicherheit. Ein politisch-metaphysisches Problem', in H. Fink-Eitel and G. Lohmann (eds) *Philosophie der Gefühle*, Frankfurt: Suhrkamp: 218–43.
Bryden, A. and Caprini, M. (eds) (2006) *Private Actors and Security Governance*, Münster: Lit.
Buzan, B., Weaver, O. and de Wilde, J. (1998) *Security: A New Framework for Analysis*, Boulder: Lynne Rienner.
Checkel, J. T. (1998) 'The Constructivist Turn in International Relations Theory'. *World Politics*, 50 (2):, 324–348.
Daase, C. (2010) 'National, Societal, and Human Security: On the Transformation of Political Language', *Historical Social Research*, 35 (4): 22–37.
Daase, C. and Friesendorf, C. (eds) (2010) *Rethinking Security Governance: The Problem of Unintended Consequences*, London: Routledge.
Daase, C. and Kessler, O. (2007) 'Knowns and Unknowns in the War on Terror: Uncertainty and the Political Construction of Danger', *Security Dialogue*, 38 (4): 411–36.

Dalby, S. (1997) 'Contesting an Essential Concept: Reading the Dilemmas in Contemporary Security Discourse', in K. Krause and M.C. Williams (eds) *Critical Security Studies*, Minneapolis: University of Minnesota Press: 3–31.

Douglas, M. and Wildavsky, A. (1982) *Risk and Culture: An Essay on the Selection of Technical and Environmental Dangers*, Berkeley: University of California Press.

Elkins, D. and Simeon, R. (1979) 'A Cause in Search of its Effect, or What Does Political Culture Explain?', *Comparative Politics*, 11 (2): 127–45.

Finnemore, M. (1996) *National Interest in International Society*, Ithaca: Cornell University Press.

Galtung, J. (1969) 'Violence, Peace and Peace Research', *Journal of Peace Research*, 6 (3): 167–91.

Glaser, C.L. (1997) 'The Security Dilemma Revisited', *World Politics*, 50 (1): 171–201.

Haglund, D.G. (2011) '"Let's Call the Whole Thing Off"? Security Culture as Strategic Culture', *Contemporary Security Policy*, 32 (3): 494–516.

Herz, J. (1950) 'Idealist Internationalism and the Security Dilemma', *World Politics*, 2 (2): 157–80.

IAEA (1986) International Nuclear Safety Advisory Group: Summery Report on the Post-Accident Review Meeting on the Chernobyl Accident, Safety Series No. 75-INSAG-1, Vienna.

Janis, I. (1982) *Groupthink: Psychological Studies of Policy Decisions*, Boston: Houghton Mifflin.

Jepperson, R.L., Wendt, A. and Katzenstein, P. (1996) 'Norms, Identity, and Culture in National Security', in P. Katzenstein (ed.) *The Culture of National Security: Norms and Identity in World Politics*, New York: Columbia University Press: 33–73.

Jervis, R. (1978) 'Cooperation under the Security Dilemma', *World Politics*, 30 (2): 167–214.

Johnston, A.I. (1995) 'Thinking about Strategic Culture', *International Security*, 19 (1): 32–64.

—— (1998) *Cultural Realism: Strategic Culture and Grand Strategy in Chinese History*, Princeton: Princeton University Press.

Katzenstein, P. (ed.) (1996) *The Culture of National Security: Norms and Identity in World Politics*, New York: Columbia University Press.

Kier, E. (1996) 'Culture and French Military Doctrine Before World War II', in P. Katzenstein (ed.) *The Culture of National Security: Norms and Identity in World Politics*, New York: Columbia University Press: 186–215.

Koselleck, R. (1979) 'Begriffsgeschichte und Sozialgeschichte', in R. Koselleck (ed.) *Vergangene Zukunft. Zur Semantik geschichtlicher Zeiten*, Frankfurt: Suhrkamp.

Krahmann, E. (2003) 'Conceptualizing Security Governance', *Cooperation and Conflict*, 38 (1): 5–26.

Lapid, Y. and Kratochwil, F. (eds) (1997) *The Return of Culture and Identity in IR Theory*, Boulder: Lynne Rienner.

Mandelbaum, M. (1988) *The Fate of Nations: The Search for National Security in the Nineteenth and Twentieth Centuries*, Cambridge: Cambridge University Press.

Mearsheimer, J.J. (1983) *Conventional Deterrence*, Ithaca: Cornell University Press.

Meyer, J. (1999) 'Changing Cultural Content of Nation-States: A World Society Perspective', in G. Steinmetz (ed.) *State/Culture: State-Formation after the Cultural Turn*, Ithaca: Cornell University Press: 123–43.

Mueller, J. and Stewart, M. (2015) *Chasing Ghosts: The Policing of Terrorism*, Oxford: Oxford University Press.

Münch, R. (1996) *Risikopolitik*, Frankfurt: Suhrkamp.

Posen, B.R. (1993) 'The Security Dilemma and Ethnic Conflict', in M.E. Brown (ed.) *Ethnic Conflict and International Security*, Princeton: Princeton University Press: 103–24.

Rauer, V., Junk, J. and Daase, C. (2014) 'Konjunkturen des Kulturbegriffs: Von der politischen und strategischen Kultur zur Sicherheitskultur', in H.-J. Lange, M. Wendekamm and C. Endreß (eds) *Dimensionen der Sicherheitskultur*, Wiesbaden: Springer VS: 33–56.

Risse-Kappen, T. (1991) 'Public Opinion, Domestic Structure, and Foreign Policy in Liberal Democracies', *World Politics*, 43 (4): 479–512.

Ruighaver, A.B., Maynard, S.B. and Chang, S. (2007) 'Organizational Security Culture: Extending the End-User Perspective', *Computers and Security*, 26 (1): 56–62.

Skinner, Q. (1989) 'Language and Political Change', in T. Ball, J. Farr and R.L. Hanson (eds) *Political Innovation and Conceptual Change*. Cambridge; Cambridge University Press: 6–23.

Slovic, P. (1992) 'Perception of Risk: Reflections on the Psychometric Paradigm', in S. Krimsky and D. Golding (eds) *Social Theories of Risk*, Westport: Praeger: 117–52.

Snyder, J. (1973) 'The Soviet Strategic Culture: Implementation for Nuclear Options', *R-2154-AF*, Rand Corporation, Santa Monica.

Sperling, J. (2010) 'National Security Cultures, Technologies of Public Goods Supply and Security Governance', in E.J. Kirchner and J. Sperling (eds) *National Security Cultures: Patterns of Global Governance*, London: Routledge: 1–18.

Vertzberger, Y.Y.I. (1998) *Risk Taking and Decisionmaking: Foreign Military Intervention Decisions*, Stanford: Stanford University Press.

Walt, S.M. (1987) *The Origins of Alliances*, Ithaca: Cornell University Press.

Waltz, K.N. (1979) *Theory of International Politics*, New York: Random House.

—— (1989) 'The Origin of War in Neorealist Theory', in R.I. Rothberg and T.K. Rabb (eds) *The Origin and Prevention of Major Wars*, Cambridge: Cambridge University Press: 39–52.

Weaver, O. (1995) Securitization and Desecuritization, in R. Lipschutz (ed.) *On Security*, New York, N.Y.: Columbia University Press: 46–86.

5 An ethics of security

J. Peter Burgess

In a sombre press conference at the US Department of Defense on the eve of the US invasion of Iraq in February 2002, then-Secretary of Defense Donald Rumsfeld was queried about the absence of evidence in support of the official justification for the invasion, namely the possession by Saddam Hussein's regime of a significant stock of weapons of mass destruction. Rumsfeld – apparently dodging the question – answered by lecturing the press corps on the nuances of the notion of 'knowns' and 'unknowns' in security. The statement, which provoked both laughter and annoyance at the time, is one of the most viewed statements on YouTube of the last decade:

> As we know, there are known knowns. There are things we know we know. We also know there are known unknowns. That is to say, we know there are some things we do not know. But there are also unknown unknowns, the ones we don't know we don't know.[1]

Say what one will about former Secretary of Defense Donald Rumsfeld's politics and the policy choices that led to the invasion and Second Iraq War, but in this moment he was a steely-eyed epistemologist putting his finger directly on the nature of security, insecurity, and the reality of threats. As set out in the editors' Introduction, this is the aim of the present volume (cf. also Daase and Kessler 2006).

Rumsfeld was right to point out that there is a fundamental difference between these two types of unknowns – those that we know we don't know and those that we don't know we don't know. In other words, there is a difference between answers we do not have to intelligible and meaningful questions, and answers we do not have to as-yet-unasked questions. To be sure, the answer to an unknown question is a strange thing to know. But the *unknown* answer to an *unknown* question has an epistemological status that is quite remarkable indeed. The idea of an *unknown unknown* requires us to imagine a kind of ignorance beyond knowledge, an ignorance of our own ignorance.

The first degree of ignorance is straightforward: 'Where are the weapons of mass destruction?', we ask, and receive the answer, 'Well, we *don't know*, but we are able to find out'. We let science or intelligence do its work, based on rational hypotheses and factual confirmation or falsification, until sooner or later we come to an answer. The answer itself may be uncertain, but we are certain of the question's answer-ability.

The other type of ignorance, call it second degree ignorance, is far more complex: 'What are the dangers lurking, the threats we cannot yet name, can only imagine?', we ask. This question targets, by its very questioning, an entirely different sort of knowledge. It cannot be answered empirically by presenting facts collected and ordered according to standard scientific methods. The unknown unknown does not belong to the world of facts and experience. It is knowledge of the abyss, or perhaps from the abyss. It is knowledge, in any case, from an entirely different place, from inside us, or perhaps beyond us.

What is *politically* important about both types of questions is that they both support a certain kind of *action*. Indeed Rumsfeld's aim in waxing philosophical was to make legitimate the invasion of Iraq in the absence of any evidence – or evidence of evidence – of weapons of mass destruction. In short, he advanced an ethics of action based on an epistemology of ignorance.

What kind of ethics is born of ignorance? What kind of policy can be formulated on the grounds of what we do not know? What does interaction between security and knowledge tell us about the present and future of security studies? How can this re-tooling of security as epistemology give us insight into our own present, our own security culture? This chapter will revisit the basic premise for understanding security in our time to answer these questions. It will suggest that the foundation for the politics of security today is a certain epistemology of the unknown, and that this epistemology imposes changes in the way that we are to understand ethics in general, and the ethics of security in particular.

The fragmentation and internalization of security

As the framing of this volume makes clear, security studies as it is practiced today is characterized by its diversity. While volumes have been written on the security provided by the state, security which is assured by virtue of the state's ability to protect and preserve the values unified under its name, less reflection has been given to the notion that security itself may involve a kind of fundamental fragmentation. This fragmentation of discourse, scope and knowledge can be tracked along several registers, many of which are developed in this book (cf. also Burgess 2009).

We can observe it in the inflation and uneven differentiation of the *objects* of security, of the things we experience as being under threat, the objects of security measures. While the perennial nation-state still holds sway over our political imaginaries as the privileged object of threat and thus security measures, as evinced in Chapter 1 by Glaser, Chapter 6 by Masala and Chapter 7 by Geis and Wagner in this volume, a range of objects have entered and orbit the discourse of security. We speak of financial security (see Chapter 9 by Boy in this volume), IT security, food security, water security, climate security (see Chapter 8 by Methmann and Oels in this volume), airport security, road security, human security, societal security, health security, legal security, home security, etc. Each of these objects of security forms a node in a different matrix of security, an different assemblage of the structuring and enabling elements for experiencing, assessing, and communicating and taking measures against threat: social and cultural settings, value premises, emotional and spiritual ties, availability and cost of measures, access, resistance, etc. (Burgess 2010).

We can also find fragmentation in the *subject* positions from which security is experienced, assessed, declared, and operationalized. Whereas only twenty years ago the voice of security was spoken in a more-or-less unified way from a more-or-less unique place – the state – today the subject of security is split into multiple voices, sometimes overlapping, sometimes conflicting, and sometimes reinforcing each other. Public and private agencies, local and global authorities, NGOs and IGOs, celebrities and religious leaders, doctors and lawyers, have unequal but significant access to the control positions of the security discourse. (Both Fierke and Fehl emphasize the diversification of subjects of security, although in different ways.)

Finally, we can also see the fragmentation in the *practice* of security. With a security object identified and insecurity declared from one or several subject positions, the measures available to address the security issue have also multiplied and differentiated from one or several subject positions. In particular, processes of privatisation and popularisation of security services generate a multiplicity of practices. Once considered a right and the basic entitlement of citizenship, security has become a commodity, merchandise that can be bought or sold on a more-or-less open security market. Commercial security guards replace public police forces, the number of tasks carried out by contracted security consultants has increased sharply, and mercenaries replace national security forces. Security merchandise circulates across borders, social classes, services, organizations, interests and allegiances (Abrahamsen and Williams 2011; Leander 2010a, 2010b, 2013).

The decline of prophylactic security and the rise of risk

Security has undergone a fundamental shift in the last decades from an outward focus on a known enemy threatening the sovereign state, to a general inward focus on a new constellation of threat that is at once globalized and localized, both ubiquitous and intensely individual. During the course of the 1980s and 1990s the understanding of security shifted away from a logic of national security that opposed one state to other states. (While Glaser, in Chapter 1 of this volume, claims that threats posed by states are still key to security studies, Masala, in Chapter 6 this volume, opens for a broader understanding of the need for a new security agenda.) This logic, based on a range of conceptual oppositions – between self and other, the safe and the unsafe, the pure and the impure, Good and Evil, etc. gradually began to wane. Instead, over the last thirty years, security as both concept and experience has been shifting an internal logic, in which security threats and the measures necessary to address them are more proximate, more common and more intimate. As a consequence, the politics of security has gradually shifted from being entirely about a foreign 'other' to being about us and, most significantly, about the other *in* us. Security politics concern increasingly threats that do not respect borders and barriers. Rather, they are more ambient and more ubiquitous. Thus a range of globalized and localized security threats have changed their configuring of security from an optic whereby a border demarcates the end of security and the beginning of danger, to an experience of the growing porosity of the security border. This shift has significant consequences for the way in which we understand a threat. Today, danger is increasingly perceived as residing among us, whether we speak of climate change, pandemic, data viruses, the danger is not a simple threat on the horizon, beyond the city walls, or a well-guarded border. It is in some sense already here, already among us, *already in us*. It is thus easy to imagine that ubiquitous threats such as climate change, pandemics, cyber insecurity, or food quality worries come to replace the classical geostrategic threats that characterized the Cold War, or that terrorism carried out by a state's own nationals is more menacing than the military threats that oppose one state to another.

Security and insecurity are gradually being internalized. It is no longer a question of shutting the threat out in order to assure security within – what we might term *prophylactic security* – but rather of living with threat, and the management of omnipresent danger.

In a prophylactic configuration of security, the primary figure or symbol is the barrier. Security is understood as protection, shielding, refuge, a barrier against something 'other'. The prophylactic conception of security necessarily lends itself to a binary logic of threat, dividing the world in to situation of security *here* and insecurity *there*, of *us* and *them*, friend and enemy, refuge and threat, and so on. Prophylactic security encapsulates the place or space of safety, dividing reality into an inside and an outside. The function of any security measure in this paradigm is to assure separation, that there is no leakage, contamination, or corruption of the inside by the outside.

In this configuration, security measures take either the form of real separation actions – higher walls and thicker glass – surveillance measures which assure that the other remains where it belongs; or armed measures intended to force the 'other' to remain where it belongs. Non-physical and virtual prophylactic measures, while not playing out in space, nonetheless also apply a logic of othering to the danger or threats. Most consequential of these are the various forms of personal data-gathering, -sorting and -sharing practices that have come to dominate immigration policy in particular. The paradigms of classic war give considerable weight to this conception, and the now more-or-less discredited 'War on Terror' has done much to revitalise and retool it.

More than ever before, security concerns *us*. As a consequence of the facts on the ground, the technologies that mediate the facts, and the conceptual tools with which we connect our experience of the world and our embracing of or resistance against it, security has mutated into a reflexive enterprise. It has become self-ransacking in that we ourselves are accomplices in our own insecurity. At the level of high politics this takes the form of the blurring of internal and external security matters. In fields dominated by information technology, such as global finance or communication, it is a question of becoming precariously dependent upon the very systems that threaten our stability.

Consequently we can observe the concept of *risk* replacing the notion of *threat* in more and more contexts. The implication is that in today's 'security environment', even though we do not know what the danger is, we can respond to that *ignorance* by using *risk* as a kind prosthesis of *knowledge*. Every unknown danger can be integrated into the calculus of how to respond as though it were a kind of known danger. This implementation of risk thinking is a response to the rise of non-conventional, non-national, non-contiguous threats, exactly those that have brought ambiguity to the interpretation of security threats.

But this difference between the known and the unknown is not merely empirical. The unknown, in addition to being empirically unknown, is accompanied by an aesthetic, emotional, and ethical *effect* of being unknown. The asymmetry of the known and the unknown lies in the shock of its potentially unexpected arrival. There is a near *moral* reaction or indignation when the unknown appears in a way that does not correspond to our preparations for it. It says something about us, our knowledge of ourselves and our surroundings and about our own moral character or disposition.

Indeed, instead of accounting for this strange meeting of pathos and fact, the social sciences deal with this phenomenon backwards. As Nassim Nicholas Taleb points out, the social sciences have feigned possession of tools capable of measuring uncertainty as though it were an empirical phenomenon since the beginnings of the conceptualisation of risk and risk analysis (Taleb 2007: xvii-xx). As Boy points out in her contribution to this volume in Chapter 9, the insurance and finance industries have brought this illusion to the highest levels: the uncertainty of loss is adequately calculated in order to entirely eliminate it from the equation of profit. Yet in a real sense, what we do not know is far more historically consequential than what we do know. When what we do not know happens against all conceptualized likelihoods, its meaning is immense.

Clearly this situation has important ethical consequences as well. For example, to take *responsibility* in any given situation implies relating to the unknown. To take responsibility in a strong ethical sense is to act in the *absence* of knowledge. Complete and integral knowledge makes responsibility meaningless. Knowledge sets aside the ethical imperative. *Knowing*, by contrast, and particularly in the realm of protecting from the non-perceived dangers of the unknown, requires no *ethical* insight. The transparent self-evidence of knowledge is factual, and empirical, not normative, ethical or value-oriented. True responsibility takes the form of a kind of improvisation, of invention, of making something from nothing at all. Empirical or statistical knowledge about past occurrences can support our reflections, but cannot tell us about what we should do. Hegre and Kristiansen, for example, explain in Chapter 12 of this volume how empirical analysis can contribute to explaining how factors converge to bring about certain events, but can only support speculation about the future. Empirically-based analyses can in this sense not fully contribute to ethics. Empirical knowledge does not participate in the ethical moment of decision-making.

In other words, the rise of risk in our time and the expansion of the governance of dangers in place of a posture of protection against threats, is an ethical turn, a turn inward towards the self. It seems clear that with the internalization of danger in our time and the position of the social, cultural or political subject as the axis around which security and insecurity are experienced and pronounced, the constellation of ethical values is key. Yet we lack a way to grasp the relation between security and the subject that it contributes to shaping or even generating.

Security as knowledge

The increasing reflexivity of our insecurity fundamentally changes the equation of danger and protection that structures and justifies a range of social, political, economic and cultural institutions on both the national and international planes. More crucially, it disrupts a deeply entrenched understanding of how the self is constituted, and how the subject of politics understands itself and the horizon of reference and meaning available to it. Moreover, it reconfigures the very notion of what protection, danger and potential damage might be, how the vulnerable self, encapsulated in the vulnerable material borders of the body, meets the world of dangers. The decline of the prophylactic concept of security opens space for new insights into the self, new questions, uncertainties and insecurities.

This paradigm shift is not entirely complete. Despite this reflexive turn, the prophylactic impulse to deal with dangers by keeping them at bay remains in operation. We cling to the metaphysics of danger as a logic of presence-absence, whereby the aim of security measures is to remove threat, and make absent the thing whose presence is endangering. At the same time we remain haunted by the reality that danger is at hand in the very thought of its absence: fear arises as much from the thought of danger as it does from the presence of 'real' danger. This thought, perhaps even more than any material menace, is the primary cause of unease and insecurity.

In this sense, a certain degree of naiveté plays a role in the psychic management of insecurity. We can, for example, easily see ourselves as secure when we actually stand in immanent danger. Inversely, we can be convinced of our own insecurity while at the same time being in no danger at all. Security, in the shallowest sense, is inseparable from our own *certainty* of real and potential threats. Indeed, as the speed of politics and public expectations of political action in a media-driven public sphere increases, the old-fashioned distinction between the secure self, potentially threatened only by the contingent facts of a stable, factual world, the objective or true source of threat, becomes less tenable. The experience of 'threat', just like that of 'security', obeys the structures of an important and influential phenomenology. Threats are unlike others: They are not known, do not have force of presence, and do not impact us as an imminent damage or destruction might.

In other words, security and insecurity only 'happen' in the future. Security and insecurity are not experiences of the immediate present, but of a possible destructive future. The contingency of insecurity, its status as possible but not inevitable, lies at the heart of its meaning and is the key to its force. If a destructive event is certain and if we know of this unavoidability, then the destructive event is no longer a source of insecurity. It is *already* destruction, *already* the presence of the worst, *already* damage or death. Those who experience insecurity as *certainty* are, strictly speaking, not insecure because they are already injured or dead. The only option for eliminating the insecurity of our imaginaries is the end of experience. This is not to downplay the 'experience' of death – if such a thing is understood as the end of biological life – but rather to say that the experience of the disaster and 'death', is displaced in time toward the present. For practical purposes – notwithstanding post-death paranormal or spiritual activities that are beyond the scope of our reflection – insecurity is entirely played out before the event, but *as the event*. In other words, security is a singular experience of something that has not yet happened, but which haunts our minds and shapes our actions with its inevitability. Obviously the certainty of death cannot be experienced: the person who experiences death can longer reflect upon the experience nor relay it to others. It is this non-experience – and not death itself – that is the foundation of insecurity and the motivation for security measures of all kinds.

Uncertainty thus becomes not only the basic epistemological support for experiences of and claims about security and insecurity. It is also its moral force, the source of its meaning, the support of the cultural, social and political differences in the way it is addressed, and, to a large degree, the foundation for the political legitimacy of measures carried out in its name.

Security, in this sense, is a kind of prosthetic knowledge, knowledge of an unknown threat, knowledge of an unknown future. Security is knowledge of something about which, by any ordinary measures, we have no knowledge. An odd kind of knowledge indeed! Security is knowledge that builds on everything except what epistemologists would call a sound basis for knowing. It is based on previous experience, traditions, culture, intuition, insight, wisdom, beliefs, superstition, etc.

'Politics' in this sense is a discussion about what we don't know, about the unknown. It is about the unknown consequences of certain actions, unknown attitudes about what is 'best' for society, uncertain assumptions about the will of the people, etc. Were we to know with certainty what people wanted, what was possible, what the consequences of certain actions would be, then there would certainly be no role for politics.

Both classical epistemology and ethics maintain a fundamental and stable distinction between claims about what the world is and claims about what the world should be, between descriptive and normative claims. In addition to organizing reality along the dividing line of the normative (to which we will return), this distinction also structures and supports the division of labour between academic fields and faculties. Much ink has been spent on this crucial question and much more can be expected. It is impossible to do justice to this debate here other than to draw attention to the fact that it stems from the assertion that it is a matter of assertions. 'Knowledge' is reduced to assertions about 'knowledge' and, simultaneously, 'ethics' is reduced to assertions about 'ethics'. The question of the status, the reality, or the being of knowledge and ethics is of particular interest. Is ethics, the theory of principles that govern behaviour, a kind of knowledge? Does knowledge itself possess the force of normativity? Behind these questions lies another set of postulates and a world of assumptions about what the world is, what its being entails, the divisibility of its being, not least being knowledge about the being of the world.

The core question for an ethics of security is: in what way can that which is not – that which is not *yet* – oblige us to certain kinds of actions? How can future events that is formed and supported in the interstices of probability and supposition, whose ethos is couched in fear and an inability to effectively or successfully act provide normative guidelines for action (Burgess 2011: 4–5)?

I have argued that the basic premise of this distinction is a metaphysical insistence on the distinction between what is and what is not, even if 'what is not' actually exists in the form of a judgement about the future or the formulation of a normative claim. Yet, as we will see in a moment, risk-thinking in our time transcends this notion. Risk analysis, management and communication is confronted – today more than ever before – with a future that lives itself out fully and powerfully in the present. More than ever before, value judgements involved in risk calculations not only reflect our past and characterize our present: they reach into our future, link to what we cannot yet know and what cannot yet guide us in our conduct. In other words, how the status of knowledge about the world seems to give us indications about how we should act in the world.

I am not referring to certainty in normative statements (for example, what I *should do* if I acquire the knowledge that the dishes need to be washed). I am referring to the inherent certainty or uncertainty of knowledge itself, whose normative effects mobilize action. The force of not knowing something has itself enormous power, arguably more so than what we do know. This force of the unknown lies partly in the fact that we cannot plan for everything, that we must reconcile ourselves with the insecurity that lies in our inability to control events. There is always some degree of chance, of uncertainty in our future. We are aware that we always see 'through a glass darkly'. This is the very nature of consciousness. On the other hand, our lives are not governed by randomness, falling upon us in a purely accidental way, adding a layer of uncertainty or insecurity to everything we think or do.

The 'space' between these two kinds of normative claims, of necessity and randomness, is where ethics 'happens'. Ethics, from a certain point of view, is nothing other than making decisions in the absence of certainty. If there were certainty about our actions, if we actually knew without doubt what to do, then this could be many things, but it would not be called ethics. It might not even be part of human consciousness. Ethics lives in the world of inadequate knowledge and randomness. This is also the home of risk analysis.

Security as ethics

The relation between security and ethics is an old one. Particularly in the area of international relations, from the moment insecurity was formulated as a concern for the future with an implicit appeal to political or other action, it has been formulated in terms of implicit or explicit ethical claims. Indeed, one of the premises of realist international relations theory is the bracketing of ethical issues. The international arena is structured by networks of power in which value orientations are invisible. More recently, the maturing of the one variant or another of liberal internationalism has brought an influx of works and debates about the ethics of international actors.[2] Already in *Inside/Outside*, Walker critiqued this rapidly growing niche in IR theory, which called itself 'ethics and international relations' (Walker 1993: 50). However unlike Walker, who regards 'ethics' and 'international relations' as two autonomous discourses, too far afield from each other to have any conceptual communication, we consider ethical values and the international as inseparable (Burgess 2011: 11–13).

The term 'ethics' has a broad range of meanings, which are the objects of innumerable historical and systematic debates (Steele 2013). At the risk of over-generalizing, ethics, in the vast majority of philosophical perspectives, corresponds to one or another systematization of substantial, stable, coherent, understandable, autonomous value – of good and evil, virtue and vice, right and wrong, and so on. Different ethical theories set out different criteria and procedures for arriving at knowledge of what this value is, but all presume that it is a kind of knowledge, knowledge that is knowable by virtue of metaphysical assertions, deductive claims, consensus, political deliberation or tacit social or cultural processes. A variety of discourses of ethics are in play in such debates, far too many to canvass here. All such discourses of ethics share the aim of providing a stable platform for decision-making about human action, a system that is portable from one empirical setting to another and from one individual to another. The grandiose presumption of ethical theory understood in this conventional way is that ethics is knowledge, and that 'doing' ethics is a straightforward, empirically-grounded process. Ethics is about discovering what is already out there, uncovering, exposing, or casting light on the right, the good, the just, the appropriate in all its ideal, contextual or pragmatic diversity. Even though many ethical theories would take some kind of subjective moral faculty as a central support of ethical judgment, this subjectivity is, in the course of moral reasoning, inevitably recast as an object of ethical reasoning and argument. It becomes the crystallized anchoring point of a deduction based on observable facts and unwavering ideas.

The necessary assumption behind such discussions is a Cartesian subject of ethics whose premises are generally passed over in silence. The Cartesian subject – one of an endless range of the possible forms of the subject of ethics – is well-known and well-documented in other critiques of modernity, but seldom applied to a critique of philosophical ethics.[3] It is rational, autonomous, sovereign, self-conscious, self-present, unified, stable, and above all free. In short, the subject of ethics is – by nature or by principle – *secure*. When we take as our point of departure the assumption of a timeless, universal Cartesian subject of ethics (but also of politics, humanity, civilization, etc.), we are making an assumption about the inviolability, the incorruptibility and unassailability of the subject of ethics. In short, we are making assumptions about its *security*. The traditional subject of ethics is one whose own security does not come into question.

The *post-Cartesian* subject of ethics, by contrast, is one guided and structured by *insecurity*. Thus, long before any observation or assertion can be made about the security of an individual, a group, a state, the planet, or anything at all, the insecurity of the subject position from which such an observation or assertion is made is already in play. The security of the subject is already suspended. The insecurity of the subject, its fragility and vulnerability, the question or doubt about the security of the subject is already active in any observation or predication. It is possible, even important, to develop the status of the subject in modern history Western subjectivity as less than self-evident; that its position, stability and certainty are themselves subject to a certain kind of fragility.

To bring together this observation about the fragility of the subject of security and our insights about security as knowledge, a new conceptualization of ethics itself is needed. A useable ethics must account for the reflexivity of security knowledge at the end of modernity without taking the status of the subject of ethics for granted.

'Ethics' is thus defined as *the principle governing conduct in the absence of adequate knowledge of the future.* This definition contains both a commonplace about the situation of ethics in time and a provocation about the relation between ethical judgement and knowledge.

First, ethics is always about the future. The terms and conditions for action, for deciding on how to behave are by necessity set out in reference to acts not yet carried out. Ethics is always future-oriented, organized around events that have not yet taken place, around facts that do not yet have status of facts, relative to conditions that are not yet fulfilled and consequences that can only take the shape of potential.

Second, as a consequence of being about the future, the epistemological foundations of ethics in general and of security in particular are unlike any other. Ethics starts and ends in knowledge we do not have. Like security it makes up a set of *ad hoc* principles not only about what has not yet happened, but, more importantly, based on what has not yet happened. If security is 'knowledge' about the future, then assuring security is already a kind of ethics, already a way of deploying a certain set of ideas or principles in the face of the unknown. What is novel and crucial here is that the 'unknown' of the future and its way of being both unknown and unknowable is not some contingency, not some inconvenience that we can prepare for or hope to overcome. The unknown-ness of the future is the condition of security. Assuring the security of a future that is known (bracketing for a moment the fact that the future can by definition never be known) would simply not be security. As we cannot know what the empirical setting for future actions will be, nor what consequences our actions will have, *inadequate*, incomplete or imperfect knowledge is not the exception but rather the only available foundation for ethical judgement.

If we supplement these insights with a more general understanding of security as both an experience of the compression or acceleration of time and a function of precaution in the face of an unknown and dangerous future, we arrive at a new understanding of the ethical subject of security.

By its very character, security does not organize knowledge as a function of certainty about imminent dangers. A threat that is 'imminent' – so imminent that it can be regarded as certain – is no longer within a logic of security (or insecurity). If the actualization of a threat is utterly unavoidable, if its damage is on the order of necessity, it has – in the logic of security, based as it is on the modalities of fear and the practices of precaution – for all practical and conceptual purposes *already* happened; there is no security-relevant difference between judgement of imminence and the disaster itself. This is because at such a point in the actualization of threat, fear is *absolutely justified* and precaution is no longer a functional option. Fear that is factual, whereby the imagined catastrophe in fact corresponds to reality, is, strictly speaking, not fear. For fear depends, for its very coherence, on some minimum degree of *unreality* in order for the power of the imaginary to do its work. Precaution is equally incoherent and impracticable at the moment of imminence. For the margin of time in which to exercise caution is reduced to immediacy. In other words, at the moment of imminence, in conceptual terms the damage or destruction is *already done*. If the floodwaters are already rising, if the pandemic has arrived, if the bullet has already left the barrel of the gun, then we are in more or less severe peril, but we are no longer insecure. (Bracketing for the sake of argument the various knock-on-wood forms of insecurity, such as the economic insecurity caused by floodwaters, the immune system insecurity caused by pandemics, or the insecurity of others caused by murder by bullet.)

Insecurity and the ethics it supports thus obey a logic of contingency. They function in a frame of multiple futures. Security is a question of what options we have for saving ourselves, protecting ourselves, for preparing for what might come. It is a configuration of the present and future wherein the possibility of choice can lead to one or another varying futures, differing results to a possible course of events. Insecurity is the space of choice, of the aleatory, of alterity, of a certain liberty. It is, in other words, the space of ethics. When danger is imminent, when there are no alternatives to the catastrophe, when the thought of options is absorbed into the careening locomotive of the necessary, then choice too disappears.

Insecurity is the experience of holding forth when we are unsure of the dangers, when the danger and its consequences still lie outside of the necessary. If we know what catastrophe awaits us, then the experience does not belong to insecurity. It is far more an experience of certainty, certainty of the kind that surely belongs to the order of the aesthetic, perhaps of the theological. It is for this reason that we conclude that security is itself ethics.

Conclusion

If we understand ethics as the principles governing behaviour in the absence of adequate knowledge, then surely security is an ethics. For security is simply an approach to the future that not by chance, but by necessity, is unknown and rife with dangers.

Thus when the title of this chapter announces 'an ethics of security' it is being somewhat disingenuous. For what we now describe as an 'ethics of security' does not correspond in its structure, concepts or content as a simple 'ethics of'. Indeed the more general consequence of our reflection is that there is no sense in saying 'ethics of'. It cannot be a question of an ethics of security.

We might understand by 'ethics of' that an autonomous set of principles for action or behaviour can be unproblematically brought to bear on a discrete object called security, such that the properties of the thing called security trigger the subjective principles in the *dispositif* called ethics, by consequence letting itself be governed by these principles. But this is at best problematic because security itself is an ethical *dispositif*, a set of tools and arrangements that organize the future as an experience of the unknown, of unknown dangers, the very knowledge of which is an imposition of the choice with certainty with which the subject of security is necessarily made up.

If, as I argue, ethics is about the range of acceptable and appropriate actions grounded in a lack of adequate knowledge about the future, then security is no less than an ethics of danger.

Security is the moral, cognitive, and aesthetic encapsulation of the horizon of danger that derails and re-rails the circuits of the self, the means, measures and logics by which the self sees itself, knows itself, values itself, and takes measures in the world in order to advance and preserve what is of value to it. This means something more than simply asking and adequately answering the question, 'Who am I?' or 'Who are we?' It means a continuous reorganizing of both the question and the political meaning of the question.

Paradoxically, for risk analysis in the narrow sense of the term, ethics is not simply an alternative. By this I do not mean that it would be advantageous to incorporate ethics into risk analysis: rather that risk analysis is ethics from start to finish, if we define ethics, as I do, as making decisions under conditions of inadequate knowledge, decisions in which it is the incalculable, the entirely human, that takes responsibility.

This preoccupation with certainty naturally has consequences for the way that we study security, what kind of security research questions are asked, by whom and for whom, and what kind of status the answers to such questions can actually have. Given the rise in risk studies as a sister field to security studies, it is unsurprising that security knowledge itself shifts toward an assessment of risk, which by definition reflects future realities.

As we know, the recent engagement of security studies with risk studies draws force from a scientific tradition growing out of the actuarial sciences. The reliance of security on science and technology, and its easy adoption of the gadget fetishism of technological security management and less material techniques of governance, is both odd and disquieting. The epistemological lineage of the natural sciences is organized by a straightforward logic of the *episteme*, the opposition between the unknown and the known. Science derives its rationality, but also its normative force and legitimacy, from the primacy of the known or the immediately-to-be-known over the unkown. And yet, security is by definition excluded from this field. For security concerns precisely what we do not know. As soon as the unknown becomes known it ceases to be a question of security.

The entire rationality of its politics revolves around one epistemological aberration: security is by nature a relation to what is unknowable. The moment the unknowable threat becomes known, it ceases to be a threat.

Notes

1 Donald Rumsfeld, Department of Defense, 12 February 2002, available at http://youtu.be/GiPe1OiKQuk (accessed 28 July 2012). Also reproduced in Seely (2003).
2 See, for instance: Appadurai 2001; Barkan 2000; Barry 1998; Bleiker 2001; Cochran 1999; Crawford 2002; Doyle and Ikenberry 1997; Finkielkraut, Badinter and Daniel 2000; Gasper 2001; Graham 1997; Gregg 1998; Harbour 1999; Hurrell 2002; Hutchings 1992, 1999; Jabri and O'Gorman 1999; Lefever 1998; McElroy 1992; Oppenheim, Carter and Ricciardi 2001; Robinson 1999; Seckinelgin and Shinoda 2001; Segesvary 1999; Shaw 1999; Smith 2000; Smith and Light 2001; Sutch 2001; Thomas 2001.
3 A catalogue of attempts would include Bauman (1993); Caputo (1993); Ferré(2001); Geuss (2005); Park (2008); Wren-Owens (2007).

References

Abrahamsen, R. and Williams, M.C. (2011) *Security Beyond the State: Private Security in International Politics*, Cambridge: Cambridge University Press.
Appadurai, A. (ed.) (2001) *Globalization*, Durham: Duke University Press.
Barkan, E. (2000) *The Guilt of Nations: Restitution and Negotiating Historical Injustices*, New York: Norton.
Barry, J.A. (1998) *The Sword of Justice: Ethics and Coercion in International Politics*, Westport: Praeger.
Bauman, Z. (1993) *Postmodern Ethics*, Cambridge (MA): Blackwell.
Bleiker, R. (2001) *The Ethics of Speed: Global Activism after Seattle*, The Hague: Institute of Social Studies.
Burgess, J.P. (2009) 'There Is No European Security, Only European Securities', *Cooperation and Conflict*, 44 (3): 309–28.
—— (2011) *The Ethical Subject of Security: Geopolitical Reason and the Threat against Europe*, London and New York: Routledge.
—— (ed.) (2010) *The Routledge Handbook of New Security Studies*, London and New York: Routledge.
Caputo, J. (1993) *Against Ethics*, Indiana: Indiana University Press.
Cochran, M. (1999) *Normative Theory in International Relations: A Pragmatic Approach*, Cambridge: Cambridge University Press.

Crawford, N.C. (2002) *Argument and Change in World Politics: Ethics, Decolonization, and Humanitarian Intervention*, Cambridge: Cambridge University Press.
Daase, C. and Kessler, O. (2006) 'Knowns and Unknowns in the War on Terror: Uncertainty and the Political Construction of Danger', *Security Dialogue*, 38 (4): 411–36.
Doyle, M.W. and Ikenberry, G.J. (1997) *New Thinking in International Relations Theory*, Boulder: Westview Press.
Ferré, F. (2001) *Living and Value: Toward a Constructive Postmodern Ethics*, Albany: State University of New York Press.
Finkielkraut, A., Badinter, R. and Daniel, J. (2000) *La morale internationale entre la politique et le droit, Répliques*, Geneva and Paris: Tricorne/France Culture.
Gasper, D. (2001) 'Global Ethics and Global Strangers. Beyond the Inter-national Relations Framework: An Essay in Descriptive Ethics', Institute of Social Studies Working Paper No. 341, The Hague.
Geuss, R. (2005) *Outside Ethics*, Princeton: Princeton University Press.
Graham, G. (1997) *Ethics and International Relations*, Oxford and Cambridge (MA): Blackwell.
Gregg, R.W. (1998) *International Relations on Film*, Boulder: Lynne Rienner.
Harbour, F.V. (1999) *Thinking about International Ethics: Moral Theory and Cases from American Foreign Policy*, Boulder: Westview Press.
Hurrell, A. (2002) 'Ethics and Norms in International Relations', in W. Carlsnaes, T. Risse and B.A. Simmons (eds) *Handbook of International Relations*, London: Sage: 147–54.
Hutchings, K. (1992) 'The Possibility of Judgment: Moralizing and Theorizing in International Relations', *Review of International Studies*, 18 (2): 51–62.
— (1999) *International Political Theory: Rethinking Ethics in a Global Era*, London: Sage.
Jabri, V. and O'Gorman, E. (1999) *Women, Culture, and International Relations: Critical Perspectives on World Politics*, Boulder: Lynne Rienner.
Leander, A. (2010a) 'Practices (Re)Producing Orders: Understanding the Role of Business in Global Security Governance', in M. Ougaard and A. Leander (eds) *Business and Global Governance*, London and New York: Routledge: 57–78.
— (2010b) 'Risk and the Fabrication of Apolitical, Unaccountable Military Markets: The Case of the CIA 'Killing Program', *Review of International Studies*, 37 (5): 1–16.
— (ed.) (2013) *Commercialising Security in Europe: Political Consequences for Peace Operations*, London and New York: Routledge.
Lefever, E.W. (1998) *The Irony of Virtue: Ethics and American Power*, Boulder: Westview Press.
McElroy, R.W. (1992) *Morality and American Foreign Policy: The Role of Ethics in International Affairs*, Princeton: Princeton University Press.
Oppenheim, F.E., Carter, I. and Ricciardi, M. (2001) *Freedom, Power, and Political Morality: Essays for Felix Oppenheim*, Basingstoke and New York: Palgrave.
Park, J.Y. (2008) *Buddhism and Postmodernity: Zen, Huayan, and the Possibility of Buddhist Postmodern Ethics*, Lanham: Lexington Books.
Robinson, F. (1999) *Globalizing Care: Ethics, Feminist Theory, and International Relations*, Boulder: Westview Press.
Seckinelgin, H. and Shinoda, H. (2001) *Ethics and International Relations*, Basingstoke and New York: Palgrave.
Seely, H. (2003) *Pieces of Intelligence: The Existential Poetry of Donald H. Rumsfeld*, New York: Free Press.
Segesvary, V. (1999) *From Illusion to Delusion: Globalization and the Contradictions of Late Modernity*, San Francisco: International Scholars Publications.

Shaw, M. (1999) *Politics and Globalisation: Knowledge, Ethics and Agency*, London and New York: Routledge.
Smith, H. (2000) *Democracy and International Relations: Critical Theories/Problematic Practices*, Basingstoke and New York: Macmillan Press and St. Martin's Press.
Smith, K. and Light, M. (2001) *Ethics and Foreign Policy*, Cambridge and New York: Cambridge University Press.
Steele, B.J. (2013) *Alternative Accountabilities in Global Politics: The Scars of Violence*, Abingdon and New York: Routledge.
Sutch, P. (2001) *Ethics, Justice, and International Relations: Constructing an International Community*, London and New York: Routledge.
Taleb, N.N. (2007) *The Black Swan: The Impact of the Highly Improbable*, London: Penguin.
Thomas, W. (2001) *The Ethics of Destruction: Norms and Force in International Relations*, Ithaca: Cornell University Press.
Walker, R.B.J. (1993) *Inside/outside: International Relations as Political Theory*. Cambridge: Cambridge University Press.
Wren-Owens, E. (2007) *Postmodern Ethics*, Newcastle: Cambridge Scholars Publishing.

Part II
Subjects of Security

6 Power politics revisited

Are realist theories really at odds with the new security threats?

Carlo Masala

Introduction

The end of the Cold War and the emergence of the so-called new security threats associated with it gave the impression that realism, formerly the leading paradigm of International Relations (IR) theory, especially in Europe, has lost relevance. While realism still plays a strong role in US academia (see Chapter 1 by Glaser in this volume), European scholars stated that the discipline had been 'hypnotized' (Fozouni 1995: 508) for more than forty years by a wrong-headed theory, which, as an American historian added, 'should not continue to command the intellectual energy and resources of the field' (Vasquez 2003: 90). In academia, the historical turn of 1989–90 boosted various non-positivist theories,[1] while the appearance and lingering of the unipolar momentum – which most realists had considered transitory (Waltz 2000a)[2] – made it seem as though the theory which had 'occupied the intellectual energy' of IR scholars for more than three decades no longer had anything to offer (Halliday 1994: 11). The question of whether realist theories could productively contribute to twenty-first century security politics was answered by many scholars in the negative.

However, this chapter intends to make an argument for the continuing relevance of realist theories in addressing the new security threats or risks that states, societies, and even individuals, now face. Two aspects of realism support this: first, that a realist view on security studies, defined by Joseph Nye and Sean Lynn-Jones as the study of the threat, use and control of military force (Nye and Lynn-Jones 1988), is closely connected to the concept of national security. Although the term is highly contested, national security puts the state at the forefront of any security studies analysis. According to the classical definition realist scholars subscribe to, national security 'has a more extensive meaning than protection from physical harm; it also implies protection, through a variety of means, of vital economic and political interests, the loss of which could threaten fundamental values and the vitality of the state' (Jordan et al. 1999: 3)[3]. In times when most security studies scholars deal with non-military, societal and individual, regional and global security issues,[4] realist security studies scholars remind us of the centrality of the use of force and the state in world politics (see Chapter 1 by Glaser in this volume).

Second, as this volume deals with new security issues, realist security studies scholars can help to bring more logical rigor to the debates by pointing out that some (but not all) of the issues scholars label as 'new' security issues are in fact rather old. Failed states, ethnic conflicts, the return of religion, the rise of new great powers, global and regional power shifts – all these phenomena have characterized the international systems for centuries. Realist scholars, especially those who work with historical case studies, make the point that most of the issues labeled as new are actually 'not-so-new', having already been a part of the security concerns of policy makers in the past.

For these reasons, security studies can profit from realist scholarship in the future. Yet this will also require an openness to dialogue on the part of realist scholars, as this chapter argues.

The first part of this chapter argues that realism is not a paradigm or a coherent theory. Instead I will make the point that realist scholars share some minimal theoretical assumptions, but are otherwise members of a broad church instead of a homogeneous school of thought. The second section of this chapter will show that realist theories have a hard time explaining the unipolar moment because of a fundamental misreading (or misinterpretation) of the effect that the structure of the international system has on great powers.

From here, the third section will claim that realist theories do have a relevance (or explanatory power) when it comes to some new security threats, which the introduction of this volume by Schlag et al. outlines and this section's chapters on financial security (Chapter 9 by Boy), democratic peace (Chapter 7 by Geis and Wagner) and environmental security (Chapter 8 by Methmann and Oels) elaborate in greater detail. I will argue that those are rather new permutations of old threats (the rise of major powers and the increasing irrelevance of international security institutions).

It may be a surprise that part four argues that realist theories also have a normative role to play with regard to recent developments in international security policy (e.g. liberal or neoconservative interventionism, securitization moves with regard to international terrorism and other 'new' threats). However, in order to do this, realist scholars must be aware that their theories have a hidden normative agenda (Masala 2011a). Admitting the normative bias of their theoretical designs would enable realists to engage with other schools of thought in security studies, namely post-positivist scholars, who – despite epistemological and ontological differences – come to very similar conclusions with regard to real-world policy issues.

Finally, I will make the point that realist scholars should redefine their future role within the universe of IR theories. Instead of seeking to regain the paradigmatic high ground, realists should consider themselves as a kind of 'IR guerrilla', reminding established theories that material power and the use of force still play a major role in today's real-world international relations.[5] At the same time, realists are well-equipped to remind policy makers of the potential negative consequences of their actions.

Is anybody still a realist? About the core and the peripheries

For more than three decades realist scholars portrayed themselves as a unified research program based on Kenneth Waltz's seminal book *Theory of International Politics* (1979). The standard neorealist narrative can be framed by Imre Lakatos' famous description of scientific research programmes. According to Lakatos, every research program has a 'hard core' of theoretical assumptions that cannot be abandoned or altered without abandoning the program altogether. If the hard core seems to be under threat, more modes or specific theories are developed in order to protect it (Lakatos 1977). If realism is evaluated against this standard, one could rightly ask whether anyone still is or ever has been a realist (Moravcsik and Legro 1999). Yet this is a reading of realist theory which says very little about the actual development of realist theories. I argue instead that realism is a group of theories which share a central core of assumptions, but developed – and are still developing – outward in different directions or trajectories from this core.[6] It's not the aim of any realist scholar to protect Waltz's seminal work, and it was not Waltz's idea back in 1979 when he wrote *Theory of International Politics* to create a research program.[7]

If one accepts the notion that realist theories have a common core out of which they each developed differently, the idea of multiple realist theories is acceptable, and there is no such thing as a unified realist research program.

But what does this core consist of? In reference to William Wohlforth (2009: 9), I argue that all realist scholars share three assumptions:

a) *Groupism*. Politics take place within and between groups. Group solidarity is essential to domestic politics, and conflict and cooperation between polities is the essence of international politics.
b) *Egoism*. When individuals and groups act politically, they are driven principally by narrow self-interest.[8]
c) *Power-centrism*. The key to politics in any area is the interaction between social and material power, an interaction that unfolds in the shadow of the potential use of material power to coerce.[9]

But outside these commonalities, there is a lot of disagreement within Realism itself: between offensive (Copeland 2001; Mearsheimer 2002) and defensive realists (Snyder 1991; van Evera 1999); structural (Waltz 1979) and neoclassical realists (Mercer 1996; Schweller 1998); hegemonic stability (Gilpin 1981) and power transition realists (Kugler and Lemke 1996); structural and second image realists; and between balance of power (Waltz 1988), balance of threat (Walt 1987) and unipolar realists (Brooks and Wohlforth 2008). This incredible diversity of approaches ought to remind the reader that realism is a varied and philosophical way of thinking about international relations (see Chapter 1 by Glaser in this volume).

Realism and the unipolar moment

Since polarity is an important variable to explain the security policies of major (and sometimes mid-range and minor) powers in most realist theories, one would expect realist security studies scholars to be well suited to deal with the occurrence of the unipolar moment in the 1990s. However, most realists failed to explain security politics under unipolarity, especially the behaviour of the United States. In a nutshell, most realists argued that unipolarity would be brought to an end by other states or a coalition of states due to the 'iron law' of balance of power (Art 2004; Pape 2005a; Paul 2005). Only Wohlforth countered this argument by pointing out that the United States were simply too powerful to be balanced (Wohlforth 1999). The dominance of this argument stems from the importance assigned to it in the *Theory of International Politics*, where Waltz identified balance of power as the only law in international relations (Waltz 1979: 126). Other now nearly forgotten realists like Robert Gilpin, Raymond Aron or A.F.K. Organski and his power transition school, expressed doubts about whether balance of power was really the 'chief operating mechanism' as Waltz had claimed (Waltz 1979: 124). Wohlforth recently reminded us that realists like Robert Gilpin developed much more sophisticated theories of international relations than Waltz:

> Had Robert Gilpin's *War and change in world politics* been given equal billing, international relations research would have unfolded quite differently over the past three decades. Scholars would not have been bewildered by change, bewitched by the balance of power, blind to numerous potentially powerful realist theories, and bothered by endless and unproductive zero-sum debates among representatives of competing paradigms. And had all those pathologies been absent, we would be far better prepared today for the intellectual and policy challenges of a world in which underlying power balances appear to be changing quickly, and the status quo inter-state order is ever more contested.
>
> (Wohlforth 2011: 502)

The hegemonic position of Waltz and Mearsheimer's version of realist theory blinded realists (and even their critics) to two facts: First, that Unipol, which, like other states, acts and interacts under the condition of anarchy, faces fewer structural constraints than second-rank powers, and domestic politics are thereby more important to explain the actions of the preponderant power; and second, that every hegemon in history turned out to be a revolutionary power trying to shape its environment to its own favour (Tenenbaum 2012). Had realists been able to see these two arguments, they would not have been so optimistic about changes in the global distribution of power and would not have been surprised by the policies of the George W. Bush administration.

After being wrong on an issue they themselves would claim to be well suited to deal with despite the fact that their theories could explain a great deal about security policies under unipolarity, it comes as no surprise that critics questioned the relevance of realism to twenty-first century security studies.

Realism and not-so-new security threats

As previously mentioned, there is, especially in European academia and to a lesser extent in the US, a widely shared assumption that realism has almost nothing to offer with regard to twenty-first century security politics. The security and survival bias of realist theories seemed incapable of explaining the loss of relevance of military power and the rise of economic and 'soft' power within the international system.[10] This view has been relaxed in the years since the rise of new regional powers (e.g. India, Brazil, Nigeria) and one potential peer competitor to the United States – China – brought hard security issues back to the IR agenda. Especially in the US, some offensive versions of neorealism have experienced a revival, since they point to the competitiveness of the international system. The most extreme prediction comes from the godfather of offensive neorealism, John Mearsheimer, who argues that a future military confrontation between the United States and China is almost unavoidable (Mearsheimer 2010: 395). But this is only one realist view on future relations between the United States and China. As I have shown elsewhere, other realisms have different, sometimes more modest takes on the future of this relation (Masala 2011b). Even for realists, the rise of China and the potential for a future bipolarity (or even power transition) does not necessarily lead to a head-on confrontation between the two powers. Hegemonic stability or power transition realists make convincing arguments that the rise of China may lead to strong tendencies towards conflict-generating power politics, but not necessarily to war. The benefits of realism in dealing with the rise of China and other regional powers is that realist scholars remind us that great powers are concerned with their territorial security and that, from the point of view of their leaders, military power still matters.

Realist scholars may also be able to productively weigh in on the observable tendency that international institutions and organizations (especially in the field of security policy) are being increasingly side-lined by the major powers among their member-states. While institutional theories taught us that international institutions are actors in their own right and can permanently influence the behaviour of their members (Keohane 1988), all realist theories have expressed scepticism about the extent to which international institutions are able to act independently from the policies of its most powerful members. Hence, to realists it was no surprise that the end of the post-Second World War order has been accompanied by an increase of informal fora for security cooperation between great and major powers (PSG, RMSC, etc.), or in realist vocabulary, the establishment of directorates (Daase and Kessler 2008). These directorates are set up to deal with specific policy issues, they have no (or minimal) organizational structures and they are dissolved once a policy is implemented successfully (see Chapter 2 by Fehl in this volume). Realist theories remind us 'that institutions are based on the self-interested calculations of great powers, and they have no independent effect on state behaviour' (Mearsheimer 1994/1995: 7). However, what remains understudied is the relation between these directorates and the still-existing institutions. From the perspective of a great power, are they legitimate alternatives or just tools to exert pressure on international institutions and organizations in order to reform them (Williamson 2009)? Studying these questions would require more interaction between realist and institutional theories. So far this development has not taken place from either side (see Chapter 2 by Fehl in this volume).[11]

These two examples – the rise of new great powers and the increasing weakness of international security institutions – serve as examples to illustrate the continuing relevance of realist theories to security studies. And it seems obvious that the old realism horse can run this course, since the above outlined security challenges are – from a realist perspective – not new but rather old and centred around states and institutions, subjects familiar to realist theories. In this debate (about the not-so-new security challenges) realist scholars can contribute knowledge derived from the use of historical case studies (Walt 1991: 217) and, more importantly, by focussing on the central role of the state and military power in dealing with these issues. The insight that International Relations, and especially security studies, deals with repeating patterns is something realist theories can offer the debate. The question of what realist theories can contribute to explaining 'really new' security threats or risks lies at the heart of the next section.

Realism and really new security threats

The preceding section argued that some of the so-called 'new' security threats are indeed not-so-new and that realism has explanations to offer in regards to these kinds of security threats. However, other so-called new threats are indeed new to the extent that they are de-territorialized and emanate from non-state actors. The classic examples of these are international terrorism or global epidemics. Until now, realist theories have remained silent about these new security threats. With the exception of Robert Pape's realist-inspired analysis on suicide terrorism (Pape 2005b) and Barry Posen's attempt to adopt the power and security dilemma to ethnic conflicts (Posen 1993), realist theories have a hard time grasping these new security threats. This is partly because all realist theories are state-centric and largely ignore the relevance of non-state actors in twenty-first century security policy. This disregard of new security threats by realist scholars stems from a misunderstanding of one of the realist theory fundamentals: the role of the state. The central role of states in all realist theories is the result of the historical prominence and centrality of states in international relations since the creation of the Westphalian system. But the central role of the state is not carved in stone. The system, according to Waltz, can be populated by 'tribes, nations, oligopolistic firms, or street gangs' (Waltz 1979: 67). Which group is the most relevant for the structure of the system is a matter of the distribution of capabilities. But until 'non-state actors develop to the point of rivalling or surpassing great powers' (Waltz 1979: 95), states remain the most important actors. Hence, realism is actually a *group-centric* rather than state-centric school of thought. If realist scholars took this insight seriously, there would be no major difficulties in applying their theories to every social group which acts and interacts in the arena of international politics. So the absence of strong realist voices in analysing new security threats is the result of the scholar's bounded understanding of the basic assumptions of realist theories rather than an inherent weakness of realist theories.

However, this failure of realist scholars to readjust their theories has not led realists to remain silent about these new security threats.[12] On the contrary, realist scholars have actively participated in and even led government policy debates over the past two decades.

In the following short overview I will pick up on two subjects in which realist scholars are prominently engaged and argue that their engagement is driven by a hidden realist normative agenda (Masala 2011a). The two areas in which realists raise their voices are the interventionist agenda of liberal democracies (see Chapter 7 by Geis and Wagner in this volume) and the securitization (see Chapter 3 by Fierke in this volume) of certain issues. This might come as a surprise since both issue areas are commonly known as being rooted into two different theoretical approaches: the liberal one (humanitarian interventions/democratic peace) and the constructivist one (securitization).

With regard to the growing tendency of liberal democracies to intervene militarily to spread democracy and human rights across the globe, realists are concerned that such policies contribute to a growing instability in the international system. Their concern is driven by three fundamental observations, which derive directly from the philosophical foundation of their theories:

a) The attempt to universalize norms and values and thereby contribute to global justice faces the problem that justice cannot be objectively defined. For realist scholars, 'justice' is the fighting word of the powerful (Waltz 1979: 201). The task of realist scholars is to show that the true nature of policy is concealed by moral justifications and rationalizations (Morgenthau and Thompson 1985: 101; see also Cozette 2008).
b) Overwhelming power leads to growing instability in the international system because unbalanced power tends to use its power to promote change abroad for the sake of its own security.
c) The use of military and economic power will face resistance since it will be confronted with growing nationalism within the societies subject to change (Mearsheimer 2011).

For the above-mentioned reasons realist scholars recommend that liberal democracies, especially the United States, cultivate a 'security culture of restraint' (Walt 2005: 224), sometimes labelled a strategy of 'offshore balancing' (Layne 1997, 2006).

For most scholars unfamiliar with the philosophical foundation of realist theories it comes as a surprise that realists are not 'warmongering Neanderthals' but actually are rather sceptical about the use of force (Edelstein 2010). As one prominent realist recently argued:

It turns out that contrary to the conventional wisdom, realists are much less willing to use military force than most people on either the left or the right in the US. When I say the left, I'm talking about liberals. When I talk about the right, I'm basically talking about neo-conservatives. The fact is that when you look closely at the American national security elite, and this includes academics, you discover that many liberals and neo-conservatives are powerfully disposed to using military force around the world to serve US interests. Realists, on the other hand, tend to be much more wary about using military force. This means that in many situations – and we saw this in the run-up to the Iraq war – the realists end up opposing hawkish policies being pushed by liberals and neo-conservatives. In those circumstances, what you often find is that realists have more in common with people on the far left, and here I am talking about individuals who are clearly outside of the mainstream or the consensus.

(Mearsheimer 2012)

The other area where realists are engaged in policy debates is the growing number of issues which are securitized by governments in order to justify 'the use of extraordinary means in the name of security' (Buzan et al. 1998: 15; for a constructivist criticism see Chapter 3 by Fierke in this volume). Realists worry about two tendencies: that securitization undermines the democratic foundation of societies by gradually turning them into garrison states (Laswell 1941), and that it is used to legitimize military adventures abroad. From a realist perspective, 'states, like people, are insecure in proportion to the extent of their freedom. If freedom is wanted insecurity must be accepted' (Waltz 1979: 129).

This kind of policy engagement by realist pundits seems to contradict the realist claim of being a moral- and value-free theory which 'only' describes the world as it is. Their aim to change governmental policies seems to be at odds with their philosophical claim that the 'real political world cannot be changed' (Oren 2009: 283) and that realism 'doesn't take a normative or ethical position […] and […] is essentially amoral' (Walt 2009). Engaging in the marketplace of ideas seems contradictory to the realist belief that the international system has a deep structure that constrains states to behave in a certain way (Kaufmann 2004). This public engagement of realist scholars in conjunction with their scholarly work is criticized by other academics. As Samuel Barkin, a political scientist from the University of Massachusetts complained, 'some contemporary realists want to have it both ways,' i.e. to both explain states' behaviour and dictate how they ought to behave (Barkin 2009: 203). This kind of ontological critique calls upon realism to abandon its positivist epistemology and ontology and introduce more reflexivity. Both Oren and Barkin recommend that contemporary realists go back to the more 'sophisticated epistemological thinking of classical realists like Carr or Morgenthau (Oren 2009: 283; Barkin 2009: 243–5). From their point of view, if realists abandoned their claims to objectivity, their public engagement would be in line with their scholarly work (Ish-Shalom 2009). Following this train of thought, realism could then enter into a fruitful dialogue with modern theories of security studies.

But is there no middle ground that would allow contemporary realists to stick to their positivist epistemology while contemporaneously engaging in such a dialogue?

The concept of 'Weberian activism' Daniel Drezner has introduced might help open a venue for more dialogue between realist and non-positivist approaches (Drezner 2009: 6). According to Patrick Jackson and Stuart Kaufmann, 'Weberian activism' is characterised by the attitude to inform policy debates by educating stakeholders and the public about the relevant empirical relationships underlying pressing policy decisions and global processes (Jackson and Kaufman 2007: 96; see also Carpenter 2013). Under the notion of Weberian activism, scholars engage in policy advocacy as an epistemic community rather than 'adopting an explicit normative position' (Drezner 2009: 6). If this notion is accepted, then realists do not have to abandon their positivist epistemology in order to engage in policy discourse. As part of an epistemic IR community, realist scholars can object to distortions of their scholarship and take responsibility to ensure that their theories are not distorted in the public sphere. And if governments reference realism to advance non-realist goals, it is part of the realist's duty to cry out publically.

Interestingly, some of the realist warnings are quite similar to postmodernist policy advocacy. Chantal Mouffe, for example, calls upon a multipolar world in order to balance overwhelming power. In her words, 'the only conceivable strategy for overcoming world dependence on a single power is to find ways to "pluralize" hegemony' (Mouffe 2005: 118). And postmodernist Italian philosopher Danilo Zolo argues in favour of the establishment of regional blocks in order to balance US supremacy in the twenty-first century (Zolo 2002: 85). Recently Giorgio Agamben (2013) proposed the creation of a Latin empire under French leadership in order to balance Germany and the Nordic countries in Europe. This comes pretty close to the standard realist analysis, and is even compatible with the realist policy advice that only a multipolar world could balance the United States' tendencies to structure the world along their own moral principles and security goals (Waltz 2000b). Peter Gowan, a Marxist historian, surprisingly noticed that the left can learn more from John Mearsheimer's *Tragedy of Great Power Politics* than from any number 'of treaties from the coming wonders of global governance' (Gowan 2002: 67).

At first sight, problem-solving theories and critical theory look like strange bed fellows.[13] But a closer look, especially when it comes to policy advocacy, reveals that both share the attitude of 'challeng[ing] the existing order' despite the fundamental difference that realists are utterly sceptical about the possibility of 'human emancipation' (Cox 1996: 53). Realists have to accept that their theories have an analytical and a normative dimension. Finding out the truth behind power describes best their desire to explain. Speaking truth to power on the other hand is the critical potential that is inherent in realist theories and explains their public engagement. Once realist scholars can accept this double dimension of their scholarly works, the discursive floor for a potentially fruitful dialogue with critical theory is at least partly open. For their part, critical theorists should accept that having positivist epistemology is not an impediment to engaging in public discourse.

Conclusion: the realist as guerrilla

This chapter shed light on the question of whether realist theories in the field of security studies have something to offer in the twenty-first century. The record is mixed. If one accepts the notion that there is no single realism, but instead many realist theories, then these theories surely have something to offer IR in the analysis of what I have called not-so-new security threats. The rise of great powers, the still-existing concern of states with their territorial security, the importance of military power, all these are subjects where realist theories can help explain and understand real-world events.

However if we talk about 'really new' threats, realism has difficulty dealing with them if it does not take one of its core assumptions more seriously, namely that international politics are characterized by groupism.

With regards to both phenomena, realism has to reach out to interact more with other theoretical schools or approaches. But to do this, realists need to recognize the contingent nature of their own theory, as well as its explanatory limits. This might be a problem for 'die-hard realists' à la Mearsheimer and it might be a problem for 'realist bashers' à la Moravcsik. But in general such an engagement would produce better results in answering real-world questions. Secondly, realist scholars should give greater voice to the critical potential of their theories. By focusing on the aspect of speaking 'truth to power', realists would be able to engage in a dialogue with other critical approaches – postmodern approaches are well-suited candidates for such a dialogue. However there are also obstacles, which, even if they did engage in such dialogue, would set limits to this. First, realists do not believe in the potential for human emancipation and second, they will not abandon their positivist epistemology (as some critical scholars would like them to do).

But it takes two to tango. Even with realists willing to engage in such a dialogue there needs to be preparedness on the other, postmodernist side to see the critical potential of contemporary realist theories and to approach realist theories with fewer prejudices. Surely this engagement won't be easy, but nevertheless it seems promising to try.

Finally, realists ought to redefine their self-understanding as scholars. The declining salience of paradigm wars and the relative decline of realism's centrality in the discipline (especially in Europe) offer unique advantages to realist scholars, which some of them have not yet fully embraced. Since they are no longer forced to maintain or to strive for the theoretical high ground, realists can behave like guerrillas, operating in academic territory mainly controlled by other theoretical forces, reminding other theoretical schools of their deficits, pointing to the still existing importance of material power and the national interest, and criticizing governments for foolish policies. Since it is widely believed that realists are status quo defenders and supporters of militarized foreign policies, challenging such policies and their theoretical foundations (e.g. humanitarian intervention and cosmopolitanism, external democratization and democratic peace theory) has the effect of a surprise attack. Besides realism's already existing impulse to explain, a sceptical interpretation of real world policies and an attitude of speaking truth to power should be characteristic of future realist scholarly work. The advantage of being at the margins of IR theoretical debates is obvious and very similar to guerrilla tactics: You win just by not losing.

Notes

1. See, for example, Kurki (2006), Lapid (1989), Linklater (1995), Buzan and Little (2001), Barkawi and Laffey (2006), Jackson and Sorenson (2003).
2. A realist exception is Wohlforth (1999).
3. See this book for a debate of the various definitions of national security.
4. See the graphic (Figure 1) in the introduction to this volume by Schlag et al.
5. I am fully aware that in the recent past classical realism has been re-discovered by critical scholars who aim at excavating the critical potential of classical realism. But their intentions differ fundamentally from mine. Critical scholars aim to deconstruct the myth that there is a linear train of thought from classical to contemporary (especially Waltzian) realism trying to tie classical realism to constructivist theories (see Williams 2008). When I talk about realists as guerillas I intend to advocate a research strategy in which realists concentrate on speaking truth to power and pointing to the importance of material factors in explaining real world events (just to mention two things). Hence, while critical scholars intend to deconstruct realist theories I aim for re-positioning realist theories in the field of IR.
6. The reason why I think that realist theories (like other theories) cannot be judged against Lakatos' criteria is that, firstly, scholars of IR rarely consider themselves as part of a sect where defending the 'true religion' is the main purpose of their scholarly existence, and secondly, that Lakatos himself used to be extremely sceptical when his description of a scientific research program was applied to the discipline of social science.
7. 'First, a research program is not fashioned by the creator of the initiatory theory but by the creator's successors. The original theory may be a good one, but the successor theories weak and defective. If the program should run off the tracks, we would still want to know how good the original theory may be. Second, the problem of evaluating a theory endures, whether or not the theory spawns a succession of theories. Third – an acute problem in the social sciences in applying the "novel facts" test – how are we to decide which facts are to be accepted as novel ones? Some will claim that their theories revealed one or two; others will say, we knew that all along. Fourth, if assaying a theory in itself is not possible, then how can anyone know whether launching a research program is worthwhile?' Quoted from Waltz (2003: xi).
8. At first sight it might appear a-logical that selfish individuals would sacrifice their lives for selfish collective actors. Classical Realism, especially Reinhold Niebuhr, has dealt with that problem extensively. According to him (Niebuhr 1932), individuals in their personal dealings are often able to transcend 'self'interest. But collective actors such as nations dealing with other nations, or social classes with other social classes, have little or no capacity for 'self'transcendence. 'They have a limited understanding of the people they harm by their unjust "self"assertion; they lack appreciation for the often complicated laws and institutions through which such injustice is perpetuated; and they are more inclined to embrace rationalizations of "self"interest than prophetic denunciations' (Berke 2000).
9. As connoisseurs of IR will notice, structure is not included. Structural realism is one branch of realism, which for a long time has been dominant in the realist theory family. But ultimately structural realism is just one brand of realism, not a defining characteristic.
10. For more on the security and survival bias, see Chapter 1 by Glaser in this volume, for more on soft power, see *Nye* (2011).

11 I am not arguing to revitalize the boring neo-neo debate of the 1990s. Instead I advocate for a more fruitful dialogue along concrete empirical research questions.
12 While Glaser sees this as the strength of a parsimonious theory, I consider it a weakness of realist scholarship. See the contribution of Charles Glaser in Chapter 1 of this volume.
13 See the famous distinction by Ashley (1986).

References

Agamben, G. (2013) 'Se un impero latino prendesse forma nel cuore d' europa', *La Repubblica*, 15 March.
Art, R.J. (2004) 'Europe Hedges its Security Bets', in T.V. Paul and J.J. Wirtz (eds) *Balance of Power: Theory and Practice in the 21st Century*, Stanford: Stanford University Press: 179–213.
Ashley, R. (1986) 'The Poverty of Neorealism', in R.O. Keohane (ed.) *Neorealism and its Critics*, New York: Columbia University Press: 255–300.
Barkawi, T. and Laffey, M. (2006) 'The Postcolonial Moment in Security Studies', *Review of International Studies*, 32 (2): 329–52.
Barkin, S. (2009) 'Realism, Prediction, and Foreign Policy', *Foreign Policy Analysis*, 5 (3): 233–46.
Berke, M. (2000) 'Reinhold Niebuhr, Moral Man and Immoral Society', available at: http://www.firstthings.com/article/2000/03/reinhold-niebuhrmoral-man-and-immoral-society (accessed 16 January 2015).
Brooks, S.G. and Wohlforth, W.C. (2008) *World out of Balance: International Relations and the Challenge of American Primacy*, Princeton: Princeton University Press.
Buzan, B. and Little, R. (2001) 'Why International Relations has Failed as an Intellectual Project and What to Do About It', *Millennium – Journal of International Studies*, 30 (1): 19–39.
Buzan, B., Wæver, O. and Wilde, J.d. (1998) *Security: A New Framework for Analysis*, Boulder: Lynne Rienner.
Carpenter, C. (2013) 'From Kingdonian to Weberian Activism: A Shifting Stance', Blog entry, *Duck of Minerva*, 3 July, available at: http://www.whiteoliphaunt.com/duckofminerva/2013/07/from-kingdonian-to-weberian-activism-a-shifting-stance.html (accessed 22 November 2014).
Copeland, D.C. (2001) *The Origins of Major War*, Ithaca: Cornell University Press.
Cox, R. (1996) 'Realism, Positivism and Historicism', in R. Cox and T.J. Sinclair (eds) *Approaches to World Order*, Cambridge: Cambridge University Press: 49–59.
Cozette, M. (2008) 'Reclaiming the Critical Dimension of Realism: Hans J. Morgenthau on the Ethics of Scholarship', *Review of International Studies*, 34 (1): 5–27.
Daase, C. and Kessler, O. (2008) 'From Insecurity to Uncertainty: Risk and the Paradox of Security Policy', *Alternatives*, 33 (2): 211–32.
Drezner, D.W. (2009) 'Defending the Realist Interest: Policy Advocacy and Policy Planning in an Anarchical World', Paper presented at the Conference on Power in a Contemporary World, Stanford University.
Edelstein, D.M. (2010) 'Why Realists Don't Go for Bombs and Bullets', Blog post, 20 July, http://walt.foreignpolicy.com/posts/2010/07/20/why_realists_don_t_go_for_bombs_and_bullets (accessed 21 July 2010).
Fozouni, B. (1995) 'Confutation of Political Realism', *International Studies Quarterly*, 39 (4): 479–510.

Gilpin, R. (1981) *War and Change in World Politics*, Cambridge: Cambridge University Press.
Gowan, P. (2002) 'A Calculus of Power', *New Left Review*, 16: 47–67.
Halliday, F. (1994) *Rethinking International Relations*, Basingstoke: Macmillan.
Ish-Shalom, P. (2009) 'Theorizing Politics, Politicizing Theory, and the Responsibility that Runs Between', *Perspectives on Politics*, 7 (2): 303–16.
Jackson, P.T. and Kaufman, S.J. (2007) 'Security Scholars for a Sensible Foreign Policy: A Study in Weberian Activism', *Perspectives on Politics*, 5 (1): 95–103.
Jackson, R. and Sorensen, G. (2003) 'Methodological Debates: Classical versus Positivism Approaches', in R. Jackson and G. Sorensen (eds) *Introduction to International Relations: Theories and Approaches*, Oxford: Oxford University Press: 227–46.
Jordan, A.A., Taylor, W.J. and Mazarr, M.J. (1999) *American National Security*, 5th edn, Baltimore: John Hopkins University Press.
Kaufmann, C. (2004) 'Threat Inflation and the Failure of the Marketplace of Ideas: The Selling of the Iraq War', *International Security*, 29 (1): 5–48.
Keohane, R.O. (1988) 'International Institutions: Two Approaches', *International Studies Quarterly*, 32 (4): 379–96.
Kugler, J. and Lemke, D. (eds) (1996) *Parity and War: Evaluations and Extensions of the War Ledger*, Ann Arbor: University of Michigan Press.
Kurki, M. (2006) 'Causes of a Divided Discipline: A Critical Examination of the Concept of Cause in International Relations Theory', *Review of International Studies*, 32 (2): 189–216.
Lakatos, I. (1977) *The Methodology of Scientific Research Programmes: Philosophical Papers* (Volume 1), Cambridge: Cambridge University Press.
Lapid, Y. (1989) 'The Third Debate: On the Prospects of International Theory in a Post-Positivist Era', *International Studies Quarterly*, 33 (3): 235–54.
Laswell, H.D. (1941) 'The Garrison State', *The American Journal of Sociology*, 46 (4): 455–68.
Layne, C. (1997) 'From Preponderance to Offshore Balancing: America's Future Grand Strategy', *International Security*, 22 (1): 86–124.
—— (2006) 'The Unipolar Illusion Revisited: The Coming End of the United States' Unipolar Moment', *International Security*, 31 (2): 7–41.
Linklater, A. (1995) 'Neo-Realism in Theory and Practice', in K. Booth and S. Smith (eds) *International Relations Theory Today*, Cambridge: Polity Press: 241–62.
Masala, C. (2011a) 'Warum (Neo-)Realisten (meistens) keinen Krieg mögen', *Zeitschrift für Außen- und Sicherheitspolitik*, 4: 253–69.
—— (2011b) 'Die Erklärung zwischenstaatlicher Konkurrenz im Neorealismus', in T. ten Brink (ed.) *Globale Rivalitäten: Staat und Staatensystem im globalen Kapitalismus*, Stuttgart: Steiner: 29–43.
Mearsheimer, J.J. (1994/1995) 'The False Promise of International Institutions', *International Security*, 19 (3): 5–49.
—— (2002) *The Tragedy of Great Power Politics*, New York: Norton.
—— (2010) 'The Gathering Storm: China's Challenge to US Power in Asia', *The Chinese Journal of International Politics*, 3 (4): 381–96.
—— (2011) 'Kissing Cousins: Nationalism and Realism', Paper prepared for the Yale Workshop on International Relations, May.
—— (2012) 'Theory Talk #49', 24 June, available at: http://www.theory-talks.org/2012/06/theory-talk-49.html (accessed 24 June 2012).
Mercer, J. (1996) *Reputation and International Politics*, Ithaca: Cornell University Press.

Moravcsik, A. and Legro, J.W. (1999) 'Is Anybody still a Realist?', *International Security*, 24 (2): 5–55.
Morgenthau, H.J. and Thompson, K. (1985) *Politics Among Nations*, 6th edn, Boston: McGraw-Hill.
Mouffe, C. (2005) *On the Political*, London and New York: Routledge.
Niebuhr, R. (1932) *Moral Man and Immoral Society: A Study in Ethics and Politics*, New York: Charles Scribners & Sons.
Nye, J.S. (2011) *The Future of Power*, New York: Public Affairs.
Nye, J.S. and Lynn-Jones, S. (1988) 'International Security Studies: A Report of a Conference on the State of the Field', *International Security*, 12 (4): 5–27.
Oren, I. (2009) 'The Unrealism of Contemporary Realism: The Tension between Realist Theory and Realists' Practice', *Perspectives on Politics*, 7 (2): 283–301.
Pape, R.A. (2005a) 'Soft Balancing against the United States', *International Security*, 30 (1): 7–45.
—— (2005b) *Dying to Win: The Strategic Logic of Suicide Terrorism*, New York: Random House.
Paul, T.V. (2005) 'Soft Balancing in the Age of U.S. Primacy', *International Security*, 30 (1): 46–71.
Posen, B.R. (1993) 'Security Dilemma and Ethnic Conflict', *Survival*, 35 (1): 27–47.
Schweller, R.L. (1998) *Deadly Imbalances: Tripolarity and Hitler's Strategy of World Conquest*, New York: Columbia University Press.
Snyder, J.L. (1991) *Myths of Empire: Domestic Politics and International Ambition*, Ithaca: Cornell University Press.
Tenembaum, Y.J. (2012) 'It's Time to Revise How We Talk about Revisionist Powers', *Georgetown Journal of International Affairs*, 29 October, available at: http://journal.georgetown.edu/2012/10/29/its-time-to-revise-how-we-talk-about-revisionist-powers-by-yoav-j-tenembaum/ (accessed 26 May 2013).
van Evera, S. (1999) *Causes of War: Power and the Roots of Conflict*, Ithaca: Cornell University Press.
Vasquez, J.A. (2003) 'The New Debate on Balancing Power: A Reply to my Critics', in J.A. Vasquez and C. Elman (eds) *Realism and the Balancing of Power: A New Debate*, Upper Saddle River: Prentice Hall: 87–113.
Walt, S.M. (1987) *The Origins of Alliances*, Ithaca: Cornell University Press.
—— (1991) 'The Renaissance of Security Studies', *International Studies Quarterly*, 35 (2): 211–39.
—— (2005) *Taming American Power: The Global Response to U.S. Primacy*, New York: Norton.
—— (2009) 'Realism on a Rack', Blog post, 13 January, available at: http://walt.foreignpolicy.com/posts/2009/01/13/realism_on_the_rack (accessed 13 January 2009).
Waltz, K.N. (1979) *Theory of International Politics*, Reading: Addison-Wesley.
—— (1988) *The Balance of Power and NATO Expansion*, Berkeley: University of California Press.
—— (2000a) 'Structural Realism after the Cold War', *International Security*, 25 (1): 5–41.
—— (2000b) 'Intimations of Multipolarity', in B. Hansen and B. Heurlin (eds) *The New World Order*, London: Macmillan: 1–18.
—— (2003) 'Thoughts about Assaying Theories', in C. Elman and M.F. Elman (eds) *Progress in International Relations Theory: Appraising the Field*, Cambridge (MA): MIT Press: vii–xii.

Williams, M.C. (ed.) (2008) *Realism Reconsidered: The Legacy of Hans Morgenthau in International Relations*, Oxford: Oxford University Press.

Williamson, C. (2009) 'Informal Institutions Rule: Institutional Arrangements and Economic Performance', *Public Choice*, 139 (3): 371–87.

Wohlforth, W.C. (1999) 'The Stability of a Unipolar World', *International Security*, 24 (1): 5–41.

—— (2009) 'Realism and Security Studies', in V. Mauer and M.D. Cavelty (eds) *The Routledge Handbook of Security Studies*, London and New York: Routledge: 9–20.

—— (2011) 'Gilpinian Realism and International Relations', *International Relations*, 25 (4): 499–511.

Zolo, D. (2002) *Invoking Humanity: War, Law, and Global Order*, London: Continuum.

7 Democratic distinctiveness and the new security agenda

Anna Geis and Wolfgang Wagner

Introduction

The issue of peace and war has traditionally been the domain of (neo-)realist perspectives on international politics.[1] Since the 1980s, liberal International Relations (IR) researchers have established a counter-perspective on this core security issue by developing the 'Democratic Peace' research as an encompassing and 'progressive' research programme (Chernoff 2004). The core finding of the Democratic Peace thesis, namely, that democracies rarely if ever wage war against one another, has been widely debated and does not require another detailed discussion here.[2] Instead, this chapter aims to take stock of the research programme that has emanated from the Democratic Peace thesis and that is best described as a 'democratic distinctiveness programme' (Owen 2004). This usage emphasizes the finding that democracies tend to differ from non-democracies in the conduct of their external relations. Liberal researchers maintain that this 'peculiarity' is no coincidence but instead the result of democratic domestic institutions and norms.

We are particularly interested in how successfully the 'democratic distinctiveness programme' has dealt with the new security agenda that has arisen since the end of the Cold War. Put differently: to what extent does its key insight that security policy is influenced by domestic institutions and political culture apply to the new security agenda? To answer this question, we will review the literature that is inspired by the 'democratic distinctiveness programme' and that addresses three prominent developments in post-Cold War security politics – the broadening of the concept of security, the changing nature of Western warfare and the internationalization of security politics – and examine the extent to which democracies – rather than functional requirements, technological innovation, or shifts in the global distribution of power – have been put forward as the driving force behind these developments. Before we delve into these various dimensions, the next section provides a very brief overview of Democratic Peace theory and the emergence of a democratic distinctiveness programme.

We will argue in this contribution that, although rooted in the state-centric world of pre-globalization international relations, the 'democratic distinctiveness programme' has done remarkably well in applying its key causal mechanisms to a changing security agenda. It should be noted, however, that scholars who established the narrower field of 'Democratic Peace' or 'Kantian peace' in the 1980s and 1990s are not necessarily in a dialogue with scholars investigating democratic distinctiveness issues. These communities partly overlap, but the latter relies upon a large extension of the original Democratic Peace puzzle, i.e. the absence of war between democracies. Our argument is that a 'democratic distinctiveness' perspective is, *in principle*, apt to generate explanations for a whole range of security issues beyond inter-state war. Given the extensive research on Democratic Peace and inter-state war over the last decades, it seems more rewarding to replace the Democratic Peace research programme with a much more comprehensive liberal approach to security challenges in a globalizing world. In addition, a broader perspective focusing on the impact of democratic politics on foreign policy choices reflects the hegemony of liberal-democratic states in shaping the post-1990 world order. Although this hegemony might currently be in decline (e.g. Mahbubani 2008), we still consider it worthwhile to pursue a critical democracy-centred research.

In our conclusion, we make recommendations for the continued development of the democratic distinctiveness programme. We will argue that the 'democratic distinctiveness programme' should pay more attention to the 'dark sides' of democracies' security policies. The programme would benefit from the inclusion of more self-reflexive Critical Theory approaches.

From democratic peace to democratic distinctiveness

The state-centric roots of the democratic peace

Democratic Peace theory was developed on the assumptions of the 'old security agenda': an international system in which the major actors are nation-states and the dominant form of armed conflict is inter-state war. In hindsight, of course, the harbingers of a new security agenda were already present when Michael Doyle published *Kant, liberal legacies and foreign affairs* in 1983: intrastate wars were already more numerous than international wars and almost as many people lost their lives in the former as the latter.[3] However, the possibility of a nuclear war between major powers implied that the main threat to security was another inter-state war. As a consequence, the Democratic Peace thesis was tested with the help of two datasets firmly rooted in the methodological nationalism of pre-globalized international relations: Correlates of War (COW) and POLITY.

Remarkably, evidence from non-inter-state relations was already present in the early stages of the Democratic Peace debate: together with William Antholis, Bruce Russett (1993) argued that a Democratic Peace could be found among the city states of Ancient Greece; Neta Crawford found that 'the five democratic nations that formed the Iroquois League exemplify Immanuel Kant's idea of a system for "perpetual peace"' (Crawford 1994: 346); and Spencer Weart (1994) presented evidence for the Democratic Peace in medieval Switzerland. However, these contributions have remained footnotes to the main debate over the absence of inter-state war among democracies. Democratic Peace theory clearly owes its successful establishment to its ability to explain this key security puzzle of pre-globalized International Relations.

In order to explain the phenomenon of Democratic Peace, a variety of rationalist and constructivist explanations have been developed, pitting democratic institutions against democratic norms,[4] although they are better understood as mutually reinforcing: some rationalist explanations have focused on democratic institutions that render government policy responsive and accountable to a citizenry pictured as eager to preserve their lives and property, and who thus abhor war. In a more formal vocabulary, it has been argued that democracies are characterized by large 'selectorates' (the proportion of society selecting the leadership). Because political leaders' staying in power depends on a broad winning coalition, they are better off providing public goods (such as peace and economic growth) instead of private goods.[5] In a similar vein, Dan Reiter and Allan Stam have argued that democratic leaders are not only constrained by voters' ex post evaluation of their policies ('electoral punishment model') but that they are 'constantly monitoring and campaigning for public support, even when there is no election immediately impending' ('contemporary consent model') (Reiter and Stam 2002: 198). As a consequence, democratic leaders 'virtually never initiate war that is unpopular at the time' (Reiter and Stam 2002: 200). An early wave of institutionalist theorizing also argued that 'institutional constraints – a structure of division of powers, checks and balances – would make it difficult for democratic leaders to move their countries into war' (Russett 1993: 38). More recently, scholars have de-emphasized the constraining effects of domestic institutions and have instead highlighted that elections, open political competition and free media improve a government's ability to send credible signals of its resolve (Schultz 2001: 23–115).

An alternative, 'constructivist' account emphasizes democratic norms and culture instead of democratic institutions (cf. Doyle 1983; Owen 1994; Risse-Kappen 1995). From this perspective, democratic decision-makers will prefer negotiation over the use of force in international politics because they try to follow the same peaceful norms of conflict resolution they have internalized within their domestic political processes.[6] However, this pacifist preference only translates into peaceful relations with other democracies. As Thomas Risse-Kappen (1995) argued, democratic actors 'recognize' each other as actors who have learnt to solve conflicts by peaceful means and who adhere to similar norms. The security dilemma is thus mitigated by trust and ultimately the development of a common identity.[7]

Broadening the agenda: democratic distinctiveness

The successful defence of its core finding against a multitude of theoretical, methodological and empirical critiques not only helped to establish Democratic Peace theory in security studies but also inspired two closely interwoven developments in peace and conflict research.[8] First, research on the pacifying effects of trade and international institutions gained new momentum as these venerable research traditions became subsumed under a 'Kantian peace' (Russett 1998). In both areas, inconclusive results have stimulated the search for context conditions, and various studies have pointed to democracy as a prime context condition. Thus, high levels of commerce and joint memberships in international institutions do not necessarily contribute to peace *per se* but empirical studies suggest that they do so among democracies.[9] Second, and closely related to the first development, the causal mechanisms used to explain the absence of war among democracies were applied to a growing number of further puzzles. These studies demonstrated that the peculiarities of democracies in a broad range of issues can be traced back to institutions of accountability and liberal norms such as the protection of the individual. These studies put the absence of war among democracies in a broader context by treating it as one of many peculiarities that set democracies apart from non-democracies. It is important to note that this broadening is not limited to the pacifist and cooperative effects of democratic politics but also includes its belligerent and exclusive sides (Geis *et al.* 2013). Taken together, these studies have established democratic politics as the centre of gravity in liberal theorizing about conflict. While embracing both rationalist and constructivist approaches using quantitative and post-positivist methods, the unifying theme has been the peculiar impact of democratic politics on a wide range of (security) issues.

Democratic distinctiveness and the 'new security agenda'

This edited volume explores the contributions of various approaches and IR theories to the ever-expanding field of 'security' (see the introduction to this volume by Schlag *et al.*). Given its origins in pre-globalized international relations, one may have expected Democratic Peace theory not to cope very well with the 'new security agenda'. However, as outlined in the previous section, a growing number of scholars have demonstrated the value-added of using insights from Democratic Peace theory to interpret and explain key developments and patterns in post-Cold War (security) politics. In the same way as Masala demonstrated in the foregoing section for realist approaches, the extension of the notion of security has been both a challenge and an opportunity for the democratic distinctiveness perspective: It had to react to the state increasingly losing its security monopoly, but its core assumptions proved resilient. Space constraints do not allow for a comprehensive review. Instead, we will focus on three areas that stand out as particularly prominent post-Cold War developments, namely: the broadening of the concept of security, the changing nature of Western warfare and the internationalization of security politics. It is important to note, however, that a democratic distinctiveness perspective has also been applied to other issues, including defence spending, arms control policies, civil wars and terrorism.[10]

Democratic distinctiveness and the broadening of the concept of security: fighting wars for liberal norms

As liberal Democratic Peace theory has focused on the IR puzzle of the absence of inter-state war, it has had major difficulties explaining the militant 'dark side' of democracies: Democracies *do* fight wars against non-democracies, and from time to time they even initiate wars and other militarized conflicts with them (Rousseau

2005). Since the end of the Second World War a more common type of war fought by democracies has been *interventions* into ongoing violent conflicts (Chojnacki 2006: 19–23). The end of the Cold War gave rise to a distinct form of 'liberal interventionism,' which evolved in the 1990s. During this liberal heyday (and beyond), Western democracies substantially contributed to the global transformation of war via their armament and arms control policies, risk-sensitive style of warfare, alignment policies, normative justifications of war, and interpretations of international law (Evangelista *et al*. 2008; Shaw 2005).

These wars left a strong imprint on the regions concerned and ultimately on international order; and the Western democracies' use of liberal norms and principles to justify them warrants the parlance of a specific *liberal* interventionism. This was most clearly seen in so-called 'humanitarian interventions' justified by altruistic claims of 'saving strangers' (Hasenclever 2001; Wheeler 2000). Such 'liberal wars' have attracted attention from scholars outside the Democratic Peace community (e.g. Chandler 2006; Freedman 2005; Shaw 2005), but also from scholars of a democratic distinctiveness programme who outlined a research agenda of 'democratic wars' (Geis *et al*. 2006; Geis *et al*. 2013; Müller 2004).

A democratic distinctiveness perspective on 'liberal' or 'democratic' wars enables us to understand democracies' military engagements not as 'alien' or 'exceptional' to Democratic Peace but to recognize a specific liberal-democratic propensity to fight a certain type of war – one in the name of norms and values cherished by liberal-democratic polities, such as the protection of minority rights and human rights or democracy promotion. Seen from the perspective of Western democracies, the end of the Cold War opened up the possibility to transform the world order into a largely liberal one, reflecting originally *liberal* norms in the first place but rendering these into values held *universally* around the globe.

Democracies have been the driving force behind the broadening of the United Nations Security Council's interpretation of what constitutes a 'threat to international peace and security' (Article 39 of the UN Charter) and therefore warrants coercive force. The interpretation has been broadened to include gross violations of human rights (Brock 2005: 21). Initially limited to cases of imminent acts of aggression, the Security Council considered the consequences of the repression of the Kurdish population in Northern Iraq (1991), the human tragedy in Somalia (1992) and the humanitarian crisis in Rwanda (1994) as threats to international peace and security (Frowein and Krisch 2002: 724). The controversy over NATO's self-empowered 1999 intervention in Kosovo, which was not mandated by the UN Security Council, triggered an intense debate over future decisions on 'humanitarian interventions': on improving the criteria and further developing international law norms to deal with humanitarian crises more appropriately.

The resulting deliberation process can be read as an attempt to strengthen the concept of 'human security' within the international community. The Canadian government convened an International Commission on Intervention and State Sovereignty (ICISS) to review the relationship between sovereignty and human rights. By interpreting sovereignty as responsibility, the ICISS aimed at overcoming the contradictions between sovereignty and human rights. Liberal democracies were at the forefront of establishing a 'responsibility to protect' (R2P), according to which the international community should take timely and decisive action if states fail to protect their populations against genocide, war crimes, ethnic cleansing, or crimes against humanity (Bellamy 2009). Although the status of R2P in international law remains contested, democracies were instrumental in having the United Nations Security Council justify the use of military force against the Libyan government of Muammar Gaddafi with reference to the principle of R2P.

A democratic distinctiveness perspective also addresses the domestic side of international norm change: how democratic governments (or societal actors and media) attempt to justify and legitimate the use of force with reference to liberal norms. In contrast to traditional Democratic Peace explanations, which point out the peaceful effects of liberal-democratic norms, such analyses underline that liberal norms are inherently ambivalent, able to legitimate both the use of force and military restraint (Brock 2002; Geis *et al.* 2013; MacMillan 2005; Müller 2004). Implied in such a perspective is an increased attention to the numerous ethical dilemmas and legitimacy problems such a foreign policy generates:

> (I)t is the efforts by democratic states to exercise and/or justify the use of force in terms of higher values – the pursuit of higher goods – than the pursuit of state interests alone that add layers of politically significant complexity and create tensions and dissonance between the proclaimed ends of foreign policy and the means through which these are pursued
> (MacMillan 2005: 3)

Democratic distinctiveness and the changing nature of Western warfare: privatization and the 'revolution in military affairs'

The previous subsection indicated that liberal democracies are quite active in military engagements.[11] The relative frequency and the changing nature of their interventions are accompanied by changes in their way of warfare. Two recent trends in Western warfare have been debated intensively in IR security studies and peace and conflict research: the increasing employment of Private Security and Military Companies (PSMCs) and the transformation of Western militaries through high-tech weaponry and casualty-averse military strategies. A democratic distinctiveness perspective can highlight the central domestic motives and driving forces underlying these two recent trends.

Democratic distinctiveness and the privatization of security

The rise of professional 'corporate warriors' and the 'privatization of security' has attracted much scholarly and political attention during the last years, primarily due to the US government's heavy reliance on such contractors in their Iraq and Afghanistan military missions (Singer 2008; Schwartz 2010).[12] A democratic distinctiveness perspective offers powerful explanations for why democratic governments engage in the outsourcing of logistical, maintenance, training, protection, intelligence and – to a much lesser extent – combat tasks to private companies. One set of explanations focuses on the demand side, another set on the supply side of contracting.

As the demand-side explanation would have it, in rationalist Democratic Peace theory both democratic governments and their citizens are modelled as risk averse. The democratic public eschews the material and human costs of war, which it would have to bear, and a rational government interested in its re-election will respect these preferences. Importantly, the public is modelled in many Democratic Peace accounts as 'casualty averse' (Schörnig 2007). The validity of the argument, however, is dependent on context: If the material and human costs of war can be shifted from the population at large to a specific small group (professional armies, contractors) or if they can be kept from the public's scrutiny, governments might be able to win the consent of a majority of citizens or at least to increase their autonomy *vis-à-vis* the public.

Contracting implies a reduction of political risks and costs in several regards (Binder 2007). The problematic practices of contracting under the George W. Bush administration have shown how fatal such practices are for democratic control of military-related activities in the US (Avant 2006; Avant and Sigelman 2010). By employing highly intransparent practices of acquiring, splitting and monitoring of contracts, the US executive has permanently bypassed Congress and public. Contracting can also help governments to conceal the real human costs of war and thus 'circumvent' the public's 'casualty aversion': Studies show that media coverage on casualties among regular soldiers – who are considered 'our boys and girls' – is much more frequent and detailed than on casualties among contractors – who often remain 'faceless' deaths. In general, news coverage on the regular troops is much higher than on the PSMCs, and the public has hardly any access to information about the PSMCs' activities in the theatre (Avant and Sigelman 2010: 244–8). As dead contractors are not listed in the official record, the number of official casualties can be kept lower. In sum, contracting promises a democratic government more autonomy and flexibility in its foreign policy (Avant 2006: 510–5).[13]

Given the enhanced interventionism of liberal democracies since 1990, there has not only been an increased demand for outsourcing on the part of democratic governments, but also an increased supply by contractors themselves. A supply-centred liberal explanation is as follows: The PSMCs, interested in maximizing their profit, represent a particularistic interest within the democratic society. The structures of political interest mediation within contemporary democracies provide ample opportunities for special interest groups to exert disproportionate influence on the policy-making process (Czempiel 1996: 86). The top levels of many PSMCs are staffed by former military personnel and since they offer 'security goods' that concern the core of state sovereignty, private security companies benefit from a special 'closeness' to state agencies and policy-makers (Binder 2007). They can exert direct influence on decision-makers and engage in lobbying practices in order to increase the demand for their goods. In a liberal theory perspective, political decision-makers are 'besieged' and 'captured' by powerful special interest groups who seek to pursue their self-interests at the cost of the general public interest. The debate on the influence of PSMCs on the US government's decision-making reminds one of the debate on the influence of a 'military-industrial complex' that took place in the US in the 1960s and 1970s. In the case of the George W. Bush administration, one can show that PSMCs *did* exert influence. The top level staff of PSMCs possess social capital due to their former positions in the regular military. Many state agencies used information and reports provided by PSMCs, who attempt to praise their unique services and goods (Avant 2006: 512–4).

In sum, a democratic distinctiveness perspective can highlight democracy-specific motives of Western governments' privatization of security strategies.

Democratic distinctiveness and technology and science developments

Whereas the Cold War revolved around huge arsenals of nuclear weapons that were capable of devastating the entire planet, precision-guided missiles and Unmanned Aerial Vehicles (UAVs or drones) have become the icons of the post-Cold War period. In the same way that we analysed the privatization of security from a democratic distinctiveness perspective, we argue that the 'revolution in military affairs' is best understood as a development driven at least in part by democratic politics, rather than being an entirely exogenous challenge.

Whereas many civil wars are still fought with small arms and light weapons, the 'Western way of war' has come to be characterized by high-tech weaponry (Shaw 2005). The so-called 'revolution in military affairs' (RMA) refers to advances in 'signature management' (i.e. the undetectability by radar and other detection methods), precision warfare (using laser and satellite guidance), improved intelligence and reconnaissance (with the help of satellites and drones) and the provision of detailed real-time information to troops as well as decision-makers ('network-centric warfare') (Schörnig 2007).

To be sure, developments in armaments would not be possible without innovations in science and technology that are inherently difficult to plan. However, it is not technology *per se* but its integration into military strategy that makes RMA politically relevant (Rasmussen 2006: ch. 2). Moreover, because military research and development is heavily dependent on government funding, it also reflects political priorities (Reppy 1990; Sauer and Schörnig 2012: 364).

Since the end of the Cold War, the main political priority of democratic governments has been the advancement of technologies that minimize the risk of casualties, first and foremost among its own armed forces, but also among civilians in a conflict zone (Shaw 2005: 79–80, 84ff.). Because of the pivotal role of risks and their management, post-Cold War military missions have been analyzed from the perspective of risk society theory (Beck 2009: ch. 9; Rasmussen 2006; Shaw 2005). It is important to note, however, that the public expectations of casualty minimization so typical of risk societies become particularly politically relevant in the presence of free media and institutions of accountability. Thus, even though the focus of risk society theory has been post-industrial, late-modern

'Western' societies, there has been an underlying assumption that these are, by and large, democracies.[14] Therefore, at least in the realm of military missions, the theories of risk society and of democratic distinctiveness complement each other. For example, from both perspectives, drones appear as 'weapons of choice' because they do not endanger armed servicemen and, if armed, allow for precise strikes (Beck 2009; Sauer and Schörnig 2012). At the same time, the case of drones also serves as a reminder that democracies do not have a monopoly on casualty-minimizing technologies. Instead, several non-democracies have followed suit and invested heavily in RMA technology (Sauer and Schörnig 2012: 371–2). Nevertheless, a democratic distinctiveness perspective can shed additional light on one key driving force of the RMA, namely the attempt to minimize the risk to one's own troops.

Risk society and democratic distinctiveness scholars concur that the RMA has had a facilitating effect on the use of force by democratic governments. According to Rasmussen, the effects of the RMA can be understood as a case of risk compensation, i.e. a situation in which a reduction of risk leads to more risky behaviour: liberal democracies are 'able to fight more wars because the risks are lower' (Rasmussen 2006: 73; Müller 2004: 500; Sauer and Schörnig 2012: 373).

Democratic distinctiveness and the internationalization of security politics

Internationalization and globalization are generally not associated with the 'high' politics of security but rather with the 'low' politics of governing the economy, the environment, migration etc. However, the end of the Cold War has paved the way for unprecedented levels of internationalization in security politics, giving rise to notions of 'security governance' (Kirchner 2006; Krahmann 2003). Whereas the changing nature of armed conflict challenges the notion that inter-state war is the main threat to security and thus the main puzzle in international relations, the internationalization of security politics questions the methodological nationalism underlying the initial Democratic Peace proposition: If the nation-state is no longer the main locus of decisions about war and peace, how can the concept of democracy, which is intimately tied to the nation-state, retain explanatory value? In this section we do not dispute that internationalization is indeed a challenge to democratic control. However, we argue that the very process of internationalization is best understood not as an exogenous shock but as a process emanating from democratic politics.

To an unprecedented degree, contemporary security politics has become politics within international organizations. Important exceptions such as the 2003 Iraq War notwithstanding, international organizations have become the main locus to decide about military missions and to assume responsibility for their implementation. While internationalization is a globally discernible trend, it has been particularly pronounced in the North Atlantic area, i.e. within the remit of NATO and the European Union. Established as an alliance against the

Soviet Union, NATO has responded to the dissolution of its antagonist by taking on additional tasks such as peace support missions and security sector reform. Since the late 1990s, the European Union has followed NATO by evolving into a military actor as well. During the Cold War, NATO's highly integrated command structure was designed to signal resolve in case of an armed attack, but it had the side-effect of fostering cooperation and trust among the militaries of the member states (Wallander 2000). Appreciation for this side-effect was a main factor in adapting – rather than dissolving – NATO to the post-Cold War security agenda, and the establishment of similar structures within the European Union. Spending scarce defence budgets as efficiently as possible has been a further motivation for maintaining and even deepening the integration of the armed forces. Both organizations have therefore encouraged role specialization and the establishment of integrated military units.

To be sure, the internationalization of security politics poses a challenge to the notion of democratic control that lies at the heart of Democratic Peace theory. If decisions on the use of military force are no longer made in the national capitals but in international fora, it becomes more difficult to hold the government accountable. As in other policy areas, internationalization in security politics shifts political resources from parliaments, courts and civil society institutions to the executive branch, because international fora offer executives privileged access to information (Moravcsik 1994; Wagner 2006; Wolf 1999).

However, it would be misleading to regard the internationalization of security politics as exogenous to democratic politics. Instead, the internationalization of security politics is better understood as driven by forces which are particularly pronounced in democracies (Wagner 2011). First, democracies have been found to be particularly capable of and interested in international cooperation. The transparency of decision-making and the high esteem for the rule of law make commitments by democracies particularly credible and thus make democracies particularly reliable partners (Lipson 2003; Martin 2000). Second, the large size of the selectorate comes with incentives to spend scarce resources on public goods such as the welfare state. In the absence of a major military threat, democratic governments find it difficult to make a case for high levels of defence spending. Possible gains in efficiency by engaging in role specialization and multinational integrated military structures therefore seem particularly attractive to democracies.

'Democratic distinctiveness': a resilient approach?

Without doubt, Democratic Peace theory is firmly rooted in pre-globalized international relations. Geared towards the explanation of inter-state wars, the 'new security agenda' appeared as a challenge to the validity of its main causal mechanisms. However, as demonstrated in the previous section, distinctly democratic features such as accountability to a large selectorate and the prevalence of liberal norms and values contribute to a comprehensive understanding of main features of the 'new security agenda'.

Since we have only highlighted the potentials of a democratic distinctiveness research programme so far, we will conclude our contribution with a more critical outlook addressing three lacunae. In our view, liberal IR research on the link between democracy and security politics would benefit, *firstly*, from drawing on Critical Theory traditions (see also Chapter 3 by Fierke in this volume). Research from Western scholars about their own polities and policies requires a high degree of self-reflexivity and sensitivity towards the numerous ambivalences generated by liberal-democratic actors and policies. To be sure, Critical Theory encompasses a diverse field of approaches such as, for example, Marxist, feminist, discursive or recognition-based writings (Calhoun 1995), which highlight quite different aspects of society, democracy and politics. But all of them provide theoretical tools to probe ambivalences, paradoxes and contingencies of democratic politics and problematize the insoluble nexus between knowledge production and power, thereby promoting reflexivity of scholarship (Hobson 2011a).

This does, of course, neither imply that Critical Theory should replace any of the other existing approaches in democratic distinctiveness research, nor that it is methodologically possible to connect it easily with these other approaches. Pleading for the inclusion of Critical Theory does not suggest a specific normative position on the ambivalence of liberal norms or on policy recommendations but calls on the individual researcher to make his or her normative assumptions explicit and reflect upon the consequences of this research for policy issues.

The more demanding challenge is to translate such an inspiration by Critical Theory traditions into a substantive research agenda (Hobson 2011b). The Peace Research Institute Frankfurt (PRIF) has attempted to develop such an agenda within its research programme 'The Antinomies of Democratic Peace' (Müller 2004). One central field of empirical and theoretical study was the investigation of 'democratic wars' as they denote the flipside of Democratic Peace most clearly: their domestic and international legitimation, their parliamentary control, and peculiarities of democracies' weapons systems and warfare.[15] Following traditions of the Frankfurt School of Critical Theory, PRIF examined ambivalences, paradoxes and 'dark sides' that come with Enlightenment ideas and concepts. Instead of assuming a virtuous circle of all good things going together, PRIF highlighted the multifarious dilemmas which are created and faced by a liberal foreign policy that conceives of itself as being ethical, i.e. as realizing goals beyond the narrow self-interest.

Such a 'critical' substantive research agenda has not been exhausted yet, and we would like to suggest that future research on democratic distinctiveness should, *secondly*, definitely stretch beyond IR approaches and tie in with studies on the domestic condition of democracies done in democratic theory, comparative politics and political sociology. If we trace a democracy's 'distinctiveness' back to domestic institutions, norms and preferences, then it is advisable to take seriously the diagnosis of a 'democratic melancholy' in consolidated democracies (Offe 2008): as observed since the 1990s, there is a strange duality of democratic triumphalism *and* melancholy in the West. While the regime-type democracy has been spreading around the globe, the citizens in consolidated democracies feel discontent with their institutions and ruling elites. The processes of globalization pose new challenges for the domestic legitimacy of democratic regimes. If democracy and civilian attitudes erode from within under the pressure of globalization, the foundations for Democratic Peace would rest on very shaky grounds.

A further challenge to 'democratic distinctiveness' research might, *thirdly*, arise from a shift in global power relations. Debates on the 'decline of the West' and the 'rise of authoritarian powers' such as China and Russia have become a prominent topic in policy journals and IR conferences. An analytical perspective tailored to a specific regime type and reflecting the specific historical moment and (putative) 'triumph' of democracy after the end of the Cold War can thus expect to soon be outdated (Ish-Shalom 2006: 581). Although we might indeed witness a substantial loss of power for the Western democracies in the future, we contend that research on 'democratic distinctiveness' will remain a useful perspective to understand the dynamics of international conflicts as well as cooperation. (Liberal) democracies will neither vanish from the scene of world politics nor can they blindly trust in the global 'triumph' of their kind. The conflicts that arise from such constellations will still be shaped by democracies.

With regard to a dialogue with other subsections of security research in IR, we have argued that 'democratic distinctiveness' is, *in principle*, an approach that can be linked to a variety of the approaches and methods in security studies assembled in this volume – be it the institutional approach by Fehl in Chapter 2, the critical discourses of security studies as summarized by Fierke in Chapter 3, or the interdisciplinary method combinations as discussed by Junk and Rauer in Chapter 13. However, as a basically 'liberal' perspective focussing on domestic norms, institutions, actors and processes in democracies, 'democratic distinctiveness' requires more than a dialogue with other IR sections – research should stretch out over political theory and comparative politics. Drawing more extensively on research from comparative politics could inspire more research on questions of how 'hybrid regimes' that are neither democracies nor autocracies behave in their external relations. Apart from the much-cited study by Mansfield and Snyder on the increased war-proneness of democratizing regimes (Mansfield and Snyder 2005), 'democratic distinctiveness' literature has largely neglected the persistence of 'hybrids' in international politics. To be sure, the large universe of regime types is more complexly designed than just assembling 'democracies' and their 'non'-counterparts, be they autocracies or dictatorships.

Notes

1 See the contributions of Glaser, of Masala, and of Hegre and Kristiansen in this volume.
2 For a comprehensive discussion see Russett and Oneal (2001).
3 On the descriptive statistics of armed conflict see Gleditsch et al. (2002); on descriptive statistics of battle deaths see Lacina and Gleditsch (2005).
4 For an overview see Müller and Wolff (2006).
5 For an outline of the 'selectorate theory', see Bueno de Mesquita *et al.* (2003).
6 The 'extension hypothesis' of Democratic Peace, see Friedman (2008).

7 We cannot discuss the merits and flaws of rationalist or constructivist explanations of Democratic Peace here, see, e.g., Müller and Wolff (2006) and Rosato (2003).
8 For a more comprehensive discussion see Geis and Wagner (2011: 1559).
9 For democracy as a context condition of the commercial peace see Bliss and Russett (1998); for democracy as a context condition of peace by international institutions see Pevehouse and Russett (2006).
10 For democratic distinctiveness as applied to defence spending, see Goldsmith (2007); to arms control policies, see Müller and Becker (2008); to civil wars, see Krain and Myers (1997); Hegre *et al.* (2001); Lacina (2006); and to terrorism, see Abrahms (2007).
11 It should be noted that only a limited number of democracies is particularly active in this regard – we cannot deal with the huge differences among democracies here. See Geis *et al.* (2013).
12 There is a huge body of literature on this issue today, to name but a few: Avant (2005); Chesterman and Lehnardt (2007); Krahmann (2010); Leander (2009); Singer (2008).
13 We cannot discuss here that such promises are misplaced and that outsourcing entails diverse new costs and risks, instead of reducing them. See, e.g., Deitelhoff and Geis (2009).
14 Thus, Shaw defines the Western way of war as 'the specific way of fighting [...] that democracies – chiefly the USA and Britain – developed' (Shaw 2005: 4). In a similar vein, Rasmussen introduces the object of his study as 'Western societies' which, among other things, are characterized by an 'almost universal consensus on the values of liberal democracy' (Rasmussen 2006: 1). Finally, Ulrich Beck's essay on the political logic of 'risk wars' refers to 'electoral risks for the belligerent governments' (Beck 2009: 152).
15 See, among others, the contributions in Evangelista *et al.* (2008); Geis *et al.* (2006); Geis *et al.* (2013) and Geis *et al.* (2007).

References

Abrahms, M. (2007) 'Why Democracies Make Superior Counterterrorists', *Security Studies*, 16 (2): 223–53.
Avant, D. (2005) *The Market for Force: The Consequences of Privatizing Security*, Cambridge: Cambridge University Press.
—— (2006) 'The Implications of Marketized Security for IR Theory', *Perspectives on Politics*, 4 (3): 507–28.
Avant, D. and Sigelman, L. (2010) 'Private Security and Democracy: Lessons from the US in Iraq', *Security Studies*, 19 (2): 230–65.
Beck, U. (2009) *World at Risk*, Cambridge: Polity Press.
Bellamy, A. (2009) *Responsibility to Protect*, Cambridge: Polity Press.
Binder, M. (2007) 'Norms versus Rationality: Why Democracies Use Private Military Companies in Civil Wars', in T. Jäger and G. Kümmel (eds) *Private Military and Security Companies*, Wiesbaden: VS: 307–20.
Bliss, H. and Russett, B. (1998) 'Democratic Trading Partners: The Liberal Connection, 1962–1989', *Journal of Politics*, 60 (4): 1126–47.
Brock, L. (2002) ' "Staatenrecht" und "Menschenrecht". Schwierigkeiten der Annäherung an eine weltbürgerliche Ordnung', in M. Lutz-Bachmann and J. Bohman (eds) *Weltstaat oder Staatenwelt? Für und wider die Idee einer Weltrepublik*, Frankfurt/M.: Suhrkamp: 201–25.
—— (2005) 'The Use of Force in the Post-Cold War Era: From Collective Action Back to Pre-Charter Self Defense?', in M. Bothe, M.E. O'Connell and N. Ronzitti (eds)

Redefining Sovereignty: The Use of Force After the Cold War, Ardsley: Transnational Publishers: 21–52.
Bueno de Mesquita, B. et al. (2003) *The Logic of Political Survival*, Cambridge (MA): MIT Press.
Calhoun, C. (1995) *Critical Social Theory*, Oxford: Blackwell.
Chandler, D. (2006) *From Kosovo to Kabul and Beyond: Human Rights and International Intervention*, London: Pluto Press.
Chernoff, F. (2004) 'The Study of Democratic Peace and Progress in International Relations', *International Studies Review*, 6 (1): 49–78.
Chesterman, S. and Lehnardt, C. (eds) (2007) *From Mercenaries to Market*, Cambridge: Cambridge University Press.
Chojnacki, S. (2006) 'Democratic Wars and Military Interventions, 1946–2002', in A. Geis, L. Brock and H. Müller (eds) *Democratic Wars: Looking at the Dark Side of Democratic Peace*, Basingstoke and New York: Palgrave Macmillan: 13–39.
Crawford, N. (1994) 'A Security Regime Among Democracies: Cooperation Among Iroquois Nations', *International Organization*, 48 (3): 345–85.
Czempiel, E.-O. (1996) 'Kants Theorem, oder: Warum sind die Demokratien (noch immer) nicht friedlich?', *Zeitschrift für Internationale Beziehungen*, 3 (1): 79–101.
Deitelhoff, N. and Geis, A. (2009) 'Securing the State, Undermining Democracy: Internationalization and Privatization of Western Militaries', TranState Working Paper No. 92, University of Bremen.
Doyle, M.W. (1983) 'Kant, Liberal Legacies and Foreign Affairs', *Philosophy and Public Affairs*, 12 (3): 205–35.
Evangelista, M., Müller, H. and Schörnig, N. (eds) (2008) *Democracy and Security: Preferences, Norms and Policy-Making*, London and New York: Routledge.
Freedman, L. (2005) 'The Age of Liberal Wars', in: D. Armstrong, T. Farrell and B. Maiguashca (eds) *Force and Legitimacy in World Politics*, Cambridge: Cambridge University Press: 93–107.
Friedman, G. (2008) 'Identifying the Place of Democratic Norms in Democratic Peace', *International Studies Review*, 10 (3): 548–70.
Frowein, J. and Krisch, N. (2002) 'Article 39', in B. Simma (ed.) *The Charter of the United Nations: A Commentary*, Oxford: Oxford University Press: 717–29.
Geis, A., Brock, L. and Müller, H. (eds) (2006) *Democratic Wars: Looking at the Dark Side of Democratic Peace*, Basingstoke and New York: Palgrave Macmillan.
Geis, A., Müller, H. and Schörnig, N. (eds) (2013) *The Militant Face of Democracy: Liberal Forces for Good*, Cambridge: Cambridge University Press.
Geis, A., Müller, H. and Wagner, W. (eds) (2007) *Schattenseiten des Demokratischen Friedens. Zur Kritik einer Theorie liberaler Außen- und Sicherheitspolitik*, Frankfurt/M.: Campus.
Geis, A. and Wagner, W. (2011) 'How far is it from Königsberg to Kandahar? Democratic Peace and Democratic Violence in International Relations', *Review of International Studies*, 37 (4): 1555–77.
Gleditsch, N.P. et al. (2002) 'Armed Conflict 1946–2001: A New Dataset', *Journal of Peace Research*, 39 (5): 615–37.
Goldsmith, B.E. (2007) 'Defense Efforts and Institutional Theories of Democratic Peace and Victory: Why Try Harder', *Security Studies*, 16 (2): 189–222.
Hasenclever, A. (2001) *Die Macht der Moral in der internationalen Politik*, Frankfurt/M.: Campus.
Hegre, H. et al. (2001) 'Towards a Democratic Civil Peace? Democracy, Democratization, and Civil War 1816–1992', *American Political Science Review*, 95 (1): 33–48.

Hobson, C. (2011a) 'Towards a Critical Theory of Democratic Peace', *Review of International Studies*, 37 (4): 1903–22.
— (2011b) 'The Sorcerer's Apprentice', *International Relations*, 25 (2): 171–7.
Ish-Shalom, P. (2006) 'Theory as a Hermeneutical Mechanism: The Democratic-Peace Thesis and the Politics of Democratization', *European Journal of International Relations*, 12 (4): 565–98.
Kirchner, E.J. (2006) 'The Challenge of European Union Security Governance', *Journal of Common Market Studies*, 44 (5): 947–68.
Krahmann, E. (2003) 'Conceptualizing Security Governance', *Cooperation and Conflict*, 38 (1): 5–26.
— (2010) *States, Citizens and the Privatization of Security*, Cambridge: Cambridge University Press.
Krain, M. and Myers, M.E. (1997) 'Democracy and Civil War: A Note on the Democratic Peace Proposition', *International Interactions*, 23 (1): 109–18.
Lacina, B. (2006) 'Explaining the Severity of Civil Wars', *Journal of Conflict Resolution*, 50 (2): 276–89.
Lacina, B. and Gleditsch, N.P. (2005) 'Monitoring Trends in Global Combat: A New Dataset of Battle Deaths', *European Journal of Population*, 21: 145–66.
Leander, A. (2009) 'The Privatization of Security', Copenhagen Business School Working Paper No. 10.
Lipson, C. (2003) *Reliable Partners: How Democracies Have Made a Separate Peace*, Princeton: Princeton University Press.
MacMillan, J. (2005) 'Introduction: The Iraq War and Democratic Politics', in A. Danchev and J. MacMillan (eds) *The Iraq War and Democratic Politics*, London and New York: Routledge: 1–19.
Mahbubani, K. (2008) *The New Asian Hemisphere: The Irresistible Shift of Global Power to the East*, New York: Public Affairs.
Mansfield, E.D. and Snyder, J. (2005) *Electing to Fight: Why Emerging Democracies Go to War*, Cambridge (MA): MIT Press.
Martin, L. (2000) *Democratic Commitments: Legislatures and International Cooperation*, Princeton: Princeton University Press.
Moravcsik, A. (1994) 'Why the European Union Strengthens the State: Domestic Politics and International Cooperation', Center for European Studies Working Paper No. 52, Harvard University.
Müller, H. (2004) 'The Antinomy of Democratic Peace', *International Politics*, 41 (4): 494–520.
Müller, H. and Becker, U. (2008) 'Technology, Nuclear Arms Control, and Democracy: Reflections in the Light of Democratic Peace Theory', in M. Evangelista, H. Müller and N. Schörnig (eds) *Democracy and Security: Preferences, Norms and Policy-Making*, London and New York: Routledge: 102–19.
Müller, H. and Wolff, J. (2006) 'Democratic Peace: Many Data, Little Explanation?', in A. Geis, L. Brock and H. Müller (eds) *Democratic Wars: Looking at the Dark Side of Democratic Peace*, Basingstoke and New York: Palgrave Macmillan: 41–73.
Offe, C. (2008) 'Political Disaffection as an Outcome of Institutional Practices?', in A. Brodocz, M. Llanque and G.S. Schaal (eds) *Bedrohungen der Demokratie*, Wiesbaden: VS: 42–60.
Owen, J.M. (1994) 'How Liberalism Produces Democratic Peace', *International Security*, 19 (2): 87–125.

(2004) 'Democratic Peace Research: Whence and Whither?', *International Politics*, 41 (4): 605–17.
Pevehouse, J. and Russett, B. (2006) 'Democratic International Governmental Organizations Promote Peace', *International Organization*, 60 (4): 969–1000.
Rasmussen, M.V. (2006) *The Risk Society at War: Terror, Technology and Strategy in the Twenty-First Century*, Cambridge: Cambridge University Press.
Reiter, D. and Stam, A. (2002) *Democracies at War*, Princeton: Princeton University Press.
Reppy, J. (1990) 'The Technological Imperative in Strategic Thought', *Journal of Peace Research*, 27 (1): 101–6.
Risse-Kappen, T. (1995) 'Democratic Peace – Warlike Democracies', *European Journal of International Relations*, 1 (4): 491–517.
Rosato, S. (2003) 'The Flawed Logic of Democratic Peace Theory', *American Political Science Review*, 97 (4): 585–602.
Rousseau, D.L. (2005) *Democracy and War: Institutions, Norms, and the Evolution of International Conflict*, Stanford: Stanford University Press.
Russett, B. (1993) *Grasping the Democratic Peace: Principles for a Post-Cold War World*, Princeton: Princeton University Press.
—— (1998) 'A Neo-Kantian Perspective: Democracy, Interdependence and International Organizations in Building Security Communities', in E. Adler and M. Barnett (eds) *Security Communities*, Cambridge: Cambridge University Press: 368–94.
Russett, B. and Oneal, J. (2001) *Triangulating Peace: Democracy, Interdependence, and International Organizations*, New York: Norton.
Sauer, F. and Schörnig, N. (2012) 'Killer Drones: The "Silver Bullet" of Democratic Warfare?', *Security Dialogue*, 43 (4): 363–80.
Schörnig, N. (2007) 'Visionen unblutiger Kriege. Hightech-Antworten zur Umgehung der Opfersensibilitätsfalle', in A. Geis, H. Müller and W. Wagner (eds) *Schattenseiten des Demokratischen Friedens. Zur Kritik einer Theorie liberaler Außen- und Sicherheitspolitik*, Frankfurt/M.: Campus: 93–122.
Schultz, K. (2001) *Democracy and Coercive Diplomacy*, Cambridge: Cambridge University Press.
Schwartz, M. (2010) *Department of Defence Contractors in Iraq and Afghanistan: Background and Analysis*, Washington: Congressional Research Service Report.x
Shaw, M. (2005) *The New Western Way of War*, Cambridge: Polity Press.
Singer, P.W. (2008) *Corporate Warriors: The Rise of the Privatized Military Industry*, Ithaca: Cornell University Press.
Wagner, W. (2006) 'The Democratic Control of Military Power Europe', *Journal of European Public Policy*, 13 (2): 200–16.
—— (2011) *Die demokratische Kontrolle internationalisierter Sicherheitspolitik. Demokratiedefizite bei Militäreinsätzen und in der europäischen Politik innerer Sicherheit*, Baden-Baden: Nomos.
Wallander, C.A. (2000) 'Institutional Assets and Adaptability: NATO after the Cold War', *International Organization*, 54 (4): 705–35.
Weart, S. (1994) 'Peace Among Democratic and Oligarchic Republics', *Journal of Peace Research*, 31 (3): 299–316.
Wheeler, N. (2000) *Saving Strangers: Humanitarian Intervention in International Society*, Oxford: Oxford University Press.
Wolf, K.D. (1999) 'The New Raison d'État as a Problem for Democracy in World Society', *European Journal of International Relations*, 5 (3): 333–63.

8 Securing the environment
From defense to resilience

Chris Methmann and Angela Oels

Introduction

The story of environmental security has often been told as one of progress and emancipation, with a happy end in store. In this chapter, we offer a new and different reading of environmental security, based on Foucault's concept of governmentality. In a genealogical reading, we show that the meaning of the 'environment' and the practices of securing it have changed over time. We demonstrate that far from simply leading to emancipation or progress, each and every mode of securing has its own more or less undesirable policy implications, including the most recent form, resilience.

As outlined in the introduction to this edited volume, the end of the Cold War created the conceptual space to 'redefine security' in a globalizing world (Ullman 1983). At around the same time, environmental activists and concerned scientists decided to intensify the debate about environmental problems by arguing that the environment itself was a security issue. They claimed that environmental change would trigger unprecedented waves of migration or cause conflicts over scarce resources (Myers and Kent 1995; Tuchman Mathews 1989).[1] The securitization of the environment was an effort to mobilize public support for environmental policies. This started the scientific debate spinning, but it turned out that claims concerning environmental conflict could not be easily empirically substantiated (Barnett 2000). On a normative level, some began to suspect that couching environmental issues in the language of national security could actually do more harm than good (Deudny 1990). Therefore, an increasing number of scholars began to reconsider environmental security. This coincided with the emergence of the concept of human security. Now it was claimed that all harmful effects of securitizing the environment could be circumvented once the environment was produced as a threat to human security. However, for quite a while, no one was interested in hearing about the human security implications of environmental change and it remained an abstract and academic debate with little if any political impact (Floyd 2008). This lasted until the mid-2000s, when climate change made it to the top of the policy agenda. Disguised as climate security, the human security agenda featured prominently in UN Security Council sessions in 2007 and 2011. What a career: from (indefensible) claims about environmental conflicts to the high politics of climate security, the history of environmental security reads like a success story, both in terms of political influence and a 'consequentialist' evaluation of security (Floyd 2007). Today, many advocate climate security as a safe and effective means of pushing for more ambitious climate change mitigation and adaptation policies (Brauch 2009).

In this chapter, we question whether climate security discourse is really desirable. First, we argue that what has been called a broadening of security still implies an essentialized concept of security. The genealogy of environmental security shows that securitizing the environment can imply a range of very different practices enforced by diverse actors. In this sense, we show how the broadening of security has transformed its very meaning. Drawing on a Foucauldian notion of security, we trace three corresponding modes of how the environment has been rendered governable that have emerged over the last three decades and still co-exist today: environmental conflict, environmental security and resilience. We discuss the underlying conceptions of environment and security of each of these discourses as well as the political implications that flow from them. This allows us to cast doubt on the thesis of environmental security as an increasingly emancipatory and therefore 'innocent' discourse. Although today's debates about climate security are far from centered on military or national conceptions of security, the policies associated with them are equally undesirable. We argue that policies related to climate security render affected populations responsible for their own survival in a world where climate change wreaks havoc. Yet before we embark on our genealogical journey to this argumentative destination, we briefly introduce our theoretical vessel, sailing under the flag of Michel Foucault.

For traditional security analysts, security refers to the narrow field of high politics. This conception is invoked when the existence of the nation-state is at stake (e.g. Walt 1991). But even constructivist accounts of security, such as the Copenhagen School, often rely on an essentialized notion of security (Stritzel 2007). Foucault's concept of governmentality, by contrast, allows us to distinguish between different modes of securing, each of which is linked to characteristic practices.[2] From a Foucauldian perspective, security – understood as governmentality – is organized as a dispersed web of institutions, practices and agencies, all of which problematize certain referent objects as endangered and legitimize action upon these referent objects in the name of their security (Dean 2010: 29). The Foucauldian notion of security has been usefully employed by a range of different approaches, among them the Paris school, the biopolitics literature and the governmentality approach to security (Aradau and van Munster 2011; Balzacq 2010; Dillon and Reid 2009). In the following genealogical analysis of environmental security, we trace how the relationship between environment and security is problematized and hence how the modes of governing the environment as a security issue have changed over time. We distinguish between three modes of securing, each of which is linked to a particular governmentality. First, what Foucault calls sovereign power[3] is the use of violence (or the law backed by sovereign violence) for the protection and defense of an environment understood in terms of scarce environmental resources. Secondly, what Foucault calls biopower is the use of statistics in order to identify risk groups whom governmental interventions will then target. In the case of the environment, biopower or so-called 'green governmentality' calculates 'safe' levels of emissions in order to stabilize the human-earth-system at an equilibrium (Oels 2005). The third mode is what Dillon has termed 'governing through contingency', or seeking to utilize life's ability to adapt and evolve in the face of environmental change (Dillon 2007); in our case, seeking to make social and natural systems resilient to external shocks caused by a terroristic environment.

Redefining security: the rise of environmental conflict in security studies

The end of the Cold War led large military establishments to wonder what their new role could be in a post-Cold War world. As a result, the conceptual space emerged to widen and deepen the meaning of security. There were frequent attempts to 'redefine security', i.e. to bring new issues into the realm of security (Ullman 1983). Environmental activists and concerned scientists, such as Jessica Tuchman Mathews and Norman Myers, contributed to the greening of the national security agenda (Mathews 1989; Myers 1989). They painted an apocalyptic picture of environmental degradation, predicting wars and migration triggered by environmental change. These were the early days of what we term an environmental conflict discourse. As a result of these and other efforts, global economic and environmental issues started to appear on the security agenda.

Scientists sought to corroborate the environmental conflict thesis. The Toronto Group, led by Thomas Homer-Dixon, studied the relationship between environmental degradation and actual conflict (Homer-Dixon 1999). The group concluded that resource scarcity could indeed lead to conflicts. However, there was no direct or even deterministic causality between the two, and a number of variables intervened in each case. Others were less cautious and claimed, for example, that conflicts would necessarily emerge as fresh water supplies dried up (Gleick 1989). Myers and Kent (1995) published a still-influential study predicting that climate change alone would uproot more than 200 million refugees by 2050. In 1993, the ideas of the Toronto Group became known to a wider public through an article in *Scientific American* (Homer-Dixon et al. 1993). The breakthrough for this discourse came with the essay 'The coming anarchy' published by well-known travel-writer Robert Kaplan in the *Atlantic Monthly* in 1994. United States President Bill Clinton confessed that he 'was so gripped by many things that were in that article and by the more academic treatment of the same subject by Professor Homer-Dixon' (cited in Betsy Hartmann 2006). Homer-Dixon briefed Vice-President Al Gore and military officers several times throughout the 1990s – a harbinger of Gore's later engagement in the climate security discourse.

The environment as resource

In this discourse, conflict is thought to emerge through competition over depleting resources. Obviously, therefore, the environment is understood first of all as a resource for human life. This marks a clear departure from the 1970s and the early 1980s where the environment was still understood in terms of its 'components', e.g. water, air, soil, forests, etc. (Hajer 1995). Yet when sustainable development became the dominant discourse in environmental politics at the end of the 1980s, the environment was established as a 'resource' for human (economic) activities (Escobar 1996). This is mirrored in the environmental conflict literature. It assumes that 'growing scarcities of renewable resources can contribute to social instability and civil strife' (Homer-Dixon et al. 1993), linking human behavior to the availability of resources in a neo-Malthusian fashion (Hartmann 2006). As a result, a depleted environment necessarily becomes a national security issue. *Conflict is thus likely to emerge where resources are becoming most scarce: in developing countries.* The world appears bifurcated: affluence vs. decline, North vs. South (Dalby 1996). This also holds true in the writings of Homer-Dixon who – in a more academic tone – suggests that environmental conflict will mostly occur in developing countries (Homer-Dixon 1991: 79). The bifurcation of the globe thus perfectly supports the emerging geopolitical vision that replaced competition between superpowers in the 1990s: that of 'tame' zones of economic globalization surrounded by 'wild' zones of mass poverty, political upheaval and violence (Tuathail and Luke 1994), the latter becoming a source of security threats for Northern homelands.

Sovereign security

It comes as no surprise that this discourse represents a modified version of traditional notions of national security, mobilizing defense as a strategy of securing. This discourse clearly resembles the notion of sovereign power in Foucault. Today, however, sovereign power has been governmentalized. This means that in the era of biopower, which is about fostering life, killing life can only be justified under certain circumstances. Only when the survival of the human species is at stake can sovereign power be legitimized in a liberal society, for example in the form of humanitarian interventions (Dillon and Reid 2009). Thus, the bifurcation of the world into 'tame' and 'wild' zones creates spaces for legitimate sovereign interventions. However, military interventions are just one possibility for the exercise of sovereign power. Governmentalized sovereignty, for example, also functions through the assignment of citizenship, binding individuals to a particular territory and restricting their mobility. Fences and border-controls keep 'dangerous life' out. Finally, sovereign power also appears in the form of exceptions to the rule of law, such as the temporary suspension of basic liberties. The environmental discourses, especially those around climate change, often compare the fight against climate change to US mobilization efforts during the Second World War, when presidential decree obliged all car manufacturers to produce war supplies instead of cars. In sum, the environmental conflict discourse, by couching security in national terms, reflects a neo-Malthusian conception of the environment as scarce resource that enables sovereign forms of power.

Environmental conflict and the Northern security agenda

The environmental conflict discourse has gained considerable influence despite the fact that there is no empirical evidence to substantiate the claim that environmental change will lead to actual conflict or migration (Barnett 2000; Gleditsch 1998; Jakobeit and Methmann 2012; Suhrke 1994). Whether or not this is true, this debate highlights the fact that questions of political economy and political ecology are excluded from the environmental conflict equation (Harvey 1996; Peluso and Watts 2001). As Dalby points out, the apocalyptic picture painted by Kaplan's 'The coming anarchy' neglects the many (commercial, financial and political) connections between North and South, between the 'tamed' and 'wild' zones of the globe (Dalby 1996). In this sense, sovereign power detaches the causes of environmental conflicts from their social and economic context. As Jon Barnett puts it, the environmental conflict literature is 'theoretically rather than empirically driven, and is both a product and legitimation of the Northern security agenda' (Barnett 2000: 171). Finally, the environmental conflict discourse revives colonial and racist stereotypes (Baldwin 2012). It reinvigorates the colonial idea of the non-European populations not being able to handle their own affairs or use their resources rationally (Hartmann 2006). Given this plethora of criticism, it comes as no surprise that this discourse has lost traction in both academic and political debates and has been complemented, if not frequently replaced, by the notion of environmental security.[4]

Environmental security and the production of victims

In the 1990s environmental change was redefined as a threat to human security. The shift from environmental conflict to human security was facilitated by two developments: First, this was a decade of 'humanitarian' military interventions with, and without (as in the case of the Kosovo), the backing of the UN Security Council (Chandler 2012a). A second important influence was the political campaigning for a redefinition of security in terms of human security. The motivation behind this was the hope of freeing up substantial resources for development, which at the time were used for defense. In 1994 the UNDP (1994) published a report entitled *New Dimensions of Human Security*. This report redefined security from the security of *states* to that of *people*. Human security successfully became the dominant discourse in development policy and was influential within the UN system, though often without the explicit use of the term (Chandler 2012a). Since the environment is one of the seven components of this concept, environmental change was soon re-conceptualized as a threat to human security (Barnett 2001; Dalby 2002). However, the concern with conflict did not disappear. Instead, it was redeployed within the larger discursive framework of human security and used to justify the need for humanitarian interventions and increased efforts in development policy (see also Chapter 7 by Geis and Wagner on human rights protection as legitimate reason for military interventions by democratic states).

The environment as a coupled human–ecological system

With the emergence of human security, the 'environment' in environmental security changed. It was no longer understood simply in terms of resources for human societies. The environment became part of a coupled human–ecological system. Characterizing our geological age as the anthropocene emphasizes that, for the first time in the history of the planet, human societies have become a significant driver of large-scale geo-physical change (Crutzen 2002). As a result, we have to understand men and nature as a joint 'earth system', with the associated scientific discipline of 'earth system sciences' (Lövbrand et al. 2009). This system is understood to have a stable natural equilibrium that can be scientifically determined. The task of ecosystem managers then, is to preserve the equilibrium by restricting the extraction of resources from a system. Combined with advances in computer modeling, this allows the scope and scale of global environmental change to be predicted. Climate science, and therefore also climate politics, depend on a 'vast machine' of scientific calculations and measurements (Edwards 2010).

Liberal–biopolitical security

Securing the environment understood in such a way implies the preservation of the natural equilibrium of ecosystems by determining 'safe' emission or extraction levels. This corresponds to the human security approach that frames environmental security as an attempt at 'peacefully reducing human vulnerability to human-induced environmental degradation by addressing the root causes of environmental degradation and human insecurity' (Barnett 2001: 129). According to the crucial concept of vulnerability (Methmann and Oels 2013), environmental change does not deterministically lead to security concerns. Whether this occurs depends on the vulnerability of human livelihoods. Vulnerability is shaped by a broad range of social, economic and political factors. Accordingly, the aim of vulnerability research is to build models and predictions about the vulnerability of certain portions of the global population. Costly political interventions can then be targeted at the most vulnerable in order to protect them (O'Brien 2004).

This resonates with Foucault's notion of biopolitics. Biopolitics is related to the emergence of statistics and demography, which allowed governmental authorities to understand the population as a living organism in need of constant management and optimization (Rose 2001). Governing security means targeting those risk groups that deviate statistically from the norm and directing governmental interventions towards them. Biopolitics is a subtle and liberal form of management that intervenes indirectly to achieve desired results. It seeks to influence the choices made by people using education programs, financial incentives and the like. However, not all subjects and objects are amenable to being rendered governable in a liberal way. In the end, all liberal forms of government are backed by the threat of force. Governmentalized sovereignty enables liberal interventionism for risk groups or exceptional cases that have been found to 'fail' liberal government (Dillon 1995). Repressive measures can be enacted upon failing states as well as failing individuals. This means that sovereign power is not replaced by biopolitics, but is reconfigured as the force necessary to deal with (constructed) existential threats to the survival of the population.

'Saving' the victims

Compared to the environmental conflict literature, the emergence of environmental security has been welcomed by many since it focuses on the social, economic and political context of environmental changes. Instead of seeing environmental change as a deterministic driver of threats which needs to be countered with sovereign power, environmental security suggests a broader palette of political options. Human environmental security is believed to rule out the promotion of military means, and to instead foster emancipation, development and environmental protection (Floyd 2010).

However, in light of our analysis, we take a more skeptical stance. In the case of human trafficking, Claudia Aradau (2004) has highlighted how the 'politics of pity' endorsed by human security feeds into a politics of risk prevention and precaution. Translated to our case this means: the point of Northern intervention is not primarily to 'save' the affected populations, but to prevent them from disrupting global circulation at large. In the case of development policy, Duffield and Waddell (2006) have shown convincingly that the human security of Southern populations is only taken into consideration to the extent that it contributes to Northern homeland security. This is said to be particularly true since the attacks of 11 September 2001. The vulnerable are framed as being constantly on the brink of becoming dangerous to Northern security. In this sense, human security can in fact be understood as enabling sovereign power, by paving the way for the 'security-development complex' (Duffield and Waddell 2006). What is more, even if emergency is not invoked in the name of humanity, those deemed to be vulnerable to environmental change are often rendered as helpless and passive victims in need of Western care and intervention. The debate on climate-induced migration is one example of this (Oels 2013). At best, environmental security renders those affected by environmental change as mere objects of global governance. At worst, it produces them as a 'back door' security threat.

Climate security: making people fit for survival in times of apocalyptic change

The renaissance of global warming at the beginning of the twenty-first century again reconfigured the discourse on security and the environment. A number of events that were associated with climate change revitalized the environmental security debate that had slowed down in previous years, among them: Hurricane Katrina in 2004, the publication of the 2006 *Stern Review* and the 2007 IPCC *Fourth Assessment Report*, and release of the films *The Day after Tomorrow* (2004) and Al Gore's *An Inconvenient Truth* (2006) (on visual representations of security see Chapter 11 by Schlag in this volume). Global warming was becoming popular again, and so was the concern with its security implications, particularly in the global South. Climate change no longer ranked alongside other environmental problems. Instead, it began to be understood as an overarching danger, often painted with bold, apocalyptic strokes (Methmann and Rothe 2012; Swyngedouw 2010). In a similar move, the environmental security discourse was condensed into 'climate security'.

Climate change entered the realm of high politics. The United Kingdom put climate change on the UN Security Council agenda in 2007. In 2009, UN Secretary General Ban Ki-Moon was asked to prepare a report on 'Climate change and its possible security implications' to the UN General Assembly, in which he framed climate change as a 'threat multiplier' of other pre-existing vulnerabilities (UN Secretary General 2009). In 2011, Germany used its UN Security Council presidency to pass a Presidential Statement officially recognizing climate change as a security issue, especially for the existence of small island states but also in terms of food security (UN Security Council 2011). Since then, climate change has been included in many national security strategies. Brzoska (2012) found references in two-thirds of the 24 countries he surveyed, usually couched in the language of human security requiring improved capacity building for disaster response. It featured as an issue of national security in just four cases (Finland, Russia, UK, US).

Climate security amalgamates previous strands of the environmental security discourse (Dalby 2013). For example, the 2003 Pentagon scenario planning study projects nothing less than global war and the end of civilization as potential outcomes of unmitigated climate change, thereby mobilizing the environmental conflict discourse. The Security Council debate in 2007 was characterized by the environmental conflict and human security discourses, in which the human security discourse has been dominant (Detraz and Betsill 2009; Oels 2012). Climate security, in this sense, is evidence of the success of the human security discourse in capturing the environmental debate. This is reflected in the rather strong consensus in the academic literature that climate change will not immediately trigger conflicts (Gleditsch et al. 2007).

Terroristic environments

The underlying notion of the environment, however, changes with the advent of climate change. The scientific construction of climate change increasingly recognizes the global climate system as a non-linear entity with tipping points that could lead to the collapse of the Gulf Stream or the death of the Amazonian rainforests (Lenton et al. 2008). As a result, climate change is increasingly considered to be radically uncertain and unpredictable (Methmann and Rothe 2012, on the epistemology of the unknown see Chapter 5 by Burgess in this volume). In the words of Mike Duffield (2011: 763), climate change has turned into 'environmental terror', 'an environment that, operating through uncertainty and surprise, has itself become terroristic.'

The relationship between human and ecological systems is reconfigured in terms of complex systems science (Holling 1973). In his ground-breaking paper, 'Resilience and the stability of ecological systems', C.S. Holling distanced ecology from the notion that 'there exists a "balance of nature" to which life will return eventually if left to self-repair' (Walker and Cooper 2011: 145). Instead, ecological systems were redefined as complex adaptive systems that contained multiple equilibria. The resilience of ecosystems, then, is not defined in terms of returning to an initial state after external stress, but as 'a measure of the ability of these systems to absorb changes of state variables, driving variables, and parameters, and still persist' (Holling 1973: 17). This is the notion of the environment that surfaces in the discourse about apocalyptic climate change and security.

From security to resilience

Complex adaptive systems require a very different strategy of securing than one based on preservation. Rather than stabilizing a certain status quo, 'a management approach based on resilience would emphasize the need to keep options open' and 'to devise systems that can absorb and accommodate future events in whatever unexpected form they may take' (Holling 1973: 21).

If uncertainty prevails, if we cannot predict, prevent or preempt a shock, then we have to invest in the 'preparedness' of those potentially affected by the threat (Collier and Lakoff 2008). Fostering resilience is a strategy of preparing for environmental terror – a 'paradigm of prudence' (Diprose et al. 2008). Security governance must thus invest in the resilience of social systems like 'critical infrastructure' (Lundborg and Vaughan-Williams 2011). In this sense, security does not seek to tame contingencies but governs 'through contingency', creating adaptive and resilient life that is able to sustain and transform itself in the face even of dramatic environmental change (Dillon 2007). What is more, '[l]ife that is exposed to environmental uncertainty can properly develop the desirable attributes of foresight, enterprise, and self-reliance' (Duffield 2011: 758).

Resilience perfectly dovetails into neo-liberal modes of thought (Reid 2012). As the term implies, resilient life does not need to be saved, and is rendered as self-reliant and responsible. Northern interventions are therefore much more limited in scope: They are about helping the affected populations help themselves. This also implies new roles for those doing the securing, since no conceptual distinction is made between the empowering practices of the domestic state and those of international interveners, as both are constructed as pursuing the same tasks of dispersing the power or agency to secure, rather than as acting as securing actors per se (Chandler 2012a: 224). Thriving on this emancipatory note in human security, resilience is now promoted as a key means of reducing human vulnerability.[5]

The diffusion of responsibility

The changed nature of the environmental security paradigm that emerges with the climate security discourse has a number of political implications, some of which persist today and are transforming previous forms of securing the environment. First of all, the resilience paradigm results in an individualization of the problem. Notably, the global political economy that produces vulnerability in developing countries in the first place is left out of the picture and 'naturalized':

> The view that climate change, rather than underdevelopment, is responsible for poverty, results in an outlook that tends to blame local survival strategies, such as cutting down trees to make some money from selling charcoal.
> (Chandler 2012b: 128)

The subject of resilience is a:

> politically debased subject which accepts the disastrousness of the world it lives in as a condition for partaking of that world and which accepts the necessity of the injunction to change itself in correspondence with the threats and dangers now presupposed as endemic.
> (Reid 2012: 75)

There is no longer any discussion of the fact that Northern fossil fuel-based lifestyles are responsible for climate change. Instead, the debate focuses on how Southern populations can survive in a world where apparently unavoidable climate change wreaks havoc.

Secondly, and as a result, the resilience paradigm lowers Northern expectations. The aim is no longer to raise absolute wealth levels or to fight poverty. Instead, development policy focuses only on increasing the self-reliance of the poor and ensuring that they are resilient to shocks (Chandler 2012a; Duffield 2011). This approach complements increased skepticism concerning the ability of official development assistance to foster development.

Thirdly, it is important to acknowledge that this version of security, like the previous ones, is not innocent when it comes to the use of violence. Its focus on resilience does not imply that there will no longer be military interventions. Those who fail to comply with advanced liberal government, those who fail to adapt to climate change in preconceived ways, may be tackled with military violence if considered necessary. Such use of violence is then however not framed as overriding the sovereignty of affected states. Instead, the intervening forces are represented as working hand in hand with the government conceptualized as in need of support.

152 *Chris Methmann and Angela Oels*

It does mean, however, that even when military intervention takes place, it is discursively framed as an act of facilitating, empowering or capacity-building the vulnerable subjects on the ground (Chandler 2012a: 225). In this sense, climate security develops the emancipatory notion contained in human security, but at the same time integrates it into a neo-liberal scheme that focuses on making people fit for survival in times of apocalyptic change.

Conclusion

In this chapter, we have sought to challenge the dominant narrative of environmental security as one of progress and emancipation. Through our genealogy of environmental security, we have revealed three different but interrelated discourses. First, environmental conflict sees the environment as a resource and links it, through a neo-Malthusian logic, to the traditional toolkit of sovereign security. Second, environmental security is tied to the notion of human security. Understanding the environment as a coupled human–ecological system, it argues for targeted biopolitical interventions into particularly vulnerable populations. Finally, climate security doubts that such targeted governance will be possible at all, as future environmental change is deemed radically uncertain and complex. Instead of a top-down governance of affected populations, it seeks to foster the resilience of Southern (and to some extent Northern) populations to make them fit for survival in times of an apocalyptic climate change. All three, however, do not rule out the use of force and military interventions, as the vulnerable are always on the brink of becoming dangerous.

Concluding our analysis, we think that the Foucauldian approach to security adopted here is able to overcome two pitfalls. First, it safeguards against a state-focused (see Chapter 1 by Glaser in this volume) or essentialized notion of security which is implied in the notion of broadening the security agenda. We have identified that not only the reference object of security – here the environment – can adopt different shapes, but that this also results in a transformation of what it means to secure. Whereas other, even constructivist, approaches such as the Copenhagen School take security for granted, Foucault allows us to distinguish between three different modes of securing. Second, the Foucauldian approach has advantages from a normative point of view, as it allows us to empirically extract the broader policy implications embodied in the conceptions of both 'environment' and 'security' for those affected by the policies. In this sense, Foucault allows us to recognize the story of environmental security for what it is: not a success story with a happy ending in store, but a never-ending disaster movie.

Notes

1 For environmental conflicts see Homer-Dixon (1991); for environmental migration see El-Hinnawi (1985).
2 For a comparison of different approaches to security see Oels (2012).
3 In contrast to Realist notions of power as repressive (see Chapter 6 by Glaser and Masala in this volume), Foucault conceptualizes power as productive. For Foucault, power

works through discourse(s). Discourses constitute certain subject positions, they enable certain modes of making sense of the world and they encourage certain practices. As a result, they are in a quite material sense productive of 'reality'. At the same time, they disable or make more difficult other subject positions, practices and realities.

4 A case in point for this shift is the dominance of environmental security in recent UN Security Council debates on climate change and security, see Detraz and Betsill (2009).
5 An example of this is WRI (2008).

References

Aradau, C. (2004) 'The Perverse Politics of Four-Letter Words: Risk and Pity in the Securitisation of Human Trafficking', *Millennium – Journal of International Studies*, 33 (2): 251–77.

Aradau, C and van Munster, R. (2011) *Politics of Catastrophe: Genealogies of the Unknown*, London: Routledge.

Baldwin, A. (2012) 'Orientalising Environmental Citizenship: Climate Change, Migration and the Potentiality of Race', *Citizenship Studies*, 16 (5–6): 625–40.

Balzacq, T. (2010) 'A Theory of Securitization: Origins, Core Assumptions, and Variants', in T. Balzacq (ed.) *Securitization Theory: How Security Problems Emerge and Dissolve*, London: Routledge: 1–31.

Barnett, J. (2000) 'Destabilizing the Environment-Conflict Thesis', *Review of International Studies*, 26 (2): 271–88.

(2001) *The Meaning of Environmental Security: Ecological Politics and Policy in the New Security Era*, New York: Zed Books.

Brauch, H.-G. (2009) *Facing Global Environmental Change: Environmental, Human, Energy, Food, Health and Water Security Concepts*, Berlin: Springer.

Brzoska, M. (2012) 'Climate Change as a Driver of Security Policy', in J. Scheffran, M. Brzoska, H.G. Brauch, P.M. Link and J. Schilling (eds) *Climate Change, Human Security and Violent Conflict: Challenges for Societal Stability*, Berlin: Springer, 165–84.

Collier, S.J. and Lakoff, A. (2008) 'Distributed Preparedness: The Spatial Logic of Domestic Security in the United States', *Environment and Planning D: Society and Space*, 26 (1): 7–28.

Chandler; D. (2012a) 'Resilience and Human Security: The Post-Interventionist Paradigm', *Security Dialogue*, 43 (3): 213–29.

Chandler, D. (2012b) 'Development as Freedom? From Colonialism to Countering Climate Change', in J.S. Sörensen and F. Söderbaum (eds) *The End of the Development-Security Nexus? The Rise of Global Disaster Management, Development Dialogue*, 58: 115–129.

Crutzen, P.J. (2002) 'Geology of Mankind', *Nature*, 415 (6867): 23.

Dalby, S. (1996) 'The Environment as Geopolitical Threat: Reading Robert Kaplan's "Coming Anarchy"', *Ecumene*, 3 (4): 472–96.

(2002) *Environmental Security*, Minneapolis: University of Minnesota Press.

(2013) 'Security,' in C. Death (ed.) *Critical Environmental Politics*, London: Routledge.

Dean, M. (2010) *Governmentality: Power and Rule in Modern Society*, London: SAGE.

Detraz, N. and Betsill, M.M. (2009) 'Climate Change and Environmental Security: For Whom the Discourse Shifts', *International Studies Perspectives*, 10 (3): 303–20.

Deudny, D. (1990) 'The Case against Linking Environmental Degradation and National Security', *Millennium – Journal of International Studies*, 19 (3): 461–76.

Dillon, M. (1995) 'Sovereignty and Governmentality: From the Problem of the "New World Order" to the Ethical Problematic of the World Order', *Alternatives: Global, Local, Political*, 20 (3): 323–68.

(2007) 'Governing through Contingency: The Security of Biopolitical Governance', *Political Geography*, 26 (1): 41–7.

Dillon, M. and Reid, J. (2009) *The Liberal Way of War: Killing to Make Life Live*, London: Routledge.

Diprose, R. et al. (2008) 'Governing the Future: The Paradigm of Prudence in Political Technologies of Risk Management', *Security Dialogue*, 39 (2–3): 267–88.

Duffield, M. (2011) 'Total War as Environmental Terror: Linking Liberalism, Resilience, and the Bunker', *South Atlantic Quarterly*, 110 (3): 757–69.

Duffield, M. and Waddell, N. (2006) 'Securing Humans in a Dangerous World', *International Politics*, 43 (1): 1–23.

Edwards, P.N. (2010) *A Vast Machine: Computer Models, Climate Data, and the Politics of Global*, Cambridge (MA): MIT Press.

Escobar, A. (1996) 'Constructing Nature: Elements for a Post-Structuralist Political Ecology', *Futures*, 28 (4): 325–44.

El-Hinnawi, E. (1985) *Environmental Refugees*, Nairobi: UNEP.

Floyd, R. (2007) 'Towards a Consequentialist Evaluation of Security: Bringing Together the Copenhagen and the Welsh Schools of Security Studies', *Review of International Studies*, 33 (2): 327–50.

(2008) 'The Environmental Security Debate and its Significance for Climate Change', *The International Spectator*, 43 (3): 51–65.

(2010) *Security and the Environment: Securitisation Theory and US Environmental Security Policy*, Cambridge: Cambridge University Press.

Gleditsch, N.P. (1998) 'Armed Conflict and the Environment: A Critique of the Literature', *Journal of Peace Research*, 35 (3): 381–400.

Gleditsch, N.P., Nordas, R. and Salehyan, I. (2007) *Climate Change and Conflict: The Migration Link*, New York: International Peace Academy.

Gleick, P.H. (1989) 'The Implications of Global Climatic Changes for International Security', *Climatic Change*, 15 (1–2): 309–25.

Hajer, M.A. (1995) *The Politics of Environmental Discourse: Ecological Modernization and the Policy Process*, Oxford: Oxford University Press.

Hartmann, B. (2006) 'Liberal Ends, Illiberal Means: National Security, "Environmental Conflict" and the Making of the Cairo Consensus', *Indian Journal of Gender Studies*, 13 (2): 195–227.

Harvey, D. (1996) *Justice, Nature, and the Geography of Difference*, Cambridge: Blackwell Publishers.

Holling, C.S. (1973) 'Resilience and Stability of Ecological Systems', *Annual Review of Ecology, Evolution, and Systematics*, 4: 1–23.

Homer-Dixon, T.F. (1991) 'On the Threshold: Environmental Changes as Causes of Acute Conflict', *International Security*, 16 (2): 76–116.

(1999) *Environment, Scarcity, and Violence*, Princeton: Princeton University Press.

Homer-Dixon, T.F., Boutwell, J.H. and Rathjens, G.W. (1993) 'Environmental Change and Violent Conflict', *Scientific American*, February: 38–45.

Jakobeit, C. and Methmann, C. (2012) '"Climate Refugees" as a Dawning Catastrophe? A Critique of the Dominant Quest for Numbers', in J. Scheffran et al. (eds) *Climate Change, Human Security and Violent Conflict*, Berlin: Springer: 301–14.

Kaplan, R.D. (1994) 'The Coming Anarchy', *The Atlantic Monthly*, 273 (2): 44–76.

Lenton, T.M. et al. (2008) 'Tipping Elements in the Earth's Climate System', *Proceedings of the National Academy of Sciences (PNAS)*, 105 (6): 1786–93.

Lövbrand, E., Stripple, J. and Wiman, B. (2009) 'Earth System Governmentality: Reflections on Science in the Anthropocene', *Global Environmental Change*, 19 (1): 7–13.
Lundborg, T. and Vaughan-Williams, N. (2011) 'Resilience, Critical Infrastructure, and Molecular Security: The Excess of "Life" in Biopolitics', *International Political Sociology*, 5 (4): 367–83.
Mathews, J.T. (1989) 'Redefining Security', *Foreign Affairs*, 68 (2): 162–77.
Methmann, C. and Rothe, D. (2012) 'Politics for the Day after Tomorrow: The Logic of Apocalypse in Global Climate Politics', *Security Dialogue*, 43 (4): 323–44.
Methmann, C. and Oels, A. (2013) 'Vulnerability', in C. Death (ed.) *Critical Environmental Politics*, London: Routledge: 277–86.
Myers, N. (1989) 'Environment and Security', *Foreign Policy*, 74 (Spring): 23–41.
Myers, N. and Kent, J. (1995) *Environmental Exodus: An Emergent Crisis in the Global Arena*, Washington: Climate Institute.
O'Brien, K. et al. (2004) 'Mapping Vulnerability to Multiple Stressors: Climate Change and Globalization in India', *Global Environmental Change*, 14 (4): 303–13.
Oels, A. (2005) 'Rendering Climate Change Governable: From Biopower to Advanced Liberal Government', *Journal of Environmental Policy and Planning*, 7 (3): 185–207.
—— (2012) 'From "Securitization" of Climate Change to "Climatization" of the Security Field: Comparing three Theoretical Perspectives', in J. Scheffran et al. (eds) *Climate Change, Human Security and Violent Conflict*, Berlin: Springer: 185–206.
—— (2013) 'Rendering Climate Change Governable by Risk: From Probability to Contingency', *Geoforum*, 45 (March): 17–29.
Peluso, N.L. and Watts, M. (2001) *Violent Environments*, Ithaca: Cornell University Press.
Reid, J. (2012) 'The Disastrous and Politically Debased Subject of Resilience', *Development Dialogue*, 58: 67–80.
Rose, N. (2001) 'The Politics of Life Itself', *Theory, Culture & Society*, 18 (6): 1–30.
Stritzel, H. (2007) 'Towards a Theory of Securitization: Copenhagen and Beyond', *European Journal of International Relations*, 13 (3): 357–83.
Suhrke, A. (1994) 'Environmental Degradation and Population Flows', *Journal of International Affairs*, 47 (2): 473–96.
Swyngedouw, E. (2010) 'Apocalypse Forever? Post-Political Populism and the Spectre of Climate Change', *Theory, Culture & Society*, 27 (2–3): 213–32.
Tuathail, G.Ó. and Luke, T.W. (1994) 'Present at the (Dis)integration: Deterritorialization and Reterritorialization in the New Wor(l)d Order', *Annals of the Association of American Geographers*, 84 (3): 381–98.
Ullman, R.H. (1983) 'Redefining Security', *International Security*, 8 (1): 129–53.
UNDP (1994) *Human Development Report: New Dimensions of Human Security*, New York: United Nations.
UN Security Council (2011) '6587th meeting', July 20, Part 1.
UN Secretary General (2009) *Climate Change and its Possible Security Implications*, New York: United Nations.
Walker, J. and Cooper, M. (2011) 'Genealogies of Resilience from Systems Ecology to the Political Economy of Crisis Adaptation', *Security Dialogue*, 42 (2): 143–60.
Walt, S.M. (1991) 'The Renaissance of Security Studies', *International Studies Quarterly*, 35 (2): 211–39.
WRI (2008) *Roots of Resilience: Growing the Wealth of the Poor*, Washington: WRI.

9 Financial security[1]

Nina Boy

As the Introduction to this volume reminds us, the meaning of security has undergone a fragmentation, or extension, since the end of the last century. A growing awareness of transnational security actors and threats has given rise to a plethora of new security concepts such as human security, environmental security and societal security. In particular since the financial crisis of 2007–2010, these also often include 'financial security' as a new non-state security concept (see Chapter 5 by Burgess in this volume). While the financial crisis has certainly sparked new interconnections between finance/ financialisation and security/ securitisation, financial security denotes a meaning of security in its own right both as 1) pledge, or collateral and 2) financial contract, or commodity. This chapter argues that these two different senses of financial security have taken a peculiar overlap in the government bond that critically transformed Western statehood: sovereign debt not only turned into the *safe asset* of the financial system, but it has also become the most common form of collateral, that is, security for other financial transactions (Riles 2011). The chapter thus returns the focus of security studies to the state. Yet rather than with the military state (see Chapter 6 by Masala in this volume), the concern is with the credible sovereign. This 'version' of state security is traced in four particular manifestations: the historical term of *public credit*; the *liquid government bond*; the *risk-free asset* of financial-economic textbooks; and the '*safe haven*' role assumed by the bond market in times of 'uncertainty'. As such, it finds itself at the intersection of the various disciplines of security studies, political economy, economic sociology, economic history and literature studies.

A growing literature has begun to explore the intimate relations of finance and security concealed by the disciplinary and professional segregation of the two fields (Amoore 2011; de Goede 2005, 2010, 2012; Langley 2013, 2015; Lobo-Guerrero 2011, 2012; Martin 2007; see also the contributions in the *Security Dialogue* Special Issue 2011 42(2) and Boy *et al.* 2011). These have tended to conceive of the relationship either as a securitisation (in the Copenhagen sense of the term[2]) of finance or as a financialisation of security. The *securitisation of finance* has been observed in two respects: first, the fight against terrorist finance has led to the increased policing of the financial system in regimes of financial surveillance (Amicelle 2011; de Goede 2012). Second, the financial crisis has been argued to not only have been governed as a crisis of the economy, but also as a crisis of security (Langley 2013, 2015). The reassigning of funds of the US Fed TARP Programme from absorbing 'toxic assets' to recapitalising banks is seen as indication of a shift from risk-based regulation to a logic of preparedness and resilience (Langley 2013).

If security and finance converge in a common paradigm of crisis governance, security rationales and practices have also been said to be subject to *financialisation*. Aitken (2011), for example, read the increasing significance of political prediction markets as an attempt to employ the market mechanism as best possible coordinator under uncertainty. The US-led *War on Terror* has been said to emulate a financial logic of risk management (Martin 2007), while UK border security is governed by algorithmic programmes that follow the logic of financial derivatives (Amoore 2011).

In contrast to these, sovereign creditworthiness is here described as a *securitisation in the financial sense*, that is, the becoming liquid and credible of debt. This difference is primarily analytical, if not heuristic, since these different securitisations not only overlap in practice but it is precisely the question of their correspondence that is at stake in discussions of political and financial security.[3] The chapter will begin with a historical tracing of the two financial senses of security, both of which remain central to the operation of financial markets today. The next sections will discuss the notions of *public credit*, *liquid bond*, *risk-free asset* and *safe haven* in more detail. The remaining two sections discuss the analytical relation between these different terms as one of *translation* and conclude with some reflections on political and financial security.

Financial security: pledge and bond

'Security' in the legal sense of collateral or pledge, or 'securities' as the common term for stocks and bonds in financial discourse, seem to bear no or only distant reference to political understandings of security as protection or freedom from danger. Conceptual histories of security barely mention the financial-legal sense of security, if at all (cf. Conze 1984; Rothschild 1995; Wæver 1997, 2004).[4] Early contributions to critical security studies that do so refer to the financial sense of security in an admittedly 'descriptive' manner mainly to illustrate different intelligibilities of security. The main impetus here has been to undermine the 'ontotheology' of international relations' axiomatic understanding of state security, not to enquire much further into their relation or relevance (cf. Der Derian 1995).[5]

The connotation of 'security' as pledge or collateral dates back to antiquity. In his *Histories*, Herodotus remarks that Egyptian creditors 'required as a condition of loan that the debtor pledge the mummy of his father to secure the loan', a pledge deemed of such 'intense religious concern' to satisfy the debt (Squillante 1982: 618). In archaic Greek law, pledge or pawn corresponds to the term *symbolon*: At the time of barter the consent of two contractors was not sufficient to establish a contract of exchange and required a *symbolon* to serve as witness to the transaction (Shell 1978: 34). A 'symbolon' (from Greek *symbállein* – to put together) was a token of recognition in the form of an object – such as a coin, bone or picture – that was 'divided specifically for the purpose of later comparison' (Shell 1978: 33). Alternatively, the parties exchanged a small item like a ring as mutual security for the agreement but, importantly, the coin or ring serving as *symbola* did not function as money but merely as 'a necessary symbol of credit or trust' for the actual transaction (Shell 1978: 33). Similarly, for oral agreements in thirteenth century England, 'a penny, or a larger amount, called a handsel, would be paid "in hand" or "in earnest", to set a seal to a transaction' (Muldrew 1998: 106). Security as the means of securing an obligation was also signified by the Roman *cautio* and the old French word mortgage. Curiously, all three terms – pledge, *cautio* and mortgage – carry an ambivalence of referring to the means of securing an obligation and to the obligation itself (Long 1875: 259). With the rise of monetary transactions and written contracts – 'neither of which', as Shell points out, 'require witnesses' – all *symbola* became down-payments in the modern (Roman) sense of the word and as such 'invisible' (Shell 1978: 33). Yet even when expressed in the same medium, and despite the ambivalent usage, the conceptual difference and autonomy of pledge was retained.

A pledge or collateral initially derived its value – and hence its capacity to secure – from the quality of being manifest as opposed to mobile (cf. Schuhl, quoted in Shell 1978: 32), a common example being fixed property, such as land. Even if 'chattel' explicitly referred to movable collateral other than real estate, it was at first exchanged for safekeeping and entailed a personal, and not alienable, relationship.[6] A first mobilisation of collateral occurred with London goldsmith banking in the mid-seventeenth century, where receipts issued by goldsmiths for gold deposited with them began to be traded on the credit of individual goldsmith bankers. Today the high mobility of collateral is complicated by its *re-use*. As Riles notes:

> if, as is permitted under the law of some countries, the pledgee (the party that receives collateral) "repledges" the collateral to yet another party to satisfy its own obligations, which then repledges it again, then lawyers are left to make sense of a constant global movement of collateral in and out of accounts in many jurisdictions in terms of legal rules created to address a far more stationary and localized conception of property and contract rights.
> (Riles 2011: 43)

Even if mobile, however, collateral retains a conceptual difference as 'accessory' or 'auxiliary' obligation to the promise to pay (Slovenko 1958: 63). Just as 'collateral circulation' in medical discourse refers to 'circulation carried on through lateral or secondary channels after stoppage or obstruction in the main vessels' (OED 1989) and thus stands for latent, but potent, counterfactual circulation, the value of collateral consists in its unactualised, yet guaranteed, capacity to secure either contractual performance, or the solvency of the issuer in the case of non-performance.[7]

From the end of the seventeenth century the English term 'security' itself has evolved from the sense of pledge to also denoting the obligation itself: both 'a document held by a creditor as guarantee of his right to payment' and a common term for debt as well as equity ('securities') (OED 1989). Whether or not 'securities' should refer to equity has been an issue of content since equity implies a *contingent* return – the *Penguin Dictionary of Commerce* thus condemns the indiscriminate 'misuse' of the term for shares and apart from a 'safeguard for a loan' reserves it for negotiable instruments and certificates of liability whose repayment is *guaranteed* (Greener 1970: 296). But shares played a crucial part in rendering sovereign bonds liquid, as will be elaborated below, and 'security' acquiring the meaning of financial commodity in the seventeenth century is closely bound up with the securitisation, that is, the institutionalisation and accreditation of sovereign debt.

Public credit

The peculiar phenomenon of public credit refers to the gradual establishment of sovereign creditworthiness: from sovereign debt being charged a significantly higher rate than commercial loans in the Middle Ages to circulating 'unsecured', that is, no longer requiring additional security in the form of either collateral or a high interest rate but trading merely on 'full faith and credit'.[8] 'Public credit' is the historical term under which a permanent institutionalised government debt was debated in Britain and other Anglophone countries from the end of the seventeenth century until the early twentieth century. Financial phenomena such as bonds, long-term debt and secondary markets in government debt were already features of the Italian city-states to fund wars, and thus some date the invention of public debt to the late Middle Ages (Ferguson 2009). Because of the *coercive* nature of the loans and the uncertain return of principal and interest, others however argue that public credit as a primary and voluntary market in government bonds only developed in post-revolutionary Britain, with what has been termed 'credible commitment' (North and Weingast 1989). The constitutional amendments that instituted Parliament as guarantor turned the royal debt into a national debt and marked a decisive break from the 'financial and commercial distractions which prevailed when States openly violated their solemn contracts, laughed at their obligations, and appeared insensible of the disgrace of disregarding their plighted honour' (The New York Times 1865). Rather than a sudden discovery of virtue, however, the 'mastery of Lady Credit' was the result of manifold factors, including the contested 'invention of financial man' through the disciplining techniques of double-entry bookkeeping (de Goede 2005); the reform of tax collection and administration (Brewer 1990); the moral validation of the insurance trade (Lobo-Guerrero 2012)[9]; and the dramatic increase of the credibility of contract as such during the eighteenth century (Muldrew 1998). Beyond the incorporation of a long-term debt in the creation of the Bank of England in 1694, public credit further implied 'publick Faith' in new monetary instruments, a sense of not only economic but political credibility, and a collective consent to authority. Bolingbroke wrote in 1749 that:

it was said that a new government, established against the ancient principles and actual engagements of many, could not have been so effectually secured any way, as it would be if the private fortunes of great numbers were made to depend on the preservation of it; and that this could not be done unless they were induced to lend their money to the public.

(quoted in Dickson 1967: 19)

Initially the 'security' of public securities was contested repeatedly, and in turn both tested and transformed contractual relations of mutuality. Yet from the mid-nineteenth century, social critique began to focus on the bankruptcy of private individuals and country banks, while the national debt strangely eludes this criticism (Brantlinger 1996). Despite a variety of default experiences of nearly all advanced economies in the first half of the twentieth century (Reinhart and Rogoff 2014), sovereign debt came to be perceived as 'safe'. Thus the investment company Blackrock, in a recent re-assessment of sovereign bonds, identifies four 'traditional' elements characterising sovereign debt: 1) an apparently riskless rate of return upon which all other assets trade at a risk premium; 2) a very high degree of liquidity, whereby government debt assumed high-powered money characteristics; 3) its function as a reference point for the valuation of virtually all other asset categories; and 4) its role as a safe-haven asset during times of market stress (Blackrock 2011). The next sections will consider the different aspects of *liquidity*, *risk-free asset* and *safe haven* status of sovereign debt in more detail.

Liquid government security

The term 'liquidity' has only been in use as a metaphor for the condition of financial markets since the end of the nineteenth century (OED 1989), but the association of monetary circulation with fluid dates back to the Hobbesian imagination of circulating money as the blood of the *body politic* (de Goede 2005: 23). Liquidity can be seen as a direct expression of the credit commanded by a financial instrument, marked by a similar price for buying and selling. As Carruthers and Stinchcombe elaborate, British government debt was 'liquidified' through indirect capitalisation via the three main joint-stock companies: the Bank of England, the South Sea Company and the East India Company. These companies issued shares on the stock market and loaned funds to the government, so that buying a share represented an indirect investment in the national debt (Carruthers and Stinchcombe 1999: 373). The London stock market had been highly 'illiquid' during the seventeenth century due to high transaction costs and the cumbersome procedures for transferral of title, but by 1710 had turned 'very active, highly centralised, and extremely liquid' while direct forms of government lending, such as annuities and lotteries, remained illiquid.[10] Regardless of the huge losses of the South Sea Bubble in 1720, the number of national creditors continued to rise and despite his general condemnation of the public debt, Hume acknowledged in 1752 that 'public securities are with us become a kind of money, and pass as readily at the current price as gold or silver – no merchant now thinks it necessary to keep by him any considerable cash' (quoted in Brantlinger 1996: 92).[11]

The phenomenon of *liquid debt* consists in a peculiar merging of the present and the future: it both expresses actual circulation and reflects the perceived *potential* to circulate. If debt as a 'conditionality spanning the future' (Lepinay 2007: 95) entails uncertainty, the price of which is paid in the form of interest, liquid debt has come to be imbued with the certainty (and unprofitability) of the present. As Keynes held, interest is not a reward for saving but for parting with liquidity (Keynes [1936] 2008: 108). It is illuminating to contrast the phenomenon of a liquid bond with Zygmunt Bauman's conception of liquidity (Bauman 2000, 2002). For Bauman, the predictability of the fixed institutions of classic modernity has been superseded by the uncertainty of 'liquid modernity'. In the 'fluid world of globalisation, deregulation and individualisation' (Bauman 2002: 19), primarily driven by unbridled financial markets, nothing keeps its shape and social relations undergo constant change. In this state, 'bonds' as constraining and uniting forces of mutuality secured by the law and 'bonding' as 'a term that signifies the stability of solids' (Bauman 2000: 2) have become cumbersome, ineffective and possibly 'harmful' arrangements that demand costly maintenance and are eschewed in favour of novel 'liquid' techniques of power of the present that neither 'fix space nor bind time' (Bauman 2000: 2). Bauman's conception almost stands in direct opposition to the financial meaning of liquidity, which 'dries up' when confronted with irredeemable uncertainty and the flows of which depend on plausible narratives and trust. As Lepinay notes, liquidity is 'an index of a common world', while periods of high volatility are described as 'moments of high uncertainty about the definition of individuals and goods, moments in which stable ontologies crumble' (Lepinay 2007: 99). It is not the (im)materiality of a product but the uncertainty of its definition that has adverse effects on liquidity. Rather than the 'paramount source of uncertainty' (Bauman 2000: 121), liquidity follows from the accommodation of contingency into calculable risk: the successive innovations of modern finance theory to price financial instruments as well as credit ratings and structured finance decisively contributed to an era of 'liquid finance'. Yet what distinguishes the liquid government security from other 'bull markets' is that it remains liquid, and even thrives, when all else fails, as will be elaborated in the *Safe haven* section. Simply equating liquidity with capital mobility therefore overlooks a paramount difference between markets and between different market attitudes towards the future.

Risk-free asset

As de Goede (2005) has shown, early debates on public credit formed a critical first moment in the rationalization of finance and economics as scientific truth-telling domains. In the twentieth century, sovereign creditworthiness assumes an explicit function *within* modern finance theory with Tobin's introduction in 1958 of a 'risk-free asset' to modern portfolio theory. Markowitz (1952) had laid down the foundations of modern portfolio theory by developing a systematic approach to investment that distinguished between the riskiness of an individual security and

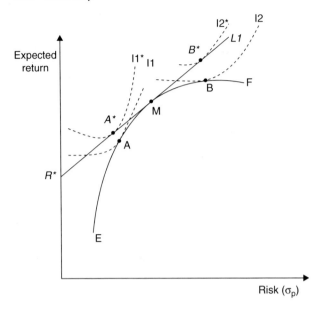

Figure 9.1 The Capital Market Line and the Market Portfolio[12] (Pilbeam 2005: 194)

the riskiness of a portfolio. An efficient portfolio, i.e. the highest return for any given level of risk, or the lowest risk for any given level of return, was achieved by the optimal *correlation* between different assets. The ideal combination of two risky assets was mapped out as the 'efficiency frontier'. Tobin (1958) extended Markowitz's analysis by introducing a riskless asset, based on the assumption of the certain return of a government bond, which investors could either borrow or lend. The effect of including the risk-less asset produced 'the striking result that the efficient set become[s] a linear line known as the capital market line' (Pilbeam 2005: 178). The Capital Market Line (corresponding to line R*L1 in Figure 9.1) dominated positions on the efficiency frontier and improved the risk-return ratio for both risk-averse and risk-embracing investors: people investing a share of their portfolio in bonds (lending to the government) could hereby lower their overall portfolio risk, while investors borrowing at the risk-free rate could achieve an excess market return according to the model (see Figure 9.1: both the risk-averse investor A and risk-embracing investor B achieve a better risk-return trade-off when lending/ borrowing at the risk-free rate, corresponding to the points A* and B* on the Capital Market Line). If the long-contested activity of speculation had been rationalised during the nineteenth century as professional risk-bearing, supporting economic production by offsetting the risk of the majority of hedgers (de Goede 2005), the introduction of a risk-free asset can be said to have provided a rationale for *leveraged* speculation.

Tobin was awarded the Nobel Prize in Economics in 1981 'for his analysis of financial markets and their relations to expenditure decisions, employment, production and prices' (Nobel Prize Website 1981) partly based on his seminal 1958 paper. Yet the concept of the risk-free asset by no means constitutes the central focus or innovation but rather takes the place of a helpful instrumentalisation and 'given' means to improve the risk/return efficiency of portfolio investment. The risk-free rate continues its elemental but 'backstage' function in the 1973 Black-Scholes option pricing formula that set off the tremendous post-Bretton Woods growth in derivatives trading.[13] While options had been traded since the seventeenth century, 'scientific finance' conceived a way to calculate the value of an option by linking stock price, option price, stock volatility, the riskless rate of interest and time, based on the price of the underlying asset moving according to the 'random walk' model of the normal distribution. The impact of the formula consisted in particular in a novel methodology which, in order to value a derivative, 'identif[ied] a "replicating portfolio" or perfect hedge' and then 'invoke[d] the fact that a position that consists of a perfectly hedged derivative is riskless, and thus can earn only the riskless rate of interest' (MacKenzie 2007: 59).[14] The riskless position of the hedge – achieved by neutralising a 'long position' in the underlying asset with a 'short position' in positions – differs from the risk-free rate because it is based on the negative correlation of market risk, while the risk-free asset is by definition uncorrelated with any other asset. That is, the entire edifice of option theory hinges on the equivalence of two fundamentally different derivations of safety: the offsetting of a potential negative market movement with the opposite position – the perfect hedge – and the positive assumption of the safe asset based on public credit.

Modern finance theory and its remarkable practical influence thus rest as much on the probabilistic quantification of uncertainty as on the stipulation of a risk-free asset, and the latter is not only a critical element in the pricing of stocks and derivatives but serves as benchmark for valuing *any* financial asset: its inconspicuous existence, subsumed by the general focus of modern finance theory on asset pricing and the calculability of the future, has only somewhat been brought to the fore by the sovereign debt crisis in the wake of the global financial crisis. In what might be called the first systemic debt crisis of 'advanced' economies, the riskless asset has been discovered as the 'bedrock of finance and investment theory' (Peebles 2012), one of the 'cornerstones of the global financial system' (Viñals 2011) and historically the 'rock around which a financial system is built' (*The Economist* 2012a).

Safe haven

Under conditions of 'market stress' and uncertainty investors leave risky assets in a 'flight to safety' to the bond market. This condition can be read from the inverse bond price–yield relationship: increased demand for bonds raises the price and thus lowers the yield, and vice versa. Safe haven yields below three per cent are considered a sign of general market fear and doubt but the more confidently investors assess future prospects the more government bond demand will fall, lowering the price and raising the yield. Raised bond yields of safe havens can, however, signify two opposite conditions: either the imposition of a risk premium due to an increase in the perception of sovereign risk; or prospects of economic growth and an 'ebbing of the panic' that motivates investors to leave unprofitable safety. Borrowing costs for the government may therefore rise due to a better outlook for the economy, while the greater a crisis, the cheaper it is for safe haven countries to borrow, but at the same time the fates of 'state' and 'economy' remain intertwined.

The perception of sovereign creditworthiness indicated by such metaphors as 'safe haven', 'flight to safety' and 'bond shelter' (*The Economist* 2012b) plays a *systemic role of securing value*. This is somewhat different from the regulatory acts of securing financial stability via the stipulation of adequate reserves and collateral at financial institutions. If these regulations have often been circumvented by financial innovation – the credit default swap for example was motivated by the outsourcing of credit risk in order to require less in the way of capital reserves – safe havens draw a more voluntary and unregulated refuge of capital. Yet the regulatory requirement of sovereign debt as collateral also leads to the phenomenon of 'captive buyers'. In the aftermath of the sovereign debt crisis there are 'fewer havens to choose from' (*The Economist* 2012b).[15] The increased demand for safety in an environment where the perception of sovereign creditworthiness is becoming scarce leads to such paradoxical effects as bond yields of the US, Germany and other states going negative in 2012 and 2013. This phenomenon reverses the logic of debt into its antithesis, where creditors pay debtors in order to lend to them.

Analytical relation: translations

How should the relation between public credit, the liquid bond, the risk-free asset and the safe haven role be conceived in analytical terms? The various facets of sovereign creditworthiness seem to be marked by a peculiar relation of both *equivalence* and *difference*. This heterogeneous equivalence may best be captured, without avowing to an essentialist concept of financial security, as instances of *translation*. Translation can be said to describe two levels: first, it expresses the both contingent and equivalent relation between the liquid government security, the epistemic variable and the systemic function of sovereign creditworthiness. Second, implicit in all of these is a translation from debt into credit.

The first usage of the word 'translation' in English referred to the physical removal from one place to another and the standard linguistic connotation of the term is therefore 'already figurative, metaphorical, a carrying over or transfer of meaning from one context to another' (Freeman 2009: 433). A prominent question in literature studies concerns the relationship between that which is translated and that into which it is translated, or the relation between the *translatum* and the *translandum* (Langenohl 2014: 94). The concept of translation carries the conundrum that the 'equivalence', 'adequacy' or 'fidelity' of a translation can never be vouched for, while the theoretical aspiration of equivalence can never be discarded (Langenohl 2014: 94). In other words, translation fails perfect equivalence and yet creates equivalence by definition.

A translational perspective on security has been suggested by Stritzel (2011) in a contribution to the literature on securitisation in the Copenhagen sense of the term (cf. Buzan, Wæver and Wilde 1998; see also Chapter 3 by Fierke in this volume). Securitisation here refers to the performative framing of a socio-political issue in terms of security, thus legitimising certain actions and discarding others. Stritzel proposes a definition of security as a process and result of a translation instead of security as a process and result of a speech act (cf. Wæver 1995), as well as an open meaning of security defined in practice instead of what he submits to be Wæver's traditionalist, ahistorical and non-empirical concept of security (Stritzel 2011: 346). Akin to Stritzel's understanding of translation as a 'bounded' or 'constrained' innovation (Freeman 2009: 433), in which the idea, in Bakhtin's words, does not 'forget its own path and cannot completely free itself from the power of those concrete contexts into which it has entered' (Bakhtin 1984: 201, quoted in Stritzel 2011: 345), the translation between the different terms of public credit, financial instrument and epistemic variable is shaped by both origin and context. In this process the framing in terms of bond market dynamics or in terms of the financial model 'reveal[s] new properties of the idea, object or action and discard[s] others' (Freeman 2009: 432). For example, in the translation of liquid government debt to the parameter of the risk-free asset the representation of sovereign creditworthiness is conceived in relation to and in terms of the previous model of the efficiency frontier of risky assets, revealing a new function in optimising both the safety and efficiency of portfolios while discarding the risk of inflation.

Yet it seems there is a stronger sense of equivalence between the different aspects of financial security than Stritzel maintains for the securitisation of political-social issues, since what is at stake is a translation of 'safety' itself. It is the safe return on government debt that is converted into the riskless asset and generally synonymous to creditworthiness. Although the risk-free asset acquires a distinct form and mode of operation in portfolio theory, it does not become riskless through translation but references a prior perception of safety. This does not mean that the translation is not productive in both ways: Callon (1991: 143) noted that translation transforms both the 'source' and the 'target' in a process of *mutual* definition and inscription. Yet in this case, the translations between the different terms imply and rest on a translation from debt into credit, or in other words, a financial securitisation. This translation of the real absence of debt into the fictive presence of credit entails a concrete, if somewhat imaginary, referent of state security.

Conclusion: political and financial security

Wæver (1995) pointed out that the so-called 'widening debate' still assumed the meaning of security itself as self-evident and merely changed the specifications of the referent of security from the state to a different entity. Rather than redefining security, these approaches were primarily redefining policy agendas (Baldwin 1997)[16]. On the other hand, Huysmans (1998) argued that the alternative competing hierarchy of security referents was formulated in opposition to a clear-cut and uncontested notion of the state. The notion of security described in this chapter relates to both of these concerns: rather than a neologism, it is one of the oldest security concepts around (de Goede 2010). And rather than defining security against the axiomatic state of IR, it presents a different version of the state in terms of a perception of sovereign creditworthiness.

At first glance, security seems to possess a rather different value in political and financial contexts: while protection from danger has a strongly positive connotation, security in finance is associated with low yields, conservation/conservatism or stagnation. In this vein, Buzan's (1983) account of security in the context of the market had defined it in zero-sum relation to efficiency and freedom and Cooper (2004) described the legitimacy of the liberal state in the service of a higher order of insecurity. Yet what is missing in these accounts is the underwriting role of public credit as collateral, epistemic benchmark and safe haven, based on a differentiation of 'risky' and 'riskless' assets that would have had no basis in the seventeenth century.

Despite these differences, financial and political security however also share certain commonalities. First, they both take transitive and intransitive meanings[17]: Just as all early formulations of financial security signify both the means to secure a contract and the contract itself, security in a political sense has alternatively referred to the means of securing a particular value or expectation (for example safe passage, the state, society, the human, population, life) and a condition or norm of being secure. This normative understanding of security as a positive and desirable condition in itself in fact only emerged in the twentieth century in the course of the interwar perception of a 'lost' security. As such it sparked the paradigm of national security of the emerging discipline of international relations (Kaufmann 2003). Second, securitisation as translation from debt into credit, and more broadly understood as 'gaining currency', somewhat resonates with the Copenhagen definition as legitimisation. The 'original' financial meaning of securitisation as the becoming liquid, becoming credible, becoming plausible may thus in fact have more in common with political securitisation than has so far been noted.

Notes

1 This title is the same as de Goede (2010) but where de Goede provides a broad analysis of finance–security relations in the disciplines of IR, IPE and modern finance, this chapter is specifically concerned with the financial sense of security and its relation to the state. The chapter partly draws on my article 'Sovereign safety', *Security Dialogue* (2015) first published on August 7, 2015 as doi:10.1177/0967010615593038, which develops the argument in relation to the Foucaultian *dispositif* of securing circulation.
2 Cf. Buzan *et al.* (1998).
3 For example, prediction markets transform political insecurities into marketable securities and thus also constitute a form of financial securitisation.
4 Conze briefly alludes to the Roman 'civil law technical terminus' of *securitas* as a debt security similar to *cautio* but although he notes that this sense is still alive he does not consider it relevant for the conceptual history of security. See Conze (1984: 832).

5 Der Derian (1995: 28) refers to the sense of 'pledge, bond, surety, sought in the face of danger or debt' as mediating between two other historic meanings of security as 'condition of being protected, free from danger, safety' and 'false or misplaced confidence'.
6 The specific kind of security was specified as *fiducia*, *hypotheca* or *pignus*, implying different conditions for the transfer of security: '*Fiducia* indicated the transfer of ownership to the creditor, who generally but not always retained possession as well; *pignus* indicated the retention of ownership by the debtor, but the transfer of possession to the creditor; and *hypotheca* indicated the retention of both ownership and possession by the debtor but with the creation of a possessory interest in the creditor' (Goebel 1961–62: 29). Mortgage, chattel and pledge continue these different variations of security.
7 A different mechanism for securing the circulation of maritime trade emerged from the thirteenth century with the development of insurance (Lobo-Guerrero 2011: 16). Insurance was fostered by the 'probabilistic revolution' which marshalled a new argument against the Church's condemnation of usury because the new form of measurement provided a justification for the price of interest (Lobo-Guerrero 2011: 29).
8 In the fifteenth century, Italian banks charged Charles VIII of France an interest rate of 100% on war loans while charging Italian merchants 5–10%. The Bank of England's first loan to the government carried double the interest than that at which it discounted trade bills. See Haldane (2009: 1).
9 Maritime insurance both served as instrument in military strategy and fuelled the national debt as merchants and underwriters invested their profits in the 'funds'.
10 The most active trader in Royal Africa Company stock (John Bull) traded 13 times from 1672 to 1679. See Carruthers and Stinchcombe (1999: 370).
11 From 11,000 in 1709, creditors rose to 25,000 in 1737 and 60,000 in 1756. In Muldrew (1998: 116).
12 Keith Pilbeam, *Finance and Financial Markets*, published 2010 [Palgrave Macmillan] reproduced with permission of Palgrave Macmillan.
13 An option is a contract that gives the right, but not the obligation to buy (or sell) a set quantity of assets at a set price.
14 This equation of positions is based on the 'no-arbitrage' stipulation of the efficient market hypothesis, where any price difference would be eliminated by market participants.
15 This resonates to some degree with Bauman's argument that 'safe ports for trust are few and far between, and most of the time trust floats unanchored vainly seeking storm-protected havens' (Bauman 2000: 135–36) yet his juxtaposition of the liquefying power of capital and trust remains problematic.
16 Even if these agendas evidently bear connections to historical conceptions of security – Rothschild (1995) for example relates the 'new' pluralist approach to security of the 1990s to historical liberal understandings of security.
17 I owe this terminology to Andreas Langenohl.

References

Aitken, R. (2011) 'Financialising Security: Political Prediction Markets and Uncertainty', *Security Dialogue*, 42 (2): 123–42.
Amicelle, A. (2011) 'Towards a "New" Political Economy of Financial Surveillance', *Security Dialogue*, 42 (2): 161–78.
Amoore, L. (2011) 'Data Derivatives: On the Emergence of a Security Risk Calculus for Our Times', *Theory, Culture & Society*, 28 (6): 24–43.
Bakhtin, M.M. (1984) *Problems of Dostoevsky's Poetics*, Minneapolis: University of Minnesota Press.
Baldwin, D. (1997) 'The Concept of Security', *Review of International Studies*, 23:5–26.

Bauman, Z. (2000) *Liquid Modernity*, Cambridge: Polity Press.
    (2002) 'The 20th Century: The End or the Beginning?', *Thesis Eleven*, 70: 15–25.
Blackrock (2011) 'Sovereign Bonds – Reassessing the Risk Free Rate', BlackRock Investment Institute, April.
Boy, N., Burgess, J.P. and Leander, A. (2011) 'The Global Governance of Security and Finance: Introduction to the Special Issue', *Security Dialogue*, 42 (2): 115–22.
Brantlinger, P. (1996) *Fictions of State*, Ithaca: Cornell University Press.
Brewer, J. (1990) *The Sinews of Power: War, Money and the English State, 1688–1783*, Cambridge (MA): Harvard University Press.
Buzan, B. (1983) *People, States and Fear: The National Security Problem in International Relations*, Brighton: Wheatsheaf Books.
Buzan, B., Wæver, O. and Wilde, J.d. (1998) 'Security Analysis: Conceptual Apparatus', in B. Buzan, O. Wæver and J.d. Wilde (eds) *Security: A New Framwork for Analysis*, Boulder: Lynne Rienner: 21–47.
Callon, M. (1991) 'Techno-Economic Networks and Irreversibility', in J. Law (ed.) *A Sociology of Monsters: Essays on Power, Technology and Domination*, London and New York: Routledge: 132–61.
Carruthers, B. and Stinchcombe, A. (1999) 'The Social Structure of Liquidity: Flexibility, Markets and States', *Theory and Society*, 28: 353–82.
Conze, W. (1984) 'Sicherheit, Schutz', in O. Brunner, W. Conze and R. Koselleck (eds) *Geschichtliche Grundbegriffe: Historisches Lexikon zur politisch-sozialen Sprache in Deutschland*, Vol. 5, Stuttgart: Klett-Cotta.
Cooper, M. (2004) 'On the Brink – From Mutual Deterrence to Uncontrollable War', *Contretemps*, 4: 2–18.
de Goede, M. (2005) *Virtue, Fortune and Faith: A Genealogy of Finance*, Minneapolis: University of Minnesota Press.
    (2010) 'Financial Security', in J.P. Burgess (ed.) *The Routledge Handbook of New Security Studies*, London and New York: Routledge: 100–9.
de Goede M. (2012) *Speculative Security: The Politics of Pursuing Terrorist Monies*, London: University of Minnesota Press.
Der Derian, J. (1995) 'The Value of Security: Hobbes, Marx, Nietzsche and Baudrillard', in R. Lipschutz (ed.) *On Security*, New York: Columbia University Press: 24–45.
Dickson, P.G.M. (1967) *The Financial Revolution in England*, Macmillan: St Martin's Press.
Ferguson, N. (2009) *The Ascent of Money*, London: Penguin Books.
Freeman, R. (2009) 'What is "Translation"?', *Evidence & Policy*, 5 (4): 429–47.
Goebel, R.J. (1961–62) 'Reconstructing the Roman Law of Real Security', *Tulane Law Review*, 36: 29–66.
Greener, M. (1970) (ed.) *The Penguin Dictionary of Commerce*, Harmondsworth: Penguin.
Haldane, A.G. (2009) 'Banking On the State', *BIS Review*, 139: 1–20.
Huysmans, J. (1998) 'Security! What do You Mean?', *European Journal of International Relations*, 4 (2): 226–55.
Kaufmann, F.-X. (2003) 'Sicherheit: Das Leitbild beherrschbarer Komplexität', in S. Lessenich (ed.) *Wohlfahrtstaatliche Grundbegriffe. Historische und aktuelle Diskurse*, Frankfurt/M.: Campus: 73–104.
Keynes, J.M. ([1936] 2008) *The General Theory of Employment, Interest and Money*, Macmillan: Cambridge University Press.
Langenohl, A. (2014) 'Scenes of Encounter: A Translational Approach to Travelling Concepts in the Study of Culture', in D. Bachmann-Medick (ed.) *The Trans/National Study of Culture*, Berlin: De Gruyter: 93–118.

Langley, P. (2013) 'Toxic Assets, Turbulence and Biopolitical Security: Governing the Crisis of Global Financial Circulation', *Security Dialogue*, 44 (2): 111–26.

—— (2015) *Liquidity Lost: The Governance of the Global Financial Crisis*, Oxford: Oxford University Press.

Lepinay, V.A. (2007) 'Decoding Finance', in D.A. MacKenzie, F. Muniesa and L. Siu (eds) *Do Economists Make Markets? On the Performativity of Economics*, Princeton: Princeton University Press: 87–127.

Lobo-Guerrero, L. (2011) *Insuring Security: Biopolitics, Security and Risk*, Abingdon: Routledge.

—— (2012) *Insuring War: Sovereignty, Security and Risk*, London and New York: Routledge.

Long, G. (1875) 'Cautio' in W. Smith (ed.) *A Dictionary of Greek and Roman Antiquities*, London: John Murray: 259–60, transcribed online by Thayer, W. (2006), available at: http://penelope.uchicago.edu/Thayer/E/Roman/Texts/secondary/SMIGRA*/Cautio.html (accessed 13 June 2013).

MacKenzie, D. (2007) 'Is Economics Performative? Option Theory and the Construction of Derivatives Markets', in D.A. MacKenzie, F. Muniesa and L. Siu (eds), *Do Economists Make Markets? On the Performativity of Economics*, Princeton: Princeton University Press: 54–88.

Markowitz, H.M. (1952) 'Portfolio Selection', *The Journal of Finance*, 7 (1): 77–91.

Martin, R. (2007) *An Empire of Indifference: American War and the Financial Logic of Risk Management*, Durham: Duke University Press.

Muldrew, C. (1998) *The Economy of Obligation: The Culture of Credit and Social Relations in Early Modern England*, Basingstoke and New York: Palgrave Macmillan.

Nobel Prize Website (1981) 'James Tobin', available at: http://www.nobelprize.org/nobel_prizes/economic-sciences/laureates/1981/ (accessed 13 June 2013).

North, D.C. and Weingast, B.R. (1989) 'Constitutions and Commitments: The Evolution of Institutions Governing Public Choice in Seventeenth-Century England', *Journal of Economic History*, 49: 803–32.

Peebles, D.J. (2012) 'Do "Risk-Free Assets" Still Exist?', *context / The AllianceBernstein Blog on Investing*, 12 January, available at: http://blog.alliancebernstein.com/index.php/2012/01/12/do-risk-free-assets-still-exist/ (accessed 13 June 2013).

Pilbeam, K. (2005) *Finance and Financial Markets*, 2nd edn, Basingstoke and New York: Palgrave Macmillan.

Reinhart, C. and Rogoff, K. (2014) Financial and Sovereign Debt Crises: Some Lessons Learned and Those Forgotten In: Claessens S., Kose M.A., Laeven L. and Valencia F. (eds) *Financial Crises: Causes, Consequence and Policy Responses*. Washington, DC: International Monetary Fund, 141–156.

Riles, A. (2011) *Collateral Knowledge: Legal Reasoning in the Global Financial Markets*, Chicago: University of Chicago Press.

Rothschild, E. (1995) 'What is Security?', *Daedalus*, 124 (3): 53–98.

Shell, M. (1978) *The Economy of Literature*, Baltimore: Johns Hopkins University Press.

Slovenko, R. (1958) 'Of Pledge', *Tulane Law Review*, 33: 59–129.

Squillante, A.M. (1982) 'The Pledge as Security Device, Part I', *Commercial Law Journal*, 87: 618–621.

Stritzel, H. (2011) 'Security, the Translation', *Security Dialogue*, 42 (4–5): 343–55.

The Economist (2012a) 'Sovereign Bonds: Oat Cuisine: A Stodgy Asset Class has Become More Complex and More Dangerous', *The Economist*, 11 February, available at: http://www.economist.com/node/21547245 (accessed 13 June 2013).

The Economist (2012b) 'Bond Shelter: America's Ability to Issue Debt is Helped by a Resemblance between Treasuries and Money', *The Economist*, 10 March, available at: http://www.economist.com/node/21549919 (accessed 13 June 2013).

The New York Times (1865) 'Government Securities the Public Credit', *New York Times*, 1 December, available at: http://www.nytimes.com/1865/12/01/news/government-securities-the-public-credit.html (accessed 13 June 2013).

The Oxford English Dictionary (OED) (1989), Oxford: Clarendon Press.

Tobin, J. (1958) 'Liquidity Preference as Behaviour Towards Risk', *The Review of Economic Studies*, 25 (2): 65–86.

Wæver, O. (1995) 'Securitisation and Desecuritisation', in R. Lipschutz (ed.) *On Security*, New York: Columbia University Press: 46–86.

(1997) *Concepts of Security*, Copenhagen: Institute of Political Science, University of Copenhagen.

(2004) 'Peace and Security: Two Concepts and their Relationship' in S. Guzzini and D. Jung (eds) *Contemporary Security Analysis and Copenhagen Peace Research*, London and New York: Routledge: 53–66.

Viñals, J. (2011) 'Government Bonds: No Longer a World Without Risk', *iMFdirect*, 24 March, available at: http://blog-imfdirect.imf.org/2011/03/24/government-bonds-no-longer-a-world-without-risk/ (accessed 13 June 2013).

Part III
Methodologies of Studying Security

10 Imaging security

A visual methodology for security studies

Gabi Schlag

Introduction

On 2 May 2011, President Barack Obama officially announced that Osama bin Laden had been killed by US special forces, concluding his speech by saying, 'on nights like this one, we can say to those families who have lost loved ones to Al-Qaeda's terror, justice has been done' (Obama 2011). Earlier that day, a photo purporting to show a dead Bin Laden, his face smeared with blood, had circulated through the internet and news outlets. This image, however, was a digital collage. In an interview, President Obama said his administration would not publish a photo of the dead body. He argued that the image embargo was to prevent pictures from being presented as trophies or seen as offensive to Muslims, and that the burial of Bin Laden's body at sea would avoid the memorial opportunity of a gravesite. This denial of a documentary picture – an iconoclastic act by the US government – was supplemented by the later release of a series of documentary videos from Bin Laden's hideaway in Pakistan showing him as an old man watching TV and some photos from the mission, his house and the 'crime scene'. Beside the release of these images, which were arguably official 'stand-ins' for the missing documentary photo of the dead body, *Time* magazine found its own iconic substitute for the events: the front cover of a special issue published on 20 May 2011 featured a painted portrait of Bin Laden crossed out with a dripping red X (Time 2011a). With this image, Bin Laden was included in a series of *Time* covers featuring America's most wanted enemies all crossed out with a large X: Abu Muzad az-Zarqawi (19 June 2006), Saddam Hussein (21 April 2003), the Japanese flag (20 August 1945) and Adolf Hitler (7 May 1945) (Time 2011b). Despite the fact that the actual killing of Bin Laden remained invisible, this cover image symbolized more than his bodily death; it restored a state of security and collective identity for the US society and marked a crucial victory in the 'war on terror'.

This story exemplifies that the question of images poses an important dimension of (international) politics. In recent years there has been a growing academic interest in the visual politics of security, in particular since the iconic images of 11 September 2001. It is often assumed that images construct social reality and influence political decision makers, that visual representations are central when legitimacy is claimed in the 'war on terror' (Shepherd 2008). In addition to this, images are used to enforce and criticize contested policies and their usage has repeatedly been accused of propaganda efforts and digital manipulation. The question how powerful images are, however, is nothing new. In the case of the copied dead Bin Laden picture, many essential aspects come together: it is a digital montage, it spread rapidly in the social media networks, it provoked harsh criticism in the Arab world and facilitated a reflection on the legitimacy of the US operation where Bin Laden was killed. Images of dead people are a distinct and ambivalent genre. On the one hand, they give visual form to the limits of inciting sympathy and mercy but also satisfaction when tyrants and dictators are shown dead.[1] On the other hand, the artificial picture of Bin Laden's dead body partly invoked a discourse of war imaginaries showing (presumably) justified enemies as well as (presumably) innocent atrocities while the *Time* cover's X treatment of his death incorporated him into America's most wanted enemies. Bearing such polyphony and ambiguity of the 'war on terror' in mind, it seems that President Obama and the editors of *Time* magazine thoroughly understand that 'a picture is worth a thousand words'.

While the relevance of visual culture to International Relations (IR) and security studies is apparent, it has been a rather recent development to discuss the conceptual and methodological challenges of researching images. I argue that acts like these, of (not) showing and (not) seeing a picture of the dead Bin Laden, direct our attention to the performative power of visual culture. Picture theory, an approach well-known to art historians and students of visual culture, conceptualizes this genuine power of images as an *iconic act* (Bredekamp 2010). The main merit of such an approach is twofold: first, it takes visuality seriously, acknowledging that images have an inherent, symbolic meaning. Thus images are neither subordinated to discourse nor do they serve as mere illustrations or representations of reality; second, picture theory does not deny the discursive embeddedness of images and thus draws our attention to the relation between visuality, discourse and power. It points out how imaginaries are invented, mobilized and re-inscribed by and through the discursive and iconic practices at play (Heck and Schlag 2013).

In this chapter, I will present a brief state of the art of what is increasingly described as a new, 'iconic' turn in critical security studies.[2] Such a turn not only strengthens interest in the well-known question of the power of images, but directs our attention to the constitution of visual regimes in our (post-) modern time. What we are seeing (or *not* seeing) and how 'things' are shown is highly influenced by discourses which enable and constrain what can be meaningfully said and known (for a similar approach, see the contributions by Fierke and by Methmann and Oels in this volume). Thus, the 'iconic turn' does not stand in opposition to what is called the 'linguistic turn' in IR but complements it. A turn to visuality, in particular pictures, is highly relevant to IR and critical security studies because it helps to reveal the social constructedness of security in a broader way. It opens the rather narrow perspective on speech acts and gives more attention to the symbolic and cultural practices which constitute the very meaning of security in the first place.[3]

The first part of the chapter provides an overview of this recent turn to visuality in IR and discusses the different epistemological and ontological positions which come along with picture theory. In addressing the more precise term of an 'iconic turn', I will give a brief overview of an iconic act theory for theorizing images for security studies in an innovative way. However, the most profound challenge to security studies' growing interest in visuality is that of methodology. How to take images seriously? How to analyze images as images *and* as being embedded in discourses and practices? The second part of this chapter will address these aspects and outlines a user's manual.

Imaging security

In recent years, IR scholars have addressed the relation between visuality and politics in different ways and this literature is steadily growing (most recent: Hansen 2015). Within the field of critical security studies, these debates have furthered our conceptual and methodological understanding of the alleged 'power of images', including political memory and war photography, political cartoons, cartographies, films and popular culture, and in particular images from 11 September 2001.[4] The social constructions of securities and insecurities are increasingly dependent on the availability of images: images of the risks and dangers, enemies, casualties, violence, pain and suffering, all with the potential to mobilize public support for contested political decisions. These images are now not just produced by professional journalists any more but are often shot and uploaded by citizens setting the news agenda in Western democracies (Mortensen 2011). Most scholars would agree that, to a broad extent, images shape and frame our understanding of political conflicts. Students of media studies have argued that images, thanks to their effect on public opinion, play a crucial role when governments decide whether to give aid to other countries, use force to end human rights violations or withdraw troops after military interventions. However, the so-called CNN-effect is an oft-cited but rarely proved hypothesis in IR.[5]

Keeping the influence of media representations on politics (and *vice versa*) in mind, it has become commonplace in critical security studies to state that security is a social construction (see Chapter 3 by Fierke and Chapter 8 by Methmann and Oels in this volume). The invocation of security, as Ole Wæver prominently argued, is part of a securitizing move wherein normal procedures of political decision-making are seen in the light of an existential threat to a referent object (Wæver 1995).[6] The conceptual and empirical debate on securitization theory has developed into an extremely fruitful research field in the last 15 years. Scholars are paying more and more attention not only to speech acts in a narrow (linguistic) sense but also to symbolic and visual constructions of security. Lene Hansen and Michael C. Williams in particular have argued that securitization theory should move beyond its exclusive focus on speech acts (Hansen 2011; Williams 2003). Taking these approaches into account, images can play two different roles in processes of securitization and de-securitization: images might become securitized as representations of referent objects, as found in Hansen's analysis of the Danish cartoon crisis. Then, visual securitization directs our attention to processes, 'when images constitute something or someone as threatened and in need of immediate defense or when securitizing actors argue that images "speak security"' (Hansen 2011: 51). Moreover, there might be images that possess the power to securitize referent objects, such as the *Time* cover of a tortured young Afghan woman or as the Doomsday clock of the Bulletin of the Atomic Scientists exemplifies (Heck and Schlag 2013; Vuori 2010). Thus there is strong evidence for a growing tendency towards recognizing images as a genuine research object in IR generally and in critical security studies in particular (Andersen et al. 2015; Hansen 2015). While the social sciences have a long tradition of analyzing media representations and their impact on national and international politics, this new interest in visuality moves beyond a merely illustrative usage of images and directs our attention to the symbolic and iconic dimension of visual culture.

For heuristic purposes, one might distinguish between two different approaches to visuality within the field of critical security studies. On the one hand, links to surveillance studies and the work of Michel Foucault on governmentality have become more prominent in recent years; regimes of seeing and being seen, regulation, control and the disciplinary effects of visual technologies are of interest here (Andersen and Moeller 2012). On the other hand, the more prominent and broader approach to visuality has been an interest in popular culture, which started in IR in the mid 1990s. Movies and photography, and occasionally pieces of art and music, are used to illustrate IR theories. Research approaches often come either with a primarily pedagogical impulse, to illustrate how power, gender, war and otherness are visually constructed (Engert and Spencer 2012; Holden 2006; Offermann and Engelkamp 2012) or with a critical move to re- and deconstruct visual representations and their political implications (for example: Bleiker and Kay 2007; Campbell and Shapiro 2007; Shepherd 2008; Shim 2013; Veeren 2011). While media and visual culture studies are still leading this research field, more and more IR students are becoming interested in the visual construction of security. Thus, the iconic turn complements the linguistic turn by expanding its core argument of 'x is socially constructed'. It is not a rejection of discourses, but an inclusion of forms of articulation other than the spoken and written word (on language and materialism, see also Chapter 3 by Fierke).

Such an approach to visual security, however, raises some difficult questions: Is there a difference between an iconic act and a speech act? And what is unique about images, are they special at all?

The iconic turn, or: 'what is an image?'

It was Susan Sontag's seminal essay *On Photography*, first published in 1977, which prompted a growing academic interest in the political power of images, in particular documentary photography (Sontag 1977). Sontag wrote: 'Photographs furnish evidence. Something we hear about, but doubt, seems proven when we're shown a photograph of it' (Sontag 1977: 5). Nevertheless, she also admitted that taking pictures is not an innocent act of objectivity. Rather: 'To photograph is to appropriate the thing photographed. It means putting oneself into a certain relation to the world that feels like knowledge – and, therefore, like power' (Sontag 1977: 4). In her essay, Sontag goes as far as to argue that taking pictures is an 'act of non-intervention' expressing a voyeuristic interest in the *status quo*, whether it is someone's joy or pain (Sontag 1977: 12). Sontag's remarks resonate with the typical reading of poststructuralist thinking in IR, in particular what Foucault argued about the nexus between power and knowledge. There is no objective and/or neutral depiction of 'reality' – mimesis is an illusion and a powerful myth of IR's 'scientific' approach (Jackson 2011: 9). With these debates in mind, a mimetic approach to visuality has been largely dismissed, either by referencing its epistemological naiveté or to the replicatory potential of digital technologies.[7]

While Sontag seems to be highly critical of photography as a form of knowledge and an instrument of emancipation, students of visual and cultural studies have developed a more analytical approach to visuality since the 1950s (Mirzoeff 2002, 2009). From their perspective, it is assumed that pictures and films are part and parcel of societal and political power relations. Contingent visual regimes influence the way societies interpret norms and values – for example what counts as 'beauty' or a 'just war' – visual media constructs images of 'Otherness' and enmity, and photography documents the good and bad shades of life, often with contentious political implications.[8] The recent turn to visual artifacts in IR and security studies revives the prominence of (critical) constructivist approaches in the social sciences and humanities while moving beyond their often narrow focus on language and text-based discourse.

At the beginning of the 1990s, cultural theorist W. J. T. Mitchell proclaimed the 'pictorial turn' and stated that '[a]lthough we have a thousand of words about pictures, we do not have a satisfactory theory of them' (Mitchell 1994: 9). Such an interest in pictures, images and visuality, however, should not be misunderstood as in opposition to the linguistic turn so much as a *re*-turn to the metaphysics of presence and correspondence (Mitchell 1994: 16). While Mitchell emphasized the discursive embeddedness of images, Gerhard Boehm has argued that images possess a self-contained visual quality that cannot be subordinated to discourses and genealogies. In other words: if one takes the renaissance of images in IR seriously, the turn to visuality constitutes a turn to the performativity of the image as an iconic act. There is something done by seeing/showing an image and this power grows out of its original *visual* forms (Boehm 1994, 2007).

The art historian Horst Bredekamp, who is closely associated with the German discipline of *Bildwissenschaften* (picture theory) that Boehm belongs to, compares the act of showing an image to Searl's influential definition of a speech act. Searl's example was that something happens when one utters the words 'yes, I do' in a specific context, i.e. two people become wife and husband. Bredekamp argues that an image supplements the speaker, that the image literally speaks to the audience and thus performs an act by showing and seeing 'some-thing'. The image embraces a kind of 'auto-activity', an agency which cannot be reduced to the creator or the recipient of visual artifacts (Bredekamp 2010: 52).

Iconic acts are thus socially and politically consequential performances because they constitute a powerful relation between the producer, the image and the spectator. This relation regulates how we see what we see. It's because of this ontology that we should care about images as images instead of analyzing them exclusively as representations of or illustrations within discourses. Theorizing images as iconic acts helps explain the mutual process of showing and seeing, in particular how images are constituted through their *relation* to spectators and producers. Thus, images are neither reduced to objective representations of a subject/object nor overrated as a substitute for 'reality' itself.

Although references to visuality have increased in IR, scholars have only implicitly theorized the images – or to be more precise, the icon – as a genuine research object (Hansen 2015). The image is mostly seen as an representation within a larger discourse and interpreted as an symbolic expression of how images are part and parcel of social constructions. Although such a perspective has strengthened our knowledge of the political implications of visuality, it often subordinates images to discourse. Taking the image seriously requires a methodological sensibility to the performativity of iconic acts as acts of showing and seeing. This statement implies that images – in particular pictures – are not mere depictions of 'reality' (either true or false) but construct powerful reality frames within their symbolic forms (Butler 2010). Their ambivalence and affectiveness makes it even more difficult to systematically interpret the various meanings they produce and their possible 'impact' on politics. As discourse analysis requires a methodology of how to interpret spoken and written words and sentences, a turn to visuality obligates us to reflect on how to analyze the iconic dimension of images and pictures, their stylistic and symbolic forms. The second part of this chapter deals with this question in more detail and suggests a visual methodology, which should not be seen as a value-neutral technique but rather as a way of critically engaging with the visual politics of security (Aradau and Huysmans 2014).[9]

Visual methodologies, or: 'how to interpret images?'

There exist a variety of visual methodologies which appear to be obvious candidates for analyzing and interpreting images (Rose 2012). Scholars have recently attempted these methodological questions in different ways (Andersen et al. 2015; Moore and Farrands 2013). In this contribution, I will focus on the intersection between two approaches: discourse analysis and iconology. Most interpretative methodologies intend to conceptualize the image in relation to the social, political and cultural discourses which give them meaning and power. They differ, however, in the extent to which they focus on the site of the image's production, the site of audiencing or the site of the image itself (Rose 2012: 43).

By site of production, Gillian Rose refers to the circumstances under which an image is produced and how these circumstances might themselves produce effects. The differences between digital and analog media, for example, have fostered a debate on the manipulation and simulation potential of images. Some scholars go so far as to argue that how an image is produced, in particular its technologies, determines 'its form, meaning and effect' (Rose 2012: 20). Because most images are produced to be seen, the site of audiencing directs our attention to a 'process by which a visual image has its meanings renegotiated, or even rejected, by particular audiences watching in specific circumstances' (Rose 2012: 30). Hence, reception analysis has a long tradition in media studies, emphasizing common and diverse practices and structures of 'reading' images.

To my mind, the most neglected site of how IR and critical security studies have approached visuality has been the image itself as a research object (Rose 2012: 27).[10] Here, composition, style and symbols play a crucial role in producing visual meanings. Understanding images and their often-contentious and polyphonic meanings is to some extent comparable to learning a language, including its grammar, vocabularies and practical usage. Thus, understanding an image requires knowledge not only of structural visual elements but also how they are (and have been) used differently. Most approaches to visual representations in IR and security studies focus on the site of audiencing and the question *what kind* of visual meanings and narratives images construct. For example, the growing literature on movies mostly addresses questions of how identity, gender, and war are socially constructed and how movies express some of the key concepts IR and security studies grapple with (and thus are useful in the classroom). While movies are seen as one expression of these socially constructed concepts and IR theories, their original visual qualities as films (*mis en scène*, time and space etc.) are barely of interest. Interpretation is mostly done with the help of discourse analysis, in which the image is conceptualized as part of structures of meaning in use, and the researcher discloses the production of power relations, dichotomies and hierarchies. While the broad inter-textual approach on discourses makes a turn to images easy, most discourse approaches to visuality run the risk of underestimating the visual qualities of the image itself, i.e. its iconic and symbolic characteristics. This narrow focus could easily be overcome by using an existing methodologically refined approach, iconology, as a toolbox to direct our attention to the genealogy and usage of symbolic forms. A connection between the insights from discourse analysis and iconology might help us more fully understand the political power of images.

Discourse analysis

In the last two decades, IR has witnessed a proliferation of discourse approaches within its many subfields, including critical security studies (Holzscheiter 2014; Milliken 1999). Often associated with the label 'post-structuralism' a main goal of discourse analysis is to reconsider the implications and consequences of textual representations for the possibility of action, which means understanding the constitutive relation between agency and structure (George 1994: 191). Although there are many differences between authors who use discourse analysis, the perspective is broadly based on three assumptions: First, discourses are systems of signification where the dominant narrative 'is a representation that arrests ambiguity and controls the proliferation of meaning by imposing a standard and standpoint of interpretation that is taken to be fixed and independent of the time it represents,' as Richard Ashley has put it (Ashley 1989: 263). Representations try to fix meaning in relation and difference to other signifiers (Hansen 2006: 20, 41–6; Milliken 1999: 229, 231–4). In other words: meaning is always about power because these relations lead to (implicit) value judgments whereby one side of the opposition is privileged over the other (Ashley 1988: 230; Milliken 1999: 229, 231ff.). Second, a discourse is productive because it defines subjects authorized to act through knowledgeable practices. A discourse regulates what can be meaningfully said and produces groups and spaces as objects which can be acted upon. Thus, discourse analysis is interested in the ways 'in which power works to constitute particular modes of subjectivity and interpretative dispositions' (Doty 1996: 4). Hence, subjects and objects are more the effects of discourses than pre-existing facts. Third, while discourses might rely on a strong continuity of central representations, their structures are essentially contingent and dependent on the play of practices, i.e. how words are used (Doty 1996: 6). Because language as a differential system lacks an unquestioned foundation of meaning, disciplinary practices, by excluding alternative discourses and thereby limiting the contingent play of practices, are essential to stabilize representations (Ashley 1989: 263; Milliken 1999: 230, 240–4). Well-established hierarchies between a developed ('Western') world and an undeveloped ('non-Western') world, for example, have been a widely used disciplinary practice which made interventions possible, even legitimate. Such representations naturalize self/other relations and might give actors a reason to act in a specific way. Discourses, however, are not exclusively about disciplinary practices in which hierarchy and dominance is imposed on social relations. Heterodox practices direct our attention to the contingency of social representations and help to understand how stable representations can be challenged, de-centered, or even replaced.

As a methodology for interpreting visual representations, discourse analysis directs our attention to: (1) power relations, (2) the construction of identities, and by default, difference, and (3) the contingent meanings audiences might ascribe to images, including the different usage of visual representations for political reasons. If we return to the fictional image of the dead Osama bin Laden as an illustration, a discourse approach could certainly highlight the ambivalence between the 'war on terror'-discourse on the one hand, and a historical 'war casualty'-discourse on the other – both discourses are mobilized by the image. While a documentary picture would be closer to a discourse on war casualties, or even war crimes of torture and killings, the symbolism of the *Time* cover clearly mobilized alternative narratives of collective remembrance within the US public. Knowing that Bin Laden is dead, seeing visual evidence doctored or not, symbolically expresses the victory over one of their most wanted enemies. Hence, some spectators see this image as Obama's political success over Bush, who failed to catch Bin Laden, strengthening his legitimacy as President and the 'leader of the free world'. Other spectators might see this image as an evidence of the unjust and cruel policies of the US administration, killing and executing Muslims in their global 'war on terror'.[11] While some understood Obama's decision to deny an image of the dead Bin Laden as an act of reconciliation and respect, this also helped his administration to avoid a public debate on the mission's legality and legitimacy. Accordingly, Obama's iconoclasm responded to Bin Laden's own careful control over his public image in his video messages. Further research could focus in more detail on the intersection between these discursive and visual artifacts because images are important due to their mimetic and affective powers in shaping our knowledge and remembrance of the 'war on terror'.

Critics might respond that students of IR and security studies should stick to the business of analyzing 'objective' security threats. There is a widely-shared belief that the inclusion of visual data delimits the discipline at the expense of an identifiable core of 'key puzzles' that IR and security studies should deal with if they intend to be relevant to 'real world politics' (Walt 1991; see also Chapter 1 by Glaser). Hence an attitude of 'Oh, just leave images to cultural and visual studies' – the alleged experts on visuality. This is not a reliable or appropriate position for two reasons. First, no one would doubt that we live in a world where (global) media networks play a powerful role in shaping our perceptions of and attitudes towards politics. In fact, it is surprising that IR and security studies are basically latecomers to the 'visual/iconic turn'. Second, constructivism lays increasing emphasis on the social constructedness of identities and communities, gender, race, and conflicts. It remains puzzling why one essential kind of 'data' – visual representations – has only occasionally been included in constructivist (and post-structuralist) work. Symbolic forms do themselves constitute meaning and cannot be reduced to the spoken or written word alone. The main challenge for any student of IR and security studies is not whether the images have an impact on politics but *how*. How do images matter? How does the interpretation of images make a difference for understanding international relations? As Axel Heck and I have argued elsewhere, iconology is a useful approach to visual representations well-known to students of art history that might provide a methodological toolbox for taking images in IR and security studies more seriously (Heck and Schlag 2013). Iconology is not an alternative to or competitor with discourse approaches, instead it fits nicely into the overall concept of a discourse as a 'structure of meaning in use'.

Iconology

The term iconology was prominently framed by Erwin Panofsky (1892–1968), a German-born art historian and expert on Renaissance art who immigrated to the USA in the 1930s and taught at Princeton University. In his essay, 'Iconography and Iconology', first published in 1939 and republished in 1955 and 1970, he defined the latter as a 'method of interpretation which arises from synthesis rather than analysis' (Panofsky 1970: 58).[12] While icono*graphy*, the dominant method of his time, referred to the knowledge of types and styles, Panofsky advocated icono*logy* as a method of synthesis for understanding the meaning of symbolic forms. Hence, the aim of iconology is to reconstruct the symbolic content of images understood in their historical and social context. As a systematic process of interpretation, iconology is based on three stages: (1) the pre-iconic description, (2) the iconographic analysis and (3) the iconological interpretation.

The pre-iconographic description deals with the apparent subject of an image and the objects which are shown to us. To understand an image in its factum, we need practical experiences in order to decode the subjects and objects at hand. Iconographic analysis understands an image based on the conventional and allegorical content which arises from our knowledge of literary sources and historical documents. While an iconographic approach stops here, and focuses on identifying and describing types and styles, Panofsky argues that an iconological interpretation goes a step further, trying to figure out the meaning of an image through its symbolic form. Iconology thus requires a 'history of cultural symbols', i.e. an 'insight into the manner in which, under varying historical conditions, the general and essential tendencies of the human mind were expressed by specific themes and concepts' (Panofsky 1970: 65).

Although iconology is first and foremost a method used to analyze art, its systematic three-step interpretation process is not limited to the world of museums and galleries. One could say that iconology is highly compatible with the discursive approach to visuality advocated by Lene Hansen, who distinguishes between four components of analysis: the visual itself, the immediate inter-textual context, the wider policy discourse and the constitutions of the image (Hansen 2011: 55). While iconography helps to understand the specific stylistic aspects of the image itself and its practical context, an iconological approach enables us to see how images symbolically perform how we see what we see. It's the systematic focus on visuality in its iconic, social, and historical context that makes iconology a valuable method far beyond the work of art historians. Together, discourse analysis and iconology help to understand *how images matter*. The concluding section of this chapter will address how images matter *for security studies*.

A user's manual – understanding *how* images matter for security studies

It's nothing new to argue that images are an important part of politics, that they construct identities, that they influence the perception of conflicts and that they are able to foster political interventions. However, it might be necessary to take a more thorough and reflected view of visual artifacts and their alleged power in international relations to show how, under what circumstances and with what kind of consequences images matter. Picture theory and visual methodologies such as discourse analysis and iconology are starting points – not ends unto themselves. It's not that any student of IR interested in visuality should become a trained art historian. Instead, I would propose extending available approaches to security, in particular securitization theory and its focus on discourses and practices, to the interpretation of visual data. How images matter would remain a question to be answered *in research*. Some general themes might include: (1) visual representations of insecurities, (2) visual representations of identity and otherness, and (3) visual representations of violence and pain.

First, an understanding of how dangers and risks are visually constructed is important to understand the impact images have (or not) on politics. For governments, it might be easier to legitimize a military intervention in the name of 'saving strangers' if disturbing pictures of human rights violations making suffering and pain visible, recognizable and to some extent intelligible are distributed through global media networks. However, the link between pictures and politics is not simply causal but rather *constitutive*. Sometimes we see images of insecurity but do not act; other times we do not see images of threats and act. While studies on the CNN-effect often imply a causal relation between media and politics, it might be more useful to analyze how insecurities are visually constructed and how they confine the limits of political agency. Take the attacks of 11 September 2001 as an example: The picture of the falling man symbolized the ontological insecurity caused to US citizens by terrorism – it made the unthinkable visible. Photographs from September 11, Moeller argues, are not only a 'legitimacy provider for security policy but also part of every person's visual reservoir and pictorial memory, on which the successful articulation of security in part depends' (Moeller 2007: 179). In other words, images can also imbue a de-securitizing potential which can be used to criticize and oppose security politics.

Second, visual representation of self/other relations construct collective identities and can reiterate and/or transform power relations. Hence, how 'the US', 'China' or 'Bin Laden' are visually represented enables and constrains policy options through constructions of identity and difference. The greater the gap between the imagined self and the constructed 'Otherness', the easier it becomes to legitimize extraordinary measures in order to defend one's own community and eliminate its alleged enemies. Historical research on enemy constructions at the start of the First and Second World Wars suggests that images can serve as indicators of escalation and anchors of legitimacy (Hase and Lehmkuhl 1997). Shim and Nabers, for example, have recently argued that our imagination of North Korea as a mostly isolated and excluded pariah state is vastly shaped by visual data, including satellite pictures and photography (Shim 2013; Shim and Nabers 2012). They are interested in 'how images determine the realm of the visible and, no less importantly, the invisible, which render specific actions and statements as legitimate or nonlegitimate' (Shim and Nabers 2012: 7). Images of North Korea shown in Western media stipulate its military 'strength' and internal 'weakness' as the main characteristic of its Otherness, representing it as the 'main antithesis […] of modern globalization' (Shim and Nabers 2012: 9). The way the US public coped with the September 11 terror attacks also reveals the variety of visual representations which are able to restore and unsettle a collective identity: the 'falling man', the collapsing Twin Towers, or President Bush at Ground Zero. But this visual suite also includes images from later on in the 'war on terror': human rights abuses and torture in Fallujah, Abu Ghraib and Guantanamo (Steele 2008; Veeren 2011).

Finally, visual representations of violence and pain raise highly difficult questions of responsibility, moral obligation and even censorship in order to preserve the dignity of those who have been harmed, tortured, and killed. Media networks are often criticized for their displacement and (mis-)use of documentary photos. Image-text-relations are extremely influential when the political consequences of discursive and visual representations of insecurity, identity, and violence are at stake. David Campbell's collaborative study on the representations of famine suggests that documentary photography regularly reaches its limits when suffering and pain are depicted.[13] The close-up of a 'starving black child' or 'a tortured woman' excites primarily pity, and certainly anger; however, it does not necessarily cause a political intervention. The reproduction of stereotypes and the voyeurism associated with documentary photography raises ethical and moral questions which should be reflected on not only within media networks but also by the public who consumes these images.

Students of critical security studies (and IR) have already proven that there are many ways to analyze the oft-cited 'power of images'. A user's manual for understanding how images matter would never be able to encompass the variety of approaches, but I would like to outline some general and essential steps to a visual approach:

- *Step 1*: According to Rose, a visual methodology has to acknowledge the different sites of visuality, i.e. the production, the image and the audience, and its different technical, compositional and social modalities. These sites and modalities share various interdependencies. However, what kind of visual data is relevant and what sites and modalities are of further interest is not a question one can answer in abstract terms, but must instead be related to the overall research question. This may seem obvious, but needs to be clearly established at the outset.
- *Step 2*: Iconology provides clear guidelines how to approach visual data through its iconographic and iconological content. It also requires a 'reading' of more than just the image. Other textual and visual documents become part of a research process on how symbols have been used in different social and historical contexts. One should remember that the main goal of this tool is not art historical, but to pay more attention to the performative power of the iconic act. Since speech act theory provides a specific perspective on what matters and how to analyze it, iconic acts share the family resemblance of a performative approach but require a peculiar vocabulary of description. Iconology provides one systematic and transparent tool to analyze visual data and thus counters many prejudices about the 'non-scientificness' of interpretative methodologies. However, it is not the authoritative and exclusive method for analyzing visual artifacts.

- *Step 3*: The final, and most compelling, step is connecting the results of this interpretation of visual data with questions relevant to scholars in IR and security studies. The three general themes I suggested earlier – representations of security, identity and violence – have been of major interest in the discipline. I believe that the analysis of images, by connecting visual and textual representations of politics, can tell us a lot about these themes. Here, the iconic turn is closely connected to a growing interest in emotions, memory and legitimacy where images do play an important, yet barely factored role in constituting meaning and agency (see Chapter 3 by Fierke).

Many visually-oriented students of IR have been party to conversations in which they were urged to prove the added value of their approach and the relevance of their research questions to the discipline. It is certainly discouraging to hear that 'your research interest is irrelevant to IR, it belongs to art history'. Yet any student must give some compelling (or at least accountable) reasons for why image analysis benefits an understanding of security politics. As mentioned in the introduction to this chapter, the 'war on terror' and its iconic images is certainly one of the most persuasive arguments for the *visual* politics of security. How political decisions are legitimized and symbolic power is exercised through images gives the analysis of visual culture therefore a dedicated political heft.

Conclusion

The global 'war on terror' has certainly revitalized the academic interest in the political relevance of images. It is, as Mitchell points out, an image of war fueled by governments, terrorists, global media networks and everyday people who upload pictures and videos to Facebook, Tumblr and Flickr (Mitchell 2011). Thanks to digital technologies, the production and distribution of images is getting easier while control and decoding is becoming more complicated. International security relations cannot be analyzed without understanding these developments and their impact on politics, in particular in Western democracies. Their publics are highly sensitive to stories and pictures they receive about conflicts and violence and they have the powers to influence their governments through democratic politics.

Looking beyond the narrow focus on speech acts – particularly in security studies and securitization theory – brings to mind how politics are *visually* constructed: the power of images to 'speak security'. In fact, students of visual culture and art history could learn a lot from students of IR and security studies when it comes to how politics are legitimized through the mobilization of discursive and visual practices of security. While visual culture and art history deal with the ontological and methodological aspects of visuality, IR and security studies provide a clear focus on the political relevance of visual culture(s) to the possibilities and limits of agency.

Notes

1 Images of dead people have been taboo in many cultures, including the taboo of showing the dying and/or the faces of slaughtered people; yet, media often show such disturbing images in order to attract attention. Accordingly, there is often a cult of the dead leader presenting his body to the public, a practice well-known to Western societies through the artistic presentation of royals and clerics since the Middle Ages.
2 This turn has also been labeled the 'visual' or 'pictorial' turn. I prefer the notion 'iconic' here because it is more precise and directs our attention to the material and symbolic dimension of a picture
3 Due to space limitations there will be no systematic interpretation of images and/or pictures in this chapter. For different accounts of how insights from visual methodology can be used in critical security studies, see Hansen (2011, 2015), Heck and Schlag (2013), Bleiker and Kay (2007), Andersen et al. (2015).
4 See for example, Campbell (2003); Campbell and Shapiro (2007); Hansen (2011); Moeller (2007); Neumann and Nexon (2006); Rauer (2006); Shapiro (2007); Weber (2006); Vuori (2010).
5 See for example, Robinson (2002); Carruthers (2011); Bahador (2007); Livingston (1997).
6 For a recent elaboration on securitization theory, see the special issue of *Security Dialogue*, December 2010.
7 The impact of digitization and simulation is a major theme in the work of James Der Derian.
8 One of the most prominent examples is Dorothea Lange's work for the US Resettlement Administration in the 1930s. Her image of the 'migrant mother' has become an icon of a socially engaged form of documentary photography but also been criticized for its stereotypes and partiality. For pictures, see Lange and Taylor ([1939] 2000).
9 Aradau and Huysmans (2014: 598) write: 'Understood as devices, methods are seen to enact social and political worlds. Understood as acts, methods can become disruptive of social and political worlds. This dual reconceptualization also allows us to derive an understanding of *critical methods*.'
10 However, Rose's excellent introduction does not refer to IR.
11 It might be worthwhile to compare the different fictional accounts of Bin Laden's hunt in more detail, in particular *Zero Dark Thirty* (2012) and *Seal Team Six* (2012).
12 For the work and life of Panofsky, see Elsner and Lorenz (2012) and Holly (1984).
13 For example, a finished project by David Campbell ('Imaging Famine', accessed November 2014).

References

Andersen, R.S. and Moeller, F. (2012) 'Engaging the Limits of Visibility: Photography, Security, and Surveillance', *Security Dialogue*, 44 (3): 203–21.

Andersen, R.S., Vuori, J.A. and Mutlu, C.E. (2015) 'Visuality', in C. Aradau, J. Huysmans, A. Neal and N. Voelkner (eds) *Critical Security Methods: New Frameworks for Analysis*, Abingdon and New York: Routledge: 85–117.

Aradau, C. and Huysmans, J. (2014) 'Critical Methods in International Relations: The Politics of Techniques, Devices and Acts', *European Journal of International Relations*, 20 (3): 596–619.

Ashley, R. (1988) 'Untying the Sovereign State: A Double Reading of the Anarchy Problematic', *Millennium – Journal of International Studies*, 17 (2): 227–62.

(1989) 'Living on Border Lines: Man, Poststructuralism and War', in J.D. Derian and M.J. Shapiro (eds) *International/Intertextual Relations: Postmodern Readings of World Politics*, Massachusetts: *Lexington Books*: 259–321.

Bahador, B. (2007) *The CNN Effect in Action: How the News Media Pushed the West Toward War in Kosovo*, Basingstoke and New York: Palgrave Macmillan.

Bleiker, R. and Kay, A. (2007) 'Representing HIV/AIDS in Africa: Pluralist Photography and Local Empowerment', *International Studies Quarterly*, 51 (1): 139–63.

Boehm, G. (1994) 'Die Bilderfrage', in G. Boehm (ed.) *Was ist ein Bild?*, München: Fink: 324–43.

Boehm, G. (2007) *Wie Bilder Sinn erzeugen*, Berlin: Berlin University Press.

Bredekamp, H. (2010) *Theorie des Bildakts*, Berlin: Suhrkamp.

Butler, J. (2010) *Frames of War: When Life is Grievable?*, London and New York: Verso.

Campbell, D. 'Imaging Famine', available at: http://www.david-campbell.org/photography/imaging-famine/ (accessed 18 November 2014).x

Campbell, D. (2003) 'Cultural Governance and Pictorial Resistance', *Review of International Studies*, 29 (1): 57–73.

Campbell, D. and Shapiro, M.J. (2007) 'Securitization, Militarization and Visual Culture in the Worlds of Post-9/11', *Security Dialogue*, 38 (2): 131–8.

Carruthers, S. (2011) *The Media at War*, 2nd edn, Basingstoke and New York: Palgrave Macmillan.

Doty, R.L. (1996) *Imperial Encounters: The Politics of Representation in North-South Relations*, Minneapolis: University of Minnesota Press.

Engert, S. and Spencer, A. (2012) 'International Relations at the Movies: Teaching and Learning about International Politics Through Films', *Perspectives*, 17 (1): 83–103.

Elsner, J. and Lorenz, K. (2012) 'The Genesis of Iconology', *Critical Inquiry*, 38 (3): 483–512.

George, J. (1994) *Discourses of Global Politics: A Critical (Re)Introduction to International Relations*, Boulder: Lynne Rienner.

Hansen, L. (2006) *Security as Practice: Discourse Analysis and the Bosnian War*, London, and New York: Routledge.

Hansen, L. (2011) 'Theorizing the Image for Security Studies: Visual Securitization and the Muhammad Cartoon Crisis', *European Journal of International Relations*, 17 (1): 51–74.

Hansen, L. (2015) 'How Images Make World Politics: International Icons and the Case of Abu Ghraib', *Review of International Studies*, 41 (2): 263–288.

Hase, R.F.v. and Lehmkuhl, U. (1997) *Enemy Images in American History*, Providence and Oxford: Berghahn Books.

Heck, A. and Schlag, G. (2013) 'Securitizing Images: The Female Body and the War in Afghanistan', *European Journal of International Relations*, 19 (4): 891–913.

Holden, G. (2006) 'Cinematic IR, the Sublime, and the Indistinctness of Art', *Millennium – Journal of International Studies*, 34 (3): 793–818.

Holly, M.N. (1984) *Erwin Panofsky and the Foundations of Art History*, Ithaca: New York University Press.

Holzscheiter, A. (2014) 'Between Communicative Action and Structures of Signification: Discourse Theory and Analysis in International Relations', *International Studies Perspectives*, 15 (2): 142–162.

Jackson, P.T. (2011) *The Conduct of Inquiry in International Relations*, London and New York: Routledge.

Lange, D. and Taylor, P. ([1939] 2000) *An American Exodus: A Record of Human Erosion*, Paris: Jean-Michel Place Editions.

Livingston, S. (1997) *Clarifying the CNN-Effect: An Examination of Media Effects according to Type of Military Intervention*, Boston: Harvard University Press.

Milliken, J. (1999) 'The Study of Discourse in International Relations: A Critique of Research and Methods', *European Journal of International Relations*, 5 (2): 225–54.

Mirzoeff, N. (2002) *The Visual Culture Reader*, 2nd edn, London and New York: Routledge.
Mirzoeff, N. (2009) *An Introduction to Visual Culture*, 2nd edn, London and New York: Routledge.
Mitchell, W.J.T. (1994) *Picture Theory: Essays on Verbal and Visual Representation*, Chicago: Chicago University Press.
Mitchell, W.J.T. (2011) *Cloning Terror: The War of Images, 9/11 to the Present*, Chicago: University of Chicago Press.
Moeller, F. (2007) 'Photographic Interventions in Post-9/11 Security Policy', *Security Dialogue*, 38 (2): 179–96.
Moore, C. and Farrands, C. (2013) 'Visual Analysis', in L.J. Shepherd (ed.) *Critical Approaches to Security*, Abingdon and New York: Routledge: 223–35.
Mortensen, M. (2011) 'When Citizen Photojournalism Sets the News Agenda: Neda Agha Soltan as a Web 2.0 Icon of Postelection Unrest in Iran', *Global Media and Communication*, 7 (1): 4–16.
Neumann, I.B. and Nexon, D. (2006) *Harry Potter and World Politics*, Lanham: Rowman & Littlefield.
Obama, B. (2011) 'Obama's Remarks on Bin Laden's Killing', *New York Times*, 2 May, available at: http://www.nytimes.com/2011/05/02/world/middleeast/02obama-text.html?ref=asia (accessed 18 November 2014).
Offermann, P. and Engelkamp, S. (2012) 'It's a Family Affair: Germany as a Responsible Actor in Popular Culture Discourse', *International Studies Perspectives*, 13 (3): 235–53.
Panofsky, E. (1970) *Meaning in the Visual Arts*, Harmondsworth: Penguin Books.
Rauer, V. (2006) 'Symbols in Action: Willy Brandt's Kneefall at the Warsaw Memorial', in J.C. Alexander, B. Giesen and J.L. Mast (eds) *Social Performance: Symbolic Action, Cultural Pragmatics, and Ritual*, Cambridge: Cambridge University Press: 257–82.
Robinson, P. (2002) *The CNN Effect: The Myth of News, Foreign Policy and Intervention*, London and New York: Routledge.
Rose, G. (2012) *Visual Methodologies: An Introduction to Researching with Visual Materials*, Los Angeles et al.: SAGE.
Shapiro, M.J. (2007) 'The New Violent Cartography', *Security Dialogue*, 38 (3): 291–313.
Shepherd, L.J. (2008) 'Visualising Violence: Legitimacy and Authority in the 'War on Terror', *Critical Studies on Terrorism*, 1 (2): 213–26.
Shim, D. (2013) *Visual Politics and North Korea: Seeing Is Believing*, London and New York: Routledge.
Shim, D. and Nabers, D. (2012) 'Imaging North Korea: Exploring its Visual Representations in International Politics', *International Studies Perspectives*: 1–18.
Sontag, S. (1977) *On Photography*, New York: Farrar, Straus and Giroux.
Steele, B.J. (2008) 'Ideals that Were Never Really in Our Possession: Torture, Honor and US Identity', *International Relations*, 22 (2): 243–61.
Time (2011a) 'The End of Bin Laden', 20 May, available at: http://content.time.com/time/covers/0,16641,20110520,00.html (accessed 18 November 2014).
Time (2011b) 'TIME's "X" Covers: A Gallery of Americas Most Hated Enemies', available at: http://content.time.com/time/photogallery/0,29307,2069764_2272406,00.html (accessed 18 November 2014).
Veeren, E.v. (2011) 'Captured by the Camera's Eye: Guantanamo and the Shifting Frame of the Global War on Terror', *Review of International Studies*, 37 (4): 1721–49.
Vuori, J. (2010) 'A Timely Prophet? The Doomsday Clock as a Visualization of Securitization Moves with a Global Referent Object', *Security Dialogue*, 41 (3): 255–77.

Wæver, O. (1995) 'Securitization and Desecuritization', in R.D. Lipschutz (ed.) *On Security*, New York: Columbia University Press: 46–86.

Walt, S.M. (1991) 'The Renaissance of Security Studies', *International Studies Quarterly*, 35 (2): 211–39.

Weber, C. (2006) *Imagining America at War*, London and New York: Routledge.

Williams, M.C. (2003) 'Words, Images, Enemies: Securitization and International Politics', *International Studies Quarterly*, 47 (4): 511–31.

11 Global, state, and individual security in quantitative conflict research[1]

Håvard Hegre and Idunn Kristiansen

Introduction

This chapter looks at security from the perspective of the quantitative literature on armed conflict. Quantitative studies make it possible to identify patterns that are less visible in studies that are rich in detail. For example, as we show below, fewer people have been killed in war during the last decade than in any other decade measuring has been feasible. This is an important complement to common (subjective) perceptions of security that tend to give current events disproportionate weight. In this sense, quantification introduces a particular type of objectivity into the security debate.[2] At the same time, variation in the magnitudes of wars complicates quantitative research on armed conflict since all cases are treated as in principle similar.

Quantitative studies, which typically focus on observable instances of the use of violence for political purposes, such as civil wars, militarized interstate disputes, or acts of terrorism, rarely explicitly use the term 'security'.[3] Furthermore, 'peace research' rather than 'security studies' is mostly used to label them. Still, 'security' as a concept is obviously also relevant to this literature.

In this chapter, we define security on three levels – from global, state, and individual perspectives – while restricting our attention to political violence. Seen from a global perspective, 'security' entails a low risk for states and individuals of being targeted in acts of political violence. From a state perspective, 'security' carries a low risk of becoming involved in political events that threaten the security of citizens, leaders, or decision-making institutions. Interstate and internal wars and violence by rebel groups against civilians are threats to both citizens and leadership. Military coups and changes to political institutions primarily threaten the leadership, but often also affect citizens indirectly. For individuals, we define 'security' as a low risk of being killed in acts of political violence by states (their own or others) or armed non-state groups. This includes interstate and internal armed conflicts, conflicts between non-state armed groups, as well as organized armed groups targeting civilians in 'one-sided violence'.

In the following, we first summarize developments in global security over time, showing that security has largely improved over the past decades and that internal armed conflicts have become more prevalent than other forms of conflict. We then review the quantitative literature in light of our definition of security and discuss how well-known measures to improve security – namely those related to *compellance* and *compliance* – fare empirically. We also briefly discuss challenges facing quantitative studies of armed conflict, especially when it comes to dealing with war escalation. We conclude that policies that induce compliance from potentially threatening actors, such as poverty reduction, are more effective than those that seek to compel them through military force.

We conclude that policies that induce compliance from potentially threatening actors, such as poverty reduction, are more effective than those that seek to compel them through military force. A strong pattern emerging from the quantitative literature is that the security of individuals is at least as relevant as that of states.[4] As the editors highlight in the introduction, the use of the term security has expanded from focusing exclusively on state security to include individuals, especially within the human security literature. This is reflected in a gradual shift within the quantitative conflict literature over the past couple of decades, from a focus on interstate armed conflicts to internal ones, largely due to the empirical observation that interstate conflicts have become very rare. Moreover, given that the political and economic reduction of vulnerabilities and risk management both seem more effective in achieving security than military means, studies of security could therefore focus more on these issues than what has been done so far.

Trends in global security

In this first section, we present some trends in global security in terms of the number of political violence events and the number of people killed. More specifically, we look at the number of armed conflicts and coups, and the number of people killed in state-based and non-state violence. We also look at trends in democracy and regime changes, since in the section on democracy below we suggest that this is important for security. In the next section, we will also discuss possible causes behind these trends.

Figure 11.1 displays the number of state-based armed conflicts by type in the period 1946–2013.[5] It shows that internal armed conflict (dark grey), which involves the government of a state and one or more internal rebel groups, has been the most frequent type of conflict since the 1960s. The number increased dramatically up to 1991, and decreased thereafter. 'Extrasystemic' or colonial conflicts (light grey) were relatively frequent compared to the other conflict types until the mid-1970s, by which point most colonies had gained independence. Interstate conflicts (second darkest grey) have decreased and almost disappeared in the post-Cold War period, while internationalized conflicts (i.e. internal conflicts with foreign state intervention; second lightest grey) now constitute a larger share of the total number of conflicts than before. Since the 1990s, internal and internationalized internal conflicts have been the most common forms of conflict. Most of these conflicts occur in low-income countries in Africa and Asia (Themnér and Wallensteen 2014).

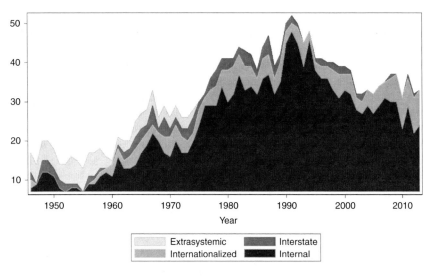

Figure 11.1 Number of state-based armed conflicts by type, 1946–2013

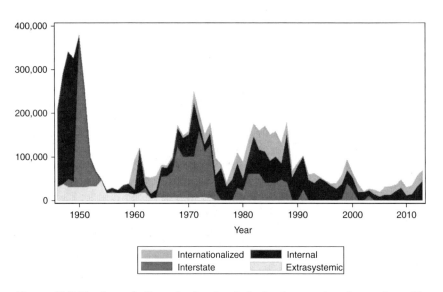

Figure 11.2 Number of direct battle-related deaths in state-based armed conflicts, 1946–2013

Figure 11.2 shows the number of people killed in the types of conflicts displayed in Figure 11.1.[6] Here, the trend of growth up until 1991 is less clear. The most lethal periods were the years around 1950 and 1970, as well as the 1980s. A handful of conflicts added considerably to the total number of battle deaths – in particular the Chinese civil war, the Korea and Vietnam wars, and the war between Iran and Iraq.

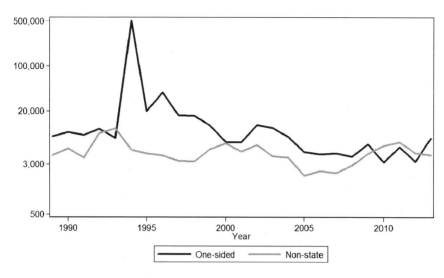

Figure 11.3 Battle-related deaths in non-state and one-sided conflicts, 1946–2013

Figure 11.3 displays the number of battle-related deaths in one-sided and non-state conflicts in the period 1989–2013 on a log-transformed scale, seeing security mainly from the perspective of individuals.[7] There are no clear trends in these types of conflict (if we disregard the 1994 genocide in Rwanda, in which almost half a million people were killed). The decline in state-based conflicts cannot be explained by an overall shift toward these less organized types of conflicts.

Figure 11.4 displays the number of attempted and successful coups in the period 1950–2013.[8] One can infer that states have gradually become more secure from coups over the past decades, since the number of attempted and successful coups has decreased substantially. The number of attempted coups peaked in the mid-1960s. In 2013, there was only one – the successful military coup in Egypt.

Figure 11.5 shows the percentage of the world's total regimes that are democratic, semi-democratic, and non-democratic.[9] The percentage of democratic regimes has increased substantially, from zero in 1800 to 59 per cent in 2013. States have also become more secure from adverse regime changes (Dahl et al. 2013). Since the mid-1970s, changes toward democracy have outnumbered those toward non-democracy, resulting in the increase in the number of democracies shown in Figure 11.5.

Although more than 880,000 people were killed worldwide in direct battle-related deaths in state-based conflicts during the 1989–2013 period (UCDP 2014),[10] and about 865,000 died as a consequence of one-sided and non-state violence in the same period,[11] since the 1970s armed conflicts have diminished dramatically as a social problem. By comparison, every year 1.2 million people die in traffic accidents (WHO 2013) and in 2010, about 470,000 died in homicides (UNODC 2011). Since fewer people are killed in political violence than in

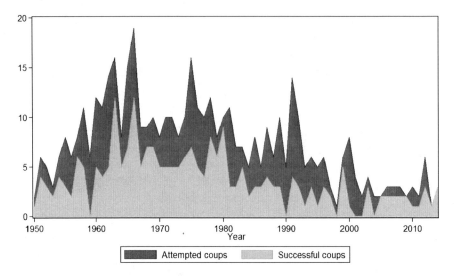

Figure 11.4 Number of coups, 1950–2013

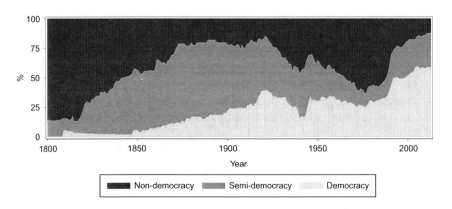

Figure 11.5 Regime types, 1800–2013

such other forms of preventable deaths, should security studies rather concentrate on these?

One reason to continue to focus on political violence is that it brings with it more serious secondary effects than other threats to personal security. Large-scale wars are routinely followed by surplus mortality due to destruction of health infrastructure, migration flows, blocking of access to safe drinking water, and breakdown of law and order with increased homicide rates, etc. According to Gates et al. (2012), a relatively small internal armed conflict in a medium-sized country, causing 2,500 battle-related deaths, reduces every citizen's life expectancy by an average of one year. For each soldier killed, approximately two infants die who would have otherwise survived (Gates et al. 2012). Civil wars also have grave economic effects; a median-sized conflict typically reduces GDP per capita by 15 per cent, and it takes at least a decade to regain the loss after a war (Gates et al. 2012). Interstate trade also suffers from both civil and interstate war (Anderton and Carter 2001; Bayer and Rupert 2004), spreading the detrimental effects widely. Another unique aspect of political violence is the risk of massive escalation, which we will return to in the section on conflict escalation and methodological limitations below.

What secures security?

As shown above, security has improved over the past decades in terms of most of our quantitative security indicators. The risk of interstate wars, coups, and adverse regime changes has declined steadily since the 1980s. In terms of the number of people killed, there has been a decline in internal armed conflicts, although the number of conflicts remains high. How can these trends be explained, and what determines security? In the following section, we discuss two sets of contributing factors: policies designed to provide security through compellance of possibly threatening actors, and policies and societal changes that instead induce actors to comply with the security needs of others.

Means of compellance

As often assumed in traditional security studies, deterring or eradicating potential enemies through the threat or use of force can improve security. In this section, we review the quantitative literature on armed conflict and discuss the security impact of three means of compellance: military expenditure, United Nations peacekeeping operations (PKOs), and military intervention for regime change.

Military expenditure

Does the money countries spend on their militaries (typically 1–3 per cent of GDP) provide security? This question is subject to much scholarly debate, and the answers remain ambiguous. One reason is that there is obviously an endogenous relationship between expenditures and security threats, so that the question of '*How much security can a dollar buy?*' (Milante 2013) always will be accompanied by the pessimistic '*How much war is caused by the search for security?*' (Van Evera 1999: 185). Another complicating issue is that the effect of military spending varies according to the source of security threats.[12] Here, we discuss the effect of domestic military spending on the risk of interstate and internal armed conflicts, as well as coups. In the end, we briefly mention some indirect effects of military expenditure on security.

HOW MUCH SECURITY CAN A DOLLAR BUY?

Regarding interstate conflict, most of the quantitative literature on the issue revolves around the relative and absolute capabilities of states' military forces.[13]

The realist balance-of-power thesis, touched upon in Chapter 1 by Glaser and Chapter 6 by Masala in this volume, maintains that wars are more likely to occur under situations of power preponderance than power parity because the gains of aggression are cheap, the risk of reprisal low, and 'there is nothing to prevent them' (Waltz 1959: 232). At the same time, equal power relations should make war less probable, since according to this thesis, the chance of easy victory is slight (Morgenthau 1967; Waltz 1959; Wright [1942] 1965). Most quantitative studies also find that relative 'power preponderance' decreases the risk of interstate conflict (e.g., Bremer 1992; Bueno de Mesquita and Lalman 1992; Hegre 2004, 2008; Lemke 2002; Oneal et al. 1996; Reed 2003). However, Hegre (2008) argues that it is necessary to see this in conjunction with absolute capabilities. He finds that an increase in the stronger party's military capabilities makes interstate conflict *more likely*, since the risk-reducing effect of increased power preponderance is weaker than the risk-inducing effect of higher capabilities. This is in accordance with Boulding's (1989) argument that strong militaries are ineffective means for deterrence, as military power rather encourages its use and initiates escalating threats and counter-threats.

It is also regularly thought that military expenditure deters and represses internal armed conflict. This, too, is related to balance of power, only in these cases between the state and insurgents. In these situations, 'dissidents are not likely to be able to organize and sustain an internal war' if the state is substantially stronger (Gurr 1970: 235). However, the strong reciprocal relationship between security threats and military spending mentioned above clearly complicates quantitative empirical analysis of the relationship.

One way to deal with this is to use income per capita as a proxy for military capabilities, as done by Fearon and Laitin (2003) and Collier and Hoeffler (1998). They interpret the negative relationship between income per capita and the risk of internal conflict as due to 'the *government's police and military capabilities and the reach of government institutions into rural areas*' (Fearon and Laitin 2003: 80, emphasis in original). They argue that weak, badly financed and corrupt counterinsurgency forces create favorable conditions for rebellion, since the state is less able to control the national territory. According to them, preventive efforts should therefore include strengthening military and police forces so that governments are better able to fight civil wars.

Although the use of GDP per capita as a proxy for military capabilities avoids the problem of reciprocal causation, this variable also captures aspects of economic development unrelated to state military capacity (see the section on poverty reduction below). This is clear from studies that look at military expenditures while controlling for GDP per capita: Hegre and Sambanis (2006) do not find military spending to have any robust effect on the risk of civil war onset, and Henderson and Singer (2000) find a significant *conflict-inducing* effect. Taydas and Peksen (2012) also show that military expenditures are not likely to affect the risk of civil conflict, and that welfare spending (i.e., public provision of education, health services, and social security) is much more efficient.[14]

Another way to avoid reciprocal causation is to use instrumental variables, thereby accounting for the potential effect of anticipated rebellion on military spending. Applying this, Collier and Hoeffler (2002, 2006) do not find any deterrence effect of military expenditure on the risk of internal conflict. Rather, 'during the inception stage of rebellion a large military response might be ineffective, or even counterproductive: excessive repression by government forces assists rebel recruitment and appears to be a common error of counter-insurgency' (Collier and Hoeffler 2002: 13).[15]

Furthermore, with regard to individuals' security, Lacina (2006) finds no relationship between the number of people killed per year in internal conflict and 'military quality' measured as military expenditures per soldier. As to the duration of internal conflict, Collier et al. (2001: 3) do not find any effect on conflict length when using instrument variables for military expenditure.

When it comes to coups, military expenditures can also be used by regimes as 'coup-proofing' – preventing coups by influencing competing elites' ability or willingness to engage in coups. Generous military salaries and grants can potentially reduce their readiness to engage in coup attempts. Collier and Hoeffler (2007) show that higher military expenditures reduce the likelihood of coups in high-risk African countries. There, 'buying off the threat of a coup is a rational use of government resources' (Collier and Hoeffler 2007: 19). Outside Africa, however, higher military spending is ineffective (Collier and Hoeffler 2007). A central reason might be that military spending also strengthens the military's ability to arrange and carry out coups. In those cases, other coup-proofing mechanisms, such as disarmament, demobilization, and division of the military are regularly used to weaken its capacity to carry out coups (Collier and Hoeffler 2007; Powell 2012: 9–10; Quinlivan 1999: 133). When these mechanisms are combined with high military spending, the military's effectiveness is reduced at the same time as resources are diverted from other security enforcing policies.

In summary, the evidence for a deterrence effect of domestic military expenditure is weak for all the security threats we consider. Although it is possible that measures other than military spending should be used to study the effect of states' counter-insurgency capabilities,[16] this also suggests that strong counter-insurgency capacity might not be an efficient way of preventing conflict at all.

INDIRECT EFFECTS OF MILITARY SPENDING ON SECURITY

In addition to the security effects of military expenditures discussed above, military spending can also indirectly affect security. It can easily lead to arms races between states, thereby possibly exacerbating international tensions (Gibler et al. 2005; Wallace 1979, 1982). Excessive military spending is also often associated with weak civilian control over the military, and militaries are more likely to distort public spending in favor of the armed forces, thereby diverting funds from other policies that may reduce the long-term risk of conflict (Collier and Hoeffler 2007). Strong military influence in politics, and weak civilian control over the armed forces, also increases the risk of civil and interstate conflict (Choi and

James 2004; Hegre and Nygård 2014; Levy 2012; Sechser 2004). Furthermore, military spending has been shown to reduce economic growth and reduce funds available to other public goods, including health, education, and poverty reduction (Gleditsch et al. 1996; Knight et al. 1996). As we will argue in the section on poverty reduction below, economic growth and poverty reduction have important, positive security implications. Additionally, Gupta et al. (2001) show a strong and positive relationship between military spending and corruption. This indicates that higher military expenditures may be associated with lower, rather than higher, levels of state capacity.

UN peacekeeping operations

The second means of compellance that we focus on, UN peacekeeping operations (PKOs), has been employed by the international community to promote peace and contain internal and interstate armed conflict since 1948. They are thought to reduce civilians' fear of victimization, mistrust and uncertainty; improve information flow; constrain political manipulation; facilitate negotiation and implementation of peace agreements; and strengthen moderate forces (Doyle and Sambanis 2006: 49–50; Fortna 2008: ch. 4). After the Cold War, they have increased considerably in size, number and mandate. While traditional peacekeeping missions were typically restricted to cease-fire monitoring, they have become more multidimensional and engaged in broad issues such as state building, human rights monitoring, security sector reform, and disarmament, demobilization, and reintegration (DDR). An increasing number of PKOs also have a mandate to use force (Human Security Centre 2005). However, do they increase security?

A number of quantitative studies of the security effect of UN PKOs, using various statistical models and datasets, conclude that they substantially and significantly extend the duration of peace after civil war (Doyle and Sambanis 2000; Fortna 2004a, 2008; Gilligan and Sergenti 2008).[17] According to Fortna (2008: 125), for example, the risk of conflict recurrence decreases 'by 75%–85% or more when peacekeepers are present'. However, the efficiency depends on mandate and size, especially in terms of budget. When it comes to mandate, Doyle and Sambanis (2000) find that traditional PKOs, characterized by very limited mandates and unarmed or lightly armed troops, do not have any effect on the risk of conflict recurrence.[18] Multidimensional PKOs on the other hand 'are extremely significant and positively associated with' peace-building success (Doyle and Sambanis 2000: 791).[19] This corresponds with Goldstein's (2011) conclusion that PKOs work when they are multidimensional, with military, police and civilian components and 'expanded powers to monitor, and in some cases even take over, the functions of states emerging from civil wars' (Goldstein 2011: 100). Related to budget, Collier et al. (2008: 473) also show that doubling PKO expenditure reduces the risk of conflict recurrence from 40 per cent to 31 per cent.

PKOs are clearly effective in post-conflict situations, but probably do fairly well in ongoing conflicts as well. Kreps and Wallace (2009) and Hultman (2010) find that PKOs with strong mandates are efficient in managing violence against civilians in armed conflicts, and Doyle and Sambanis (2000) show that UN PKOs can be effective in ending violent conflict as well – at least when they are provided with a strong enforcement mandate.[20] Beardsley (2011) also concludes that PKOs reduce the likelihood of conflict in neighboring countries. By creating stability in one country, the risk of conflict contagion is reduced (Gleditsch 2002). Hegre et al. (2010: 1) also show a strong general security effect of UN PKOs with solid mandates and budget: 'in a scenario where the UN is willing to issue PKOs with strong mandates and increase its PKO budget by 50%, the risk of armed conflict in the world in 2035 would be reduced by up to two thirds relative to a scenario without PKOs'.

In interstate conflict, PKOs appear to have a positive, although perhaps not so clear, impact on security. Fortna (2004b) finds that PKOs reduce the likelihood of recurrence of interstate conflict, and that the effectiveness is somewhat higher for armed than unarmed missions. Elsewhere, she shows that PKOs are effective in increasing the duration of post-conflict peace for both internal and interstate conflicts (Fortna 2003). However, she argues that the positive impact of peacekeepers in post-conflict situations is larger and more clearly significant for civil than interstate wars, especially 'in the most recent era of active international involvement to keep peace in internal conflicts' (Fortna 2003: 108).[21]

It is well-known that UN PKOs are deployed in conflict situations and not in military coups. However, according to Paul Collier (2009a, 2009b), UN-sanctioned military operations could also be used 'to provide a guidance system that transforms the missile of the coup d'état into an effective domestic restraint on misgovernance' (Collier 2009b: 204). He argues that coups could be reduced if 'the international community would make a common commitment that should a government that has committed itself to the international standard of [free and fair] elections be ousted by a coup d'état, they would ensure that the government was reinstated, by military intervention if necessary' (Collier 2009b: 204). Such a system would reduce the attractiveness of coups as a strategy, and encourage legitimate routes to power, which in turn would promote security, Collier argues. However, it does not appear the proposal has been taken seriously – perhaps because coups have become relatively rare.

To summarize, UN peacekeeping operations appear to be quite successful in reducing violence – especially after civil war, provided they have strong mandates and sufficient budgets. Why, then, do UN investments in military operations appear to be more effective in enhancing security than domestic expenditures? Obviously, UN PKOs are in most cases more neutral to underlying social conflicts than domestic governments involved in internal armed conflicts. UN forces are also better at keeping civilians out of harm's way than many government forces, since their mandates are regularly in terms of the protection of civilians, whereas governments have an incentive to target civilians who support or protect the armed opposition. Furthermore, UN PKOs often involve more than the use of force, including state-building efforts, human-rights monitoring, DDR, and so on, and PKO budgets are rarely used to buy political loyalty in the way that domestic military expenditures often are.

Military enforcement of regime change

As Geis and Wagner discuss in Chapter 7, military force and intervention are sometimes used to promote democratic norms and principles. In their words, there is a 'liberal-democratic propensity to fight a certain type of war – one in the name of norms and values cherished by liberal-democratic polities, such as the protection of minority rights and human rights or democracy promotion' (see Chapter 7 by Geis and Wagner in this volume p. 126). The United States, for example, has increasingly stated 'democracy promotion' as motivation for military interventions, such as in Afghanistan and Iraq (Gleditsch et al. 2007: 14). This is thought to reduce internal conflict as well as to promote interstate peace (see the section on democracy below). However, does military enforcement of regime changes – interventions 'to liberate oppressed peoples' (Pickering and Peceny 2006: 540) – actually enhance democracy (and thereby security)?

Pickering and Peceny (2006: 539) 'find little evidence that military intervention by liberal states helps to foster democracy in target countries'. Gleditsch et al. (2007: 40) show that 'democratic intervention does indeed promote democratization', but only in the short term. In the long run, 'the target states tend to end up among the unstable semi-democracies', and forced democratization could even be 'potentially harmful with regard to securing peace' (Gleditsch et al. 2007: 1). Peceny (1999) claims that US military intervention generally has no effect on democracy, but that democratization is enhanced when free and fair elections are actively supported and sponsored: 'It is the adoption of pro-liberalization policies during military interventions that generates democracy, not intervention in and of itself' (Peceny 1999: 552). Other studies similarly find a democratizing effect of US military interventions that specifically aim at liberalization (Hermann and Kegley 1998; Meernik 1996). However, Bueno de Mesquita and Downs (2006) show that although intervening states often claim that democratization of the target state is a main goal, this is rarely achieved: 'intervention does little to promote democracy and often leads to its erosion and the substitution of largely symbolic reforms' (Bueno de Mesquita and Downs 2006: 647). Pickering and Peceny (2006) also show that the UN PKOs are more likely to have a democratizing influence than other military interventions.

Achieving stable democracy after military intervention might be difficult because sustainable democracy relies on complex internal conditions and not only on the incumbent leader. Regardless of military intervention, the prospects for democracy are weak in countries that are poor, oil-dependent, and with non-democratic neighbors (Gleditsch 2002; Gleditsch et al. 2007: 41; Przeworski et al. 2000). War and instability can also potentially reduce the prospects for democracy, for example by disrupting trade and economic growth, as suggested by Gates et al. (1996: 5).

To sum up, there is no clear evidence for a democratizing effect of military intervention for regime change. This also leaves pessimistic prospects for peace as a consequence of intervention.

Means of compliance

In addition to the means of compellance discussed so far, security can also be improved if the incentives for potential enemies to use violence for political purposes diminish. Such incentives can change because hawkish decision-makers in potential adversaries are replaced by less hostile representatives through the introduction of democratic institutions, or because the cost-benefit analysis of militaristic policies change as a consequence of altered socio-economic circumstances. In the following, we discuss four means of compliance that can affect the risk of internal and interstate conflict as well as the security of individual citizens: democracy, poverty reduction, good governance, and economic globalization.

Democracy

A vast quantitative literature has dealt with the impact of democratization for international security, as Geis and Wagner highlight in Chapter 7.[22] Democracies have rarely, if ever, fought wars against each other (Doyle 1986; Russett and Oneal 2001). This may be due to particular normative and structural constraints in democracies that restrict their warlike behavior (Maoz and Russett 1993). However, the fact that democracies tend to become involved in as many wars overall as non-democracies somewhat undermines this explanation. Other explanations draw on democracies' ability to credibly signal their true intentions (Fearon 1994), and that they are particularly adept at avoiding wars they cannot win and mobilizing resources when they become involved in hostile interactions (Bueno de Mesquita et al. 2003). This makes democracies unattractive targets, since they are likely to win the wars they fight (Reiter and Stam III 1998).

Perhaps more persuasively, the democratic peace may be due to democracies failing to disagree sufficiently on international policies to be willing to suffer the costs of war. Such joint interests may be due to the fact that most democracies were on the same side during the Cold War (Farber and Gowa 1995). Joint democracy may also give rise to joint interest in the promotion of democratic regimes or, importantly, reduced incentives for political leaders to expand the territory they control. The profitability of occupation is also less certain for democratic leaders than for autocratic ones, since the benefits of occupation have to be shared between almost as many as those who bear the costs (Rosecrance 1986). Hence, joint democracy may lead to the mutual acceptance of international borders, removing an important source of war (Huth and Allee 2002). Related to this, Schweller (1992) argues that regime type affects how declining powers behave. When challenged by rising powers, realist theory posits that leading powers wage preventive wars to maintain their military hegemony, as discussed by Glaser in Chapter 1. Preventive wars are, however, less attractive to democratic leaders. If the rising power is another democracy, the historical absence of war between democracies indicates that the threat is minimal. If it is non-democratic, the public is wary of the risks and costs of a war when danger is not imminent, and the formation of alliances to counter-balance the non-democratic threat is often a preferable strategy.

The relationship between democracy and internal security threats is less clear. The developed and consolidated democracies in the Western world have had an unprecedentedly low frequency of internal armed conflicts since the Second World War, just as they have avoided war between themselves. Theoretical explanations include that democracies allow discontent to be expressed and have mechanisms to handle it, and that they facilitate effective bargaining and reduce commitment problems. Seen from the perspective of individual citizens, Lacina (2006) and Gleditsch et al. (2009) show that internal wars in democracies also tend to kill fewer people when they break out. Democratic governments also make use of less violence against civilians (Eck and Hultman 2007) and engage in less repression (Colaresi and Carey 2008; Davenport 2007b). In contrast to this, rebel groups tend to make more extensive use of violence against civilians when fighting democratic regimes (Eck and Hultman 2007). Possibly because of the stronger constraints on the use of violence against insurgents, democracies also tend to have longer internal wars (Gleditsch et al. 2009). Autocracies, on the other hand, tend to have shorter and more intense internal conflicts, and refrain less from using extensive violence against civilians (Eck and Hultman 2007; Gleditsch et al. 2009).

Moreover, countries that have political institutions that mix democratic and authoritarian traits or that have recently democratized have a higher risk of onset of internal armed conflict than completely authoritarian systems and established democracies (Cederman et al. 2010; Fearon and Laitin 2003; Hegre et al. 2001). Such political systems often fail to adequately handle social conflicts, but are also constrained from the brutal repression that autocratic rulers can engage in to prevent challenges to their rule.

There are also indications that democratic regimes are effective in reducing the risk of internal conflict only in societies with relatively high levels of socio-economic development (Collier and Rohner 2008; Hegre 2003). As we discuss below, socio-economic development implies changes that are conducive to peace itself. These changes promote better governance within democracies and non-democracies.

Poverty reduction

A large number of empirical studies find a strong link between poverty, under-development and internal conflict, measured as GDP per capita (Collier and Hoeffler 1998; Fearon and Laitin 2003), energy consumption per capita (Hegre et al. 2001; Hibbs 1973), infant mortality rates (Abouharb and Kimball 2007; Urdal 2005), and education levels (Thyne 2006).[23] This relationship cannot be attributed to other factors such as political system, former colonial power, geographical location, or a pre-existing history of conflict. Also in the short run, solid economic growth reduces the risk of internal armed conflict (Collier and Hoeffler 2004a; Miguel et al. 2004). Military coups are also less frequent in countries with higher average income (Collier and Hoeffler 2007; Londregan and Poole 1990).

There are several reasons for this link between poverty and conflict. Poverty may be a direct motivation for conflict (Gurr 1970), as a large gap between people's material wellbeing and what they expect creates frustration and anger. Dismissing the empirical importance of such direct motivations, Collier (2000) instead highlights that poverty reduces the costs for cynical 'violence entrepreneurs' to recruit soldiers and thereby sustain rebellion. As mentioned in the section on military expenditure above, such rebellions are also facilitated by the frequent low capacity of governments in poor countries to effectively control their territories (Fearon and Laitin 2003; Gat 2006). Low-income countries often have low-quality roads, poor communication networks, and militaries that are no better equipped or organized than rebel armies. The incentives to use violence for political goals are also higher in low-income economies where most of the wealth is tied to land, such as oil or agricultural production, because control of territory secures income (Boix 2008). Finally, economic development means specialization, division of labor, and internal trade. Such economic networks are vulnerable to large-scale violence. If elites depend on the revenues generated in a modern economy, they will be much more careful to prevent violence, whether incited by rebel organizations or their own coercive institutions. In the words of Gat (2006: 658), 'it was mainly the benefits of peace that increased dramatically once the Malthusian trap was broken, tilting the overall balance between war and peace for [...] industrializing and industrial societies, regardless of their regime, for which wealth acquisition ceased to be a zero-sum game.' Economic development also creates fertile ground for democratization, which in turn renders government military forces more accountable, more professional, and more effective.

A couple of studies also indicate that the negative effect of development on the risk of armed conflict is contingent on democracy (Collier and Rohner 2008; Hegre 2003). In middle-income countries, citizens often demand expanded political rights and influence on important policies. As seen in North Africa and the Middle East following the Arab Spring, such demands are often associated with intense repression and sometimes with the eruption of armed conflicts.

Good governance

Many studies of internal armed conflict also concentrate on how the psychological state of 'relative deprivation' is transformed into intergroup conflict (Davies 1962; Gurr 1968). As defined by Gurr (1968: 1104), relative deprivation is 'actors' perceptions of discrepancy between their value expectations (the goods and conditions of life to which they believe they are justifiably entitled) and their value capabilities (the amounts of those goods and conditions that they think they are able to get and keep).' When the government is seen as *responsible* for the 'expectations-ability discrepancy' among citizens, it can be ascribed to a lack of 'good governance', defined as 'the extent to which policy making and implementation benefit the population at large' (Hegre and Nygård 2015: 986).[24]

A general empirical implication of the relative deprivation-conflict hypothesis is that good governance reduces incentives for conflict. Many non-quantitative studies highlight the importance of governance factors (e.g., Zakaria 1997), and a number of quantitative studies further indicate that aspects of good governance reduce the risk of internal armed conflict.[25] For example, countries with a well-functioning rule of law have less social conflict (Taydas et al. 2010), and several studies find corruption to be associated with political instability and internal armed conflict (Fjelde 2009; Le Billon 2003; Mauro 1995; Taydas et al. 2010). Moreover, sound economic policies stabilize political institutions and ease the risk of conflict by stimulating economic growth (Collier and Hoeffler 2004b; Gates et al. 2006; Przeworski et al. 2000). Bussmann and Schneider (2007) also show that economic openness in the form of interstate trade and foreign direct investment inflows decrease the risk of internal conflict, although the process of opening up the economy is often associated with increased violence. Related to this, Dreher et al. (2012) show that economic freedom and globalization reduce governments' human rights violations.

On the other hand, heavy military involvement in government may lead to poor governance and a higher risk of conflict. Military regimes, on average, tend to have poor rates of economic performance (Knutsen 2011; Wintrobe 1998), and they have the lowest life expectancy of any type of regime (Geddes 1999). Another aspect of poor governance that is likely to turn people against their own governments is systematic exclusion from decision-making bodies (Cederman et al. 2010). When this is based on pre-existing identity markers such as ethnicity and religion, exclusion is particularly likely to lead to organized mass opposition, since such groups typically have networks that facilitate organization. Finally, repression and disrespect for human rights is also associated with political violence (Carey 2007; Davenport 2007a; Moore 1998). However, repression also increases when armed conflict breaks out.

Economic globalization

Over the past decades (and even centuries), countries have become more tightly interwoven. Globally, imported goods form a steadily increasing share of domestic consumption, and an increasing share of domestic producers are dependent on the access to international markets for their products. How does this affect security? Several studies show that interstate trade and foreign investments reduce the risk of interstate armed conflict (Bussmann 2010; Hegre et al. 2010; Gartzke et al. 2001; Russett and Oneal 2001). Gartzke (2007) even argues that capitalism is more fundamental than democratic institutions to avoid interstate conflict, stating that the positive trend of fewer conflicts over the past century is a 'capitalist peace'. International trade, after all, is an important form of the positive-sum interactions that Gat (2006) sees as the major explanation of the decline in war over the past centuries. This view is, however, disputed (Dafoe et al. 2013). Some studies also indicate that globalization reduces the risk of internal armed conflict (de Soysa and Fjelde 2010; Hegre et al. 2003), although others are more skeptical (Bussmann and Schneider 2007; Schneider 2014).

International trade and investment also have other beneficial effects that strongly influence conflict propensities in the long run. First, it promotes economic growth (Frankel and Romer 1999), which in most cases leads to poverty reduction (Collier and Dollar 2002). Second, trade has also been found to improve domestic governance (Sandholtz and Gray 2003). It is, however, possible that the beneficial effects of trade are dependent on economic development (Mousseau et al. 2003).

Conflict escalation and methodological limitations

In the sections above, we have reviewed a number of studies that apply statistical methods to systematized historical data in order to draw general inferences. These methods require that the observations we analyze be roughly similar (or that we can account for their differences by means of explanatory variables). One particular challenge to such quantitative studies is posed by the immense variation in the magnitudes of wars. For example, the Iran–Iraq war that erupted in 1980 is typically not treated as fundamentally different from the Sino–Vietnamese war the year before, despite the fact that the Iran–Iraq war killed 50 times as many people. Treating such diverse cases as similar can be problematic in some instances, especially when it comes to determining the causes of war escalation.

Lewis Fry Richardson (1960), one of the founders of quantitative research of war, discovered that the number of fatalities in wars follow a power-law distribution. This means that the number of wars with a certain number of fatalities varies as a power of the fatality of the war, or simplified, that about 20% of wars account for 80% of the people killed.[26] Power-law distributions also imply that wars are 'scale-free' – that the probability of further escalation is independent of the accumulated magnitude. This means, for example, that leaders are as reluctant to escalate a war from 100 deaths to 1,000 as they are to escalate from 10,000 to 100,000 deaths.

Pinker (2011: ch. 5) discusses some explanations of why the size of war follows such a pattern. One has to do with coalition behavior: hegemonic power structures and alliance formations can lead very large populations into war, and more people are killed when larger populations are involved. According to Pinker (2011: 236–7), however, the psychological and strategic mechanisms of wars of attrition, in combination with 'loss aversion', constitute a more persuasive explanation to war escalation: Wars are fought until one side cannot endure the costs anymore, but cost tolerance increases as the war stretches on because it becomes more valuable not to suffer loss of reputation, and more important to revenge the dead.

This indicates that the processes causing war escalation can be very different from those leading to war onset, and that the determinants of escalation are much harder to identify quantitatively than the structural factors that are conducive to onset of armed conflicts. Quantitative studies of conflict onset are less challenging, since conflicts are not so different when they break out. What triggered the declaration of war between Austria–Hungary and Serbia in July 1914, for instance, is less unusual than the world war that ensued, and any steps to prevent that war declaration might have prevented the entire cascading of violence. The quantitative studies reviewed here mostly focus on the latter. However, since any war requires that it breaks out in the first place, the factors or structural changes that reduce the risk of war onsets also reduce the risk of extremely deadly wars.

Treating wars and armed conflicts as in principle similar, 'thinly described' events (Geertz 1973) also means quantitative studies ignore a large amount of information relevant to these events, such as the psychology of core actors or the informal networks of domestic power relations they act within. Quantitative security studies will never explain more than a fraction of the variation between societies in terms of violent group behavior. On the other hand, quantitative studies allow us to identify patterns that are hard to discover in studies that are rich in detail. The declining trend shown in Figure 11.2, for instance, can only be demonstrated with simplified codification of very complex events.

Conclusion

Defining security as a low risk for states and individuals being targeted in acts of political violence, we have shown in this chapter that threats to security have shifted dramatically over the past 50 years. The number of people killed by political violence has decreased, and a larger proportion is due to internal conflicts in low-income countries. We have reviewed the aspects that the quantitative conflict literature indicates are the most important guarantors of security. According to the empirical findings of this research, means of compellance, in particular military expenditure, are inefficient and often counter-productive, both internally and internationally. An exception is the use of force by UN peacekeeping operations, which often succeed in constraining violence. The main reason for this discrepancy is probably that UN forces more often are neutral and constrained in their use of violence than domestic militaries.

On the other hand, the literature strongly suggests that policies that induce actors to refrain from the use of violence are most effective in establishing security in the long run. Most important is probably solid economic growth that reduces poverty, stimulates human capital formation, and gives rise to dense networks of positive-sum economic interactions. From such socio-economic changes follow peaceful interactions, sustainable democratization, and good governance. The past half century has also seen vast improvements in all these indicators.

The quantitative conflict research literature strongly suggests that the global security environment has changed – not because of more efficient militaries, but because governments have become much more responsive to the general well-being of their citizens. This supports the expansion of the notion of security – as shown in figure 11.2, it is particularly the security of individuals from state-sponsored violence that has improved.[27] This has implications for the field of security studies. Essentially, our findings suggest that the traditional focus on military defense against threats should partly shift towards economic and political risk-reducing policies. Furthermore, since internal armed conflicts have accounted for the most deaths over the past half century, and interstate conflicts have become completely outnumbered by internal conflicts, the poor, non-Western countries where these political violence events occur should receive more attention in security studies. Finally, this chapter has highlighted the importance of the security of individuals, not only that of states.

Notes

1 The research was funded by the Research Council of Norway, projects 217995/V10 and 204454/V10 (see http://havardhegre.net for details).
2 Quantification does not necessarily mean objectivity in all respects, though.
3 In this chapter, we do not look at international terrorism specifically, despite the importance of the 'war on terror' since 2001. Terrorism, however, often stems from the same sources as internal armed conflicts, which we give much attention.
4 See Chapter 1 by Glaser and Chapter 6 by Masala that make strong cases for focusing on states' security. The difference in emphasis is related to the more general debate between 'realism' and 'liberalism'. Incidentally, quantitative studies challenge the realism paradigm on empirical grounds – for instance, the evidence for a democratic peace is mainly quantitative.
5 State-based conflict is defined in accordance with the UCDP/PRIO Armed Conflict Dataset as 'a contested incompatibility that concerns government and/or territory where the use of armed force between two parties, of which at least one is the government of a state, results in at least 25 battle-related deaths' (Themnér 2014: 1). The UCDP/PRIO dataset is used in the figure (Gleditsch et al. 2002; Themnér and Wallensteen 2014, version 4 2014). The figure is stacked.
6 The figure is based on Lacina and Gleditsch (2005, version 3.0) and Sundberg (2008, version 5 2014). In order to merge the two datasets, we calculate the geometric mean of the datasets' best estimates for each conflict type where we have data from both, and extend this where we have only one source. Since UCDP does not provide a best estimate for Syria in 2013, we include a very conservative estimate of 25,000 battle-related deaths for Syria this year, based on UCDP's lower-end estimate. The real number may be considerably higher (see e.g. Price et al. 2014). The figure is stacked.
7 One-sided conflict refers to the use of armed force against civilians by a state's government or a formally organized group (Eck and Hultman 2007), while non-state conflict denotes armed conflict between two organized armed groups, neither of which is the government of a state (Sundberg et al. 2012), both resulting in minimum 25 battle-related deaths in a year. The data in the figure are from UCDP's One-Sided Violence Dataset (Eck and Hultman 2007, version 1.4 2014) and UCDP's Non-State Conflict Dataset (Sundberg et al. 2012, version 2.5 2014).
8 Coup attempts are defined as 'illegal and overt attempts by the military or other elites within the state apparatus to unseat the sitting executive', while successful coups are defined as the seizure and holding of power for a minimum of seven days (Powell and Thyne 2011: 252). The data used in Figure 11.4 are from an updated version of Powell and Thyne (2011), available at http://www.uky.edu/~clthyn2/coup_data/home.htm.
9 The figure is based on a categorical version of the Polity scale, taken from Marshall et al. (2014). Values larger than six are defined as democracy, values between -5 and 5 as

semi-democracy, and values below -6 as non-democracy. Interruption (-66), interregnum (-77) and transition (-88) periods are not included.
10 This number does not include the people killed in Syria in 2013.
11 746,309 died from one-sided violence and 118,259 from non-state conflicts in the period 1989–2013 (Eck and Hultman 2007, UCDP's One-Sided Violence Dataset version 1.4 2014, Sundberg, Eck and Kreutz 2012, UCDP's Non-State Conflict Dataset version 2.5 2014).
12 Military spending has been shown to systematically depend on a set of domestic and international factors, such as states' perceived security situation, arms races, military expenditures in neighboring countries, regime type, international trade, and income per capita (Albalate et al. 2012; Collier and Hoeffler 2002, 2007; Goldsmith 2003).
13 Capabilities are typically measured with the 'CINC' score (Singer et al. 1972), which is a function of population size, average income, and military expenditures.
14 These studies, however, suffer from ignoring the potential reciprocal causation.
15 Such 'backfiring' is well-known in the literatures on repression and mobilization (e.g., Moore 1998).
16 Somewhat different results are found for other measures of military capacity. Hegre and Sambanis (2006) find a robust negative relationship between the number of troops relative to the total population and the likelihood of civil war onset. Brandt et al. (2008) and DeRouen and Sobek (2004) also find that that army size divided by the total population decreases the duration of civil war.
17 Some of these also address the potential problem of endogeneity related to selection bias and nonrandom employment of PKOs (see Fortna 2008; Gilligan and Sergenti 2008).
18 Interestingly, Fortna (2004a: 283) finds that 'traditional peacekeeping missions and observer missions have been the most successful' in this regard while Doyle and Sambanis (2006: 111) find that 'traditional peacekeeping does not work well, and may even have negative effects'.
19 Sambanis (2008: 29) also argues that 'the UN has become better at peacekeeping over time', and Fortna (2004a) finds that the effect of PKOs is only significant in the post-Cold War period.
20 However, Gilligan and Sergenti (2008: 89) and Greig and Diehl (2005: 621) do not find any effect of UN interventions in ongoing civil wars.
21 This is in line with Diehl et al. (1996), who demonstrate that UN intervention has no effect on interstate conflict recurrence in the period 1946–88.
22 For a recent review, see Hegre (2014).
23 For a review, see Hegre (2015). Hibbs (1973) and Hegre et al. (2001) indicate that the relationship between development indicators and political violence or the risk of armed conflict may be curvilinear, with the highest amount of violence in middle-income countries. At least, it seems that the difference between the poorest countries and lower-middle income countries is smaller than between lower- and upper-middle income countries.
24 The link between poor governance and the two aspects discussed above – democracy and poverty – is not necessarily direct. For example, South Korea was poor in the 1960s, but not poorly governed, and Peru and the Philippines were fairly democratic in 1990, but not well governed (Hegre and Nygård 2014: 16). Likewise, Taiwan and Singapore were well governed but not particularly democratic.
25 A comprehensive review and reanalysis is found in Hegre and Nygård (2015).
26 And indeed, the 20 per cent of interstate wars with the most states participating do account for 80 per cent of the fatalities (Joyce et al. 2013).
27 The recent collapse of central government rule in Sunni parts of Iraq exemplifies how the security of states has become more dependent on the services they provide to their citizens – many commentators suggest that ISIS might have failed if Nuri al-Maliki's government had been more responsive to the Sunni population.

References

Abouharb, M.R. and Kimball, A.L. (2007) 'A New Dataset on Infant Mortality Rates, 1816–2002', *Journal of Peace Research*, 44 (6): 743–54.
Albalate, D., Bel, G. and Elias, F. (2012) 'Institutional Determinants of Military Spending', *Journal of Comparative Economics*, 40 (2): 279–90.
Anderton, C.H. and Carter, J.R. (2001) 'The Impact of War on Trade: An Interrupted Times-Series Study', *Journal of Peace Research*, 38 (4): 445–57.
Bayer, R. and Rupert, M.C. (2004) 'Effects of Civil Wars on International Trade, 1950–92', *Journal of Peace Research*, 41 (6): 699–713.
Beardsley, K. (2011) 'Peacekeeping and the Contagion of Conflict', *Journal of Politics*, 73 (4): 1051–64.
Boix, C. (2008) 'Economic Roots of Civil Wars and Revolutions in the Contemporary World', *World Politics*, 60 (3): 390–437.
Boulding, K.E. (1989) *Three Faces of Power*, Newbury Park: Sage.
Brandt, P.T., Mason, T.D., Gurses, M., Petrovsky, N. and Radin, D. (2008) 'When and How the Fighting Stops: Explaining the Duration and Outcome of Civil Wars', *Defence and Peace Economics*, 19 (6): 415–34.
Bremer, S.A. (1992) 'Dangerous Dyads: Conditions Affecting the Likelihood of Interstate War, 1816–1965', *Journal of Conflict Resolution*, 36 (2): 309–41.
Bueno de Mesquita, B. and Downs, G.W. (2006) 'Intervention and Democracy', *International Organization*, 60 (3): 627–49.
Bueno de Mesquita, B. and Lalman, D. (1992) *War and Reason: Domestic and International Imperatives*, New Haven: Yale University Press.
Bueno de Mesquita, B., Smith, A., Siverson, R.M. and Morrow, J.D. (2003) *The Logic of Political Survival*, Cambridge (MA): MIT Press.
Bussmann, Margit (2010) 'Foreign Direct Investment and Militarized International Conflict', *Journal of Peace Research*, 47 (2): 143–53.
Bussmann, M. and Schneider, G. (2007) 'When Globalization Discontent Turns Violent: Foreign Economic Liberalization and Internal War', *International Studies Quarterly*, 51 (1): 79–97.
Carey, S.C. (2007) 'Rebellion in Africa: Disaggregating the Effect of Political Regimes', *Journal of Peace Research*, 44 (1): 47–64.
Cederman, L.-E., Hug, S. and Krebs, L.F. (2010) 'Democratization and Civil War: Empirical Evidence', *Journal of Peace Research*, 47 (4): 377–94.
Cederman, L.-E., Wimmer, A. and Min, B. (2010) 'Why Do Ethnic Groups Rebel? New Data and Analysis, *World Politics*, 62 (1): 87–119.
Choi, S.-W. and James, P. (2004) 'Civil-Military Relations in a Neo-Kantian World, 1886–1992', *Armed Forces & Society*, 30 (2): 227–54.
Colaresi, M. and Carey, S.C. (2008) 'To Kill or to Protect: Security Forces, Domestic Institutions, and Genocide', *Journal of Conflict Resolution*, 52 (1): 39–67.
Collier, P. (2000) 'Doing Well Out of War: An Economic Perspective', in M. Berdal and D.M. Malone (eds) *Greed & Grievance: Economic Agendas in Civil Wars*, Boulder: Lynne Rienner: 91–111.
(2009a) 'The Political Economy of State Failure', *Oxford Review of Economic Policy*, 25 (2): 219–40.
(2009b) *Wars, Guns and Votes: Democracy in Dangerous Places*, New York: Harper-Collins.
Collier, P. and Dollar, D. (2002) *Globalization, Growth, and Poverty*, Oxford: Oxford University Press.

Collier, P. and Hoeffler, A. (1998) 'On the Economic Causes of Civil War', *Oxford Economic Papers*, 50 (4): 563–73.

—— (2002) 'Military Expenditure: Threats, Aid and Arms Races', World Bank Policy Research Working Paper No. 2927, available at: http://elibrary.worldbank.org/doi/pdf/10.1596/1813-9450-2927 (accessed 22 January 2015).

—— (2004a) 'Conflicts', in B. Lomborg (ed.) *Global Crises, Global Solutions*, 1st edn, Cambridge: Cambridge University Press: 129–59.

—— (2004b) 'Greed and Grievance in Civil War', *Oxford Economic Papers*, 56 (4): 563–95.

—— (2006) 'Military Expenditure in Post-Conflict Societies', *Economics of Governance*, 7 (1): 89–107.

—— (2007) 'Military Spending and the Risks of Coup d'Etat', available at: http://users.ox.ac.uk/~econpco/research/pdfs/MilitarySpendingandRisksCoups.pdf (accessed 22 January 2015).

Collier, P., Hoeffler, A. and Söderbom, M. (2001) 'On the Duration of Civil War', World Bank Policy Research Working Paper No. 2681, available at: http://elibrary.worldbank.org/doi/pdf/10.1596/1813-9450-2681 (accessed 22 January 2015).

—— (2008) 'Post-Conflict Risks', *Journal of Peace Research*, 45 (4): 461–78.

Collier, P. and Rohner, D. (2008) 'Democracy, Development and Conflict', *Journal of the European Economic Association*, 6 (1): 531–40.

Dafoe, A., Oneal, J.R. and Russett, B.M. (2013) 'The Democratic Peace: Weighing the Evidence and Cautious Inference', *International Studies Quarterly*, 57 (1): 201–14.

Dahl, M., Gates, S., Hegre, H. and Strand, H. (2013) 'Why Waves? Global Patterns of Democratization, 1820–2008', Typescript, PRIO, available at: http://havardhegre.net/items/why-waves (accessed 16 February 2014).

Davenport, C. (2007a) 'State Repression and Political Order', *Annual Review of Political Science*, 10: 1–23.

—— (2007b) *State Repression and the Domestic Democratic Peace*, Cambridge: Cambridge University Press.

Davies, J.C. (1962) 'Towards a Theory of Revolution', *American Sociological Review*, 27 (1): 5–19.

De Soysa, I. and Fjelde, H. (2010) 'Is the Hidden Hand an Iron Fist? Capitalism and Civil Peace, 1970–2005', *Journal of Peace Research*, 47 (3): 287–98.

DeRouen, K. and Sobek, D. (2004) 'The Dynamics of Civil War Duration and Outcome', *Journal of Peace Research*, 41 (3): 303–20.

Diehl, P.F., Reifschneider, J. and Hensel, P.R. (1996) 'United Nations Intervention and Recurring Conflict', *International Organization*, 50 (4): 683–700.

Doyle, M.W. (1986) 'Liberalism and World Politics', *American Political Science Review* 80 (4): 1151–69.

Doyle, M.W. and Sambanis, N. (2000) 'International Peacebuilding: A Theoretical and Quantitative Analysis', *American Political Science Review*, 94 (4): 779–801.

—— (2006) *Making War & Building Peace: United Nations Peace Operations*, Princeton: Princeton University Press.

Dreher, A., Gassebner, M. and Siemers, L.-H.R. (2012) 'Globalization, Economic Freedom, and Human Rights', *Journal of Conflict Resolution*, 56 (3): 516–46.

Eck, K. and Hultman, L. (2007) 'One-Sided Violence Against Civilians in War: Insights from New Fatality Data', *Journal of Peace Research*, 44 (2): 233–46.

Farber, H.S. and Gowa, J. (1995) 'Polities and Peace', *International Security*, 20 (2): 123–46.

Fearon, J.D. (1994) 'Domestic Political Audiences and the Escalation of International Disputes', *American Political Science Review*, 88 (3): 577–92.

Fearon, J.D. and Laitin, D.D. (2003) 'Ethnicity, Insurgency, and Civil War', *American Political Science Review*, 97 (1): 75–90.
Fjelde, H. (2009) 'Buying Peace? Oil Wealth, Corruption and Civil War 1985–99', *Journal of Peace Research*, 47 (2): 199–218.
Fortna, V.P. (2003) 'Inside and Out: Peacekeeping and the Duration of Peace after Civil and Interstate Wars', *International Studies Review*, 5 (4): 97–114.
—— (2004a) 'Does Peacekeeping Keep Peace? International Intervention and the Duration of Peace After Civil War', *International Studies Quarterly*, 48 (2): 269–92.
—— (2004b) 'Interstate Peacekeeping: Causal Mechanisms and Empirical Effects', *World Politics*, 56 (4): 481–519.
—— (2008) *Does Peacekeeping Work? Shaping Belligerents' Choices After Civil War*, Princeton: Princeton University Press.
Frankel, J.A. and Romer, D. (1999) 'Does Trade Affect Growth?', *American Economic Review*, 89 (3): 379–99.
Gartzke, E. (2007) 'The Capitalist Peace', *American Journal of Political Science*, 51 (1): 166–91.
Gartzke, E., Li, Q. and Boehmer, C. (2001) 'Investing in the Peace: Economic Interdependence and International Conflict', *International Organization*, 55 (2): 391–438.
Gat, A. (2006) *War in Human Civilization*, Oxford: Oxford University Press.
Gates, S., Hegre, H., Jones, M.P. and Strand, H. (2006) 'Institutional Inconsistency and Political Instability: Polity Duration, 1800–2000', *American Journal of Political Science*, 50 (4): 893–908.
Gates, S., Hegre, H., Nygård, H.M. and Strand, H. (2012) 'Development Consequences of Armed Conflict', *World Development*, 40 (9): 1713–22.
Gates, S., Knutsen, T.L. and Moses, J.W. (1996) 'Democracy and Peace: A More Skeptical View', *Journal of Peace Research*, 33 (1): 1–10.
Geddes, B. (1999) 'What Do We Know About Democratization After Twenty Years?', *Annual Review of Political Science*, 2: 115–44.
Geertz, C. (1973) *The Interpretation of Cultures: Selected Essays*, Vol. 5019, New York: Basic Books.
Gibler, D.M., Rider, T.J. and Hutchison, M.L. (2005) 'Taking Arms Against a Sea of Troubles: Conventional Arms Races During Periods of Rivalry', *Journal of Peace Research*, 42 (2): 131–47.
Gilligan, M.J. and Sergenti, E.J. (2008) 'Do UN Interventions Cause Peace? Using Matching to Improve Causal Inference', *Quarterly Journal of Political Science*, 3 (2): 89–122.
Gleditsch, K.S. (2002) *All International Politics is Local: The Diffusion of Conflict, Integration, and Democratization*, Ann Arbor: University of Michigan Press.
Gleditsch, N.P., Bjerkholt, O., Cappelen, Å., Smith, R.P. and Dunne, J.P. (eds) (1996) *The Peace Dividend*, Amsterdam: Elsevier.
Gleditsch, N.P., Christiansen, L.S. and Hegre, H. (2007) 'Democratic Jihad? Military Intervention and Democracy', World Bank Policy Research Working Paper No. 4242, available at: https://openknowledge.worldbank.org/handle/10986/7095 (accessed 22 January 2015).
Gleditsch, N.P., Hegre, H. and Strand, H. (2009) 'Democracy and Civil War', in M. Midlarsky (ed.) *Handbook of War Studies III*, Ann Arbor: University of Michigan Press: 155–92.
Gleditsch, N.P., Wallensteen, P., Eriksson, M., Sollenberg, M. and Strand, H. (2002) 'Armed Conflict 1946–2001: A New Dataset', *Journal of Peace Research*, 39 (5): 615–37.

Goldsmith, B.E. (2003) 'Bearing the Defense Burden, 1886–1989: Why Spend More?', *Journal of Conflict Resolution*, 47 (5): 551–73.

Goldstein, J.S. (2011) *Winning the War on War: The Decline of Armed Conflict Worldwide*, New York: Dutton.

Greig, J.M. and Diehl, P.F. (2005) 'The Peacekeeping-Peacemaking Dilemma', *International Studies Quarterly*, 49 (4): 621–45.

Gupta, S., de Mello, L. and Sharan, R. (2001) 'Corruption and Military Spending', *European Journal of Political Economy*, 17 (4): 749–77.

Gurr, T.R. (1968) 'A Causal Model of Civil Strife: A Comparative Analysis Using New Indices', *American Political Science Review*, 62 (4): 1104–24.

— (1970) *Why Men Rebel*, Princeton: Princeton University Press.

Hegre, H. (2003) 'Disentangling Democracy and Development as Determinants of Armed Conflict', World Bank Working Paper No. 24637, available at: http://web.worldbank.org/archive/website01241/WEB/0__CO-81.HTM (accessed 22 January 2015).

— (2004) 'Size Asymmetry, Trade, and Militarized Conflict', *Journal of Conflict Resolution*, 48 (3): 403–29.

— (2008) 'Gravitating Toward War: Preponderance May Pacify, but Power Kills', *Journal of Conflict Resolution*, 52 (4): 566–89.

— (2014) 'Democracy and Armed Conflict', *Journal of Peace Research*, 51 (2): 159–72.

— (2015) 'Civil Conflict and Development', in N. van de Walle and C. Lancaster (eds) *Oxford University Press Handbook on the Politics of Development*, Oxford: Oxford University Press.

Hegre, H., Ellingsen, T., Gates, S. and Gleditsch, N.P. (2001) 'Toward a Democratic Civil Peace? Democracy, Political Change, and Civil War, 1816–1992', *American Political Science Review*, 95 (1): 33–48.

Hegre, H., Gissinger, R. and Gleditsch, N.P. (2003) 'Globalization and Internal Conflict', in G. Schneider, K. Barbieri and N.P. Gleditsch (eds) *Globalization and Armed Conflict*, Lanham: Rowman and Littlefield: 251–76.

Hegre, H., Hultman, L. and Nygård, H.M. (2010) 'Evaluating the Conflict-Reducing Effect of UN Peace-Keeping Operations', Paper presented to the National Conference on Peace and Conflict Research, Uppsala, 9–11 September, available at: http://folk.uio.no/hahegre/Papers/PKOpredictionUppsala.pdf (accessed 22 January 2015).

Hegre, H. and Nygård, H.M. (2015) 'Governance and Conflict Relapse', *Journal of Conflict Resolution*, 59 (6): 984–1016, DOI: 10.1177/0022002713520591.

Hegre, H., Oneal, J.R. and Russett, B. (2010) 'Trade Does Promote Peace: New Simultaneous Estimates of the Reciprocal Effects of Trade and Conflict', *Journal of Peace Research*, 47 (6): 763–74.

Hegre, H. and Sambanis, N. (2006) 'Sensitivity Analysis of Empirical Results on Civil War Onset', *Journal of Conflict Resolution*, 50 (4): 508–35.

Henderson, E.A. and Singer, J.D. (2000) 'Civil War in the Post-Colonial World, 1946–92', *Journal of Peace Research*, 37 (3): 275–99.

Hermann, M.G. and Kegley Jr., C.W. (1998) 'The U.S. Use of Military Intervention to Promote Democracy: Evaluating the Record', *International Interactions*, 24 (2): 91–114.

Hibbs, D.A. (1973) *Mass Political Violence: A Cross-National Causal Analysis*, New York: Wiley.

Hultman, L. (2010) 'Keeping Peace or Spurring Violence? Unintended Effects of Peace Operations on Violence against Civilians', *Civil Wars*, 12 (1–2): 29–46.

Human Security Centre (2005) *Human Security Report 2005: War and Peace in the 21st Century*, Oxford: Oxford University Press.

Huth, P.K. and Allee, T.L. (2002) 'Domestic Political Accountability and the Escalation and Settlement of International Disputes', *Journal of Conflict Resolution*, 46 (6): 754–90.

Joyce, K.A., Ghosn, F. and Bayer, R. (2013) 'When and Whom to Join: The Expansion of Ongoing Violent Interstate Conflicts', *British Journal of Political Science*, 44 (1): 208–38.

Knight, M., Loayza, N. and Villanueva, D. (1996) 'The Peace Dividend: Military Spending Cuts and Economic Growth', *IMF Staff Papers*, 43 (1): 1–37.

Knutsen, C.H. (2011) 'The Economic Effects of Democracy and Dictatorship', PhD thesis, Department of Political Science, University of Oslo.

Kreps, S. and Wallace, G. (2009) 'Just How Humanitarian Are Interventions? Peacekeeping and the Prevention of Civilian Killings during and after Civil Wars', presented at American Political Science Association Annual Meeting, Toronto, 3–6 September, available at: http://papers.ssrn.com/sol3/papers.cfm?abstract_id=1450574 (accessed 22 January 2015).

Lacina, B. (2006) 'Explaining the Severity of Civil War', *Journal of Conflict Resolution*, 50 (2): 276–89.

Lacina, B. and Gleditsch, N.P. (2005) 'Monitoring Trends in Global Combat: A New Dataset of Battle Deaths', *European Journal of Population*, 21 (2–3): 145–66.

Le Billon, P. (2003) 'Buying Peace or Fuelling War: The Role of Corruption in Armed Conflicts', *Journal of International Development*, 15 (4): 413–26.

Lemke, D. (2002) *Regions of War and Peace*, Cambridge: Cambridge University Press.

Levy, Y. (2012) 'A Revised Model of Civilian Control of the Military: The Interaction Between the Republican Exchange and the Control Exchange', *Armed Forces & Society*, 38 (4): 529–56.

Londregan, J.B. and Poole, K.T. (1990) 'Poverty, the Coup Trap, and the Seizure of Executive Power', *World Politics*, 42 (2): 151–83.

Maoz, Z. and Russett, B.M. (1993) 'Normative and Structural Causes of Democratic Peace, 1946–1986', *American Political Science Review*, 87 (3): 624–38.

Marshall, M.G., Gurr, T.R. and Jaggers, K. (2014) 'Polity IV Project, Political Regime Characteristics and Transitions, 1800–2013', Center for Systemic Peace, available at: http://www.systemicpeace.org/inscrdata.html (accessed 20 January 2015).

Mauro, P. (1995) 'Corruption and Growth', *The Quarterly Journal of Economics*, 110 (3): 681–712.

Meernik, J. (1996) 'United States Military Intervention and the Promotion of Democracy', *Journal of Peace Research*, 33 (4): 391–402.

Miguel, E., Satyanath, S., and Serengeti, E. (2004) 'Economic Shocks and Civil Conflict: An Instrumental Variables Approach', *Journal of Political Economy*, 112 (4): 725–53.

Milante, G. (2013) 'Nov. 13: How much security can a dollar buy?', available at: http://www.sipri.org/media/newsletter/essay/milante_nov13 (accessed 4 December 2013).

Moore, W.H. (1998) 'Repression and Dissent: Substitution, Context, and Timing', *American Journal of Political Science*, 42 (3): 851–73.

Morgenthau, H. (1967) *Politics Among Nations: The Struggle for Power and Peace*, New York: Knopf.

Mousseau, M., Hegre, H. and Oneal, J.R. (2003) 'How the Wealth of Nations Conditions the Liberal Peace', *European Journal of International Relations*, 9 (2): 277–314.

Oneal, J.R., Oneal, F.H., Maoz, Z. and Russett, B. (1996) 'The Liberal Peace: Interdependence, Democracy, and International Conflict, 1950–85', *Journal of Peace Research*, 33 (1): 11–28.

Peceny, M. (1999) 'Forcing Them to Be Free', *Political Research Quarterly*, 52 (3): 549–82.
Pickering, J. and Peceny, M. (2006) 'Forging Democracy at Gunpoint', *International Studies Quarterly*, 50 (3): 539–59.
Pinker, S. (2011) *The Better Angels of Our Nature: Why Violence has Declined*, New York: Viking.
Powell, J.M. (2012) 'Coups and Conflict: The Paradox of Coup-Proofing', PhD thesis, University of Kentucky, available at: http://uknowledge.uky.edu/polysci_etds/3 (accessed 22 January 2015).
Powell, J.M. and Thyne, C.L. (2011) 'Global Instances of Coups from 1950-Present: A New Dataset', *Journal of Peace Research*, 48 (2): 249–59.
Price, M., Gohdes, A. and Ball, P. (2014) *Updated Statistical Analysis of Documentation of Killings in the Syrian Arab Republic*. Report commissioned by the Office of the UN High Commissioner for Human Rights, available at http://www.ohchr.org/Documents/Countries/SY/HRDAGUpdatedReportAug2014.pdf (accessed 25 February 2015).
Przeworski, A., Alvarez, M.E., Cheibub, J.A. and Limongi, F. (2000) *Democracy and Development: Political Institutions and Well-Being in the World, 1950–1990*, Cambridge: Cambridge University Press.
Quinlivan, J.T. (1999) 'Coup-Proofing: It's Practice and Consequences in the Middle East', *International Security*, 24 (2): 131–65.
Reed, W. (2003) 'Information, Power, and War', *American Political Science Review*, 97 (4): 633–41.
Reiter, D. and Stam III, A.C. (1998) 'Democracy, War Initiation, and Victory', *American Political Science Review*, 92 (2): 377–89.
Richardson, L.F. (1960) *Statistics of Deadly Quarrels*, Pittsburgh: Boxwood.
Rosecrance, R. (1986) *The Rise of the Trading State: Commerce and Conquest in the Modern World*, New York: Basic Books.
Russett, B. and Oneal, J. (2001) *Triangulating Peace: Democracy, Interdependence, and International Organizations*. London and New York: Norton.
Sambanis, N. (2008) 'Short-Term and Long-Term Effects of United Nations Peace Operations', *The World Bank Economic Review*, 22 (1): 9–32.
Sandholtz, W. and Gray, M.M. (2003) 'International Integration and National Corruption', *International Organization*, 57 (4): 761–800.
Schneider, G. (2014) 'Peace Through Globalization and Capitalism? Prospects of Two Liberal Propositions', *Journal of Peace Research*, 51 (2): 173–83.
Schweller, R.L. (1992) 'Domestic Structure and Preventive War: Are Democracies More Pacific?', *World Politics*, 44 (2): 235–69.
Sechser, T.S. (2004) 'Are Soldiers Less War-Prone than Statesmen?', *Journal of Conflict Resolution*, 48 (5): 746–74.
Singer, J.D., Bremer, S. and Stuckey, J. (1972) 'Capability Distribution, Uncertainty, and Major Power War, 1820–1965', in B.M. Russett (ed.) *Peace, War, and Numbers*, Beverly Hills: Sage: 19–48.
Sundberg, R. (2008) 'Collective Violence 2002–2007: Global and Regional Trends', in L. Harbom and R. Sundberg (eds.) *States in Armed Conflict 2007*, Uppsala: Universitetstryckeriet.
Sundberg, R., Eck, K. and Kreutz, J. (2012) 'Introducing the UCDP Non-State Conflict Dataset', *Journal of Peace Research*, 49 (2): 351–62.
Taydas, Z. and Peksen, D. (2012) 'Can States Buy Peace? Social Welfare Spending and Civil Conflicts', *Journal of Peace Research*, 49 (2): 273–87.

Taydas, Z., Peksen, D. and James, P. (2010) 'Why Do Civil Wars Occur? Understanding the Importance of Institutional Quality', *Civil Wars*, 12 (3): 195–217.

Themnér, L. (2014) 'UCDP/PRIO Armed Conflict Dataset Codebook, Version 4', available at: http://www.pcr.uu.se/digitalAssets/124/124920_1codebook_ucdp_prio-armed-conflict-dataset-v4_2014a.pdf (accessed 23 January 2015).

Themnér, L. and Wallensteen, P. (2014) 'Armed Conflict, 1946–2013', *Journal of Peace Research*, 51 (4): 541–54.

Thyne, C. (2006) 'ABC's, 123's, and the Golden Rule: The Pacifying Effect of Education on Civil War, 1980–1999', *International Studies Quarterly*, 50 (4): 733–54.

UCDP (2014) 'UCDP Battle-Related Deaths Dataset, Version 5.0', Uppsala Conflict Data Program, available at: http://www.pcr.uu.se/digitalAssets/124/124934_1codebook-ucdp-battle-related-deaths-datasets-v.5-2014.pdf (accessed 23 January 2015).

UNODC (2011) 'Global Study on Homicide', United Nations Office on Drugs and Crime, available at: http://www.unodc.org/documents/data-and-analysis/statistics/Homicide/Globa_study_on_homicide_2011_web.pdf (accessed 23 January 2015).

Urdal, H. (2005) 'People vs. Malthus: Population Pressure, Environmental Degradation and Armed Conflict Revisited', *Journal of Peace Research*, 42 (4): 417–34.

Van Evera, S. (1999) *Causes of War: Power and the Roots of Conflict*, Ithaca and London: Cornell University Press.

Wallace, M.D. (1979) 'Arms Races and Escalation: Some New Evidence', *Journal of Conflict Resolution*, 23 (1): 3–16.

(1982) 'Armaments and Escalation: Two Competing Hypotheses', *International Studies Quarterly*, 26 (1): 37–56.

Waltz, K.N. (1959) *Man, the State, and War: A Theoretical Analysis*, New York: Columbia University Press.

WHO (2013) 'Global Status Report on Road Safety 2013', World Health Organization, available at: http://www.who.int/iris/bitstream/10665/78256/1/9789241564564_eng.pdf (accessed 23 January 2015).

Wintrobe, R. (1998) *The Political Economy of Dictatorship*, Cambridge: Cambridge University Press.

Wright, Q. ([1942] 1965) *A Study of War*, 2nd edn, Chicago: University of Chicago Press.

Zakaria, F. (1997) 'The Rise of Illiberal Democracy', *Foreign Affairs*, 76 (6): 22–43.

12 Combining methods

Connections and zooms in analysing hybrids

Julian Junk and Valentin Rauer

Introduction[1]

The main premise of this volume is that security studies is expanding both in terms of the scope of research objects and across disciplinary boundaries. Former dividing lines such as micro versus macro, subject versus object and military versus civil have become increasingly blurred while corresponding methodological boxes have opened. As the contribution by Hegre and Kristiansen in this volume demonstrates, even well-established research fields such as conflict studies stand to benefit from integrating the insights provided by qualitative and quantitative methods. However, the challenge faced by existing research strategies becomes even more pressing when one considers the impacts of technological and digital advancements in security studies (Rauer 2012). One of the most prominent – though, from a social science perspective, yet to be completely understood – developments are drones, or 'unmanned area vehicles' (UAVs). These robotic systems are increasingly capable of autonomous action, challenging well-established patterns of assigning agency, responsibility and geographical distance. As such, drones do not represent actors in the sense of human beings but combine characteristics of humans and machines: they constitute 'hybrids' or 'actants' capable, at least in part, of intentional and autonomous decision-making (Müller and Schörnig 2010; Sharkey and Suchman 2013; Strawser 2013). Scholars have argued that the social sciences have not yet developed research methods suited to these partially overlapping and fragmented phenomena (Latour 2005). Research on phenomena such as hybridity demands the combination of methods in a controlled and systematic way, forcing researchers to abandon their own methodological camps and engage in dialogue with other areas of security studies and their research tools.

The expansion of security studies goes hand in hand with the need for more inclusive research designs that harvest a plurality of methods and integrate them into one coherent research project. One challenge for investigating hybrid phenomena is identifying systematic strategies for combining methods. This chapter proposes a set of strategies to this end. For that purpose, we take a renewed look at the assumptions made by Science and Technology Studies (STS) and the so-called Actor Network Theory (ANT), an interdisciplinary research field that places hybrid phenomena at its core. In highlighting an inherent pluralism within

STS/ANT, we extract two essential analytical lenses: zooms and connections. These lenses provide categories for systematizing and, ultimately, investigating hybridity. This chapter links these two lenses to other commonly discussed approaches for combining methods, referring to the practice and effects of the use of UAVs, so-called (lethal) 'drones'. However, we move beyond conventional terminology by distinguishing between method triangulation and method parallelization as two of the most useful strategies for combining methods. While literature on so-called mixed methods or triangulation abounds, this chapter argues that the current state of research is deficient in two ways: first, in systematizing the different approaches of combining methods and, second, in identifying the operational challenges and opportunities held by each approach. The framework presented here of linking the analytical lenses of zooms to research strategies for method parallelization and the analytical lens of connections to strategies of method triangulation seems far more capable of operationalizing the empirical research agenda of expanded security studies. Here, hybrid phenomena increasingly gain significance due to technological advances as well as inter- and sub-disciplinary expansion and specialization.

Methodological access to hybrids: connections and zooms

In recent years, ANT has gained in prominence, most notably in sociology and political science. The theory offers a pragmatic approach capable of addressing social phenomena that do not fit into the epistemological frameworks or scientific conventions of large theoretical ideologies that scholars are accustomed to – such as 'structural functionalism', 'system theory', 'radical constructivism' or 'realism'. Moreover, as this chapter argues, it offers analytical tools that help identify phenomena like hybridity, often neglected by other areas of security studies.[2] This section introduces the notion of hybridity and discusses the added-value that ANT provides for an analysis of hybrid phenomena.

Hybrids

'Hybrid' or 'hybridity' refers to phenomena that are 'composed of two diverse elements', such as something 'involving both analogue and digital methods'.[3] The term has been used to refer to various sorts of compositions since early modern times; hybridity and actants are not at all new concepts.[4] The terms are particularly salient in the context of ANT; however, according to this approach, the traditional division of natural and social sciences is at odds with the issues and phenomena that both camps study. The core of the argument is that while the social world consists of many natural and material aspects, the natural world of physics heavily relies on social rules and structures. Thus, challenges and opportunities for researchers lie in avoiding an a priori division and combining the social and natural in order to discover the extent to which materiality and sociability create hybrids containing both aspects. For Latour, though every technology transforms the ability of human action, the reverse is also true (Latour 2005). Consequently, the common dichotomy of a purely human actor on the one hand versus a purely technological advice on the other proves false. Rather, action is distributed among human actors and the involved technologies (Rammert 2008; Suchman 2007). The notion of 'hybridity' takes this distributed and technologically mediated characteristic of human action into account.[5]

Hybridity as presented by Latour (2005) and Rammert (2008) is a concept related to gradations. For example, if people engage one another in a hand-to-hand boxing fight, the degree of technology used is clearly lower than in case of using firearms or UAVs. Humans' violent interactions vary depending on the involved technology. Boxing gloves, for instance, constitute an interaction that calls for direct bodily contact between the conflicting human beings. Social interaction is, in this case, always limited to a certain spatial dimension. The site of interaction for UAVs, however, is potentially infinite – commonly spanning distances of thousands of miles. Furthermore, modern robotic systems enlarge the capability of the human senses. Facial recognition technology enables actors to identify individuals for targeted attacks and warfare without the need of 'boots on the ground'. Going one step further, it is no longer only humans who are able to wage war – technology is also becoming more and more capable of autonomous action. The impacts and ramifications of these human-machine actor networks are best represented by the concept of hybridity. It highlights gradations, not merely raising 'either-or questions' but likewise 'more-or-less relations'. Whenever a human capability – such as using the senses to see an object or detect it – is transferred or 'translated' to autonomous robotic systems like visual recognition, the share of involved technology increases compared to conventional interactions.

Taking hybridity seriously means questioning binaries and thinking in terms of relations (see Emirbayer 1997). This scepticism of relational approaches[6] towards binaries has methodological consequences for research designs: they must necessarily become more relational, not only in their conceptual basis but also in the choice of methods. A design that places research questions on nonhuman-human relations at the centre demands reflection about method combinations that are capable of integrating potentially differing types of data sources, be they qualitative or quantitative, narrative or coded, spatial or chronological.

Hence, hybridity not only refers to human–nonhuman relations but opens up various sorts of binaries that are commonly taken for granted. As Knorr Cetina states, this entails hybridity between different levels of analysis such as micro- and macro-structures (Knorr Cetina 2009; Knorr Cetina and Brügger 2002). In the realm of financial practices, Knorr Cetina demonstrates how individual actors in micro situations interact instantly with other individuals via global infrastructure. The common binary assumptions about individual actors on the micro level as well as the aggregated action of several actors that constitute macro-structures are blurred. The micro situation is directly connected to the macro-structures of a global economy. The term she uses to refer to the phenomenon in which former individual inter-subjectivity that spans from one bodily present individual to another expands to a global social situation is 'scope' (Knorr Cetina 2005). Scopes are hybrids that transcend the dichotomy of either micro-scopes or macro-scopes; as such, analysing them requires methodological considerations that transcend such a dichotomy as well.[7] The present chapter illustrates this point with reference to an analysis of the security effects of drone warfare.

Similar intertwined hybrid phenomena apply to binaries such as 'internal and external' or 'military and civilian' security. Since the 1990s, approaches to security studies have increasingly questioned the binary of war and peace by focusing on 'small wars' (Daase 1999), 'new wars' (Kaldor 1999), 'asymmetrical wars' (built upon earlier debates on asymmetrical conflicts, see Mack 1975) or 'hybrid wars' (Hoffman 2007). These studies highlighted the blurred – sometimes even subverted – nature of distinctions between internal and external security as well as civilian and military violence as the reality of conflict has changed considerably. When a conflict does not appear to be a war, based on the fact that ordinary soldiers are not involved (at least not to the public eye), debates of war and peace become untenable. Hybrid wars have serious impacts for the security cultures in question (see Chapter 4 by Daase in this volume on the notion of security culture). Replicating either controversial or empirically misleading binaries does not help in better understanding or explaining them and their consequences.

As these examples show, hybrids uncover the relation between conceptions and material artefacts, the combination of human with non-human actions, and the connections between socially interactive micro-situations and global infrastructure. Moreover, hybrids tend even to subvert institutional concepts with long cultural and moral traditions.

This chapter differentiates between three sets of hybrids: action-centred hybrids (e.g. human–machine interaction), situational hybrids (e.g. local–global or micro–macro structures) and institutional hybrids (e.g. military/police or foreign/domestic security). These hybrid types are, however, not mutually exclusive; they are empirically related to each other in their social practices. What all types of hybridity have in common is that phenomena associated with them are set to increase in importance for both constituting and understanding social practices in the context of security studies. However, designing research strategies that capture the inherent complexity of hybridity remains a challenge. Fortunately, though largely unnoticed, studies related to STS and ANT provide analytical lenses for investigating hybrid phenomena.

Even though STS and ANT are often used as building blocks for specialized methodological thinking, i.e. critical approaches and interpretative methods, and sometimes as a reminder to collect knowledge of science for the social sciences and social and political realities (see Lidskog and Sundqvist 2014), in terms of methodology, they provide us with a more pluralistic perspective. Tracing the roots of the methodological reasoning behind these approaches helps us understand phenomena associated with hybridity without restricting STS and ANT to one particular methodological camp to the detriment of a more holistic picture of the empirical object. Contrary to how they are often referenced, this methodological pluralism is inherent in STS and ANT, for they focus not on differentiations and binaries but on connections, networks and relations. These approaches are therefore not meant to deepen cleavages between nature and culture but rather emphasize their connections and the mutual dependencies of various entities. Thus, STS and ANT favor a relational and not a functional or structural approach to social reality. To retell one well-known illustration by Latour: if a police officer gestures toward a car driver to get him/her to slow down, the officer is acting intentionally as a social actor in the ordinary Weberian understanding of social action. When a speed bump on the road causes an analogous effect, the social sciences tend to overlook this instance. From an ANT perspective, this omission is problematic: the speed bump is a materialized social actant, or quasi-actor, because it is something that causes an actor to act, namely to reduce his/her speed (Latour 2005). The police officer and the speed bump alike make the car driver act as intended, i.e. to slow down the car. The speed bump is a hybrid actor – or to term it differently according to STS and ANT – a 'quasi or materialized actant'. The speed bump and the officer are actors, exhibiting a greater or lesser degree of hybridity. Both, however, are social actors and their positions in the actor-network are closely related to one another. Autonomous robotic systems are hybrid social actors as well. The social sciences excluded, by and large, such material action from their research programs in the past.

Including objects in the study of social interaction requires adjusting analytical categories and their corresponding research strategies. This chapter suggests that two terms are analytically central to this adjustment: 'connections' (instead of intentions) and 'zooms' (instead of structures, fields, systems, spaces or micro-macro lenses). Connections indicate the relational position of hybrids between poles traditionally called 'natural objects' and 'human subjects'. The aim here is to understand its synthesis into one hybrid actor. Zooms refer to analytical perspectives of understanding phenomena that have been described as scopes, i.e. conceptual inter-linkages between macro elements and micro situations of interaction. While an analysis of both requires data to be combined, they differ in the way that data (both in its generation and its analysis) is combined within the research process.

Connections

Our understanding of connections combines approaches from STS and ANT with recent ideas about the logic of 'connective action' in digitalized societies (Bennett and Segerberg 2013). One of sociology's classic assumptions is that individual actors only become social actors upon interacting with other individual actors. These interactions typically take place in 'social situations' that are temporally and spatially limited and bounded. Connective action transcends these limits and boundaries by distributing certain elements of action to material artefacts and technologies such as digital media devices. Hence, with connective action, the temporal and spatial limits and boundaries of the social situation in which the interaction takes place are not limited to the particular location where the actors actually are; rather, they are potentially connected via mediated techniques to various locations. Interactive situations are no longer limited to a single presence or to a single location, spanning past and future situations of interaction.

Combining methods: connections and zooms 221

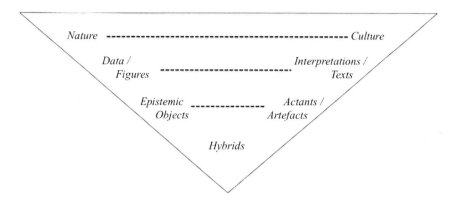

Figure 12.1 Connective actions

Since security, by definition, entails concerns about future situations as manifested in core terms such as threat, vulnerability and risk, such connective actions are of high relevance. Connections are made in textual representations, codes, discourses and technology – material practices manifested in digital and movable objects. This demands a pluralism of methods. Each method, which could be interpretations of text and discourses, interpretations of small or large coded data sets, or actions conducted by digitally driven material objects, might have its particular merits in research endeavours focusing on connections. As interactive situations are being transformed from purely human interaction to hybrid ones, methodological approaches meant to provide a toolbox for studying them ought to be pluralistic as well. If the social order is, according to the ANT perspective, not only organized by values, morals, norms and incorporated habits but likewise by material artefacts and objects, these must be incorporated within corresponding research designs. Instead of relegating materiality to the nature pole while referring to discourse, text and meaningful action as only cultural, as Latour states, we need to investigate the connections and connective action between these poles. What that means for security studies is illustrated by figure 12.1.

In order to understand the hybridity of social situations, we have to conceive of interactions as manifesting themselves in connections. Rather than dividing the social world into natural and cultural poles, this connective approach forces us to focus on the connective actions of material and cultural elements. The speed bump 'does' something. While the social effects of speed bumps can be quite simple, there are other 'materialized actors' – such as CO_2 or drones – that relate to much more complex hybridities. CO_2, for instance, connects the meteorologically measured data of a climate statistic to the morality of consumption like driving cars or eating meat; the latter might again be connected to budget-related actions like financing tree-planting campaigns in the rain forest. This chain of interactive connections is not reducible to either the cultural pole or the natural pole – it is a hybrid chain of plural interactive elements.

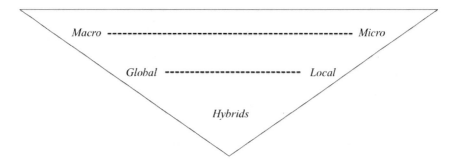

Figure 12.2 Zooms

Human actors and socially acting objects only have a socially relevant impact when they are embedded into a material network of connections. 'To connect' means also 'to act jointly' with other actors – be they material artefacts such as a speed bump, carbon dioxide molecules or UAVs. Connection connotes hybrid co-action; hybrids are actors comprised of connections. Integrating methods in order to understand this connectivity is methodologically essential. It requires an integrated interpretation of text and discourses and of small and large coded data sets or material objects to explain the result or the pattern of a given co-action.

Zooms

Focusing on connective interactions methodologically provides us with the relevant elements that comprise a hybrid. However, research access to relevant key decisions and key situations within a broad network of interactive elements is also crucial. Connective interactions can therefore only serve as a starting point for investigating the hybrid results of inter-connective action. The consequences of such actions must likewise be understood: which part of these inter-connective actions matter more and which matter less in terms of observed outcomes? 'Zooming' is the methodological approach that enables an analysis of the gradual impact of inter-connective actions. It is a technique meant to determine the scope needed to gain a comprehensive understanding of a certain object or situation (Nicolini 2009).[8] For instance, microscopes are vital in case of bacterial action, macro-scopes in cases of climate action, and meso-scopes in case of human action. However, if a given interaction combines all three scopes, methodologically speaking, there will be a need to constantly vary the size of the scope until it is evident which parts of the continuity matter more and which matter less.

In reference to Knorr Cetina, we use the term 'scope' for reflecting on this epistemic challenge. The term reveals the scaling presuppositions of micro-*scopes* or macro-*scopes*. As stated earlier, in her studies on financial markets, Knorr Cetina shows how scopes can combine both macro structures and micro situations (Knorr Cetina 2009; Knorr Cetina and Brügger 2002). The computer monitor of a trader is connected to a truly global financial market. When trading stops in the evening in Frankfurt and London, it continues in New York, when it stops in New York, it starts in Tokyo, and, on the following day, it continues again in Frankfurt and London. The financial market is a place that connects an individual actor seated in front of a monitor, in turn functioning as a macro-scope for individual action. This hybrid situation can be compared to the military scope of UAVs, which are connected with the individual pilots sitting in front of a monitor via global positioning networks. In contrast to financial trading, various teams in different locations in the world coordinate among each other to guide one of these actants. The robotic system interacts with local situations thousands of miles away from the pilot. The connective action collects data and executes action in terms of surveillance, military force and violence.

These snapshots indicate that, in the case of micro-macro hybrids, we can no longer adhere to prefixed zooms as an either-or decision. Instead, researchers need to methodologically consider the epistemic rules of the zoom itself. A reflection on how micro and macro zoom levels are conceptually interlinked is key to such a research strategy. In contrast to studying connections constituting hybrids, the methodological challenge is not to synthesize or integrate into one socially acting object but to analyse various micro and macro components and how they are conceptually interlinked.

Returning to the demand for an analytical and pluralistic reading of ANT, the analytical lens of zooming again demonstrates that ANT is misunderstood when equated with ethnographic approaches. Even though the latter is used by Latour in his empirical research when examining single places as a single researcher – which he later represents with pictures of the people he studied, sitting at a table, appearing to be working with the people in the real world – Latour is quite explicit that understanding research objects more comprehensively is only possible in combination with other methodological approaches. In his study about research on geology and pedology, the research on soils, explanatory power lies with methods that relate to coding data (see Latour 1999). Ideally, coding practices enable any researcher to connect and compare findings made at a single place or about an object with any other place or object on earth. By way of common rules for defining and naming, they connect the places and objects with calculation and statistical practices. While the power of an ethnographic approach lies in its ability to unravel false generalizations and presuppositions about causal-chains, the same holds true for more causal, analytically driven methods. Variables are connected through figures that make them comparable. Both methods connect data and situations to other forms of epistemic representations. The logic of connective action highlights how combinations of data constitute hybrids that move beyond common assumptions about binaries, both in academic methods and in the scientifically observable world.

Binaries can, however, provide researchers with a very crucial advantage, namely the reduction of complexity. Rejecting the possibility of reducing complexity with binaries confronts researchers with the challenge of how to avoid drowning in the complexity of the situations they intend to make sense of and explain in the first place. Researchers therefore require a different methodological strategy that reduces complexity without falling into the trap of biased binaries. The solution, as we argue, lies in the strategy of combining the methods of triangulation and parallelization.

Linking connections and zooms to research strategies that combine methods

Connections and zooms both require a combination of various methods to enable researchers to understand a phenomenon's hybridity. When we consider the example of UAVs again, and ask the question of whether lethal drone action increases security, binaries such as military/civilian, micro/macro or internal/external tend to be at odds with the research object being analysed. With greater density than ever before, drones link the military and the civilian sphere of war while transgressing traditional patterns of internalizing and externalizing warfare more than ever before.

In classic wars of the past, to put it simplistically, clothing mattered: Those wearing uniforms were combatants while those wearing civil clothes were civilians. Despite a number of partisan wars, this binary of civilian/militant was decisive for lethal action against actors. In asymmetric warfare, this form of interaction that we still refer to as 'war' has become increasingly hybridized. The combatants of al Qaeda and ISIS, for instance, often wear civilian clothing and fluidly change between civilian and militant institutions. This makes both target identification and information flows regarding casualties unreliable; as a consequence, it creates challenges for generating data in research about the effects of drone warfare. This challenge is aggravated by the fact that drone strikes occur in areas that offer limited access to international observers and the media. In being simultaneously characterized by closeness to non-inhabitants as well as by tremendous consequences of action committed from outside, the areas are concurrently closed and open. This hybrid situation fuels scepticism about the presupposed distinction between the civilian and the militant.

Studying hybridity in the use of drones relates to both the addressees of drone action and to the senders. Clearly, the classic binary of internal and external affairs is not analytically helpful in the illustrative case of drones. Interaction takes place at various sites such as data connection hubs (like in Ramstein, Germany), in the middle of the American heartland, and in target areas such as Waziristan. The distinction between micro and macro perspectives is similarly blurred. When zooming down onto the pilot, one might conclude that drones increase his/her safety. Zooming onto the villages of Waziristan, on the other head, leads to the conclusion that the continuous presence of drones destroys basic forms of daily certainty and hope in the power of binding human rights.

Moving beyond this binary thinking requires synthesizing hitherto divided concepts as well as combining methods in accordance with two main strategies. Going beyond the first binary of military/civilian is related to investigating connections. Consequentially, this entails a different methodological challenge than the second set of binaries described above – micro/macro and internal/external –, which involves investigating zooms. The former bears a resemblance to well-known triangulatory logic while the latter requires a parallelization of methods (see for this terminology as well: Junk 2011). While the challenge in the former binary primarily lies in synthesizing or aggregating its components in order to understand the connection, the challenge of the latter binary lies in being explicit about conceptual inter-linkages among various zoom levels.

Combining methods is essential for studying hybrid phenomena; self-reflexive scientific discourses about method combinations are nothing new. Even security studies have called for a more comprehensive use of the methodological toolboxes that have been available to social scientists and neighbouring disciplines since the 1980s (Gaddis 1987); however, the identification of distinct research strategies in this regard is still lacking.

Nevertheless, there have been numerous attempts in the social sciences to systematize a combination of methods. These include different catch-phrases and discussions of 'mixed methods' (Tashakkori and Teddlie 1998; 2003), 'integrative social sciences' (Seipel and Rieker 2003), and 'triangulation' (Flick 2011) – the latter has arguably gained the most prominence in recent years. As these different catch-phrases or labels indicate, the debates attract attention and take place within various scholarly communities with each primarily focusing on a single aspect: be it a critical discussion on whether and how to combine qualitative (small-N) and quantitative (large-N) studies (see 'integrative social sciences') or an analysis of the various mechanisms for aggregating data – the focus of the 'triangulation' camp.

As fruitful as these debates have been for advancing methodological reflections and fostering a pluralistic mind-set in the social sciences, they present certain challenges, particularly for the study of hybridity. In this context, there has existed a tendency of either being caught up in an ideological debate (a strive for pluralism and methodological non-conformism) or an over-focus on a specific subfield (data aggregation in triangulation), losing sight of the bigger picture of combining methods (Junk 2011). In this chapter, we use a typology that we believe is more useful for studying hybridity as it provides strategies for combining methods regardless of whether these are qualitative or quantitative by nature. Moreover, it maps the complete field of method combinations by looking at and delineating methods of triangulation and parallelization – not one at the expense of the other. As research strategies, these complement the analytical lenses of connections and zooms that we identified in the previous section.

Challenge and strategy I: analysing connections by means of triangulation

As discussed earlier, a binary such as civilian/military can cause problems for analysing phenomena such as autonomous robotic systems like drones: data pertaining to both sides of the binary might prove unreliable and the binary is itself highly questionable. The social effects of drone action can only be understood by considering its hybrid character, leaving aside the path dependencies associated with classic binaries. For example, researchers could investigate the extent to which hybrids can (de)legitimize lethal action and how this action is reported in the public sphere of the democratic states (see the link between democracies and security as discussed in Chapter 7 by Geis and Wagner in this volume). Are these hybrids identified as such or are they framed by binaries that present either-or categories? This requires combining numerous layers of analysis – from large-N designs to a focus on the connective power of naming and framing. Only this can create a synthetic, more comprehensive picture of the effects of armed drone use.

At least two methods converge when measuring the score of an explanatory factor or of a hybrid connection in a design such as this – this graphically forms a triangle in which two analyses meet at a point (i.e. a variable or a condition). The logic behind combining methods along the lines of connections is termed triangulation. This is by no means a new term, and the concept has been further methodologically refined since the 1970s (Denzin 1970; Fielding and Fielding 1986; Flick 2011; Strauss *et al.* 1964: 36). However, scholars often use this concept as a synonym representing every kind of method combination, neglecting the distinct vertical logic behind it. The term is also used for testing the explanatory power of one method in contrast to another. As Denzin emphasizes, it is not method competition but rather complementarity that is at the core of the combination (Denzin 1989).

Following this logic, we employ a definition of triangulation according to which a researcher taps into a variety of methods to operationalize one connection and to increase the quality of analysis. The central challenge, of course, is choosing a strategy for synthesizing or aggregating the data (for different aggregation strategies see: King *et al.* 1995: 479–80; Leuffen *et al.* 2013: 3). In terms of data generation methods, the aggregation challenge refers to minimizing measurement errors by drawing from differing sources of evidence (e.g. interviews and document analysis) and to make the scales congruent. When carrying out triangulation, a researcher must therefore beware of biases related to combining the results of two or more analyses; it is aimed at increasing validity when describing or measuring a hybrid connection.

Challenge and strategy II: analysing zooms by means of parallelization

If we relate to the second set of binaries, micro/macro and external/internal, which, for instance, comprehensive study of drones necessarily transcend, one needs to ask how to analyse zooms. We would suggest using parallelization rather than triangulation methods. The challenge here lies in the horizontal logic of combining methods: Various methods do not converge on one phenomenon (connection) but are rather used to provide an answer to the inter-linkages between its components along the micro–macro dimension. The point of reference here is not a single connection but rather the research design as a whole; it is situated in a sequential logic across various gradations between micro and macro elements (see as well Creswell

1994). Rather than data synthesis, the challenge lies in the analytical logic of a conceptual framework that combines the methods. Two subtypes – combining data analysis methods according to parallelization logic – are particularly useful in studying zooms in hybrid phenomena: research programs and causal chains.

Research programs often follow a two-step approach: combining a large-N study with a medium or a small-N study in a necessarily sequential manner. Social scientists generally either analyse a larger data set first to identify typical or outlier cases which one can investigate with more depth later in the research process (see Gerring 2007) or start with a small-N study to then expand the cases under investigation in a medium- or large-N study. This two-step approach is widely used, and it serves as a basis for case selection in a narrow sense.

Of more relevance here is the fact that this also serves to provide a more comprehensive picture of the complexity of the hybrid phenomenon under investigation as well as the validity of a given theoretical framework. This brings with it assumptions about the connectivity between micro and macro elements or of the interdependence between various zoom levels. The sequencing of methods is rooted in the conceptually based logic of the research process. Method parallelization becomes especially prevalent in analyses that focus on timing and processes. If one investigates the temporal sequence of events – which could constitute the set of hybridity relevant for one outcome – conceptual connectedness will naturally be at the core of the analysis and the combination of methods will necessarily follow this logic as well.

The combination of data analysis methods has to be chosen in light of an identification of intervening processes existent between the starting point and the outcome. Hence, the challenge of combining methods in a research design based on (causal) chains rests with the soundness of the temporal sequence of (causal) links in the conceptual framework. If we study temporal dimensions between the components of a hybrid phenomenon, we must focus on observations and corresponding methods that allow for determining comprehensive narratives. These narratives should provide a high degree of certainty when linking the observation back to the relevant hybrid set ('smoking guns', in the sense of George and Bennett: Bennett 2008: 706; George and Bennett 2005: 117), and specifying the relational processes that connect causes and effects in-depth ('confessions': Blatter and Haverland 2012: 110–8).

A mixed bag: empirical diversity and the combination of zooms and connections

When discussing research strategies and corresponding research programs linked to phenomena of hybridity in security studies, two points become evident. First, these tend to be immense scholarly endeavours. Second, zooms and connections along with parallelizations and triangulations should not always be strictly separated, let one do injustice to the complexity of the hybrid phenomena. A sequential logic of combining methods, for instance, does not exclude falling back on a triangulatory logic within the same research process. It might make sense to combine method parallelization and method triangulation within one research design. Emphasizing a sequential logic across explanatory factors does not imply that the score of a single explanatory factor cannot be triangulated beforehand.

Hence, combinations of the two sorts of logic are certainly possible, but are not without challenges.

To provide some illustrations and possible solutions to the two challenges identified above, we conclude by returning to the example that this chapter has referred to frequently: the relation between security and lethal UAVs (Galliot 2015; Strawser 2013). The exemplary research question is: to what extent do situations of interaction with lethal UAVs contribute to societal security? In answering this question, several methodological challenges can be identified. First, whose security we are zooming in on, the security of the actor A (the pilot or the sending country) or the security of the actor B (the target, victim, combatant, civilian or targeted locale)? In case we zoom in on the security of the actor A, we might compare statistics of military personnel killed in action. We will probably find that the number of UAV pilot fatalities is zero, whereas the number of jet pilot fatalities is N. However, are we actually measuring the security of actor A with this data? Should we perhaps rather connect and thus triangulate these numbers with statistics about post-traumatic stress disorder (PTSD)? We might then find that UAV pilots suffer more after their missions than their fighter flying counterparts because they are able to zoom in on the immediate interaction scenario before and after the lethal strike. Fighter pilots, on the other hand, commonly leave the target area after striking. Triangulation in this manner can prevent us from uncontrolled applications of prejudice. The number of pilot fatalities in action does not necessarily reflect their actual security. Other data sources could also be used to answer the research question more comprehensively in terms of reflexivity and validity.

An analogous point can be made concerning the security of actor B, the so-called 'targets' or the civilian victims – often cynically referred to as collateral damage. Investigations on this topic are often done by analysing the numbers of civilian and combatant fatalities. However, these numbers depend on nebulous categorizations. In hybrid wars, combatants are simultaneously civilians or switch roles on a daily basis. Thus, the number of victimized civilians might prove to be too high or low depending on the definition of the binary. Again, triangulation might provide some additional insights into these questions. Different sources of data from NGOs or from governments of targeted or sending countries could be triangulated. Should these data differ too greatly, the whole binary of combatants and civilians could be questioned or even abandoned as a valid way of measuring security outcomes of lethal drone actions.

However, answering the question of the security impact of lethal UAVs cannot simply be answered by abandoning binaries altogether. Here, parallelization can serve as an additional strategy. For instance, a researcher could continue by applying different zooms to situations of interaction. One zoom has already been mentioned: the interaction between sending actors of UAVs and their targets or victims; a research program looking at this aspect of drones would systematically parallelize an analysis of the security of actor A and one of actor B. However, we could also zoom in on the interaction of the UAV with the entire region in which the drone is present. The sound of the drone and its contingent action could force people on the ground to react. This interaction situation is much larger than the temporally and spatially very limited target situation – and the impact is different. People adapt to the constant threat by, for instance, avoiding gatherings in open spaces or refraining from speaking about them so as to not be recorded by surveillance drones, which would endanger others. A researcher could even enlarge the zoom of interactions to the situation in which the public sphere in the sending countries debate the legality and legitimacy of lethal drone action in terms of human rights. Here, signs of action, the mediated pictures and the mode of talking about experiences would have a strong impact. We might assume that drone action is much more masked than military action of humans on the ground. Thus, the threshold for public attention could prove higher than in the case of analogous warfare. The impact on global security might be that the political administrations of sending countries are less able to legally, politically or publicly be controlled by the publics affected by drone action. In this sense, drone interaction would reduce global security since masking military force undermines democratic peace. These various facets of a complex research program about the link between drone warfare and security can only be answered by parallelizing various data analysis methods.

In sum, when investigating the connections and zooms of hybrid phenomena, two distinct logics of method combination seem to both be analytically warranted yet empirically interlinked: triangulation, with the aim of synthesizing, and parallelization, with the aim of analysing. However, studying hybrids does not imply that more and more research or more and more methods help to gain a better understanding of the problem. The key is to be careful and explicit about the logic of translation and linking associated with each method combination. This is far from an easy task, as demonstrated by our illustrations of studying the social effects of the use of armed drones on security. Studying these as hybrid phenomena is challenging and does not simply entail an investigation of several aspects without prior reasoning about the translatability between those, which should inform their selection and their combinations.

Conclusion

As the illustrations about the practices and the effects of lethal drones has highlighted, there seems to be an urgent need to develop more reliable and valid approaches to hybrid actions and actors in security studies. The ethics concerning robotic systems must combine data concerned with the public sphere as well as with practices of warfare, victimhood and human rights, which are influenced and transformed by technology in action. The inter-objective situations created by robotic practices are micro situations that immediately translate to the macro-context of international relations. This chapter proposed the terms connections and zooms. The former term systematizes the methodological reasoning of approaches such as triangulating interviews with media products or governmental and NGO documents. The question of security concerning media products is wholly different than the experience of drone pilots or that of people living under constant surveillance of drones capable of lethal action. The idea of connection draws heterogenic data together, and is, in essence, an imperative to do so. The second terminological proposition is 'zooming'. The tool of zooming requires parallelizing methods for analysing micro and macro situations.

Hence, by analytically zooming and synthetically connecting, we are able to more comprehensively tackle research questions on the hybridities of global security without ignoring the micro dimensions of societal order. We must supplement connections with triangulation in order to attain a more comprehensive picture of human rights in a democratic society, and we must also parallel various zooms in relation to various micro locations and macro pictures. Utilizing both synthesized triangulation and parallelized zooms, we might be better equipped to provide answers to the methodological challenges brought about by the increasing relevance of hybrids in the field of security studies.

Notes

1 This chapter benefitted immensely from discussions at the authors workshop held in Frankfurt to prepare this volume as well as from discussions at a panel of the Annual Convention of the International Studies Association. We are especially grateful for helpful comments by Peter Burgess and Gabi Schlag. Thanks go to Johannes Haaf and Nick Gemmell for their formal and language editing.
2 For example, even the dynamic critical security studies agenda is criticized 'for positing general "logics" of securitization, and failing to grapple with the spatial and temporal specificity of security projects' (Walters 2014: 114).
3 Oxford English Dictionary accessed online via http://www.ub.uni-frankfurt.de/ (latest access: 9 March 2015).
4 The relations between hybrids, zooms and combinatory and dialogical logic was firstly discussed in the realm of computer science and linguistics (Blackburn and De Rijke 1997).
5 Besides the linguistic usage, the term has been applied to ethnic and racial studies, as well as postcolonial studies (see, for instance, Bhabha 1994).
6 Instead of relational some use the term "anti-categorial" – see, for instance, the topic of one of the conference of the German Sociological Association in 2015: "anti-categorial imperative".
7 With methodological considerations we refer to the logic of choosing methods. Levels of analysis like the micro or the macro level may each require different methods to analyse. With this emphasis of method selection this chapter employs an operational interpretation of the term methodology. The chapter by Schlag puts a slightly different emphasis on the term by highlighting the critical and reflective way of linking theory and empirical data (see Chapter 11 by Schlag in this volume).
8 Nicolini uses the concept differently by focusing on connections between different practices, not on different practices and different data-sets: 'For theorising practice, we need an appropriate methodological approach that makes us see the connection between the here-and-now of the situated practicing and the elsewhere-and-then of other practices. I will describe this second movement as "zooming out" of practice. Theorising practice thus requires a double movement of zooming in on, and zooming out of, practice obtained by switching theoretical lenses and trailing the connections between practices' (Nicolini 2009: 1393).

References

Bennett, A. (2008) 'Process Tracing: A Bayesian Perspective', in J. M. Box-Steffensmeier, H. Brady and D. Collier (eds.) *Oxford Handbook on Political Methodology*. Oxford: Oxford University Press, 702–21.

Bennett, L. W. and Segerberg, A. (2013) *The Logic of Connective Action: Digital Media and the Personalization of Contentious Politics*, Cambridge: Cambridge University Press.

Bhabha, H. K. (1994) *The Location of Culture*, London: Routledge.

Blackburn, P. and De Rijke, M. (1997) 'Zooming In, Zooming Out'. *Journal of Logic, Language and Information*, 6 (1), 5–31.

Blatter, J. and Haverland, M. (2012) *Designing Case Studies – Explanatory Approaches in Small-N Research*, Basingstoke: Palgrave Macmillan.

Creswell, J. W. (1994) *Research Design: Qualitative and Quantitative Approaches*, Thousand Oaks: Sage.

Daase, C. (1999) *Kleine Kriege – Große Wirkung. Wie unkonventionelle Kriegsführung die internationale Politik verändert*, Baden-Baden: Nomos.

Denzin, N. K. (1970) *The Research Act*, Chicago: Aldine.

(1989) *The Research Act – 3rd edn*, Englewood Cliffs: Prentice Hall.

Emirbayer, M. (1997) 'Manifesto for a Relational Sociology'. *American Journal of Sociology*, 103 (2), 281–317.

Fielding, N. G. and Fielding, J. L. (1986) *Linking Data*, Beverly Hills: Sage.

Flick, U. (2011) *Triangulation – eine Einführung*, Wiesbaden: VS Verlag.

Gaddis, J. L. (1987) 'Expanding the Data Base: Historians, Political Scientists, and the Enrichment of Security Studies'. *International Security*, 12 (1), 3–21.

Galliot, J. (2015) *Military Robots. Mapping the Moral Landscape*, Surrey: Ashgate.

George, A. L. and Bennett, A. (2005) *Case Studies and Theory Development in the Social Sciences*, Cambridge: MIT Press.

Gerring, J. (2007) *Case Study Research. Principles and Practices*, Oxford: Oxford University Press.

Hoffman, F. G. (2007) *Conflict in the 21st Century: The Rise of Hybrid Wars*, Arlington: Potomac Institute for Policy Studies.

Junk, J. (2011) 'Method Parallelization and Method Triangulation – Method Combinations in the Analysis of Humanitarian Interventions'. *German Policy Studies*, 7 (3), 83–116.

Kaldor, M. (1999) *New and Old Wars – Organized Violence in a Global Era*, Cambridge: Polity Press.

King, G., Keohane, R. O. and Verba, S. (1995) 'Review: The Importance of Research Design in Political Science'. *American Political Science Review*, 89 (2), 475–81.

Knorr Cetina, K. D. (2005) 'From Pipes to Scopes. The Flow Architecture of Financial Markets', in A. Barry and D. Slater (eds.) *The Technological Economy*. London: Routledge, 123–41.

Knorr Cetina, K. D. (2009) 'The Synthetic Situation: Interactionism for a Global World'. *Symbolic Interaction*, 32 (1), 61–87.

Knorr Cetina, K. D. and Brügger, U. (2002) 'Global Microstructures: The Virtual Societies of Financial Markets'. *American Journal of Sociology*, 107 (4), 905–50.

Latour, B. (1999) *Pandora's Hope – Essays on the Reality of Science Studies*, Cambridge: Harvard University Press.

Latour, B. (2005) *Reassembling the Social – An Introduction to Actor-Network-Theory*, Oxford: Oxford University Press.

Leuffen, D., Shikano, S. and Walter, S. (2013) 'Thinking Ahead – Measurement and Data Aggregation in Small-n Social Scientific Research'. *European Political Science*, 12 (1), 40–51.

Lidskog, R. and Sundqvist, G. (2014) 'When Does Science Matter? International Relations Meets Science and Technology Studies'. *Global Environmental Politics*, 15 (1), 1–20.

Mack, A. (1975) 'Why Big Nations Lose Small Wars: The Politics of Asymmetric Conflict'. *World Politics*, 27 (02), 175–200.

Müller, H. and Schörnig, N. (2010) 'Drohnenkrieg – Die konsequente Fortsetzung der westlichen Revolution in Military Affairs'. *Aus Politik und Zeitgeschichte*, 50, 16–23.

Nicolini, D. (2009) 'Zooming In and Out: Studying Practices by Switching Theoretical Lenses and Trailing Connections'. *Organization Studies*, 30 (12), 1391–418.

Rammert, W. (2008) 'Where the Action is: Distributed Agency Between Humans, Machines, and Programs', in U. Seifert, J. H. Kim and A. Moore (eds.) *Paradoxes of Interactivity. Perspectives for Media Theory, Human-Computer Interaction, and Artistic Investigations*. Bielefeld: Transcript, 92–109.

Rauer, V. (2012) 'Interobjektivität: Sicherheitskultur aus Sicht der Akteur-Netzwerk-Theorie', in C. Daase, P. Offermann and V. Rauer (eds.) *Sicherheitskultur – Soziale und Politische Praktiken der Gefahrenabwehr*. Frankfurt a.M.: Campus, 69–91.

Seipel, C. and Rieker, P. (2003) *Integrative Sozialforschung*, Weinheim: Juventa.

Sharkey, N. and Suchman, L. (2013) 'Wishful Mnemonics and Autonomous Killing Machines'. *Proceedings of the AISB*, 136 (May), 14–22.

Strauss, A. L., Schatzmann, L., Bucher, R., Ehrlich, D. and Sabshin, M. (1964) *Psychiatric Ideologies and Institutions*, New York: Free Press of Glencoe.

Strawser, B. J. (ed.) (2013) *Killing By Remote Control – The Ethics of an Unmanned Military*, Oxford: Oxford University Press.

Suchman, L. (2007) *Human-Machine Reconfigurations: Plans and Situated Actions*, Cambridge: Cambridge University Press.

Tashakkori, A. and Teddlie, C. (1998) 'Introduction to Mixed Method and Mixed Model Studies in the Social and Behavioral Sciences', in A. Tashakkori and C. Teddlie (eds.) *Mixed Methodology: Combining Qualitative and Quantitative Approaches*. Thousand Oaks: Sage, 3–19.

Tashakkori, A. and Teddlie, C. (2003) 'Major Issues and Controversies in the Use of Mixed Methods in Social and Behavioral Research', in A. Tashakkori and C. Teddlie (eds.) *Handbook of Mixed Methods in Social & Behavioral Research*. Thousand Oaks: Sage, 3–50.

Walters, W. (2014) 'Drone strikes, Dingpolitik and Beyond: Furthering the Debate on Materiality and Security'. *Security Dialogue*, 45 (2), 101–18.

A dialogue on the identity and diversity of security studies
A conclusion to the volume

Julian Junk, Gabi Schlag and Christopher Daase

The central aim of this conclusion is to outline possible avenues for a dialogue on the meaning and future study of security. It has been a challenge for us as well as the contributors to this volume to organise such a dialogue and to present it on paper. The limited number of chapters can only go so far in suggesting shared concepts for further debate and initiating a dialogue on the broader picture of security studies' main conceptual, empirical and methodological contributions to explaining, understanding and critically reflecting on matters of security.

One of our core assumptions stated in the introduction was that an extension of the subject matter of security studies went hand in hand with an extension of the theoretical, ontological, epistemological and methodological perspectives of security studies itself. As the chapters in this volume have confirmed, there is indeed a link between the transformation of security policies and the development of security studies. The more comprehensive the concept of security became, the more theoretical diversity and methodological pluralism characterised the state and conduct of security studies. Many sub-disciplines of political science in general, and International Relations (IR) in particular, were involved in re-shaping these agenda(s) of security and its study. Accordingly, (international) security studies has been a trans-disciplinary enterprise where neighbouring disciplines like sociology, economics, psychology, or information technology have played a crucial role from the very beginning and made security-related issues a matter of interest far beyond the scope of IR. The result of the widening of security and the different degrees of inter-disciplinarity is that security studies became at the same time more diverse, specialised and advanced in its perspectives but also gave rise to new boundaries, creating specialised groups that have not been able to communicate with each other. Given this background, the question whether security studies defines a (sub-) discipline of its own is the most obvious manifestation of its academic and political success story.

As this volume in general and the conclusion in particular demonstrate: the fear that diversity and pluralism leads to impassable boundaries in security studies does not appear to be valid; a dialogue is both possible and worthwhile. This conclusion takes in large parts the form of a dialogue of all authors contributing to this volume. This serves two goals. First, it enables us to do justice to the diversity of their conceptual, empirical and methodological backgrounds without pressing the conclusion into one final message conveying what security studies is or should be all about. A dialogical approach takes pluralism seriously and neither intends to outline a fashionable middle ground nor to conventionalise antagonist positions. Instead, it helps to clarify different perspectives, build bridges, create a common space for debate and hopefully helps to translate key concepts and arguments of one approach into the language of another (and *vice versa*) in order to strengthen mutual understanding of commonalities and differences. Second, the following dialogue explores sometimes surprising common ground among various perspectives and shows that while there might not be *one* common identity in security studies, there are different degrees of family resemblance between the authors. While identity *and* diversity are important aspects for characterising the development of security studies, the danger of fragmentation should neither be overstated nor ignored. The collection in this volume has proven that even seemingly distant perspectives might face similar challenges and come to similar conclusions – most vividly perhaps in the fact that the state is seen by many contributors as still one if not the most important reference point in security studies. We are sure that a discussion about these relations of identity and diversity is valuable and has indeed the integrating effects constituting a community of scholars that Toulmin (1972) argued to be essential for any discipline.

In this conclusion, we use an innovative dialogical approach in form and content. We asked the authors and participants of our workshop to respond to four key questions that emerged in our discussions: Should there be a core of security studies? What are the current challenges to security studies? What is the political relevance of security studies? What are the areas and challenges for a sustainable dialogue on security studies? These questions return to the issues discussed in the introduction in two ways. First, the central controversy over the status of security studies – either a (sub-) discipline of its own or a central part of IR – resonates within the question of a core. This refers not only to its factual existence but also to the question whether it would be preferable to have one. As we argued in the introduction, if there ever was and still is any conceptual core of security studies, then it is a rather formal reference to its central notion 'security' as well as the practices and discourses associated with it. Second, these questions pick up the contested relation between security studies and its subject matter, in particular how politically relevant research should or must be. While this normative impetus of being politically relevant has been more obvious for strands of peace research, security studies has long been perceived as a problem-solving research field, for example solving the problem of nuclear threats through the establishment of deterrence theory and research on strategic action.

Last but not least, a disclaimer is necessary. The following dialogue is not a transcript of a meeting of all authors and participants in one room – the documentation of a real dialogue – even though there have been joint meetings and discussions. It is an aesthetic attempt to initiate a critical conversation on security studies – hopefully far beyond the scope and limits of this edited volume.

Should there be a core of security studies?

The first question refers to a disciplinary core, in descriptive as well as in normative terms, which returns to Toulmin's definition of a discipline we outlined in the introduction (Toulmin 1972). Reactions to this question as displayed in the dialogue below show the ambivalences associated with disciplines, their boundaries and their disciplinary effects. It is worth noting that security-related research and international security studies have not always and probably are still not congruent. Internal security, societal risks and resilience measures have been excluded from IR's take on security by definition for many decades (Waltz [1959] 2001). Didier Bigo (2001), however, has argued that the boundaries between internal and external security, or to put it differently between inside and outside (Walker 1992), increasingly become blurred to an extent that IR's founding distinction loses empirical and conceptual power. The political dissolution of internal and external security certainly has reanimated the inter- and trans-disciplinary interest in security issues. This also holds true for the evolution of disciplines and their boundaries. The first decade of strategic studies with its primary focus on nuclear deterrence, game theory and formal modelling is an exemplary case of an inter-disciplinary community of scholars.

VALENTIN RAUER: My impression is that security studies is composed of so many disciplines that it cannot be understood itself as one discipline. Thus the core should be the ability to combine different fields of disciplinary approaches into a coherent analysis.

ANGELA OELS AND CHRIS METHMANN: We don't see the need to make all approaches compatible or coherent. After all, what is most important is to foster respect for the plurality of approaches within the larger field of security studies. Many approaches should not and cannot be combined because their theoretical premises contradict each other. Still they all contribute to our knowledge. It is because of this we would reject any notion of a core or coherence, because it is a normative position in itself. It would require to name and, consequentially, to marginalise a periphery.

GABI SCHLAG: I think a critical perspective on security studies' core is needed but we should distinguish a descriptive and a normative dimension here. Although I agree with the normative claim that a core is highly problematic for different reasons, it would be naive to neglect that a core is often invoked as a disciplining practice. Rather than invoking or neglecting a core, I'm interested in the practices and consequences of making a (sub-) discipline named security studies.

NINA BOY: I would add that there is a certain discrepancy between the historical meaning of security and its 'critical' contestation. Securitisation theory was partly so successful because it spanned the two, both taking the historical discourse of security seriously and revealing its performative dimension.

VALENTIN RAUER: And we see a new wave in security studies at this very moment: the study of materiality. This should not be left to natural sciences, because material conditions have a strong impact on the frames and the stories of security.

GABI SCHLAG: Just a brief response: yes, materiality is important but certainly in a different way than realists claimed. In the end, the meaning of materiality cannot be grasped without understanding discourses and practices, i.e. how agents make sense of the world.

CARLO MASALA: As you might have expected, I contradict the assumptions that there is no core or that there should be no core. For decades state security was the core – and to a large part it still is. This is not to neglect the other advances, but many of those are dealing with the empirical fact too that the state is not obsolete in our times. Therefore, we should have the courage to state that the core of security studies is and should remain the conditions under which states threaten to use or actually do use force.

CHARLES GLASER: I agree: there is a well-established debate over what should be covered by the term security studies. Probably not surprising either, I prefer a narrow traditional definition along the lines of Carlo Masala. Interstate war, the causes of war, and the means for reducing the probability of war and the damage if war occurs at all fit centrally within this traditional conception – as do questions of military competition, arms control, cooperation, and strategy development. IR provides the foundation for much of security studies.

ANNA GEIS AND WOLFGANG WAGNER: We can perhaps agree that there is at the same time a narrow and a broad definition of security studies. According to the narrow definition, which our perspective of democratic distinctiveness adheres to, it is the use of force by governments – this includes various types of the use of force, which are short of war.

CAROLINE FEHL: In my opinion, the understanding of security studies as relating to the potential or actual use of force among states or by transnational non-state actors is already quite broad. It includes discursive and institutional efforts to link policy areas not primarily designed to regulate the use of force, like environment, development, and migration, to notions of security and threat that ultimately contribute to enabling political responses resorting to the use of force.

HÅVARD HEGRE AND IDUNN KRISTIANSEN: Our perspective or point of departure is that of peace research. Hence, our research probably belongs to security studies only if defined broadly. A broad definition, we think, has some advantages and may allow explanations of phenomena of interest to security studies: While 'traditional' security studies mainly concentrates on the security of states, peace research is more attentive to the security of individuals. A wide definition would also cover political and economic risk-reducing policies such as poverty reduction, redistribution, normative change, and democratisation in addition to military measures against threats. Furthermore, a non-Western perspective receives much more attention in peace research, since most political violence events occur in the Global South. Traditional security studies still seems to concentrate on infrequent interstate disputes that involve Western countries.

CHRISTOPHER DAASE: The simple recognition that there is an extended notion of security in both the political and the academic world is telling. Traditional security studies and advances made in fields like peace research have merged already. Who talks about peace currently? The frame of security seems to be much more present.

KARIN FIERKE: I agree: if we take the premise of this book seriously, there is the phenomenon of extended security and we all agree that it exists. While there was a core, there is no longer one. It has been challenged by claims that security studies is ethnocentric, by its status as an essentially contested concept, by the increasing importance of human security and the expansion to a range of other issue areas, and by questions about whether security actually contributes to insecurity. In addition, there are more global forms of governance, which render the narrow definition focused on states increasingly problematic.

PETER BURGESS: Indeed, therefore the core of security studies, if it exists at all, takes the form of a question. It is the question of alterity as one of the foundational structures of existence. Alterity presents the world as a topology of oppositions, where the sovereignty of the one is simultaneously confirmed and threatened by the sovereignty of the other. This is the great challenge to cope with for security studies.

Keeping this conversation in perspective, it appears that there is a consensus on the notion of extended security and that this poses a challenge to scholars of security studies – a challenge that is unavoidable. Differences in perspectives are about how to cope with this challenge, whether still to take the traditional core of state security as a starting point or whether to directly start with one aspect of broader security. Most authors also raise the question whether the presence/absence of a core and a clear-cut disciplinary identity should worry us. As we argued in the introduction, we are convinced that diversity and pluralism is not the problem – rather it is the growing inability of scholars to talk to each other although they share an interest in matters of (international) security. The consequence of such a mutual silence then often is the consolidation of the hegemony of one approach where alternative approaches are dismissed as either 'unscientific' or politically irrelevant. There are obviously powerful positions within security studies which raise more attention in the academic and political world than others; a critical conversation, however, is only possible if and when the 'mainstream' is open to reflect on its blind spots and more heterodox approaches share an interest in a critical conversation on its policy relevance (whatever that might imply, c.a.s.e collective 2006).

What are the current challenges to security studies?

The discussion on the core of the security studies has indicated that the extension and widening of the security agenda, most explicitly since the 1980s, is commonly understood as the most challenging development for political decision makers, experts and security scholars. As we already argued, the widening of security was somehow mirrored in the widening of security studies itself with often ambiguous consequences. Thus, challenges to security studies are as much challenges to security politics. Accordingly, challenges come in various forms: conceptual, theoretical, empirical and methodological dimensions have been accentuated differently throughout the evolution of security studies.

CHRISTOPHER DAASE: The greatest challenge for security studies is that it is not clear what we exactly know. There are knowns and unknowns. Is there a measure of security? Is there a yardstick to distinguish good from bad security policy?

JULIAN JUNK: I agree. The arbitrariness of data is the greatest challenge. This is particularly prevalent in security studies because deliberations on security are still taking place in a very elitist environment and because in central terms like risk and danger there is an inherent element of probabilistic estimates of future occurrences of events.

VALENTIN RAUER: Indeed, this is a major problem: how to deal with the fact that security politics belongs largely to the field of arcane institutions. Often data that has been leaked is mostly arbitrary and hardly able to meet solid empirical and methodological requirements. Thus many aspects that are crucial for security studies cannot be observed empirically.

CHARLES GLASER: I would like us to focus on a challenge, which often goes hand in hand with discussing methodological challenges: the fixation on method-driven research leads us to forget or to ignore important questions.

JULIAN JUNK: Indeed, problem-oriented, empirical driven research is key. However, this does not lead us away from methodological challenges but creates new ones: how to integrate various methods into new and coherent research programmes within security studies, which do justice to the empirical challenges we identified?

HÅVARD HEGRE AND IDUNN KRISTIANSEN: We will limit ourselves to point out challenges to our own peripheral corner of 'security studies': quantitative peace research. We recognise that while our tools are powerful to answer certain research questions, they force us to leave other important issues unanswered. Many crucial matters are not quantifiable, such as the mental processes that lead individuals to make certain (observable) decisions.

NINA BOY: Security studies needs to engage with the financial meanings of security and securitisation, as well as the interrelations between finance and security in the form of the financialisation of security and the securitisation of finance. This is not only because security studies has not had a lot to say on the phenomenal impact of the financial crisis, but also because security and finance have been historically and conceptually deeply interlinked, not least in the evolution of the state. There is a need for more enquiries into the semantic history of security.

GABI SCHLAG: Not only the current financial crisis and a perceived conceptual shift from security to risk or even resilience is a challenge to security studies but also the lasting relevance of images and visual culture. Social networks, for example, where images of violence travel faster than ever before are transforming the media business. Here citizen journalists upload authentic, yet unverified images of ongoing conflicts which are seen by audiences all over the world. This gap between documented violence and political responsibility might be a particular challenge for democracies.

ANNA GEIS AND WOLFGANG WAGNER: Security studies has become a very diverse field. The various extensions of the notion of security have led to the inclusion of many topics previously excluded from being studied (energy, health, food, migration and others). At the same time, methodologists have advanced methods to studying security to an unprecedented degree. The challenge arising from this is that is becomes virtually impossible for any individual scholar to keep an overview of the manifold topics studied and the approaches and methods used to study them.

CAROLINE FEHL: I share this point: there still is a clear danger that the field becomes permanently subdivided. Therefore there should be more forums like this, which provide the opportunity to leave one's own security studies ivory tower.

PETER BURGESS: Indeed, diversity management is key for the future trajectories and impact of security studies. Its diversity extends far beyond political sciences let alone IR. A central challenge is how to open and generalise security studies as a problem of humanities and thus linking it to relevant subfields of the humanities like psychoanalysis, ethics, metaphysics, literature, etc. In short: security studies could and should be far more oriented as a set of interpretative strategies.

KARIN FIERKE: I think we should opt instead for more focus on pressing political and academic problems. Theoretical advances have tended to move in tandem with real world problems, from the contestation of both theory and political practice surrounding the demise of the Cold War, to the increased emphasis in its aftermath in both realms to humanitarian intervention and human security in the 1990s to terrorism after 9/11. The emergence of the various critical approaches to security was in many cases a response to the failure of more state-centric military approaches to deal with challenges presented in the political world, which deserves greater critical scrutiny than it has been given.

ANNA LEANDER: To add to this valid point: politics in general has indeed been transforming in ways that make security politics more central and pervasive than in the past. The core challenge is to explain, understand and intervene in this process. In particular intervention places considerable responsibility on the researcher.

ANGELA OELS AND CHRIS METHMANN: We agree, we need to critically engage with practices and processes of security and make visible their political consequences. The very selection of our research objects is already political in itself. Do we support those in power by offering them policy-relevant advice or do we undermine dominant regimes of power by denaturalising them? A poststructuralist position clearly favours irritating and destabilising taken for granted regimes of power. For this reason, it is important to study not only official practices but also resistance and opposition. For example, the process of securitisation is not always successful and never complete – raising attention to this is important. However, little research has been done on this.

GABI SCHLAG: I share this normative commitment and think that security studies should focus more on possibilities and practices of de-securitisation, reintroducing issues to a transparent and reflective decision making process where critique and contestation is possible.

CARLO MASALA: While all of this might be true, I have the plea not to forget the relevance of our research for policy-makers or other societal or economic stakeholders in the policy-making process.

This dialogue among the authors has revealed that there are particular methodological and normative challenges. The former refers to the simultaneous arcane and diverse nature of the data. Mixed methods-designs and new software-tools are a reaction to this development, something Gaddis (1987) already called for in the late 1980s. The second agreement refers to the responsibility of the researcher to reflect critically on the sensitive or potentially even conflictive nature of the study subject. The latter has been of lasting interest in IR and security studies in recent years with the inclusion of ethnographic and ethical perspectives – and this leads us directly to the third discussion: the relevance of security studies for security policy.

What is the political relevance of security studies?

Political relevance of research and the academic sophistication of approaches form two sides of the same coin. It is often claimed or even taken for granted that insights from security studies should remain relevant for policy makers and security scholars should pay attention to past and even more present political problems. The dividing line between politics and science, thus, is permeable – and, as most authors share to a different degree, should provide the common ground for an open, yet critical relationship between policy makers and security scholars. The 'ivory towers' of pure theory and methodology, however, are exposed as rather a myth than as precondition for objective knowledge. We all feel responsible – however, for different subject matters, to different referent objects and to different audiences. It is noteworthy that the old-fashioned, yet prevalent slogan of 'speaking truth to power' is not restricted to Critical/critical security studies but expresses an ideal cherished by the great majority of scholars with different backgrounds. Security studies is, as we said in the introduction, more or less problem-*driven* and not purely problem-*solving*.[1]

This ambivalent link between doing research and making politics also raises critical questions of scholarly responsibility and reflexivity: how we define security and what we select as a worthwhile research question has indeed political implications (Aradau 2004; Bueger and Gadinger 2007; Huysmans 2002).

CAROLINE FEHL: Both traditional and new approaches to international security studies claim a high political relevance of their insights. What is meant by this, however, differs markedly between various camps. To establish bridges, across which one can compare, integrate and accumulate insights across sub-field divides, would increase the attractiveness of security studies as a whole for policy-makers, who are looking for consolidated research findings to justify and guide their decisions.

VALENTIN RAUER: I would like to accentuate it differently: Not the coherence, but the gap between theoretical advances and real world problems is a necessary condition for the political relevance of security studies. The relevance is based on its ability to analyse the relation of security practices to democratic and public norms and values. Theory can always function as a starting point to question common sense in security politics.

PETER BURGESS: Indeed, security studies has the potential to interrupt dominant discourses of governance. It should thus irritate and deconstruct. Therein is its relevance.

ANGELA OELS AND CHRIS METHMANN: This critical perspective is key. The policy relevance of critical security studies lies in their ability to criticise and denaturalise dominant regimes of power and knowledge in order to create the space for alternative framings and practices. This critical security studies perspective can offer valuable advice to actors on how to frame certain issues in order to make a successful discursive intervention.

NINA BOY: Thinking and writing as such have a political dimension. The gap between theory and the 'real world' is problematic but I feel the relevance of academia lies in the reflexive conceptualisation of security governance.

ANNA LEANDER: I completely share this point of view: Security Studies is in itself already a form of politics.

GABI SCHLAG: Writing articles and books is political because with the selection of themes and approaches we already make a choice about what is worthy to engage with. Thus, the political relevance of security studies has often – maybe too often – been a 'Western' endeavour focussing on security problems in Europe and North America. If security studies intends to stay politically relevant, scholars should be more open to other perspectives.

ANNA GEIS AND WOLFGANG WAGNER: However, security studies should be more than just navel-gasing. Security studies acquire political relevance to the extent that they contribute to the critical reflection of security policies and security practices. In line with the understanding of the core of security as government-controlled, the main target of such critical reflections is what governments do. However, this should be understood widely as the activities of non-state actors, including private military companies, as well and should reflect government policies that encourage, inhibit or even outlaw certain types of activities.

KARIN FIERKE: Traditional approaches in security studies did not help to confront these problems. Nevertheless, I agree: security studies should be problem-driven and like all disciplines it should be able to adapt to current transformations in the real world. One of these real world challenges is to become much less centred on the West as global order is shifting to include emerging powers like China, India, or Brazil.

HÅVARD HEGRE AND IDUNN KRISTIANSEN: From our peace research perspective, the core problem is to understand the causes of political violence and to find means to secure peace. All answers to such complex research problems are obviously of great political relevance. Peace researchers and others engaging in security studies clearly should do more to communicate the political implications of the findings that already exist, in addition to be more attentive to the questions policy-makers want answered.

CARLO MASALA: To make the point of Karin Fierke sharper, meta-discussions are not helpful. The focus on pressing real-world problems is key. How can we achieve this: by establishing as scholars networks that go beyond our university ivory towers.

CHARLES GLASER: Carlo Masala is right here. But it matters, which types of networks. There is no guarantee of impact just by the virtue of knowing someone. The prospects for influence are increased by regular contact and interaction.

It appears that there are two takes on the notion of relevance: one views the relevance as given but warns of real world consequences of research. This has been the classical response to the post-modern movement by Walt (1991) that theoretical pluralism and intellectual innovation comes with a price. Heterodox approaches, however, seem even more politically engaged than (neo-)realists would have expected but certainly in a different kind of politics. But relevance is also based on the premise that there is no sufficient interaction between researchers and the political world. Academia and politics, as some authors implied, follow different language games where a sophisticated translator is often needed. Here, we do face a challenge for a more profound dialogue with people who are able to speak the different languages of politics and academia.[2]

What are the areas and challenges for a sustainable dialogue on security studies?

A dialogue presupposes different perspectives. It also presupposes that there is something important and valuable we should discuss. A dialogue, however, also implies that after all these debates authors might stick at least to some degree to *their* approaches, defending them against critique but also rethinking theoretical claims and empirical results. Thus, a dialogue does not intend to outline a new grand theory, but rather to strengthen the ability to talk to each other. Challenges to such a dialogue are often associated with structural and disciplinary constraints. Students of security studies, for example, are advised to define their theoretical and methodological identity when they are writing a PhD; ISA sections with reference to security related issues are organised in different ways, differences between a US-based and European-based security scholars community certainly have deepened, including the fact that some scholars in North America are more familiar with the European community, while some scholars in Europe are essentially US-centred in their research questions, theories and methodologies (c.a.s.e. collective 2006; Waever 1998). This dilemma also includes publication outlets, for example the major journals and edited volumes, which are often required to express coherence rather than an 'eclecticism' of approaches to security (for the value of eclecticism and pragmatism, see Katzenstein and Sil 2008; Kratochwil and Friedrichs 2009).

ANNA GEIS AND WOLFGANG WAGNER: Dialogue between different approaches is of utmost importance but demanding at the same time. Without dialogue, however, approaches tend to degenerate into sects.

NINA BOY: A genuine dialogue requires a degree of self-reflexivity and is only possible if the partners involved are willing to change their position or at least take a different look at their own perspective. If positions are too far removed however it can be more productive to critically engage with similar work.

ANNA LEANDER: Dialogue is much needed and it poses a simple but powerful challenge: dialogue entails two sides communicating. I think dialogue tends to be rather one-sided in security studies: the collective of 'critical scholars' of various denominations engage broadly. The other side rarely responds and if it does, it is usually not based on any detailed engagement.

KARIN FIERKE: I would go beyond this. While I share the premise that dialogue is essential, I think this dialogue should not only be between different approaches to security but between actors positioned in different global locations, both historically and at present. As the world becomes smaller and interconnected in new ways, while rapidly changing, dialogue would seem to be crucial to gaining an understanding of these changes and the potential for human agency in shaping these changes

CARLO MASALA: To specify this point from my perspective: it is of particular importance that these actors include think tanks, whose knowledge we as academics often forget to harvest sufficiently.

CHARLES GLASER: But not only think tanks are of importance: we need to draw upon the knowledge of policy-makers and decision-makers in this dialogue too. Let me add more critically to the emphatic embrace of interdisciplinary dialogue: this is important, but not all combinations will be equally productive.

ANNA GEIS AND WOLFGANG WAGNER: Indeed, as long as the basic yardstick against which claims are assessed, is contested, a dialogue does not make sense.

VALENTIN RAUER: Even though it might be difficult, I still think that we should try it: We do not need only an internal social science dialogue of among security study scholars, but one across disciplines as well. Methods can provide an avenue here.

PETER BURGESS: The epistemology of measurement, which is in our case how security is measured, determines what security is. What needs to be researched is this relation between methodology and security itself. Or to speak more like traditional international relations theory, how do epistemological issues impact ontological issues and how are forms of knowledge under duress themselves insecure or insecuritising? An acknowledgement and an understanding of the differences about these issues forms the basis for a fruitful dialogue, one being based on the recognition of difference.

ANGELA OELS AND CHRIS METHMANN: We strongly agree with that. Dialogue is valuable when it fosters respect for otherness and diversity. We have to recognise that we all pursue different aims with our research. We follow Cox in that 'theory is always for someone and for some purpose' (Cox 1981). Dialogue should not be about creating 'coherence' in the field. The push for coherence threatens to marginalise poststructuralist and critical approaches, which are not in line with positivist criteria of 'proper' research.

GABI SCHLAG: I agree with almost all what has been said so far about the value of dialogues in different directions. However, I'm skeptical that the basic career and reputation structures of IR and security studies are very helpful here. Power networks, either in the academic or in the political world, do not appreciate a conversation with the 'others'. When an article in *International Security* counts more than in *Alternatives*, and if journals embrace a certain intellectual identity of their publications (i.e. what gets published, where, how and why?), the day-to-day practice of a sustainable dialogue is more difficult than expected. Power relations do not change easily.

As we can see throughout the dialogue, there are various dividing but also connecting lines. However, by centering the book on the notion of extended security and extended security studies, a dialogue was possible because it was not ideological. Whether this notion of extended security studies is really a (sub-) discipline in its own right remains controversial. It certainly is a trans-disciplinary project that is both relevant and influential – with unintended consequences and corresponding normative questions following from this. But whether security studies is a disciplining or a trans-disciplinary project, it seems to be a worthwhile, even necessary endeavour to occasionally disrupt tendencies of over-specialised discourses and engage in a critical conversation which is stimulated by the diversity and pluralism of perspectives. Building bridges across the abyss of mutual silence, though, is possible but calls for open-minded scholars. We think there are many who are interested in a critical dialogue on the subject matter of security as well as the state and art of security studies itself. Structures and institutions where such a dialogue is supported and such a dialogical approach to mutual understanding and co-existence is valued, however, are still too little. This volume is hopefully the beginning of a continuous conversation.

Notes

1 This might sound as a picayune statement but we believe that there remains a crucial difference between problem-driven approaches and problem-solving approaches. Cox (1981: 128) described the latter as a kind of theory, which 'takes the world as it finds it [...] and make these relationships and institutions work smoothly by dealing effectively with particular sources of problems'. Such a technocratic approach was part of strategic studies first decade but even realist and institutionalist approaches have become more reflective as the contributions by Glaser and Fehl show.
2 For a different, though related, question of how concepts are translated to local discourses on security, see Stritzel (2011).

References

Aradau, C. (2004) 'Security and the Democratic Scene: De-securitisation and Emancipation', *Journal of International Relations and Development*, 7: 388–413.

Bigo, D. (2001) 'Internal and External Security(ies): The Möbius Ribbon', in M. Albert, Y. Lapid and D. Jacobson (eds) *Identities, Borders, Orders*, Minneapolis: University of Minnesota Press: 91–116.

Bueger, C. and Gadinger, F. (2007) 'Reassembling and Dissecting: International Relations Practice from a Science Studies Perspective', *International Studies Perspectives*, 8 (1): 90–110.

c.a.s.e. collective (2006) 'Critical Approaches to Security in Europe: A Networked Manifesto', *Security Dialogue*, 37 (4): 443–87.

Cox, R. (1981) 'Social Forces, States and World Orders: Beyond International Relations Theory', *Millennium – Journal of International Studies*, 10 (2): 126–55.

Gaddis, J.L. (1987) 'Expanding the Data Base: Historians, Political Scientists, and the Enrichment of Security Studies', *International Security*, 12 (1): 3–21.

Huysmans, J. (2002) 'Defining Social Constructivism in Security Studies: The Normative Dilemma of Writing Security', *Alternatives: Global, Local, Political*, 27 (suppl. 1): 41–62.

Katzenstein, P. and Sil, R. (2008) 'Analytic Eclecticism in the Study of World Politics: Reconfiguring Problems and Mechanisms across Research Traditions', in C. Reus-Smit and D. Snidal (eds) *The Oxford Handbook of International Relations*, Oxford: Oxford University Press: 109–30.

Kratochwil, F. and Friedrichs, J. (2009) 'On Acting and Knowing: How Pragmatism Can Advance International Relations Research and Methodology', *International Organization*, 63 (4): 707–31.

Stritzel, H. (2011) 'Security as Translation: Threats, Discourse, and the Politics of Localisation, *Review of International Studies*, 37 (5): 2491–517.

Toulmin, S. (1972) *Human Understanding: The Collective Use and Evolution of Concepts*, Princeton: Princeton University Press.

Waever, O. (1998) 'The Sociology of a Not So International Discipline: American and European Developments in International Relations', *International Organization*, 52 (4): 687–727.

Walker, R.B.J. (1992) *Inside/Outside: International Relations as Political Theory*, Cambridge: Cambridge University Press.

Walt, S.M. (1991) 'The Renaissance of Security Studies', *International Studies Quarterly*, 35 (2): 211–39.

Waltz, K. ([1959] 2001) *Man, the State and War: A Theoretical Analysis*, New York: Columbia University Press.

Index

Page numbers in *italics* are figures; with 'n' are notes.

accountability 129, 133, 135
Actor-Network-Theory 15, 24, 78, 216–17, 219–20, 223
Afghanistan 52, 131, 200; and NATO 64
alliance theory 18
anarchy 9, 16, 46; and constructivism 46; and the international system 36–7; and positivism 72; and unipolarity 114
anthropology 16, 17
apparatus (*dispositif*) 78
Arab Spring 76, 203
armed conflict 191–5, *192–3*, 196
Austin, John L. 71, 75

Bank of England 159, 160
Bauman, Zygmunt 161, 167n15
behaviourism 18
binaries 223–7, 228
Bin Laden, Osama 173–4, 180–1
biopolitics 147–8
biopower 144, 145
'bounded rationality' 58–9
Britain, and liquid government security 160–1
Brundtland Report 10, 88
Butler, Judith 74–5, 78
Buzan, Barry 1, 3, 4, 166

Capital Market Line 162, *162*
certainty *see* knowledge; uncertainty
challenges to security studies 237–40
changing adversary's objectives 40
Chemical Weapons Convention 62
China 115; and the United States 47–8
civil wars 194–5
classical realism 40, 41, 121n5, 121n8
climate change 148–50, 151
climate security 149

CNN-effect 175, 183
coercion, freedom from 38
cognitive research 15
Cold War 12, 14, 47, 201; and language 72–3
collateral 156, 157, 158, 166
collectivism 15
Collier, Paul 196, 197, 198, 199, 203
colonialism 146
common security 12
comparative case studies 16, 17
compellance measures for security 191, 195–200, 206
competition, between security seeking states 42–3, 45
compliance measures for security 191, 201–5
Comprehensive Test Ban Treaty 62
Conference of the Committee on Disarmament 62
conflict 84; environmental 144–6, 152; *see also* quantitative conflict research
conflict studies 23–4
connections/connective actions 220–2, *221*, 224–9, 227–9, 230
constructivism 14, 16, 46, 55, 57, 128; conventional 18; and culture 84; and Democratic Peace 128, 129
contemporary consent model 128
conventional constructivism 18, 73
cooperation: and conflicting security cultures 84; and democratic distinctiveness 135; and groupism 113; and institutions 51, 52, 54, 55, 56–8, 60, 65; and international security 11; and realism 42, 43–4, 46–7, 115; and security 5, 44, 84
Copenhagen School 71, 73, 74
corruption 198, 204

coups 193, *194*, 196–7, 199, 202
Cox, Robert 71, 241n1, 244
credible commitment 159
creditworthiness, sovereign 157
critical security studies 4, 14, 71, 73, 75, 230n2, 235; and images 176, 179–80, 184–5
Critical Theory 14, 71, 119, 127, 136
culturalism 15–16, 21, 82–91
culture: defined 82; and security studies 83–5

danger dimension of security 8, *8*, 12, 88, 99, 104
deconstructivist perspectives 18
defense, and deterrence 40
defense advantage 48
defensive realism 37, 40, 43–4, 46, 48
democracy: as means of compliance 201–2; promotion of 200
democratic distinctiveness programme 22, 126–37
Democratic Peace 22, 126–7, 130, 135, 201; and risk 132
'democratic wars' 130
de-nationalization 89
deprivation-conflict hypothesis 203–4
de-securitisation 185, 240
deterrence 3, 18, 40, 196; and language 72; and military expenditure 196–7
dialogues on security studies 24–5, 233–4; on a core of security studies 235–7; current challenges 237–40; on the political relevance of security studies 240–2; on a sustainable dialogue 242–4
dignity 76–7, 184
dimensions of security 7–12, *8*, 87–8
directorates 115–16
disciplines, defined 4–7
discourse analysis of images 179–80, 182
dispositif (apparatus) 78
domestic metaphors 73
drones 24, 134, 216, 217, 224, 225–6, 228–9

economic security 10, 22, 88
Eighteen Nation Disarmament Committee (ENDC) 61–2
emancipation 73, 89; and the environment 143
embodiment, and language 70, 80
environmental security 10, 22, 88, 142–52
epistemological dimension 13, *13*, 14
escalation in conflict 205–6
ethics 21, 94–106; and hybridity 229; security as 102–4

European Union 55–6, 134–5
extended security studies 13–19, *13*, 237, 244

fatalities in war 192–5, *192–3*, 205, 228
fear 99, 104
feminist perspectives 18, 71; and language 72
financial crisis 156–7, 238
financial security 22–3, 156–66, 238; history of 157–9; liquid government security 160–1; public credit 159–60; translations 164–5
Foucault, Michel 7, 17, 71, 74–5, 78, 142, 143–4, 152; governmentality 176; on power and knowledge 177
fragmentation of security 96
Frankfurt school 73, 75

game theory 16–17; and deterrence theory 18
gender, and language 72–3, 74
geographical dimension of security 8, *8*, 11–12, 88
globalization: economic 204–5; and human rights 204
global security 12, 88, 190–5, *192–3*
good governance 203–4
governmentality 176; and environmental security 142, 143, 144
greedy states 41, 44, 45–6
groupism 113, 116–17

Hansen, Lene 3, 4, 73–5, 175–6, 182
hierarchical institutions 58, 60
historical institutionalism 59, 64
history: of financial security 157–9; of security studies 2–4, 86–7
humanitarian security 11, 22, 39, 117, 130; and environmental change 146–7
human rights 11, 39; and hybridity 224; violations of 130–1, 184, 204
human security 9, 52, 75–7, 79–80, 87; and environmental change 146–7, 148, 152
hybridity/hybrids 24, 216–20, 224–7

iconic turn 174, 176–7
iconology 181–2, 184
identity 234; discourse analysis of images 180; and images 180, 185; and language 73
images 23, 173–85, 238; iconic turn 176–7; imaging security 175–6; and security studies 182–5; visual methodologies 178–82

Index

India, and the United States 53
individuals 236; and conflict studies 190; motivation 15
information 45–7; and rational theory 37–8
insecurity 90; contingency of 100; and ethics 103, 104; and language 73–5
institutional hybrids 219
institutional theory 20, 51–4, 56–60, 128; and multilateral arms control 60–4, 65; and rational institutionalism 54–6
internal armed conflicts 190, 191, 194, 195–6, 206; and democracy 202; and globalization 204; and good governance 203–4; and PKOs 199; and poverty 202
internalization of security 95–6
International Atomic Energy Agency (IAEA) 84
International Commission on Intervention and State Sovereignty (ICISS) 130–1
International Relations (IR) 1, 4, 14, 51, 71, 233; and ethics 102; and images 174, 175, 176, 178, 179, 181, 184; and language 78; and rational institutionalism 54
interstate armed conflict 191, 198, 204
interstate conflict, and PKOs 199
interventionism 117, 129–31
interventions, military 146–7, 151–2, 183, 200
Iran 52

justice 117

'Kantian peace' 127, 128
knowledge 79, 102; and ethics 103; security as 99–101, 105
knowns/unknowns 94–5, 98, 100, 106, 238

language 21, 70–80; and embodiment 70; speech acts 23
Latour, Bruno 217–18, 220, 223
League of Nations, Covenant 87
liberal institutionalism 14, 18; neo- 54
liberalism 75
Libya 131
liquid debt 161
liquid government bonds 23, 156, 160–1

materiality 235–6; and language 70, 71, 78, 79
Mearsheimer, John 43, 114, 118, 120
methodological dimension 13, *13*, 14, 16–17
micro-macro hybrids 219, 220, 223, 226
migration, climate-induced 148

military 9–10, 40, 44, 111; contractors 131–3; expenditure 195–8, 206; interventions 146–7, 151–2, 200; and realism 35; and regime change 200; RMA (revolution in military affairs) 133–4
military interventions 146–7, 151–2; and use of images 183
mixed methods-designs 217, 225, 240
monism 17–19
motivational realism 41–2
movies 176, 179
multilateral arms control 60–4, 65

national security 8–9, 111, 145–6; and the geographical dimension 11; statism 15
NATO 11, 18, 52, 55, 64, 89, 134–5; intervention in Kosovo 130
neoliberal institutionalism 54
neoliberalism, and resilience 150–1
neorealism 16, 41, 43, 46, 113; offensive 115
new security threats/agenda 111, 116–19, 120; and democratic distinctiveness 129–35
Non-Nuclear Weapon States (NNWS) 60, 61, 62
non-positivist theory 111
Non-Proliferation Treaty (NPT) 52–3, 60–3, 65
non-state security threats 10, 116
non-verbal communication 74
normative 100, 101
Northern Iraq 130
Northern security agenda 146, 148
North Korea 52, 183
Nuclear Weapons States (NWS) 53

objective security 89, 90, 181
objectivism 14
offensive neorealism 115
offensive realism 40, 43, 48
ontological dimension 13, *13*, 14, 15
Other/Otherness 74, 97, 244; and images 177, 180, 183

Palme Commission 12
paradox of security 88–90
parallelization methods 217, 226–8
Pareto efficiency 55, 58, 59
Paris school 143
peace 7, 85–7; and conflict studies 23; Democratic Peace 126–7; research 190, 236, 242
peacekeeping operations (PKOs) 198–9, 206

performativity 78, 177, 178
picture theory 174, 177, 182
pledges 158–9
pluralism 17–19, 234
political culture 21
popular culture 176
portfolio theory 161
positivsm 72; (neo-) 17
post-colonial perspectives 18
post-humanism 15, 18
post-positivism 17, 18–19
post-structuralism 18, 180
poverty: and conflict 202–3; and poor governance 208n24
power: balance 114, 117, 119, 195–6; and discourse analysis of images 180; 'go-it-alone power' 58; and images 180; inequalities 55; and institutions 57; and knowledge 79, 177; politics 3, 54, 111–21; and positivists 72; and realism 36–7; and security 43; sovereign 143–4
precaution 104
preventive wars 201
Private Security and Military Companies (PSMCs) 96, 131–3
privatization of security 96, 131–3
problem-solving theory 71, 119
Proliferation Security Initiative (PSI) 51, 53, 63–4
prophylactic security 96–9, 99
public credit 23, 156, 159–60, 165, 166

quantitative conflict research 190–207; compellance measures 195–200, 206; compliance measures 201–5; conflict escalation and methodological limitations 205–6; global security trends 191–5, *192–3*

R2P (responsibility to protect) 52, 131
racism 146
rational institutionalism 54–60, 64–5
rationalism 15–16, 37–8, 46–7, 128; and Democratic Peace 128, 129
realism 14, 17–18, 20, 21, 35–8; and China and the Unites States 47–8; divergent types of 40–4; and the geographical dimension of security 11; and power politics 111–21; and security 35, 38–40; and the security dilemma 45–7
reception analysis 179
reductionist theories 83
reference dimension of security 8–9, *8*
regime change, and the military 200

relevance of security studies 240–2
religious imagery 73
repression 148, 204
research: programmes 113; strategies 224–9; and theoretical assumptions 113
resilience 143, 150–1, 152
resistance 76, 77
resource, environment as 145
responsibility 98; 'to protect' (R2P) 52, 131
risk-free assets 23, 156, 161–3, *162*, 165
risk/risks 12, 88, 96–9, 101, 105–6; and Democratic Peace theory 132
risk society theory 133–4
RMA (revolution in military affairs) 133–4
robotic systems 24

safe asset 156
safe havens 156, 160, 161, 163–4, 166; and bond markets 23
science 106, 133–4, 240
Science and Technology Studies (STS) 216–17, 219–20
scope 218–19, 222
Searle, John 71, 75, 177
securitization 18, 78, 79, 88–9, 117, 118, 175, 235, 240; of the environment 142, 143; of finance 156, 157; and images 183, 185
security: defined 5–6, 7, 10, 19–20; as financial term 158–9; four dimensions of 7–12; history of concept 86; and realism 35, 38–40
security communities 11
security culture 21, 82–5, 90–1; and the security paradox 88–91; transformation of 85–8
security dilemma 20, 35, 40, 43, 44, 55; and culturalism 83; and Democratic Peace 128; and information 45–7, 48; and institutions 61; and new security threats 116
security governance 90, 134, 150
security paradox 83
security politics 239; internationalization of 134–5, 238
security-seekers 44, 45–6
security services 96, 131–3
security studies, defined 5
self-reliance 86, 151
self-sacrifice, political 76–7
September 11 attacks 90, 148, 173–4, 183–4
social networks 185, 238
societal security 9, 25n9, 87, 156, 228
Somalia 130

sovereign debt 160
sovereign power 143–4, 145–6, 148
speech acts 23, 71, 73–4, 77, 184, 185
Stanford School 84
states: and Democratic Peace theory 127, 134; and financial security 156; and new security threats 116–17; and realism 35, 36, 37
statism 15
strategic culture 21, 84, 85
strategic studies 3, 17
strategy/strategic, defined 85
structural realism 39, 40, 42–4, 121n9; and the security dilemma 45–6
subjective security 89, 90
subjectivism 14
subsuming security 74
surveillance 176; financial 156; technologies 15
Switzerland 127
symbols 184

technology 106, 133–4, 216; and hybrids 217–20
terrorism 90, 116; and finance 146
theoretical assumptions of research 113
theoretical dimension 13, *13*, 17–19
think tanks 3, 6, 243
threats 12, 98, 99, 115–16; new security 111, 116–19, 120
Toulmin, Stephen 5–6, 234, 235
trade: effect of war on 195; and interstate armed conflict 204
traditionalists 39, 165
translations, and financial security 164–5
trans-nationalization 89
triangulation methods 217, 225–6, 227–8

uncertainty 98, 100, 101
unipolarity 112; and realism 114–15
United Nations (UN) 52, 53, 56; and climate change 149; human security 9, 75, 146; interventions 130–1; on peace 87; peacekeeping operations (PKOs) 198–9, 206
United States 117–18; Atoms for Peace programme 60; and China 47–8, 115; and democracy promotion 200; and India 53; and private military contracting 132; and the PSI 63–4; TARP Programme 157; and unipolarity 114; and the 'war on terror' 157, 174, 184
unmanned area vehicles (UAVs) *see* drones

victims, and environmental security 146–8
visualisation 71
visual politics 23, 173, 178, 185
vulnerability 12, 148; and resilience 151

Wæver, Ole 1, 3, 4, 18, 165, 175
Walt, Stephen M. 4, 17, 25n4, 49n7, 242
Waltz, Kenneth 9, 11, 42–3, 47, 83, 116
'war on terror' 157, 174, 184, 185, 207n3
weapons 136; drones 24, 134
Wendt, Alexander 16, 46–7, 48n4
West: decline of 137; non-West opposition 77
window of vulnerability 12
Wittgenstein, Ludwig 17, 71, 75

Yugoslavia, and NATO 64

zooms 220, 222–9, *222*, 230